Advances in Digital Multimedia Broadcasting

Volume II

Advances in Digital Multimedia Broadcasting
Volume II

Edited by **Alicia Witte**

CLANRYE
INTERNATIONAL

New Jersey

Published by Clanrye International,
55 Van Reypen Street,
Jersey City, NJ 07306, USA
www.clanryeinternational.com

Advances in Digital Multimedia Broadcasting: Volume II
Edited by Alicia Witte

International Standard Book Number: 978-1-63240-048-2 (Hardback)

Contents

Preface

Multimedia is a combination of different types of media such as audio, video, text, animations, graphics, images, and interactive media. This field of computer technology is widespread in the present world due to its use in communication, entertainment, and academics. Multimedia involves presentation of data using multiple principles, concepts, and theories. A very important aspect of multimedia is digital broadcasting, which one can observe on television, internet, radio, cell phone communication etc. Multimedia has gained unimaginable importance over the last few decades. It has gained relevance in the field of computer science, especially in programming and communication technology.

Digital multimedia has also gained considerable importance in medical sciences, engineering, education, entertainment etc. Digital multimedia broadcasting is a technique used to distribute data over a large area by processing and transmitting the data using computer science tools. It converts data into digital forms such as bits, and then transmits the same using tools of electronics and physics.

This book has contributors from several countries, all of them leading experts in their field. All the chapters have been thoroughly written and reviewed, ensuring that the views of the contributors have been preserved in a uniform format. This effort would not have been possible without the kind cooperation of our contributors, who patiently went through revisions of their chapters. I convey my heartfelt thanks to all contributors and to the team at the publishing house for their encouragement and excellent technical assistance as and when required.

Editor

Optimization of ATSC Mobile Handheld Service Capacity

Omneya Issa

Communications Research Centre Canada (CRC), Ottawa, ON, Canada K2H 8S2

Correspondence should be addressed to Omneya Issa; omneya.issa@crc.gc.ca

Academic Editor: Dimitra Kaklamani

Mobile TV has become a reality offered on several mobile delivery systems. Among them is the Advanced Television System Committee (ATSC) system for mobile and handheld digital television services, known as ATSC Mobile DTV or ATSC M/H, which has moved from standardization to implementation. As the North American broadcast industry is preparing to provide Mobile DTV service to consumers, this work discusses important technical parameters that affect the TV service quality and capacity. Since additional error correction mechanisms were added to overcome mobile transmission problems, the available payload for M/H services is limited. This creates a need to efficiently use the available M/H bandwidth. The paper aims to optimize the Mobile DTV service capacity while maintaining an acceptable perceived quality. It presents tradeoffs between several factors affecting service capacity and signal robustness, which is prominent for designing Mobile TV broadcasting scenarios.

1. Introduction

The concept of television viewed on mobile devices has been a reality since 2005, when South Korea began satellite and terrestrial TV. Japan followed soon thereafter with US cellular carriers such as Sprint Verizon and AT & T. Content providers, such as MobiTV, Slingbox, and Hulu, offer episodes and clips from standard programs delivered on cellular networks. The North American broadcast industry formed an association called Open Mobile Video Coalition (OMVC) to assist ATSC in developing a standard for providing TV content to mobile handsets. The final standard of ATSC Mobile DTV, designated as A/153 [1], was ready in late 2009. Beside TV, the new standard provides a flexible framework for applications, such as video and audio streaming, real-time mobile commerce, participation and interactive television and advertising that allows M/H viewer to engage in real time with the program.

ATSC Mobile DTV has the potential to be the ubiquitous system for delivery of content to devices that move. The main purpose of the standard is to enable reception of DTV broadcaster's signal on handheld and mobile receivers at vehicular speeds. Based on it, a broadcaster can devote a portion of the station's assigned channel capacity to mobile service. This portion, however, is overly coded to combat rabidly the changing multipath conditions and poor signal-to-noise ratios usually associated with mobile devices and small antennas. The mobile signal is not decodable by legacy fixed receivers but is compatible as a valid legacy signal.

The overall structure of ATSC M/H is partitioned into three layers: presentation, management, and physical. The presentation layer mainly includes audio and video coding and other data as closed captions. The management layer includes all functions associated with transport, demultiplexing, and associating data with a particular service or program.

A number of existing standards and protocols were incorporated into this layer. Data, video, and audio transport is via Internet Protocol (IPv4) and User Datagram Protocol (UDP). Real-time programs, including video and audio, are further carried via the Real-time Transport Protocol (RTP) and its associated control protocol (RTCP). The UDP additionally carries Network Time Protocol (NTP) and service map tables that associate data streams with services. The payload interface between the management and physical layers is a two-dimensional block of data called an RS frame. The RS frame payload consists of concatenated IP datagrams, with each row of the frame starting with mobile/handheld (M/H) transport (TP) header that provides IP datagram locating information.

The physical layer incorporates the mobile data into the legacy ATSC transmission. It includes all the features of

ATSC signals and incorporates new features unique to ATSC M/H, which include two-dimensional block forward error correction coding (i.e., Reed-Solomon error coding) of RS frame for byte errors and serial concatenated convolutional coding (SCCC) of the mobile payload for improved signal-to-noise ratio. That is, the mobile payload data is serially coded by preceding the legacy ATSC trellis code with an SCCC code. This provides legacy receivers with a signal that is normally coded while mobile receivers can take advantage of the concatenated codes to perform iterative turbo decoding that can greatly improve the signal.

Although the ATSC mobile DTV is built around a highly robust transmission system coupled with flexible IP-based transport system and efficient video and audio coding, some of these features add to the overheads that constraint the payload carried by the channel. That is, including other protocols (i.e., IP, UDP, and RTP) introduces signalling information that needs to be carried along with the transported data. And since the RF channel capacity is the same, extra channel coding, intended for increasing signal robustness, limits the effective bandwidth, that is, the payload size available for carrying mobile data.

In fact, the total bandwidth needed for the mobile DTV service depends on several factors, including the number and type of program services, the quality level, and the level of robustness desired, typically ranging from less than one megabit per second to many megabits per second. Even, if a bandwidth portion is designated for mobile DTV, the service capacity, in terms of mobile TV services, will be affected by the same factors as well.

The specifications of the different transport and transmission features are detailed in the ATSC M/H standard, which is divided into nine parts. Among them, part 2 [2] specifies the transmission system characteristics, including the Reed-Solomon (RS) and SCCC coding, and discusses different payload data rates. Part 3 [3] covers the service multiplex and transport system, describing transport signalling and streaming. Parts 7 [4] and 8 [5] describe video and audio systems, respectively, mainly formats and codecs. There is also the recommended practice [6] (i.e., A/154), whose purpose is to explain what is enabled by the standard technically and functionally and to provide recommendations for the emission systems. However, neither the standard nor the recommended practice translates these specs into service capacity or discusses capacity usage optimality.

Beside the standards, recently the OMVC discussed some ATSC M/H broadcast scenarios based on program quality [7]. Companies, providing transmission and reception equipment, focused more on link budget and site planning [8], the inherent challenges, and the technology added to adapt the ATSC physical layer to mitigate the mobile fading channel and to enable ATSC Mobile DTV reception [9].

The study in this paper brings forward the optimization of mobile DTV service capacity, by maximizing the number of TV services without compromising the service quality. It discusses it within the boundaries dictated by the requirements for link robustness and compatibility with legacy system. The paper is organized as follows: Section 2 presents the problem modeling, Section 3 illustrates the results and discusses tradeoffs and potentials of TV quality versus robustness, and Section 4 concludes the paper.

2. Problem Modeling

Mobile DTV is carried in the same RF channel as standard digital broadcast service (i.e., main A/53-compatible service) using a portion of the total 19.4 Mbps allocated for that service. Experts in broadcasting think that the most-readily conceived service will be consumer access to free and pay television programming over a mobile device [10]. That is why, in this paper, we focus on linear TV program services, either real-time broadcast or non-real-time on-demand services, in formulating the problem. This is also done within the scope of the Core Mobile Mode (CMM) defined in [2], in which mobile DTV services are transmitted while reserving a minimum of 4.7 Mbps for main A/53-compatible services. Nevertheless, experts have recently worked on extending the standard with a new mode, called Scalable Full Channel Mobile Mode (SFCMM) that scales capacity up to the total bandwidth for M/H services [11]. It is worth noting that the work done in this study can be easily extended to cover the whole bandwidth.

As mentioned before, the ATSC bandwidth portion dedicated for mobile and handheld services carries, along with service streams, forward error coding (FEC), signalling, and transport protocol overheads. The robust channel coding has to be considered as well in order to estimate the effective bandwidth available for carrying mobile data. In fact, a major part of this bandwidth is given up for signal robustness by an SCCC coding that can hoard, to the least, half of the M/H bandwidth, and, to the most, three quarters of that bandwidth.

Thus, among the main factors affecting the effective bandwidth and, hence, the service capacity are the FEC and channel coding rates, the overhead of M/H signalling, including tables similar to that of ATSC, and the overhead of transport protocols. Of course, the number of services carried in this bandwidth depends also on the quality intended for each service and which controls the service encoding bit rate. Other parameters specified in the standard, such as the frame mode and number of groups, have also an impact on the effective bandwidth, which the standard calls the payload data rate (PDR).

The interaction of all these factors and their impact on service capacity can be depicted by understanding the composition of the data frame (i.e., RS frame) that carries the IP packets of the M/H services from and to the physical layer. Before physical transmission, video and audio in ATSC-M/H are originally transported via RTP over UDP in IP packets as most of the mobile multimedia applications.

The RS frame is the basic data delivery unit into which the IP streams are encapsulated every 986 ms. Each RS frame is composed of 187 rows of N bytes, Figure 1, where N is primarily determined by the level of robustness (i.e., channel coding rate and RS coding) selected by the physical layer. Each row of the RS frame starts with an M/H Transmission Parameter (TP) header that includes type of network protocol, whether an error is detected or stuffing bytes are included in this row,

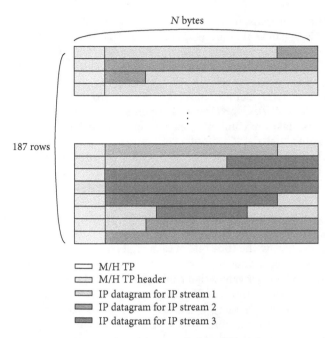

FIGURE 1: RS frame internal structure [2].

and the offset to the start of a new IP packet. After the M/H TP header, IP packets are carried within the row of the RS frame. Each row can carry multiple IP packets and IP packets can wrap from one row to another. If data is not available to fill either the current row or the remainder of the RS frame, then stuffing bytes can be used.

Another parameter that determines the value of N is the number of groups (NoG) of the M/H ensemble. In fact, the M/H data to be transmitted is packaged into a set of consecutive RS frames, where this set of RS frames logically forms an M/H ensemble. The data from each RS frame to be transmitted during a single M/H frame is split up into chunks called M/H groups and the M/H groups are organized into M/H parades, where an M/H parade carries the M/H groups from one RS frame. The maximum number of groups per parade is 8 and this number is always multiplied by 5.

PDR is the payload data rate of an RS frame and, thus, it is mainly a function of the size of an RS frame. So in its turn, the PDR also depends on the same factors, which are the level of robustness and the number of groups allocated for an ensemble. A requirement for successfully transmitting M/H services is that the PDR of the RS frame carrying these services should fit the ensemble bit rate, which is the sum of the bit rates of the services in this ensemble. However, as mentioned before, the RS frame also carries signalling tables, transport signalling packets (i.e., RTCP and NTP), and the transport protocol overhead, which is the RTP/UDP/IP headers added to the service packets before being organized in the RS frame. The study objective is to maximize the number of M/H TV services.

If we define service capacity as the number of media (in our case linear TV) services that the payload can carry, the optimization of the M/H service capacity can be described as the maximization of the number of M/H TV services Nc per ensemble. However, this was done by optimizing the media

bit rate R_i as well to ensure the best media quality for a given number of services. This objective was realized to be subject to several constraints that needed to be met, namely, the media bit rate constraint R_i, the PDR that has to fit not only the TV service bit rates, but also all the signalling overheads, and the RS frame size (consequently the PDR) defined by the required signal robustness level, that is, the RS code and the channel coding rate.

Mathematically, the problem can be formulated as follows:

$$\text{maximize}_{(Nc, R_i)} \quad Nc$$

subject to

$$PDR_{eff} \geq O + \sum_{n=i}^{Nc} 1.1 * (Rv_i + Ra_i) + \Delta_i$$

$$0 < Rv_i < (1 + O_h) * 768$$

$$PDR_{eff} = \frac{(N-2) * 187}{40 * 312 * 188 * PRC} * 19.392658 \qquad (1)$$

$$N = \left\lfloor \frac{5 * NoG * PL}{187 + P} \right\rfloor - 2,$$

$$PL = f(cr_A, cr_B, cr_C, cr_D),$$

$$cr_j \in \left\{ \frac{1}{2}, \frac{1}{4} \right\}, \quad \forall j \in \{A, B, C, D\}$$

$$P \in \{24, 36, 48\}$$

$$Nc \geq 0$$

$$PRC = 1.$$

In the optimization problem (1), the optimization variables are the number of services Nc and the service bit rate R_i. The first constraint depicts that the number of services is limited by the PDR and the overhead of signalling and transport. In other words, the PDR has to fit different types of overhead in addition to the media bit rates. Rv_i and Ra_i are the IP video and audio bit rates, respectively, of media service i. These rates include the overhead of IP/UDP/RTP headers added to media data packets. O is the fixed overhead per RS frame, consisting of the NTP packet and the fixed part of M/H signaling tables. Δ_i is the overhead added with each M/H service i, which includes extra information added for each service to the signaling tables and RTCP packets for each IP stream. The service bit rate variation is also reflected in this constraint. It is worth noting that although the video and audio service components are encoded at constant bit rates, a 10% range of bit rate fluctuation was usually observed. Accounting for this variation is important, since any overflow will result in packet loss at the receiver and service display interruption. Although researchers in [12] had recently proposed a buffering technique in the implementation of the transmitter to absorb this overflow, we saw that it is better to account for it, since it was not yet adopted by the standard.

The second constraint concerns the bit rate of video stream. The standard specifies that AVC video compression should conform to the baseline profile of AVC video at level 1.3 [4]. According to the AVC compression standard [13], 768 kbps is the maximum encoding bit rate at this level. It is worth noting that the standard has been lately amended to optionally support the main profile. O_h is the overhead percentage that needs to be added to encoding bit rate to account for IP/UDP/RTP headers.

The RS frame carries a column of 2-byte width for M/H TP headers. That is, a TP header of 2 bytes is always present for each row. This reduces the payload size available for service data to $(N − 2) ∗ 187$ bytes. That is why, in our optimization problem, payload data rate is called PDR_{eff} (i.e., effective PDR) to reflect a payload without TP headers. The PDR, as defined in [2], is the total payload bits per second of the M/H multiplex, having in its numerator the RS frame size. Thus, the third constraint depicts the PDR_{eff} with the effective payload size (i.e., $(N − 2) ∗ 187$). The PDR is also function of the parade repetition cycle (PRC), which is the frequency of transmission of the parade carrying the ensemble. This parade is transmitted in one M/H frame per PRC M/H frames. To follow the study objective, a parade needs to get the maximum possible bandwidth to give a best service quality. Thus, the PRC is set to 1; that is, the parade containing the designated ensemble is transmitted in every M/H frame.

As represented by the fourth constraint, other parameters determine N, the number of RS frame columns. N is a function of the number of groups per M/H subframe (NoG), the number of SCCC payload bytes per a group (PL), and the number of RS parity bytes per RS frame column (P) [2]. The NoG allocated for a parade depends on the bit rate required for transmitting the services of the ensemble carried by this parade. It should be selected so that the PDR_{eff} fits the ensemble data rate. To make best use of the PDR_{eff} and, hence, maximize service capacity, NoG was set to 8, which is the maximum number of groups per subframe for a parade.

PL is also called RS frame Portion Length. It depends on the RS frame mode, the SCCC block mode, and the SCCC outer code mode. The frame mode determines whether one or two RS frames are carried in the parade. A single frame mode means that there is only a primary RS frame for the parade carrying a primary M/H ensemble, while a dual frame mode indicates a primary frame and a secondary frame for the same parade carrying a primary and a secondary ensemble, respectively. The dual mode is only used in case a service has basic and enhanced components (e.g., service encoded with scalable video coding (SVC)), which means a different level of error correction is assigned to each component. It was recommended in the standard [3] to assume that receivers deployed in the initial M/H market have only the ability to decode single mode frames and, thus, to restrict each service to a single ensemble for initial M/H broadcasts.

As PL is the FEC redundancy bytes per group, another two important parameters determine its value: the SCCC block mode and outer code rate. The block processor of the M/H transmission system processes an M/H group into SCCC blocks that are mapped to 10 M/H blocks. The M/H blocks are divided into four sets called group regions (A, B, C, D). The processor has two SCCC block modes: separate and paired. In case of separate SCCC block mode, the SCCC outer code rate is set independently for each group region. Each region ($A, B, C,$ or D) may have either 1/2 or 1/4 code rate. This makes 16 combinations. However, if the block mode is paired, then the SCCC outer code rate is identical for all group regions; and therefore is given by either the all 1/2 rate case or the all 1/4 rate case. That is, the code rate combinations of the paired block mode are a subset of the code rate combinations of the separate block mode.

The fifth constraint represents PL as a function of the code rates of the four group regions cr_A, cr_B, cr_C, and cr_D, respectively. The code rate of each region cr_j can be either 1/2 or 1/4. Depending on the combination of code rates, PL takes specific integer values that can be found in [2].

P is the number of RS parity bytes per RS frame column. The RS (n, k) coding encodes the 187 bytes (column size) into one of three options: 211, 223, or 235 bytes. That is, RS encoding is performed for each of the N-columns of the RS frame payload and the RS parity bytes (P) are added at the bottom of each column. Thus, P can take one of three values: 24, 36, or 48 (bytes). The higher the P, the smaller the RS frame size.

It is worth noting that there is a tradeoff between payload size and robustness. Low code rate and high parity bytes mean highly robust signal; however, at the expenses of low data rate.

The optimization problem in (1) has continuous variables, namely the number of services and the service bit rate, and discrete variables such as PL, P, that take specific values. Also, some constraints are nonlinear. Thus, it is a Mixed Integer Nonlinear Programming (MINLP) problem. MINLP refers to mathematical programming with continuous and discrete variables and nonlinearities in the objective function or/and constraints. MINLP problems are precisely so difficult to solve, because they combine all the difficulties of both of their subclasses: the combinatorial nature of mixed integer programs (MIP) and the difficulty in solving nonlinear programs (NLP). Subclasses MIP and NLP are among the class of theoretically difficult problems (NP complete).

Nevertheless, in constrained optimization, the general aim is to transform the problem into an easier subproblem that can then be solved and used as the basis of an iterative search process. In fact, one of the most successful methods for solving MINLP problems is branch and bound [14]. It is a general framework for solving integer and combinatorial problems. The combinatorial part of the problem (determining the optimal integer assignment) is solved by a tree search in which nonlinear problems of the MINLP problem are solved and noninteger solutions are eliminated by adding simple bounds (branching). By using lower and upper bounds it is possible to limit the tree search, thus avoiding complete enumeration.

Thus, the problem in (1) was solved using a branch-and-bound algorithm that searched a tree whose nodes correspond to continuous nonlinearly-constrained optimization problems. In each nonlinear problem (node), the integer

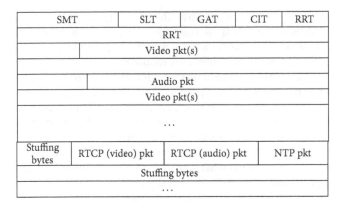

SMT	SLT		GAT	CIT	RRT
RRT					
Video pkt(s)					
Audio pkt					
Video pkt(s)					
...					
Stuffing bytes	RTCP (video) pkt		RTCP (audio) pkt		NTP pkt
Stuffing bytes					
...					

FIGURE 2: Typical RS frame payload organization.

variables (P and PL) were fixed according to the branch assignment. The nonlinear problems were solved using Sequential Quadratic Programming (SQP). SQP methods represent the state of the art in nonlinear programming methods. The author of [15] implemented and tested a version that outperformed every other tested method in terms of efficiency, accuracy, and percentage of successful solutions, over a large number of test problems.

The method mimics Newton's method for constrained optimization just as is done for unconstrained optimization. At each major iteration, an approximation is made of the Hessian of the Lagrangian function using a quasi-Newton updating method. This is then used to generate a quadratic programming (QP) subproblem whose solution is used to form a search direction for a line search procedure [16, 17]. The approximation of the Hessian matrix can be updated by any of the quasi-Newton methods. The Broyden-Fletcher-Goldfarb-Shanno (BFGS) method was used as it is considered the most popular [18].

It is worth noting that a nonlinearly-constrained problem can often be solved in fewer iterations than an unconstrained problem using SQP. One of the reasons for this is that, because of limits on the feasible area, the optimizer can make informed decisions regarding directions of search and step length.

3. Results

In order to solve the above problem, the model needs to be fed with adequate values of the parameters included in the constraints. These values were based on statistics collected form real traces, generated by an ATSC M/H signal generator and validated by the analysis of the received RS frames and in-carried services. Figure 2 shows a layout of an RS frame payload as organized by the M/H signal generator. The explanation of the content is provided below as needed.

As O is the fixed overhead per RS frame, it consists of the fixed part of M/H signaling tables and the NTP packet. The A/153 part 3 defined the MH service signaling tables carried in each MH ensemble. They include the service map table (SMT), the guide access table (GAT), the service labeling table (SLT), the cell information table (CIT), and the rating region table (RRT). The CIT is only useful for

a multifrequency network environment, so the user would be able to continue watching the same service when traveling between different coverage areas. The GAT is supposed to be transmitted every minute. RRT is much less frequent, required one time per hour. If we consider that one M/H frame spans 968 ms (~1 second), the overhead of CIT, GAT, and RRT may be negligible. The SMT and SLT delivery is more frequent though. SLT must be delivered at least once per M/H frame, while SMT must be included for the designated ensemble at least once every RS frame. So only the overhead of SMT and SLT was considered. The fixed overhead, which corresponded to the size of the tables without any service specific information, was 75 bytes.

According to the standard and the recommended practice, an NTP packet should be sent for each service in each RS frame. However, if we assume that the services of each ensemble are generated by the same encoder to fill an RS frame, one NTP packet per RS frame would be enough to designate the same timestamp for these services. In other words, all the IP streams in this RS frame would have the same local clock. The NTP packet size is normally 88 bytes.

Δ_i is the overhead added with each M/H service i. This includes specific information added for each service to the signaling tables in addition to RTCP packets for each IP stream. The linear TV services, which were the main services considered in the study, have two components representing an IP video stream and an IP audio stream per each service. Based on this, each TV service added 72 bytes to SMT and 15 bytes to SLT. In addition, two RTCP packets, one for each component, were included for each service. One RTCP packet per service component is supposed to be sent in every RS frame, as suggested by the recommended practice. An RTCP packet usually has a size of 80 bytes. These overheads were converted into percentage using the payload size of each test case.

The standard did not specify video or audio encoding bit rates. Since the video bit rate is considerably higher than the audio bit rate, the service bit rate mainly depended on the encoding rate of the video component. A HE-AAC v2 audio component of 40 kbps [9] was a reasonable compromise for good quality audio of an MH TV service. Thus, Ra_i was set to 48 Kbps, which includes the overhead of IP/UDP/RTP headers wrapping the audio packets. Hence, the service bit rate varied solely due to change in video encoding rate.

O_h is the overhead percentage that needs to be added to video encoding bit rate to account for IP/UDP/RTP headers. By analyzing several traces generated by different encoders with different bit rates, the percentage was found to have a mean value of 4%, with a confidence interval of ±0.15%. For simplicity, we fed the model with the mean value (4%) as the IP/UDP/RTP overhead.

As the standard did not recommend encoding bit rate(s) for video components, several companies and organizations have been testing different bit rates. The best study to which we had referred was [19], which was also well accepted in NAB 2010. Bit rates were selected based on the study in [19].

Although bit rates from 0 to 768 Kbps were considered in the problem solving, the results focused on bit rates starting from 230 Kbps, which corresponded to the lowest rate for fair quality and for 50% of viewer acceptability.

As stated before, to maximize service capacity, NoG was set to 8, which is the maximum number of groups per subframe for a parade. The integer parameters (PL and P) were assigned values according to [2], as mentioned in the previous section. Since the total number of groups to be transmitted for the next M/H Frame is 16 [2], TV services can span 2 parades carrying 8 groups each. However, a service should not be split over 2 ensembles unless it is coded in different components and, thus, needs a secondary ensemble. The number of TV services in the results is reported per parade; however, they may be doubled as explained.

The platform used for simulation was Matlab. The optimization problem has linear constraints whose complexity is of $O(n)$ as well as nonlinear constraints. The nonlinear ones are of low order of complexity, $O(m/n)$. As the number of groups was fixed to maximize the number of services, and the variables P, PL, and PRC had limited number of discrete values, the complexity of simulating the nonlinear constraints became of $O(1)$, which made the complexity of simulations lower than the one of the proposed algorithm.

The results gave the maximum number of TV services with respect to the service bit rate at different robustness levels. For illustration purposes, the results of only 8 robustness levels are shown in Figure 3. It is worth noting that all the services were assumed to have the same bit rate, for a certain maximum number of services. The plotted service bit rate is the one expected at the IP layer; that is, it includes all the overhead of all the upper layers and the audio component as well.

Although the maximum encoding bit rates of level 1.3 is 768 kbps, the curves of Figure 3 present the highest encoding bit rate that a TV service can have for a given number of TV services per ensemble. The increase in service bit rate was mainly attributed to video component, since the audio bit rate was sufficient for good quality. The increase goes beyond the encoding level limit reflected in the second constraint; however, it is presented for the sake of illustrating to what extent the encoding bit rate can be stretched to fill the RS frame and the corresponding video quality. Bit rates up to 1500 Kbps are plotted.

Figure 3 shows, using dotted lines, the video quality range corresponding to the service bit rate. The first one is the poor-fair range, which, in this case, represents mainly fair quality that is closed to poor, since, as mentioned above, the bit rates were chosen so that video quality remained in fair and beyond fair quality categories. The second range is fair-good, which represents fair (close to good) and good (close to fair) qualities. The last one is the good-excellent range, mainly describing good, close-to-excellent, quality. The ensemble of these quality ranges corresponds to a viewer acceptability ranging from 50 to 95% [19].

All the curves take an exponential decay shape, suggesting an important effect of low service bit rates on the maximum number of TV services per ensemble, versus a lessened effect as the service bit rate rose.

The biggest capacity, representing the highest maximum number of TV services per parade, was achieved with services

providing fair video quality. This capacity can be up to 9 services per parade if the least robust link can be tolerated. It goes down to 4 mobile TV services having fair video quality if the highest link robustness is required.

Most of the change in service capacity occurred within the range of service bit rates providing fair-good quality, which is almost 500 Kbps wide. Indeed, as the service bit rate increased in this video quality range, the maximum number of services per parade dropped considerably. At the end of this range, the service capacity of the most robust MH signal would have 3 services in less than what was spotted at the beginning of the quality range. This difference in capacity went to 4 services in less for the least error-protected signal.

Increasing service bit rate above a certain level did not considerably affect service capacity. For code rates starting with 1/2 1/2, increasing bit rates, bringing further good-excellent video quality, did not change the maximum number of services, which remained at 2. For robust code rates starting with 1/4 1/4, the same behaviour was observed for lower bit rates corresponding to good video quality. The number of services was floored to 1 for a wide range of bit rates spanning both good and good-excellent qualities.

If high signal robustness levels are targeted, good-excellent video quality will only be possible if broadcasters are comfortable with transmitting one service per ensemble. However, increasing this service bit rate to span the entire frame does not bring considerable quality advantage. Hence, if the bit rate is limited to the boundary of good-excellent video quality, a considerable part of RS frame will be stuffed with null bytes or could be used by other types of services.

Figure 4 shows the maximum number of MH TV services per parade in function of service bit rates that maximize the quality, around this bit rate, and above which the quality of the received video does not undergo noticeable enhancement. These service bit rates do not necessarily fill the whole available payload space. Thus, any remaining space of the RS frame, that is not enough for carrying an extra TV service of the same bit rate, will be filled with packets of other services, such as file transfer, or simply with null bytes. The number of services in Figure 4 is plotted for different robustness levels including four SCCC code rates and two RS codes.

Figure 4(a) illustrates results for RS code of 24. It can be seen that SCCC code rates having 1/2 in regions A and B gave the highest number of services. Code rates starting with 1/2 1/2 gave the same number of services, for IP service bit rate between 400 and 700 Kbps. However, a robustness code rate of 1/2 1/2 1/4 1/4 allowed one service in less compared to the least robust code (1/2 1/2 1/2 1/2) when service bit rate fell below (i.e., less than 400 Kbps) or above (i.e., more than 700 Kbps) this range.

The same number of services was achieved for code rates having 1/4 in regions A and B, when service bit rate was above 450 Kbps. Lower service rates gave an advantage of one extra TV service to 1/4 1/4 1/2 1/2 code rate, which offered more payload space than the most robust code rate (i.e., 1/4 1/4 1/4 1/4).

The results of 48 RS parity bytes are illustrated in Figure 4(b). Contrary to what was found with $P = 24$, the number of services achieved with codes rates starting with

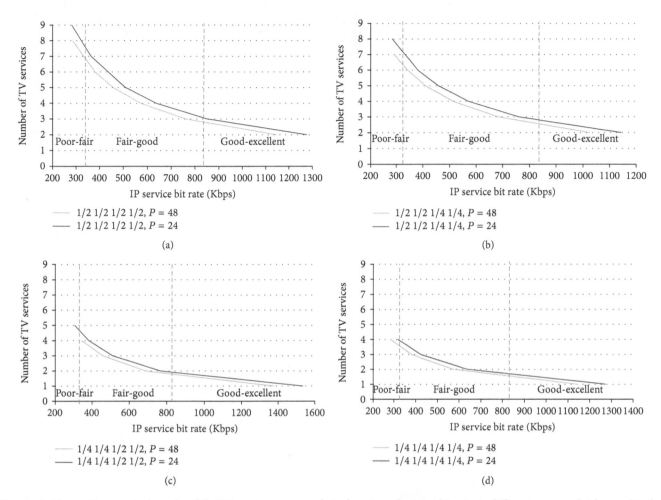

FIGURE 3: The maximum number of mobile TV services per parade in function of service bit rate in different ranges of video quality for different robustness levels.

1/2 1/2 were the same when service rates fell outside the 400–700 Kbps range. However, with the all 1/2 code rate, one more TV service could be carried, compared to 1/2 1/2 1/4 1/4 code rate, when service rates fell within this range.

Nevertheless, the same behavior, as the one observed with $P = 24$, was found for code rates starting with 1/4 1/4. In fact, the same number of services was obtained for IP service bit rates higher than 450 Kbps. It is worth noting that, at the lowest service rate (corresponding to the fair video quality boundary), the service capacity was similar for both 24 and 48 parity bytes and limited to 4 services when using these robust code rates.

In general, service capacity dropped to half when regions A and B had 1/4 code rate, compared to the number of services expected when a 1/2 code rate could be tolerated in these two regions. Moreover, the RS code had lower effect on service capacity than that of SCCC outer code rate. The parity bytes effect on number of services was mainly spotted when accompanied with less robust code rates starting with 1/2 1/2. This was when the service capacity decreased by one as the parity bytes increased from 24 to 48.

This suggests that the main player in service capacity is the SCCC outer code rates. At the most robustness level, the effect of P is almost negligible on the maximum number of services

a parade can carry. That is, as code rates start with more 1/4's, the maximum service capacity does not notably change with the variation of Reed-Solomon coding for all video quality ranges.

As mentioned above, the TV services may not fill the whole RS frame. And as described, increasing the service bit rate to span the unused space does not improve the video quality. This unused part of RS frame may represent a negligible percentage as it can be a considerable amount.

The standard suggested filling the RS frame space with TV service data. However, the results of Figures 3 and 4 suggest that filling the space, by increasing service bit rate beyond certain limits, does not bring noticeable enhancement to the service quality. Thus, the proposed algorithm sets optimal options for sending mobile TV services. These options, shown in Figures 3 and 4, optimize the space of RS frame, not only by maximizing the number of services, but also by using service bit rates that maximize the quality within a quality range while not filling the space with unnecessary packets. Thus, the unused space would be available for sending other services, mainly, non-real-time objects. The following results, presented in Figure 5 as explained in details below, show that the unused space could attain a considerable percentage that would be exploited by parallel services. These services will be

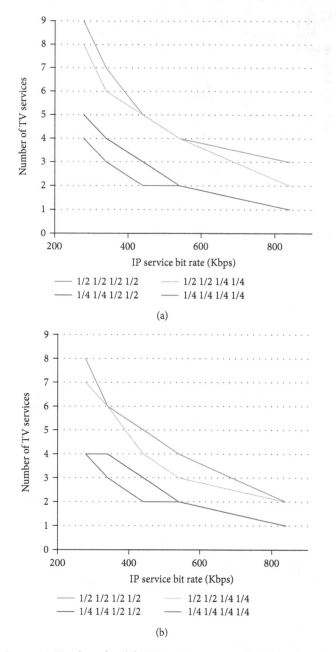

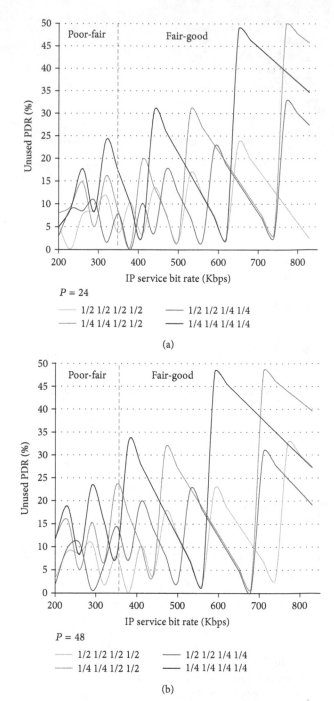

FIGURE 4: Number of mobile TV services per parade in function of minimum service bit rates guaranteeing certain video qualities for different code rates and RS codes: (a) $P = 24$, (b) $P = 48$.

FIGURE 5: Percentage of payload not used by the MH TV services, in function of the service bit rate and given that the maximum service capacity is attained at this service bit rate.

transmitted without the need of extra bandwidth, as would be the case if the conventional method of filling the frame is followed.

Figure 5 shows the percentage of data payload that is expected not to be exploited by the MH TV services, in function of the service bit rate and given that the maximum service capacity is attained at this service bit rate. The percentage is plotted when four different code rates are applied and for two RS codes.

The shape of the curves is quite interesting, suggesting that some service bit rates resulted in very small unused payload while others highly raised this unexploited portion.

Moreover, the values of these service bit rates differed according to the robustness level of the signal.

In fact, the relation took the form of oscillations that became stronger as the service bit rate increased. This may be attributed to the fact that, as the service rate increased, the number of services that could be stacked in the RS frame decreased. Hence, any small increase in the service bit rate may reduce the number of services by one, leaving a considerable unoccupied space.

With code rates having 1/2 in regions *A* and *B*, the percentage of unused payload showed lower-pitched fluctuation than what was found with code rates starting with 1/4. This is due to the fact that the service capacity, when lower code rates are used in regions *A* and *B*, is almost the double of that when the same regions have 1/4 rates.

In fair (close to poor) video quality range, the potential unused payload, for code rates starting with 1/4 and with 24 parity bytes, experienced two peaks: 18% and 24% at service bit rates of 280 Kbps and 320 Kbps, respectively. With 48 parity bytes, for the same code rates, these peaks were observed at 240 Kbps and 300 Kbps.

In fair-good video quality range, the percentage value of the peaks went above 30% with service bit rates ranging from 400–550 Kbps, and it approached 50% at 600 Kbps and up, in case of robust signals coded with 1/4 in regions *A* and *B*.

Either in fair or good quality range, for code rates starting with 1/2, the maximum percentage of unused PDR did not attain the same high values reached with code rates starting by 1/4. However, it may attain 24% at service bit rates around 600 Kbps.

It is worth noting that the RS coding did not affect the percentage of unused PDR. However, the service bit rates, at which the highest percentage values were observed, changed depending on the number of parity bytes. That is, the same percentage peaks can be obtained with lower service rate when using higher RS parity bytes.

The nonexploited payload space can be used to carry data for other mobile services, such as non-real-time (NRT) services or triggered downloadable objects (TDOs). In case that the space was filled with stuffing bytes, it can be used for iterative decoding. In fact, since the location of the stuffing bytes is known a priori to be usually carried at the end of the RS frame, a cross-layer iterative channel decoding may benefit from these bytes to improve error correction capability [20].

The amount of stuffed (unexploited) space may be important and, hence, may increase the robustness of the signal when coded with less robust code rates such as all 1/2 rate (1/2 1/2 1/2 1/2). At this code rate, up to 12% of unused PDR can be obtained for fair video quality services and up to 24% in good video quality range.

In fact, the results of Figures 4 and 5 illustrate how to get an optimal tradeoff between service capacity and the available proportion of the RS frame that can be used for other purposes, including NRT services and the iterative decoding. In a certain video quality range, an optimal balance can be achieved between the number of services and the amount of stuffing bytes that can be granted to NRT services and TDOs transmission. Another alternative would be to use the stuffing bytes to augment the effectiveness of iterative decoding in increasing the channel robustness.

4. Conclusion

The study in this paper formulated and solved the service capacity problem for ATSC mobile DTV system. The problem solution succeeded in optimizing mobile DTV service capacity, by maximizing the number of TV services without compromising the service quality. The paper presented tradeoffs between service capacity, TV quality, and signal robustness, which are important for designing Mobile TV broadcasting scenarios. The optimization technique was also found to be an effective method of tracking the unused payload space, without affecting service quality and capacity. Broadcasters may benefit from this space, which might be exploited by other services or used to increase the effectiveness of new iterative decoding techniques.

References

[1] D. T. V. ATSC Mobile Standard, A/153 Parts1-9:2009–2012.

[2] ATSC, "ATSC Mobile DTV Standard, part 2—RF/transmission system characteristics," Document A/153 Part 2:2011, Advanced Television Systems Committee, Washington, DC, USA, October 2011.

[3] ATSC, "ATSC Mobile DTV Standard, part 3—service multiplex and transport subsystem characteristics," Document A/153 Part 3:2009, Advanced Television Systems Committee, Washington, DC, USA, October 2009.

[4] ATSC, "ATSC Mobile DTV Standard, part 7—AVC and SVC video system characteristics," Document A/153 Part 7:2012, Advanced Television Systems Committee, Washington, DC, USA, July 2012.

[5] ATSC, "ATSC Mobile DTV Standard, part 8—HE AAC audio system characteristics," Document A/153 Part 8:2009, Advanced Television Systems Committee, Washington, DC, USA, October 2009.

[6] ATSC, "ATSC recommended practice: guide to the ATSC Mobile DTV Standard," Document A/154:2011, Advanced Television Systems Committee, Washington, DC, USA, April 2011.

[7] M. Simon, "Planning factors (link budget) ATSC Mobile DTV," White Paper, Rohde & Schwarz, Munich, Germany, 2010.

[8] M. Simon, "Understanding ATSC Mobile DTV physical layer," White Paper, Rohde & Schwarz, Munich, Germany, 2010.

[9] OTAG Subgroup, "ATSC M/H Broadcast Scenarios," June 2011, Open Mobile Video Coalition.

[10] S. E. Davis, "U.S. broadcaster plans for provision of ATSC Mobile DTV," *SMPTE Motion Imaging Journal*, vol. 119, no. 2, pp. 32–37, 2010.

[11] ATSC, "ATSC Mobile DTV Standard, part 9—scalable full channel mobile mode," Document A/153 Part 9:2011, Advanced Television Systems Committee, Washington, DC, USA, June 2011.

[12] S. J. Kim, K. W. Park, Y. S. Lee, K. T. Lee, and J. H. Paik, "Reducing IP packet loss in ATSC-M/H multiplexer," in *Proceedings of the IEEE International Conference on Consumer Electronics (ICCE '11)*, pp. 65–66, January 2011.

[13] ISO/IEC, 14496-10 (ITU-T H. 264), International Standard, "Advanced video coding for generic audiovisual services," 2007, with Corrigendum 1 (01/2009).

[14] R. Fletcher and S. Leyffer, "Solving mixed integer nonlinear programs by outer approximation," *Mathematical Programming*, vol. 66, no. 1–3, pp. 327–349, 1994.

[15] K. Schittkowski, "NLPQL: a fortran subroutine solving constrained nonlinear programming problems," *Annals of Operations Research*, vol. 5, no. 2, pp. 485–500, 1986.

[16] R. Fletcher, *Practical Methods of Optimization*, John Wiley and Sons, New York, NY, USA, 1987.

[17] W. Hock and K. Schittkowski, "A comparative performance evaluation of 27 nonlinear programming codes," *Computing*, vol. 30, no. 4, pp. 335–358, 1983.

[18] J. Nocedal and S. J. Wright, *Numerical Optimization*, Springer, Berlin, Germany, 2nd edition, 2006.

[19] F. Speranza, A. Vincent, and R. Renauld, "Perceived video quality and bit-rate in the ATSC Mobile DTV standard," in *Proceedings of the 63rd Annual NAB Broadcast Engineering Conference*, April 2010.

[20] Y. Wu, B. Rong, G. Gagnon et al., "Multilayer Decoding Using Persistent Bits," US Patent 20110310978, December 2011.

Multi-Resolution Multimedia QoE Models for IPTV Applications

Prasad Calyam,[1] **Prashanth Chandrasekaran,**[1] **Gregg Trueb,**[1] **Nathan Howes,**[1]
Rajiv Ramnath,[1] **Delei Yu,**[2] **Ying Liu,**[2] **Lixia Xiong,**[2] **and Daoyan Yang**[2]

[1] *Ohio Supercomputer Center/OARnet, The Ohio State University, Columbus, OH 43210, USA*
[2] *Huawei Technologies, Shenzhen 518129, China*

Correspondence should be addressed to Prasad Calyam, pcalyam@osc.edu

Academic Editor: Thomas Magedanz

Internet television (IPTV) is rapidly gaining popularity and is being widely deployed in content delivery networks on the Internet. In order to proactively deliver optimum user quality of experience (QoE) for IPTV, service providers need to identify network bottlenecks in real time. In this paper, we develop psycho-acoustic-visual models that can predict user QoE of multimedia applications in *real time* based on online network status measurements. Our models are neural network based and cater to multi-resolution IPTV applications that include QCIF, QVGA, SD, and HD resolutions encoded using popular audio and video codec combinations. On the network side, our models account for jitter and loss levels, as well as router queuing disciplines: packet-ordered and time-ordered FIFO. We evaluate the performance of our multi-resolution multimedia QoE models in terms of prediction characteristics, accuracy, speed, and consistency. Our evaluation results demonstrate that the models are pertinent for real-time QoE monitoring and resource adaptation in IPTV content delivery networks.

1. Introduction

Internet television (IPTV) is rapidly gaining popularity and is expected to reach over 50 million households in the next two years [1]. The key drivers of IPTV deployment are its cost-savings when offered with VoIP and Internet service bundles, increased accessibility by a variety of mobile devices, and compatibility with modern content distribution channels such as social networks and online movie rentals.

In spite of the best-effort quality of service (QoS) of the Internet, IPTV service providers have yet to deliver the same or better user quality of experience (QoE) than traditional TV technology. Consequently, they need to understand and balance the trade-offs involved with various factors that affect IPTV deployment (shown in Figure 1). The primary factors are: *user* (video content, display device), *application* (codec type, encoding bit rate), and *network* (network health, router queuing discipline) factors.

User factors relate to the temporal and spatial activity level of the video content. For example, a news clip has low activity level, whereas a sports clip has high activity level. Also, based on mobility and user-context considerations, the display device could support a subset of video resolutions such as quarter common intermediate format (QCIF), quarter video graphics array (QVGA), standard definition (SD), or high definition (HD). Typically QCIF and QVGA with video resolutions of 176×144 and 320×240, respectively, are suited for hand-held devices, whereas SD and HD with video resolutions of 720×480 and 1280×720, respectively, are suited for fixed displays at home and business. Application factors relate to the audio (e.g., MP3, AAC, AMR) and video (e.g., MPEG-2, MPEG-4, H.264) codecs and their corresponding peak encoding bit rates, whose selection is influenced by network factors. Network factors relate to the end-to-end network bandwidth available between the head-end and consumer sites, and consequently the network health levels are measured using the delay, jitter and loss QoS metrics.

In order to proactively deliver optimum user Quality of experience (QoE), providers and IPTV application developers need to identify network bottlenecks in real time and assess their impact on the audio and video quality degradation. While doing so, it is impractical for them to rely on actual end users to report their subjective QoE of

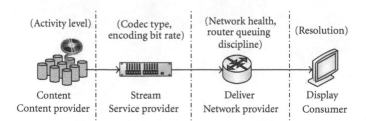

FIGURE 1: IPTV system components.

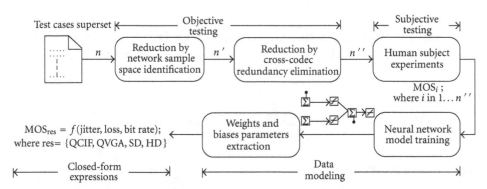

FIGURE 2: Overall architecture of proposed method for real-time multimedia QoE monitoring.

audio-visual quality. Also, they cannot rely on objective techniques such as [2, 3] that involve frame-to-frame peak-signal-to-noise ratio (PSNR) comparisons of original and reconstructed video sequences, which are computationally intensive and time consuming to perform. Hence, there is a dire need for objective techniques that can predict user QoE in *real time* for any given network health condition, while paying due considerations to salient user and application factors.

In this paper, we address this issue and propose psycho-acoustic-visual models that can predict user QoE of multimedia applications in *real time* based on online network status measurements. Our models are "zero-reference" in practice and hence do not require involvement of end users and are non dependent on actual video content. Our models pay attention to salient user and application factors by considering multi-resolution IPTV applications encoded using popular audio-video codec combinations and bit rates. More specifically, our models account for QCIF, QVGA, SD, and HD resolutions and the following codec combinations: MPEG-2 video with MPEG-2 audio, MPEG-4 video with AAC audio, and H.264 video with AAC audio. On the network side, our models account for jitter and loss levels, as well as router queuing disciplines: (i) packet-ordered FIFO (PFIFO), where packet egress of a flow is ordered based on packet sequence numbers, and (ii) time-ordered FIFO (TFIFO), where packet egress is ordered based on packet timestamps. We remark that one of the notable contributions of our study corresponds to our experiments described in this paper that show how the user QoE varies depending on whether the multimedia flows traverse PFIFO- and/or TFIFO- based routers along the network path between the head-end and the consumer sites.

Our proposed solution characteristics are shown in Figure 2. In order to develop the models, we execute a series of well-designed objective and subjective test cases in an offline closed-network IPTV testbed featuring human subject experiments. The ultimate goal of our objective and subjective testing is to come up with a set of user QoE training data from human subject experiments that can be fed to a *neural network* tool. By extracting the weights and biases parameters from the trained neural network, we obtain closed-form expressions for online prediction of user QoE. We use the popular "mean opinion score" (MOS) [4] as the subjective QoE metric during human subject experiments. The QoE prediction for a given resolution (MOS_{res}) is a function of online measurable network parameters (jitter, loss, and bit rate) obtainable from IPTV streams at monitoring points in the network.

The challenge is to significantly minimize human subject experimentation time, without compromising adequate sampling coverage necessary to achieve reasonable prediction accuracy from the neural network models. One of the minimization strategies we use is the objective testing step, in which we develop novel test case reduction schemes, namely, "network sample space identification" and "cross codec redundancy elimination". These schemes take as input the test cases superset n that includes all of the salient user, application and network factor considerations desired in the models. Using two novel objective QoE metrics at the user-level ("perceptible impairment rate") and network-level ("frame packet loss"), our schemes notably reduce the test cases set to a manageable number n'' that is suitable for human subject experimentation in compliance with the widely accepted ITU-T P.911 recommendation [4]. We evaluate the prediction performance of our models in terms of overall characteristics, accuracy, consistency, and speed. More specifically, we systematically evaluate model prediction characteristics for a comprehensive set of control inputs and verify if the prediction behavior follows expected patterns. The accuracy of the model predictions is evaluated using metrics such as the correlation coefficient and root mean square error. The consistency of the model predictions are evaluated using an outlier ratio metric. We use small-to-large scale flows simulation to measure the model prediction speeds.

The remainder of the paper is organized as follows: Section 2 presents related work. Section 3 describes our IPTV testbed setup and component configurations chosen for test cases execution. Section 4 presents the measurement methodology involved in the objective and subjective testing to collect the model training data. Section 5 describes our neural network architecture and model parameterization process. Section 6 presents our models prediction performance evaluation experiments and results. Section 7 concludes the paper.

2. Related Work

Factors that affect multimedia QoE have been extensively studied in earlier works. In [5], the effects of video activity levels on the instantaneous encoded bit rates are shown. Authors of [6, 7] show that higher activity level clips are more affected due to network congestion by 1% to 10% compared to lower activity level clips. The performance of MPEG and H.26x codecs used in IPTV applications are evaluated at various resolutions in [8]. The effects of degraded QoS conditions on multimedia QoE due to network congestion and last-mile access-network bottlenecks is presented in [9–11]. Several objective (e.g., PSNR, SSIM, PEVQ) and subjective (e.g., ACR MOS, DSIS MOS) metrics that quantify user QoE performance are described in [4, 12–14].

There already exist several objective techniques that use pyschoacoustic-visual models to predict user QoE for resource adaptation purposes in multimedia content delivery networks. One of the earliest is the E-model [15, 16], which is a pyscho-acoustic model developed to address VoIP applications. Recently, works such as [13, 17, 18] have attempted to develop pyscho-acoustic-visual models for online multimedia QoE estimation. In [17], video distortion due to packet loss is estimated using a loss-distortion model. The loss-distortion model uses online packet loss measurements and takes into account other inputs such as video codec type, coded bit rate, and packetization to estimate online relative-PSNR values. In [18], a human visual system (HVS) model is proposed that produces video QoE estimates without requiring reconstructed video sequences. The HVS model is primarily targeted for 2.5/3G networks, and consequently it only accounts for PSNR degradation for online measurements of noisy wireless channels with low video encoding bit rates. In [13], a random neural network (RNN) model is proposed that takes video codec type, codec bit rate, and packet loss as well as loss burst size as inputs and produces real-time multimedia QoE estimates. In [19],

authors use weighted values of QoS metrics within quality bounds obtained from other experimental studies and derive a numerical formula for IPTV QoE estimation. In [20], machine learning classifications are used on subjective test data for real-time QoE prediction in mobile networks. In [21], it is shown through simulations how objective QoE monitoring information can be leveraged for resource management via gradient-based routing in IPTV content delivery networks.

In comparison to above works, our novel QoE models encompass multiple video resolutions such as QCIF, QVGA, SD, and HD over a wide range of codec combinations such as MPEG-2 video with MPEG-2 audio, MPEG-4 video with AAC audio, and H.264 video with AAC audio, as well as incorporate variations in jitter, loss and router queuing disciplines on network health side. Our QoE models are able to deal with such a large combination of QoE factors than any of the earlier works due to our innovative methodologies of test-case reduction (i.e., reduction by network sample space identification and reduction by cross-codec redundancy elimination) by objective testing before conducting expensive and time-consuming subjective testing with human subjects. In addition, we have proposed two novel objective QoE metrics at the user-level ("perceptible impairment rate") and network-level ("frame packet loss") to aid in the test-case reduction steps. Moreover, we apply a feed-forward neural network [22] with an input layer, hidden layer with 2 neurons, and an output layer. Our multiple layers of neurons with nonlinear transfer functions allow the feed-forward neural network to learn both linear and nonlinear relationships between input (i.e., jitter, loss, bitrate) and output (i.e., MOS) vectors.

In addition to above academia efforts, there have lately been significant efforts in IPTV industry forums such as the Video Quality Experts Group (VQEG), International Telecommunications Union (ITU-T), Alliance for Telecommunications Industry Solutions (ATIS), and Broadband Forum to develop, validate, and standardize online multimedia QoE models [23]. To the best of our knowledge, model requirements being discussed in those forums closely match the modeling considerations in this paper.

3. IPTV Testbed and Experiments Setup

The IPTV testbed setup for our experiments is shown in Figure 3. We used the popular open-source VLC software [24] that has both the streaming server and media player components that allow streaming video content over IP networks to remote users. The Netem network emulator [25] separated two virtual LANS (VLAN 1 and 2) that were abstractions of the stream provider and consumer ends of Figure 1, respectively. For each experiment, we collected both the sender-side and receiver-side packet traces using a sniffer PC with tcpdump utility and stored them in a traffic traces repository. Our Netem was built on Linux Kernel 2.6.15 and had the following hardware: Intel Pentium 4 1.70 GHz CPU, 512 MB RAM, Debian OS, and Intel 10/100 interface card.

We now describe the user, application, and network factor component configurations used in our experiments.

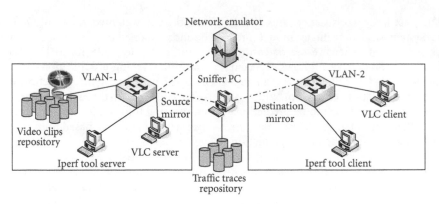

FIGURE 3: IPTV testbed setup.

TABLE 1: Peak encoding bit rates selection.

Resolution	Peak encoding bit rates (bps)
QCIF (177×140)	32 K, 64 K, 128 K, 256 K, 512 K
QVGA (340×240)	128 K, 192 K, 256 K, 512 K, 768 K
SD (720×480)	512 K, 1 M, 2 M, 3 M, 5 M
HD (1280×720)	1 M, 2 M, 5 M, 8 M, 12 M

3.1. User Factors. We generated several video clips (with audio tracks) that featured low and high activity level content with clip durations of 16–20 seconds. The video clips were extracted from a variety of sources that included conversation scenes, news telecasts, nature shows, sports telecasts, and movie trailers. Low activity level clips had little primary subject movement and little or no background movement. High activity level clips had high primary subject movement with fast changing backgrounds. Uncompressed video clips were exported to avi file format in QCIF, QVGA, SD, and HD resolutions.

3.2. Application Factors. The uncompressed video clips were then transcoded for streaming and playback with different audio and video codec combinations using the MPEG-TS container format. Specifically, the transcoding involved the following audio and video codec combinations that are popularly used: MPEG-2 video with MPEG-2 audio, MPEG-4 video with AAC audio, and H.264 video with AAC audio. For each resolution, a set of peak video encoding bit rates were chosen as shown in Table 1 based on the bandwidth consumption ranges and step sizes commonly used in practice.

3.3. Network Factors. We configured the network health, that is, delay, jitter and loss values using the corresponding commands found in Netem documentation. We did not constrain the end-to-end bandwidth capacity using Netem. In all our configurations of jitter, we set the delay value to be twice the jitter value because the delay value generally needs to be greater than the configured jitter value for proper jitter emulation. Since we are interested in only the playback quality of the IPTV content and not the channel

change time, we did not use delay as a control parameter in our experiments. We qualified our Netem jitter and loss configurations using Iperf and Ping tools and verified that Netem behavior was as expected before we commenced any of our experiments.

We also configured PFIFO/TFIFO router queuing disciplines in Netem as control parameters in our experiments. Figures 3(a) and 3(b) illustrate the comparison between the TFIFO and PFIFO router queuing disciplines. We can see that the TFIFO router processes packets of a flow F_1 at time t with interpacket jitter J as and when they arrive interleaved with packets of other flows. During the processing time δ, the router scheduler ensures the packets of flow F_1 egress the TFIFO such that the original J is retained. Given that IPTV traffic streams have small interpacket times, they are more likely to experience reordering on the Internet [26], and the consumer end may receive several re-ordered packets. Such packet reordering does not affect general TCP traffic of, for example, web file downloads. However, this seriously affects IPTV application UDP traffic because it burdens the receiver-side media player with packet ordering, and also set-top box decoders do not attempt to order packets due to their processing constraints (Figure 4).

To overcome such re-ordering effects, some network routers support PFIFO queuing that order packets at egress based on their packet sequence numbers. However, in the process, the routers change the inter-packet jitter J to J'. Depending upon the magnitude of the inter-packet jitter change $\Delta J = J - J'$, the end-to-end IPTV traffic stream jitter varies significantly, and consequently, so does the multimedia QoE at the receiver-side.

To illustrate the effects of ΔJ on the end-to-end network jitter experienced by a traffic flow and also to demonstrate the impact of PFIFO and TFIFO router queuing disciplines, we conducted a set of experiments whose results are shown in Tables 2 and 3. The experiments involved measuring end-to-end network jitter using Iperf (10 Mbps UDP mode) and Ping tools between two hosts separated by Netem configured with both PFIFO and TFIFO queuing disciplines. We can observe that both the Iperf and Ping jitter measurements correlate well with the Netem configured jitter values in the TFIFO case. However, in the case of PFIFO, Ping jitter measurements correlate well with the Netem configured jitter

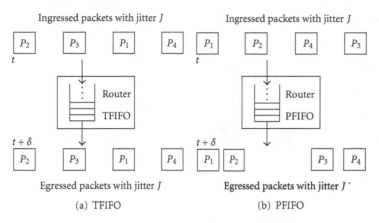

FIGURE 4: Comparison of router queuing disciplines.

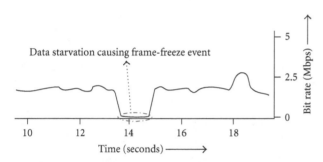

FIGURE 5: Illustration of data starvation due to high interpacket arrival time.

TABLE 2: Jitter measurements under TFIFO.

Netem configured	Iperf measured	Ping measured
6 ms	6 ms	6 ms
18 ms	18 ms	17 ms
75 ms	75 ms	69 ms
120 ms	120 ms	110 ms

TABLE 3: Jitter measurements under PFIFO.

Netem configured	Iperf measured	Ping measured
6 ms	1.861 ms	6 ms
18 ms	1.891 ms	16 ms
75 ms	1.494 ms	61 ms
120 ms	1.056 ms	105 ms

values, and Iperf jitter measurements do not correlate well. This is because the default inter-packet time in Ping is one second, which is much larger than the average PFIFO processing time. Whereas, the inter-packet times of Iperf UDP packets are small enough that the Iperf stream packets experience buffering in the PFIFO router queue and undergo processing to egress in order. The net effect of the PFIFO processing on IPTV application traffic is that the actual network-induced jitter is subsumed and the audio and video impairments perceived at the receiver end are reduced than compared to TFIFO processing.

It is relevant to note that network path processing due to PFIFO and TFIFO could sometimes hold up trains of IPTV application packets causing intermittent high inter-packet arrival times. In such cases, we observed "receiver buffer data starvation" at the client side, which causes frame-freeze impairment events at receiver-side playback. Figure 5 shows an illustration of the data starvation due to a high inter-packet arrival time case. Since data starvation cases could occur due to network processing anomalies such as network load bursts or denial of service attacks, their occurrence is probabilistic in nature on the Internet. To suitably inject frame-freeze impairment events in objective and subjective testing using Netem, we conducted a systematic set of experiments on Netem and concluded that the probability of these events occurring is well correlated with relatively high network jitter conditions under both PFIFO and TFIFO. Hence, we installed a script in Netem to randomly inject one or more frame-freeze events per video sequence in test cases with relatively high jitter settings; specifically we choose >200 ms threshold in PFIFO and >50 ms threshold in TFIFO based on our empirical observations.

4. Measurement Methodology

To systematically analyze the multimedia QoE performance in IPTV content delivery networks under PFIFO and TFIFO, we have to deal with a large sample space with several possible network health conditions. The network health conditions consist of the isolated and combined effects of jitter and loss. Obviously, it is not feasible to analyze multimedia QoE performance for all possible combinations of network jitter and loss on the Internet. Fortunately, earlier empirical studies [10, 27] have shown that multimedia QoE tends to be either in "Good", "Acceptable", or "Poor" (GAP) grades of subjective user perception for certain levels of jitter and loss values. The Good grade corresponds to cases where a human subject perceives none or minimal impairments and the application is always usable. The Acceptable grade refers to cases where a human subject perceives intermittent impairments yet the application is mostly usable. Lastly, the Poor grade refers to cases where a human subject perceives severe and frequent impairments that make the application unusable.

In this section remainder, we first describe the objective testing to reduce the number of test cases to be manageable for subjective testing. Next, we describe the subjective testing and data collection for modeling.

4.1. Objective Testing. The first goal of the objective testing is to perform QoE GAP grades mapping to QoS levels for the different resolutions. This testing enables us to determine the QoS levels that provide definitive GAP sampling ranges of network health conditions. With this knowledge of the QoS levels, we deduce the following 9 network conditions (each denoted by [⟨jitter grade, loss grade⟩] pair) that are sufficient for model coverage: [⟨GG⟩, ⟨GA⟩, ⟨GP⟩, ⟨AG⟩, ⟨AA⟩, ⟨AP⟩, ⟨PG⟩, ⟨PA⟩, ⟨PP⟩]. The second goal of the objective testing is to perform test case reduction by eliminating test cases that are redundant in the application factors. Specifically, we perform cross-codec elimination when we know that two codecs perform the same under a given network condition.

4.1.1. Objective Metrics. In each test case in the objective testing, a random activity level video clip with the corresponding resolution was streamed from VLAN 1 using the VLC streaming server at a particular bit rate with the corresponding codec. The Netem was configured with a particular network health condition and router queuing discipline. The video clip stream was made to pass through the Netem before playback using the VLC media player in VLAN 2. We collected measurements of two objective QoE metrics, one at the user-level and another at the network-level, namely, "perceptible impairment rate (PIR) events/sec" and "frame packet loss (FPL) %," respectively.

PIR is the sum of the audio impairment events (e.g., dropouts, echoes) and video impairment events (e.g., tiling, frame freezing, jerkiness, blur) counted by two human observers at the receiver end (one "listener" for audio and one "viewer" for video) divided by the length of the video clip. FPL is the percentage of the number of packets lost (audio and video combined) in a frame and is calculated from the traffic traces as a ratio of number of packets lost to the number of frames in a video clip. We used PIR as our primary metric in test case reduction experiments. To minimize learning effect of the human observers measuring PIR, we randomized the test case execution. Also, we confirmed that the PIR measurements were repeatable across diverse demographics and expertise levels with multimedia applications. From the PIR repeatability studies, we found the PIR threshold values to be: ≤0.2 for Good grade, ≤1.2 for Acceptable grade, and >1.2 for Poor grade. Further, we found a direct correlation between PIR and FPL, and hence we used the FPL measurements selectively to verify the sanity of our PIR measurements.

4.1.2. GAP Network Sample Space Identification. We conducted experiments to determine the GAP ranges of jitter and loss for the QCIF, QVGA, SD, and HD resolutions using the MPEG-4 video with AAC audio codecs. The video codec

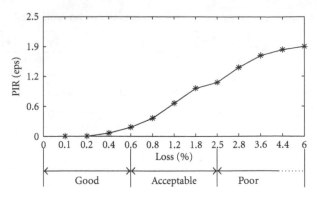

FIGURE 6: Loss GAP ranges for SD resolution under both PFIFO/ TFIFO.

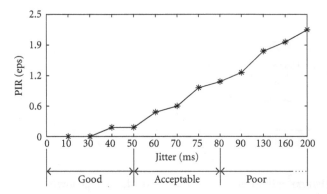

FIGURE 7: Jitter GAP ranges for QCIF resolution under TFIFO.

choice is representative and is motivated by the fact that MPEG-4 (specifically MPEG-4 part 2) is widely used and is known to have better performance than MPEG-2 and typically as good performance as H.264 (specifically MPEG-4 part 10). Also, we selected the median of the peak encoding bit rate step sizes shown in Table 1 for each of the resolutions (i.e., 128 Kbps for QCIF, 256 Kbps for QVGA, 2 Mbps for SD, and 5 M for HD). In each experiment, we gradually increased one of the QoS metric (i.e., jitter or loss) levels till PIR measurements crossed thresholds for GAP QoE grades. We stopped at PIR measurements close to 2, which is the expected human perception capability limit.

Figure 6 shows how the loss GAP boundaries were fixed for SD resolution based on the PIR threshold values. Our experiment results showed that the loss characteristics were independent of the queuing discipline, and hence the loss GAP ranges are the same for PFIFO and TFIFO. Similarly, Figure 7 shows how the jitter GAP boundaries were fixed for the QCIF resolution under TFIFO. The complete list of jitter and loss GAP ranges under PFIFO and TFIFO for the different resolutions are shown in Tables 4 and 5, respectively.

We now discuss salient observations from the above results of GAP ranges for different resolutions and queuing disciplines. We can see that higher resolutions are more sensitive to degrading network QoS conditions as evident from the narrow ranges of jitter and loss when compared to lower resolutions. For example, the loss range for Good grade

TABLE 4: Jitter and loss GAP ranges under PFIFO.

Display	Metric	Good	Acceptable	Poor
QCIF	Jitter (ms)	[0–200)	(200–400)	(> 400]
	Loss (%)	[0–2)	(2–4.4)	(> 4.4]
QVGA	Jitter (ms)	[0–200)	(200–350)	(> 350]
	Loss (%)	[0–1.4)	(1.4–2.8)	(> 2.8]
SD	Jitter (ms)	[0–175)	(175–300)	(> 300]
	Loss (%)	[0–0.6)	(0.6–2.5)	(> 2.5]
HD	Jitter (ms)	[0–125)	(125–225)	(> 225]
	Loss (%)	[0–0.3)	(0.3–1.3)	(> 1.3]

TABLE 5: Jitter and loss GAP ranges under TFIFO.

Display	Metric	Good	Acceptable	Poor
QCIF	Jitter (ms)	[0–50)	(50–80)	(>80]
	Loss (%)	[0–2)	(2–4.4)	(>4.4]
QVGA	Jitter (ms)	[0–40)	(40–70)	(>70]
	Loss (%)	[0–1.4)	(1.4–2.8)	(>2.8]
SD	Jitter (ms)	[0–30)	(30–60)	(>60]
	Loss (%)	[0–0.6)	(0.6–2.5)	(>2.5]
HD	Jitter (ms)	[0–20)	(20–50)	(>50]
	Loss (%)	[0–0.3)	(0.3–1.3)	(>1.3]

is [0–0.3) for HD, whereas the same for QCIF is [0–2). Consequently, we can conclude that higher resolution streams in IPTV deployments demand notably higher QoS levels than lower resolution streams.

Also, we can see that the PFIFO queuing makes the IPTV streams more tolerant to network jitter compared to TFIFO as evident from the higher ranges of jitter at all resolutions. For example, the jitter range for Good grade is [0–175) for SD under PFIFO, whereas the same for TFIFO is [0–30). Thus, we can conclude that having PFIFO queuing disciplines in routers at congestion points in the network or at the edges of access networks can reduce the burden of in-ordering packets for media player playback at the consumer sites. This in turn significantly increases the multimedia QoE resilience at the consumer sites towards higher network jitter levels.

4.1.3. Cross-Codec Redundancy Elimination. After the test case reduction by GAP network sample space identification, we reduced the sample space considerably by focusing on the network jitter and loss ranges that are relevant. However, due to the large number of application factors considered, the number of test cases still remains large. Specifically, owing to the 9 network conditions, 4 resolutions, 5 bit rates, and 3 codecs, we are left with 540 test cases for both PFIFO and TFIFO queuing disciplines. Obviously, it is infeasible to perform subjective testing on 540 test cases. In order to reduce the number of subjective test cases even further, we consider a "cross-codec elimination" scheme.

This scheme compares two test cases under the same network condition, resolution, and bit rate for a given queuing discipline but with different codecs and determines

if they are equivalent or different. The method we used to determine test case equivalence is based on the difference of the PIR objective QoE measurements for the two test cases under consideration. The lesser the difference in the PIR values, the greater is the likelihood that both the test cases have the same user QoE. Consequently, if two test cases are equivalent, we perform subjective testing only for one of the test cases, and assign the same MOS ranking to the other test case. If they are different, we perform subjective testing for both the test cases to obtain MOS rankings.

Since the PIR values increase with increasing severity of the network conditions as evident from Figures 6 and 7, the PIR difference ranges are relatively smaller at Good network conditions and relatively large at Poor network conditions. Hence, we derive "threshold curves" for each of the GAP curves such that the threshold curve values are 0.3 times the GAP curve values. We chose the 0.3 value because we found that differences in PIR below this value are not perceivably apparent to human observers. If the PIR difference between two cases falls below the threshold curve, we consider the two test cases to be equivalent. Whereas, if the PIR difference of the two test cases falls above the threshold curve, we consider the two test cases to be different. By employing this scheme, we reduced the subjective test cases from 540 to 280 (48% reduction) for the PFIFO queuing discipline, and from 540 to 322 (40% reduction) for the TFIFO queuing discipline.

4.2. Subjective Testing. Our subjective testing was based on online network condition emulation and not based on using presaved clips as done in most other works [13]. This enabled us to inject frame-freeze events intermittently as explained in Section 3.

4.2.1. Subjective Metrics. The collection of the subjective MOS rankings during voting periods of human subject experiments was conducted in compliance with the ITU-T P.911 standard. Note that we measured "relative MOS" and not "absolute MOS" for the different video resolutions. The absolute MOS depends on the resolution, whereas the relative MOS does not. For instance, if the absolute MOS under a close to ideal network condition for a HD resolution is 4.8, then the absolute MOS for QCIF resolution will be 4.2. By measuring relative MOS, under the same network condition, MOS will be 4.8 for both HD and QCIF resolutions. This way, video sequence transcoding to other resolutions does not impact MOS ranking for the different resolutions. The MOS rankings provided by the human subjects during voting periods were on a subjective quality scale of 1 to 5 as shown in Figure 8.

4.2.2. Compliance with ITU-T P.911. For compliance with ITU-T P.911, we developed a test administration application for the human subject experiments. The application uses the Java Socket API and consists of client and server modules that are installed on the VLC server machine and Netem machine, respectively. Upon indication of the start of a test case by the test administrator at the VLC server, the server module selects a random test video sequence for streaming to

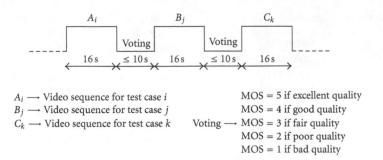

FIGURE 8: Stimulus presentation for ACR MOS collection as per ITU-T P.911.

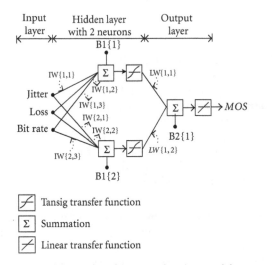

⌐⌐ Tansig transfer function

⌐Σ⌐ Summation

⌐⌐ Linear transfer function

FIGURE 9: Neural network architecture showing model parameters.

the VLC client and also notifies the Netem client to configure the corresponding test case's network condition. We adopted the most commonly used "absolute category rating" (ACR) method specified in the ITU-T P.911, which is the most commonly used method in subjective testing. The ACR method shown in Figure 8, which is a single stimulus method where test video sequences are presented one at a time using the test administration application and the human subjects rate independently. Our test administration application that implemented the ACR method had a time pattern for video sequence stimulus presentation to the human subjects.

We divided human subjects into two groups for model construction: (i) 10 human subjects for QCIF and QVGA resolution test cases and (ii) 10 human subjects for SD and HD resolution test cases. Note that ITU-T recommends 4 as a minimum number of human subjects needed for statistical soundness [13] in human subject experiments. Each of the human subjects were provided with participation instructions that included purpose, procedure, potential risks, expected duration, confidentiality protection, and legal rights. The human subjects were given generous breaks to avoid fatigue, and the testing time per human subject varied between 60–80 minutes.

5. Neural Network Modeling

We now present our modeling methodology based on neural network principles to derive closed-form expressions of multimedia QoE. After populating the human subjects MOS rankings database, we use the database to train our psycho-acoustic-visual model. We employ neural networks as our modeling technique using the Matlab Neural Network Toolbox [22]. Neural networks are essentially a system of adjustable parameters called "Weights" (i.e., IW—Initialization Weight, LW—Load Weight) and "Biases" (i.e., B). The parameters are adjusted during the training of the neural network, which results in specific weights and biases. A scalar input is multiplied by the effective weight and added to the bias to produce the target output. The network is adjusted based on a comparison of the output and the target, until the network output matches the target.

The type of neural network used in our study is a "feed-forward network", whose architecture is shown in Figure 9. The neural network consists of an input layer, hidden layer with 2 neurons, and an output layer. The output layer acts as a normalizing segment and is of the Purelin type, which covers the entire output range. Our feed-forward modeling schema allowed us to approximate both linear and nonlinear data functions. Two hidden neurons are used to perform computation of weights and biases paying due considerations to the trade-off between speed and accuracy. It is known that greater the number of hidden layers, greater is the time taken by the model to compute the weights and biases, and greater is the accuracy. The Tansig transfer function (covers range −1–1) is used to facilitate accurate modeling of nonlinear aspects of the data process. The type of training function we used is the Trainlm (Levenberg-Marquardt backpropagation algorithm), which produces suitable accuracy for the size of the network in our problem. It cuts off the model training (i.e., the number of epochs) before the model becomes overtrained with a given data set, and learns much faster than the traditional training functions such as Traingd (Gradient Descent backpropagation algorithm).

The input parameters we modeled are: (i) jitter, (ii) loss, and (iii) bit rate. The model output is the MOS ranking in the range (1–5). We developed multi-resolution neural network models for each codec combination and queuing disciplines. We developed a total of 12 models corresponding to the 3 codecs for each of the 4 resolutions

Model parameters:

	IW		B1	LW		B2
IW{1, 1}	IW{1, 2}	IW{1, 3}	B1{1}	LW{1, 1}	LW{1, 2}	B2{1}
IW{2, 1}	IW{2, 2}	IW{2, 3}	B1{2}			

MOS calculation:

$$\alpha = \text{loss} * (IW\{1,1\}) + \text{jitter} * (IW\{1,2\}) + \text{bit rate} * (IW\{1, 3\}) + B1\{1\}$$
$$\beta = \text{loss} * (IW\{2,1\}) + \text{jitter} * (IW\{2,2\}) + \text{bit rate} * (IW\{2, 3\}) + B1\{2\}$$
$$\gamma = \tanh(\alpha)$$
$$\zeta = \tanh(\beta)$$

$$\boxed{MOS = \gamma * (LW\{1,1\}) + \zeta * (LW\{1,2\}) + B2\{1\}}$$

FIGURE 10: MOS calculation using neural network model parameters.

TABLE 6: TFIFO model parameters showing weights and biases for QCIF and QVGA resolutions.

Params.	QCIF MPEG-2	QCIF MPEG-4	QCIF H.264	QVGA MPEG-2	QVGA MPEG-4	QVGA H.264
IW{1, 1}	1.5925	73.9938	0.54	−1.805	0.8271	−53.9923
IW{1, 2}	−6.6656	99.6796	0.2806	−1.1208	0.3625	0.9155
IW{1, 3}	−0.4831	−30.1671	0.0507	−17.6184	−0.0008	8.7659
IW{2, 1}	0.5170	0.7311	289.0135	−0.7044	−2.9727	−1.249
IW{2, 2}	0.5438	0.4927	88.5316	−0.3372	−16.2994	−0.5441
IW{2, 3}	0.0400	0.0803	−25.5375	−0.009	−19.3425	−0.0562
B1{1}	1.7810	65.876	0.6902	−2.9083	1.0195	−31.2057
B1{2}	1.1284	−0.2967	53.7415	−2.3335	48.4183	0.3567
LW{1, 1}	−0.7164	−0.3313	−11.176	−133.596	−19.0374	0.2548
LW{1, 2}	−31.2439	−3.2402	−0.7112	271.4444	0.2697	3.5383
B2{1}	31.5663	4.6002	12.7213	138.3723	19.9051	4.51

for each queuing discipline. Tables 6 and 7 show the model parameters for the 12 TFIFO queuing discipline models. Tables 8 and 9 show the model parameters for the 12 PFIFO queuing discipline models. Figure 10 shows how the MOS calculation is performed using the neural network model parameters. We remark that we used the Matlab Neural Network Toolbox's "training state" plots to terminate the model training and derive the weight and bias parameters that are shown in Tables 6–9; the plots help us to identify the weight and bias parameters that do not overtrain the model with a given data set.

6. Performance Evaluation

In this section we present our performance evaluation methodology used and results obtained after critical examination of our models. The results correspond to our models prediction performance in terms of overall characteristics, accuracy, consistency, and speed.

6.1. Model Characteristics. We verified the characteristics of all our multi-resolution models by observing the MOS predictions for test cases with systematically increasing jitter and loss inputs, at different bit rate settings in the resolution-specific ranges. The observations were made by plotting 3-dimensional graphs of jitter, loss, and model predicted MOS.

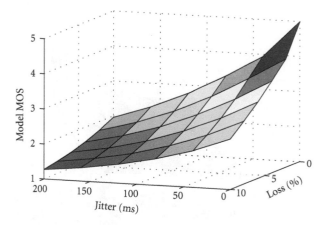

FIGURE 11: TFIFO QCIF model characteristics at 512 Kbps bit rate.

Figures 11 and 12 show example graphs, which correspond to the MOS predictions of the TFIFO models for QCIF and HD resolutions, respectively, at 512 Kbps bit rate. In each model case, we were able to confirm that the MOS predicted by the model decreases with the increase in the jitter and loss levels. Also, the predicted MOS was 5 at the best network condition with 0 jitter and 0 loss; it decreased with increasing jitter and loss and reached 1 at and after the highest value of jitter and loss used. Thus, owing to our above systematic evaluation of

Table 7: TFIFO model parameters showing weights and biases for SD and HD resolutions.

Params.	SD MPEG-2	SD MPEG-4	SD H.264	HD MPEG-2	HD MPEG-4	HD H.264
IW$\{1,1\}$	−235.618	69.198	1.9839	−2.705	18.0678	13.2719
IW$\{1,2\}$	−59.4654	66.7891	2.24103	−0.7994	−4.0983	−4.5941
IW$\{1,3\}$	−0.0141	16.6377	0.2509	−0.0137	2.0437	−0.0316
IW$\{2,1\}$	1.3085	−1.5325	−272.955	0.9113	−2.7116	2.9783
IW$\{2,2\}$	1.4055	−0.9056	−69.1575	−6.7765	−0.7866	0.276
IW$\{2,3\}$	0.1048	−0.0147	−0.0183	−4.5513	−0.0187	0.0075
B1$\{1\}$	30.533	−127.695	−2.9503	−1.4931	−14.7136	5.0295
B1$\{2\}$	−1.4295	−1.6538	35.7638	1.5997	−0.6561	1.6912
LW$\{1,1\}$	0.8211	−0.2376	−0.7411	51.6476	0.129	65.2392
LW$\{1,2\}$	−1.2851	62.1292	1.194	−26.1423	12.0581	−70.5904
B2$\{1\}$	3.0135	63.3574	2.9553	26.7493	13.1543	6.2374

Table 8: PFIFO model parameters showing weights and biases for QCIF and QVGA resolutions.

Params.	QCIF MPEG-2	QCIF MPEG-4	QCIF H.264	QVGA MPEG-2	QVGA MPEG-4	QVGA H.264
IW$\{1,1\}$	29.5296	5.1324	5.4489	0.0934	−23.7788	−4.4705
IW$\{1,2\}$	−53.6772	−1.3168	27.4114	0.1402	4.3746	2.3579
IW$\{1,3\}$	0.7985	−5.0446	−1.5200	0.0025	8.4277	0.0110
IW$\{2,1\}$	−0.0350	0.0167	−0.0479	5.6176	−0.0377	−0.0672
IW$\{2,2\}$	−0.1508	0.0736	−0.2183	−0.6570	−0.1304	−0.0397
IW$\{2,3\}$	−0.0210	0.0131	−0.0360	−26.1136	−0.0205	−0.0015
B1$\{1\}$	−15.6984	10.9947	−2.2131	−0.2708	19.0489	10.5100
B1$\{2\}$	0.8192	−0.9046	1.4721	16.4723	0.3639	1.0951
LW$\{1,1\}$	0.1918	−0.0691	−0.3595	−3.5616	0.2382	−1.6414
LW$\{1,2\}$	3.1491	−6.7489	2.2291	0.5117	3.3048	17.6250
B2$\{1\}$	2.5604	−0.3827	2.4283	4.4878	3.6572	−7.5768

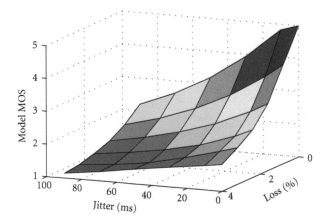

Figure 12: TFIFO HD model characteristics at 512 Kbps bit rate.

the model prediction characteristics for a comprehensive set of control inputs, we can conclude that the model prediction behavior follows expected patterns.

6.2. Model Accuracy and Consistency.
In order to validate the accuracy and consistency of our models, we choose 60 validation test cases that encompass video sequences and network conditions that are different from the ones used in the model training. Given that our model construction:

(a) considered additional factors (e.g., PFIFO/TFIFO router queuing disciplines, online network emulation, frame-freeze impairment events) and (b) was targeted specifically at multi-resolution video sequence-based IPTV applications, it is not reasonable to compare our models with existing real-time QoE models such as [13, 17, 18] that have different considerations and application contexts. Hence, we took a poll of 10 human subjects by administering the 60 validation test cases to collect Validation MOS (V-MOS) rankings using the same testbed setup explained in Section 3. We compared the V-MOS rankings with the corresponding test case model MOS predictions (M-MOS). The metrics: (i) correlation coefficient (r) and (ii) root mean square error (rmse) are used to evaluate model prediction accuracy, and the outlier ratio (or) metric is used to evaluate model consistency.

The correlation coefficient r of the pairs (x, y), where x is the V-MOS and y is the M-MOS, is calculated as follows:

$$r = \frac{n\sum xy - (\sum x)(\sum y)}{\sqrt{n(\sum x^2) - (\sum x)^2}\sqrt{n(\sum y^2) - (\sum y)^2}}. \tag{1}$$

Having r as close to 1 indicates that the model MOS ranking predictions closely match the human subject MOS rankings.

TABLE 9: PFIFO model parameters showing weights and biases for SD and HD resolutions.

Params.	SD MPEG-2	SD MPEG-4	SD H.264	HD MPEG-2	HD MPEG-4	HD H.264
IW{1,1}	0.0774	8.2689	6.0167	0.1001	0.0470	18.6600
IW{1,2}	0.3627	−47.4086	10.5060	0.9631	0.2612	1.4276
IW{1,3}	0.0256	2.1463	0.0344	0.0179	0.1268	3.4165
IW{2,1}	0.6096	163.2712	14.4661	−0.1703	−0.5565	−0.4194
IW{2,2}	−3.0682	46.1962	14.4351	−0.8077	−0.0374	−0.1042
IW{2,3}	−0.1490	−35.2372	0.1807	−0.0177	0.0179	−0.0079
B1{1}	−0.6770	−18.4515	0.7189	−1.2166	−1.0055	−48.3245
B1{2}	3.4885	−129.5034	−41.3358	1.0665	−1.1830	−0.9670
LW{1,1}	−3.5498	0.0098	−43.2699	15.4020	−0.9678	−0.2964
LW{1,2}	−0.7699	−0.9262	−0.9502	18.0452	12.9946	13.3309
B2{1}	3.7081	3.3711	46.3764	3.8736	15.0390	14.9439

The difference between the V-MOS and M-MOS for test case i is defined as the absolute prediction error P_{error} given by

$$P_{error}(i) = \text{MOS}(i) - \text{MOS}_p(i). \quad (2)$$

The rmse of P_{error} is calculated as follows:

$$\text{rmse} = \sqrt{\frac{1}{N-d}\sum_N P_{error}[i]^2}, \quad (3)$$

where N denotes the number of samples and d denotes the mapping function's number of degrees of freedom.

The outlier ratio (or) is defined as the ratio of "outlier points" to total points N and is calculated as follows:

$$\text{or} = \frac{\text{Total Number of Outliers}}{N}, \quad (4)$$

where an outlier is defined as a point for which -

$$|P_{error}(i)| > 2 * \sigma(\text{MOS}(i)), \quad (5)$$

where $\sigma(\text{MOS}(i))$ represents the standard deviation of the individual scores associated with sample i.

The performance of the model predicted MOS (M-MOS) to the human subject *MOS* rankings for the validation test cases (V-MOS) can be seen from Figure 13 for the TFIFO queuing discipline and Figure 14 for the PFIFO queuing discipline. The accuracy of the model is evaluated by determining the correlation coefficient between the M-MOS and V-MOS rankings for corresponding network conditions. The results of the average r and rmse for the TFIFO and PFIFO models are presented in Table 10. It is evident from the results that even in the worst-case scenarios, the M-MOS is very close to V-MOS because r is >0.9 and rmse is <0.7 across all the 4 resolutions for both TFIFO and PFIFO models. Upon checking the consistency of the model using the or metric, we observed that all of the models had *zero* outliers.

There is further evidence that the model predictions are consistent with what actual users experience while using multi-resolution IPTV applications on the Internet.

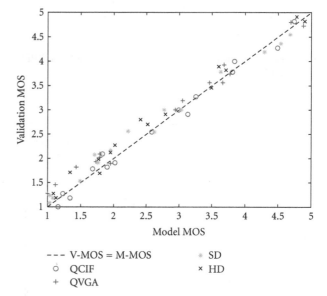

FIGURE 13: Correlation between TFIFO Model MOS and TFIFO Validation MOS.

TABLE 10: Accuracy results for TFIFO and PFIFO models.

Resolution	r (TFIFO)	rmse (TFIFO)	r (PFIFO)	rmse (PFIFO)
QCIF	0.98	0.24	0.98	0.37
QVGA	0.98	0.61	0.94	0.51
SD	0.94	0.60	0.92	0.55
HD	0.96	0.56	0.91	0.55

6.3. *Model Speed.* We evaluate the prediction speed of the models to determine if they can be successfully deployed on devices such as routers, gateways, set-top boxes, or measurement servers in a scalable manner. Specifically, even in large-scale IPTV content delivery networks, where QoE monitoring points process several tens to thousands of IPTV flows, the model speed should be small enough that it does not overburden a device's processor. The flows correspond to the measurements of numerous network paths on which critical IPTV services are provided to consumer

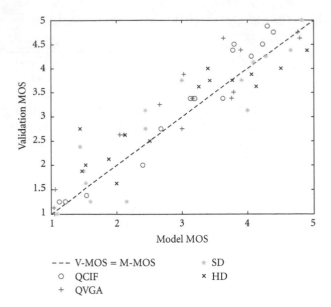

FIGURE 14: Correlation between PFIFO model MOS and PFIFO validation MOS.

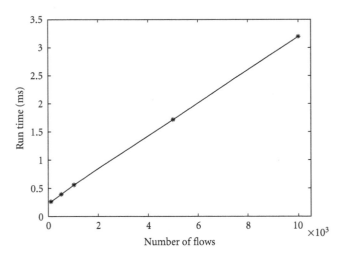

FIGURE 15: Model speed for increasing number of flows.

groups. To evaluate the model speed, we conduct a run time analysis simulation in which we calculate the amount of time taken by any of the neural network models to predict the MOS rankings for increasing number of flows with random network conditions. Four separate test runs of this simulation are conducted, and the average run-time is calculated. Representative model run time results are shown in Figure 15. From the results, we can see that even for the case of online prediction of MOS rankings for 10,000 flows, the model speed is <4 ms. Thus, the prediction speed of any of the models is negligible, making them suitable for integration even in embedded-monitoring protocols such as RTCP-extended reports (RTCP-XR) [28] in considerably large-scale IPTV content delivery networks.

7. Conclusion

In this paper, we presented a novel methodology to develop *real-time* and *zero-reference* multimedia QoE models for IPTV applications. The models were developed using neural network principles for multiple resolution (QCIF, QVGA, SD, HD) video sequences streamed with popular codec combinations (MPEG-2 video with MPEG-2 audio, MPEG-4 video with AAC audio, and H.264 video with AAC audio) and bit rates for different network health conditions. Also, we showed the impact of PFIFO and TFIFO router queuing disciplines on multimedia QoE in IPTV content delivery networks and developed separate models for each of them. The models developed can be used for online QoE estimation given measurable network factors such as jitter and loss. To develop the models, we proposed novel test case reduction schemes, namely, network sample space identification and cross-codec redundancy elimination that provided a manageable sample space to collect MOS rankings from human subject experiments in compliance with the ITU-T P.911 recommendation. Using our test case reduction schemes and two novel objective QoE metrics at the user-level (PIR) and network-level (FPL), we were able to reduce 1080 test scenarios for the modeling to 602 test cases without comprising model coverage. We evaluated our models prediction performance in terms of overall characteristics, accuracy, consistency, and speed. In worst-case scenarios, we observed our model predicted MOS rankings to have >0.9 correlation coefficient with <0.7 root mean square error and zero outlier ratio when compared with actual human subject validation MOS rankings. Also, our model speed results suggest that over 10,000 flows can be handled in <4 ms. Thus, our impressive performance of models demonstrate their suitability to be used for: (a) continuous multimedia QoE monitoring in devices such as routers, gateways, set-top boxes, or measurement servers and (b) real-time adaptation of system and network resources, in small-to-large scale IPTV content delivery networks.

References

[1] E. Jopling and A. Sabia, "Forecast: IPTV subscribers and service revenue, worldwide, 2004–2010," *Gartner IPTV Market Report*, 6 pages, 2006.

[2] J. Klaue, B. Rathke, and A. Wolisz, "EvalVid—A framework for video transmission and quality evaluation," in *Proceedings of the 13th International Conference on Modelling Techniques and Tools for Computer Performance Evaluation*, pp. 255–272, 2003.

[3] ITU-T Recommendation J.144, "Objective perceptual video quality measurement techniques for digital cable television in the presence of a full reference," 2001.

[4] "Subjective audiovisual quality assessment methods for multimedia applications," ITU-T Rec. P.911, 1998.

[5] P. Calyam, M. Haffner, E. Ekici, and C. G. Lee, "Measuring interaction QoE in Internet videoconferencing," *IEEE MMNS*, vol. 4787, pp. 14–25, 2007.

[6] G. M. Muntean, P. Perry, and L. Murphy, "Subjective assessment of the quality-oriented adaptive scheme," *IEEE Transactions on Broadcasting*, vol. 51, no. 3, pp. 276–286, 2005.

[7] X. Lu, S. Tao, M. Zarki, and R. Guerin, "Quality-based adaptive video over the Internet," in *Proceedings of the CNDS*, 2003.

[8] M. Ghanbari, D. Crawford, M. Fleury et al., "Future performance of video codecs," in Ofcom Research Report (SES2006-7-13), 2006.

[9] X. Hei, C. Liang, J. Liang, Y. Liu, and K. W. Ross, "A measurement study of a large-scale P2P IPTV system," *IEEE Transactions on Multimedia*, vol. 9, no. 8, pp. 1672–1687, 2007.

[10] M. Claypool and J. Tanner, "The effects of jitter on the perceptual quality of video," in *Proceedings of the ACM Multimedia*, pp. 115–118, New York, NY, USA =, 1999.

[11] Y. Won and M. Choi, "End-User IPTV traffic measurement of residential broadband access networks," in *Proceedings of the IEEE Workshop on End-to-End Monitoring Techniques and Services*, pp. 95–100, Salvador, Bahia, Brazil, 2008.

[12] S. Winkler and R. Campos, "Video quality evaluation for Internet streaming applications," *Human Vision and Electronic Imaging*, vol. 3, pp. 104–115, 2003.

[13] S. Mohamed and G. Rubino, "A study of real-time packet video quality using random neural networks," *IEEE Transactions on Circuits and Systems for Video Technology*, vol. 12, no. 12, pp. 1071–1083, 2002.

[14] M. H. Pinson and S. Wolf, "A new standardized method for objectively measuring video quality," *IEEE Transactions on Broadcasting*, vol. 50, no. 3, pp. 312–322, 2004.

[15] "The E-Model: a computational model for use in transmission planning," ITU-T Rec. G.107, 1998.

[16] A. P. Markopoulou, F. A. Tobagi, and M. J. Karam, "Assessment of VoIP quality over Internet backbones," in *Proceedings of the IEEE Infocom*, pp. 150–159, June 2002.

[17] S. Tao, J. Apostolopoulos, and R. Guérin, "Real-time monitoring of video quality in IP networks," *IEEE/ACM Transactions on Networking*, vol. 16, no. 5, pp. 1052–1065, 2008.

[18] F. Massidda, D. D. Giusto, and C. Perra, "No reference video quality estimation based on human visual system for 2.5/3G devices," in *Proceedings of the SPIE and T Electronic Imaging*, pp. 168–179, January 2005.

[19] H. J. Kim and S. G. Choi, "A study on a QoS/QoE correlation model for QoE evaluation on IPTV service," in *Proceedings of the 12th International Conference on Advanced Communication Technology (ICACT '10)*, pp. 1377–1382, February 2010.

[20] V. Menkovski, A. Oredope, A. Liotta, and A. Cuadra, "Predicting quality of experience in multimedia streaming," in *Proceedings of the 7th International Conference on Advances in Mobile Computing and Multimedia, (MoMM '09)*, pp. 52–59, December 2009.

[21] S. Balasubramaniam, J. Mineraud, P. McDonagh et al., "An evaluation of parameterized gradient based routing with QoE monitoring for multiple IPTV providers," *IEEE Transactions on Broadcasting*, vol. 57, no. 2, pp. 183–194, 2011.

[22] H. Demuth and M. Beale, *Matlab Neural Network Toolbox User's Guide*, The MathWorks, 2000.

[23] A. Takahashi, D. Hands, and V. Barriac, "Standardization activities in the ITU for a QoE assessment of IPTV," *IEEE Communications Magazine*, vol. 46, no. 2, pp. 78–84, 2008.

[24] "VLC media player," http://www.videolan.org/vlc.

[25] S. Hemminger, "Netem—Emulating real networks in the lab," in *Proceedings of the Linux Conference*, Australia, 2005.

[26] J. Bellardo and S. Savage, "Measuring packet reordering," in *Proceedings of the 2nd ACM SIGCOMM Internet Measurement Workshop (IMW '02)*, pp. 97–105, November 2002.

[27] P. Calyam, M. Sridharan, W. Mandrawa, and P. Schopis, "Performance measurement and analysis of h.323 traffic," in *Proceedings of the Passive and Active Measurement Workshop*, vol. 3015, pp. 137–146, 2004.

[28] T. Friedman, R. Caceres, and A. Clark, "RTP control protocol extended reports (RTCP XR)," IETF RFC 3611, 2003.

3

Towards an Automatic Parameter-Tuning Framework for Cost Optimization on Video Encoding Cloud

Xiaowei Li, Yi Cui, and Yuan Xue

Department of Electrical Engineering and Computer Science, Vanderbilt University, Nashville, TN 37235, USA

Correspondence should be addressed to Xiaowei Li, xiaowei.li@vanderbilt.edu

Academic Editor: Yifeng He

The emergence of cloud encoding services facilitates many content owners, such as the online video vendors, to transcode their digital videos without infrastructure setup. Such service provider charges the customers only based on their resource consumption. For both the service provider and customers, lowering the resource consumption while maintaining the quality is valuable and desirable. Thus, to choose a cost-effective encoding parameter, configuration is essential and challenging due to the tradeoff between bitrate, encoding speed, and resulting quality. In this paper, we explore the feasibility of an automatic parameter-tuning framework, based on which the above objective can be achieved. We introduce a simple service model, which combines the bitrate and encoding speed into a single value: encoding cost. Then, we conduct an empirical study to examine the relationship between the encoding cost and various parameter settings. Our experiment is based on the one-pass Constant Rate Factor method in x264, which can achieve relatively stable perceptive quality, and we vary each parameter we choose to observe how the encoding cost changes. The experiment results show that the tested parameters can be independently tuned to minimize the encoding cost, which makes the automatic parameter-tuning framework feasible and promising for optimizing the cost on video encoding cloud.

1. Introduction

The consensus of both academia and industry has been reached that cloud computing will be the next revolutionary progress in information technology, in which dynamically scalable and virtualized computation resources are provided as service over Internet. It has drawn extensive attention from IT giants, such as Amazon (EC2, Elastic Computing Cloud; S3, Simple Storage Service) [1], Google (GAE, Google Application Engine) [2], and Microsoft (Azure) [3]. Customers are charged based on the amount of computation resources they actually have consumed, including CPU time, memory, storage, and transferred bytes. For example, Amazon EC2 charges $0.125 per hour for standard on-demand CPU instances running Windows and $1.20 for extra-large high-CPU instances as for now [1].

Online video vendors like YouTube [4], Youku [5], and Tudou [6] have a huge number of videos of various formats uploaded by users every day, which need to be transcoded (format converted) into their desired intermediate formats, such as .flv, for storage and replay. Such transcoding work

is computing-intensive and time-consuming. It also requires storage space and bandwidth for transfer, which pose extremely high demands on hardware resources. Many content owners (libraries, traditional media production units, and governments) have the need to digitize and distribute their contents, but no technical resources/expertise to do so. With the introduction of cloud computing, a new type of Internet service termed encoding cloud emerges, which builds on the cloud infrastructure (e.g., Amazon EC2) to provide value-added video encoding service to meet the aforementioned demands. A successful example is Flix Cloud [7], which combines On2's Flix Engine encoding software with Zencoder's web-based application to provide scalable online encoding service based on Amazon EC2. Another example is http://www.encoding.com/, which offers a similar web-based "pay-as-you-go" service.

For both encoding service providers and customers, a good trade-off between quality and speed is desirable for cost saving purposes. The difficulty originates from the inherent complexity of modern video encoding technologies, most of which inherit from the block-based hybrid coding design. For example, x264, a widely adopted video encoding engine, exposes more than 100 parameters [8] for its users to balance a long list of factors including encoding speed, bitrate, objective/subjective quality, decoding buffer, and so forth. Evidently, it would be prohibitively expensive for an operator to figure out the most economically efficient "encoding recipes" for thousands of uploaded videos every day. Nevertheless, any endeavor towards this goal is imperative and essential, since the cost saving on the cloud resource consumption will simply add to the profits, whose amount would be quite considerable given the sheer volume of video being encoded. To this end, we believe that an automated mechanism for encoding parameter selection and tuning would be very valuable and timely.

In this paper, we commence our exploration towards this goal. To the best of our knowledge, there is no prior work on this front. Our study chooses H.264 as the targeted video coding standard, and specifically x264 as the targeted encoding software. The rationale of our choice is delayed to Section 2. Our empirical study makes the following important findings.

(i) Modern video encoding technology, represented by x264, is able to precisely and consistently achieve any specified numerical target on subjective/objective quality metric, such as PSNR (peak signal-to-noise ratio). This is a must-have property for any cost-optimization framework desiring to meet stringent encoding quality constraint.

(ii) While observing the quality constraint, we find that many key video encoding parameters (e.g., B-frame) are shown to be able to be independently tuned to adjust the encoding cost.

(iii) There are also strong indications that the impact of each parameter to the final encoding cost can be specified in a weighted sum fashion, in which the weight stays invariant to external factors such as cost coefficients. Combined with previous two observations, it suggests the feasibility of an automatic tuning framework over decomposable parameters, which can quickly find the optimal operation point and predict the encoding cost, if certain knowledge on encoding complexity of the video itself is available a priori.

The rest of this paper is organized as follows. Section 2 reasons our selection on x264 and reveals the internal relationship among bitrate, quality, and encoding speed. Section 3 defines a simple service model under the cloud computing environment. Section 4 presents the experimental results on key parameters in x264, such as B-frame, Ref, Subme, and Trellis. By examining critical observations made here, Section 5 discusses promises and hurdles towards an automatic cost tuning framework. Some related work are described in Section 6. Section 7 concludes this paper.

2. Related Work

Some research work [9–11] propose various algorithms, including mode ranking and learning theoretic, to optimize the R-D (rate-distortion) performance while constraining the computational complexity. Although they also address the ternary relationship between bitrate, encoding time, and quality, their approaches aim at improving the encoding technologies at the macroblock level. References [12, 13] also address the issues associated with handheld devices and power-constrained environments. The most related work to ours are the algorithms proposed by Vanam et al. [14, 15], which are employed to select the parameter settings that have comparable performances with those chosen by exhaustive search using a much fewer number of trials. Rhee et al. [16] propose a real-time encoder, which dynamically adjusts the predefined complexity level to meet the target time budget while maintaining the encoding quality and efficiency.

Both our objective and methodology are different from theirs. First, we are trying to establish a parameter-tuning framework, which can be used for optimizing the encoding cost (or resource consumption) based on a specific service model, while they aim at optimizing the R-D performance. Second, we do not touch the internal of the encoding software, but regard it as a black-box system, whose input is the encoding parameter settings and the original video. We would like to examine the correlation between different parameter settings and encoding performances regardless of the tested video, essentially how the encoding parameters affect the behavior of the encoding software. The parameter-tuning framework is established on the empirical study over a large number of videos. Given a specific video whose encoding complexity can be estimated, an optimal parameter setting which minimizes the encoding cost with satisfiable quality will be generated.

3. Encoding in x264

3.1. Rationale. In this study, we choose H.264 as the video coding standard and use x264 as the encoding software. Our choice of H.264 roots on the simple fact that it has been recognized as the most pervasive video coding standard for web videos with the support of Flash Player 10 by its outstanding compression and efficiency. Currently, the encoding cloud services have integrated a large number of encoding/transcoding software, either open-source or commercial, including On2 Flix [7], Mencoder [17], and Zencoder [18]. Among burgeoning H.264 codec, x264 [19] is one of the best performers (supported by MSU Annual H.264 Codec Comparison Report [20]) and adopted by many widely popular applications including ffmpeg [21], Mencoder, and similar x264 implements almost all of the H.264 features, which means that users have a pretty large parameter configuration space to accommodate their specific encoding requirements, a particular merit of x264. Furthermore, experiments conducted by YUV Soft [22] have shown that using x264 could achieve either excellent compression quality or extremely fast encoding speed with great flexibility, depending on the parameter settings.

3.2. Encoding Model. We model a video for encoding using two parameters:

(i) N: the number of frames;

(ii) F: the frame rate (frame per second), which is the number of frames played in one second.

We use three metrics for evaluating the encoding configuration under H.264.

(i) V: the encoding speed (second/frame), which is the time required to encode one frame. We use encoding rate and encoding speed interchangeably in this paper;

(ii) R: the bitrate after compression with container overhead (kbps), which implies the final file size and the compression ratio;

(iii) *PSNR*: the peak signal-to-noise ratio, which represents the resulting objective quality. There are two variations, average PSNR and global PSNR. Usually global PSNR is a little lower than average PSNR and we choose average PSNR in this paper.

All the above metrics can be easily obtained from the output statistics of x264.

3.3. Rate Control Modes in x264. Modern video encoding software, combined with the flexibility promised by the encoding standard such as H.264, offers handy and functional rate control methods to determine how bits are allocated within streams and tune the delicate balance among bitrate (R), encoding speed (V), and objective quality ($PSNR$). There are four rate control modes in x264, which are used most frequently, namely, CQP (Constant Quantization Parameter), CRF (Constant Rate Factor), ABR (Average Bit Rate), and two-pass VBR (Variable Bit Rate).

CQP mode specifies the same quantization values for all P-frames, meanwhile fixing the relative ratios (i.e., ipratio and pbratio) of quantization values for I-frames and B-frames in the same GOP (group of pictures). CQP mode disables adaptive quantization, a technique aiming to keep constant visual quality by imposing larger quantization values on high-complexity scenes and lower ones on low-motion scenes, based on the assumption that humans are less perceptive to high-motion scenes.

CRF mode targets a certain level of "quality" by adaptively adjusting quantization values for frames with different complexity by setting a constant rate factor. A smaller rate factor means higher quality and higher bitrate. A constant rate factor aims at consistent visual quality, while it may sacrifice some objective quality (PSNR). Generally, CRF mode produces smaller file size than CQP mode and is the most recommended one-pass mode if the quality concern overrides the strictness of the desired bitrate.

ABR and VBR modes focus on achieving the desired bitrate rather than the objective or subjective quality. Reference [23] shows that ABR mode achieves lower PSNR than CRF mode and cannot achieve the exact final file size as specified in one pass. On the same note, two-pass VBR mode

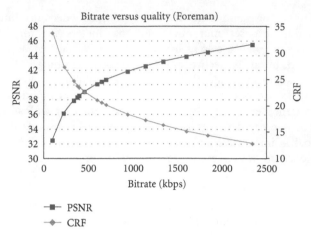

FIGURE 1: Bitrate versus PSNR and CRF (Foreman).

gives more accurate file size with possibly the highest quality. However, much more time is needed since the encoding is done practically twice, where the second pass achieves much more accurate bitrate by learning from statistics resulted from the first pass.

3.4. Bitrate, Encoding Speed, and Quality. In this section, we obtain a basic understanding of the relationship between the above three evaluation metrics. We choose the ABR mode using which we can target different bitrates and "foreman" as the example video file. Figure 1 shows the relationship between the bitrate and the resulting PSNR. We can see that the larger the bitrate, the better the quality, which is expected, although the quality improvement is becoming smaller with the escalation of bitrate. We also plot the final rate factor with varying bitrates, which is the average quantization value for all types of frames. We can see that the final rate factor is in near reverse proportional with PSNR. Since the rate factor is the major tuning parameter in CRF mode, using CRF mode can target relatively accurate video quality. Figure 2 shows the relationship between the bitrate and the encoding speed. We can see that the larger the bitrate, the longer it requires to encode a frame, since more bits are allocated. In summary, the better video quality requires larger bitrate (final file size) and longer encoding time.

4. Service Model

It is clear that changing encoding parameters simultaneously affects bitrate, encoding speed, and video quality. Thus the optimal selection of encoding parameters becomes a multiobjective optimization problem, where the tradeoffs and constraints among these objectives (e.g., bitrate, encoding speed, and video quality) are dependent on the user's preference and cost structure. Cloud service providers charge the customers based on the resource consumption. They naturally provide a unified cost structure, in which CPU usage time, memory, bandwidth, and storage expenses are represented by singular monetary value and combined as the final charges. The encoding service consumes all major resource types, including CPU usage time, memory, storage

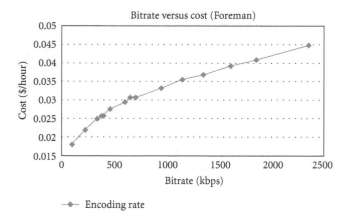

Figure 2: Bitrate versus Encoding speed (Foreman).

space, and bandwidth for data transfer. Here we omit the memory usage in our model, considering the facts that an average modern computer in the cloud (e.g., Amazon EC2 instance) has abundant memory for encoding software and memory consumption alone is not charged by current cloud service vendors. Obviously, the encoding process and the encoding results would affect the usage of various types of resource. Among the remaining three, CPU usage is only related with the encoding of the video, which is a one-time job. The CPU usage can be represented using the encoding time (T), which is calculated as

$$T = N \times V \text{ (second)}. \qquad (1)$$

Recall that N is the number of frames and V is the encoding speed as defined in Section 2. The storage and bandwidth (file transfer) usage depends on the compressed file size (S), calculated as

$$S = \frac{N}{F} \times \frac{R}{8} \text{ (byte)}. \qquad (2)$$

Recall that R is the bitrate after compression and F is the frame rate (frame per second) as defined in Section 2. Different from CPU usage, the storage and transfer costs of a video can be recurring, and dependent on different encoding service models. We define the cloud encoding cost as COST and merge the encoding time, the storage, and the bandwidth usage into a singular monetary value: operational cost of encoding (briefly encoding cost) in the cloud: COST ($)

$$\text{COST} = \alpha \times T + \beta \times S = N \times \left(\alpha V + \frac{\beta R}{8F} \right), \qquad (3)$$

where α and β are cost coefficients related with CPU usage and storage/bandwidth resources, respectively. Since different videos have different number of frames, we could normalize the above cost by eliminating N. We obtain the following normalized cost (COST′, $ per hour), which implies the cost to encode an hour long of this specific video

$$\text{COST}' = \text{COST} \times \frac{3600}{N/F} = 3600 \times \left(\alpha V F + \frac{\beta R}{8} \right). \qquad (4)$$

The new cost value, irrelevant with the number of frames, is varied with different videos, since the encoding complexity of a specific video is different from others. The cost coefficients α can be easily set as the current hourly CPU price. For example, we use $0.34/hour here, which is the price for large standard on-demand instances of Amazon EC2. On the other hand, β is dependent on the service model. For example, in the encoding-only service model, the Cloud platform is only used for the computationally extensive encoding tasks. It downloads the encoded video to its local hosting platform for long-term video storage and video distribution. In this case, the storage cost is limited to short term and there is only one-time transfer cost. For example, for transfer cost, we use the Amazon EC2's receding staircase cost starting at $0.15/GB; for the storage cost, we use $0.15/GB/month of Amazon S3 for two weeks. In the full-fledge video service model, the Cloud platform is responsible for long-term storage and distribution in addition to encoding. In this case, the storage cost depends on the storage time and the transfer cost depends on the amount of video access. Since the lifetime of the video to remain in the cloud and its popularity (hence its distribution cost) will be hard to determine, albeit a separate issue. The difficulty of predicting the above values depends on the time horizon. Nevertheless, some simple intuition developed later in this paper can be useful when uncertainty has to be dealt with.

In this work, we consider the encoding-only service model and set the goal of encoding as to maintaining the encoded quality to be acceptable by users through service-level agreement (SLA). In this way, factors other than the encoding aspect of a video (such as its popularity) are excluded.

5. Experiment Study

In the following encoding experiments, we examine the effects of parameter settings on encoding time, bitrate, and objective quality (PSNR), the collection of which determines the final cost. The test sequences we utilized are downloaded from [24], a well-recognized video test set. They are all in CIF format, 25 frames/second, and resolution of 352×288. We have tested 12 videos in total, including Bus, Coastguard, Container, Foreman, Flower, Hall, Mobile, News, Silent, Stefan, Tempete, and Waterfall. In order to minimize the stochastic errors, every set of experiments is performed five times and the results are averaged.

To align with the necessity to maintain certain acceptable level of quality, we must choose rate control methods best at controlling quality, which leaves us CQP and CRF. If purely measured by objective quality, that is, PSNR, CQP is a better candidate than CRF. But CRF brings about significant benefits, which are (1) saving more bitrate than CQP and (2) maintaining constant subjective quality, a value much appreciated by end users. As such, we believe that CRF will be commonly preferred by encoding service providers as the primary rate control method, which is also our choice in this study.

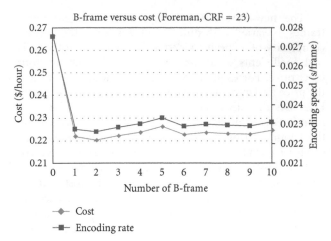

FIGURE 3: Cost and encoding speed with varying B-frame number (Foreman, crf = 23).

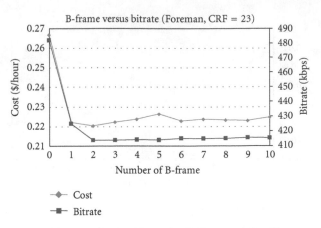

FIGURE 4: Bitrate and cost with varying B-frame number (Foreman, crf = 23).

The excellent performance of x264 is attributed to several factors, including motion estimation, frame-type decision, macroblock mode decision, and quantization. We first vary one parameter while keeping all others default, and then test multiple parameters to examine the composite effect. We note that what will frequently show up in the following figures is a parameter which is also called *CRF*. It sets the target to the CRF method to achieve the perceptual quality effect as if the same quantization value (default value is 23 in x264) is applied to the encoded video.

In the following experiments, if not clearly stated, all the test sequences exhibit similar curves as the example Foreman we will use below, under three quality levels, for concise purpose.

5.1. B-Frame. B-frame setting determines the maximum number of consecutive B-frames we can use. B-frame, different from P-frame, can use motion prediction from future frames, which enhances the compression efficiency.

Figure 3 shows the encoding cost and rate with varying B-frame numbers. We can see that the use of B-frame dramatically decreases the encoding cost, which fluctuates a little bit with higher B-frame setting. The frame-type decision algorithm in x264 for replacing a P-frame with B-frame is fast and flexible. Notice that the cost curve closely matches the encoding speed, which becomes the dominant factor using our chosen cost coefficients α and β, and the minimum cost may be achieved at different points if coefficients vary.

Figure 4 shows the bitrate and encoding cost with varying B-frame numbers. We can see that the resulting bitrate drops with the use of B-frame and down to stable level at the point of two B-frames. We speculate that the most effective number of B-frames for Foreman is 2, which is supported by the consecutive B-frame distributions extracted from x264 output statistics. The distribution of consecutive B-frames for Foreman changes from {13.4%, 86.6%} to {13.1%, 69.8%, 17.1%} if we vary the B-frame number from 1 to 2, which means with one B-frame setting, 13.4% of frames use no consecutive B-frame and 86.6% use one

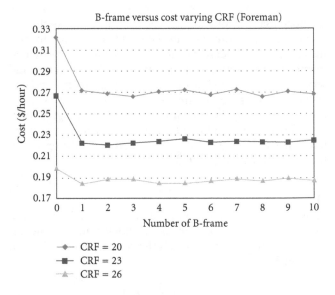

FIGURE 5: Encoding cost with varying B-frame number under different CRF settings (Foreman).

B-frame, while with two B-frame setting, 17.1% of frames use two consecutive B-frames. If we set a cutoff threshold for the cumulative distribution, say 90%, we can see the B-frame number is set to 2, which matches our observation. We also did the same experiments over other videos and conclude that it is appropriate for most videos to use 1 up to 3 B-frames to save significant bitrates as well as encoding time and cost while higher B-frame settings contribute little.

Figure 5 shows the encoding cost with different number of B-frames under varying CRF settings. We can see expected results that the encoding cost increases with CRF values and has marginal variations with higher B-frame numbers. Figure 6 shows the averaged encoding cost using 2 B-frames under different quality levels (CRF value) for all videos. We can see the cost rankings of videos under a specific CRF value are consistent for all the three quality levels (except Hall with CRF = 20). We speculate that it is the encoding complexity, the inherent characteristic of video, that leads to this phenomenon.

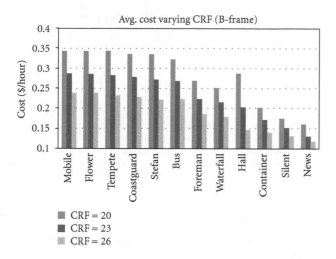

FIGURE 6: Averaged encoding cost for all videos.

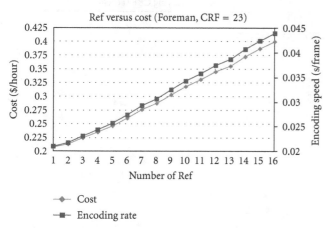

FIGURE 7: Encoding cost and rate with varying Ref number (Foreman, crf = 23).

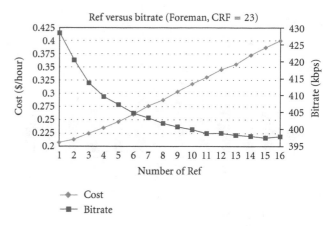

FIGURE 8: Bitrate and cost with varying Ref number (Foreman, crf = 23).

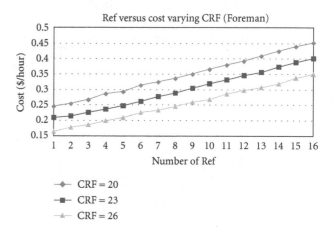

FIGURE 9: Encoding cost with varying Ref number under different CRF settings (Foreman).

5.2. *Ref.* Ref is a parameter referring to the number of previous frames that a P-frame can refer to, ranging from 1 to 16. Conceptually, each increment of Ref will bring about constant speed loss, and on the flip side, the benefit of lower bitrate, especially for highly animated videos. On the other hand, the number is dependent on both DPB (Decoded Picture Buffer) confined by ITU for specific playback devices and the preference over speed or bitrate.

Figures 7 and 8 show the encoding cost, rate, and bitrate with varying Ref numbers. As expected, a larger Ref number leads to increasing encoding time and cost, as well as decreasing bitrate. The encoding cost is mostly influenced by speed loss, and the deviation resulting from reduced bitrate is not prominent. Compared to P-frames, B-frames usually use one or two fewer reference frames. If we examine the bitrate more closely, the decreasing gradient and the relatively "stable" point for each video are different from each other.

There are two explanations. One is our choice of cost coefficients, which puts more weight on encoding speed (CPU cost) over bitrate (storage and bandwidth costs).

On the same note, it also suggests that the speed loss overshadows the bitrate benefit. The encoding time increases by about two times when Ref varies from 1 to 16, while the bitrate only drops around 30 kbps from original 430 kbps. For some videos, the bitrate variance is within 10 kbps. As such, we may suggest using as few Ref as possible for most videos, except some with high motion or complexity.

Then we vary CRF and get expected result in Figure 9 that the encoding cost increases with the quality improvement. Figure 10 displays the average cost (in most cases also the median value due to approximately linear increase) when varying CRF for all videos. Like Figure 6, the ranking is consistent with Hall being the only exception.

5.3. *Subme.* Subme controls the subpixel estimation complexity. Since H.264 has a wide range of macroblock partitions for both intra- and interpredictions, mode decision is very time-consuming. Subme levels from 0 to 5 increase the level of refinement, while levels from 6 to 9 enable a hybrid decision of SATD (sum of absolute transformed differences) and RDO (rate distortion optimization) for corresponding frame types. We do not consider level 10 since

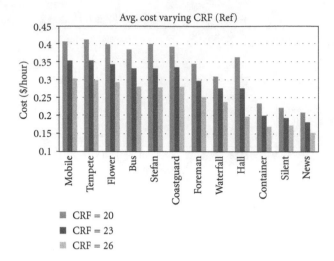

FIGURE 10: Averaged encoding cost for all videos.

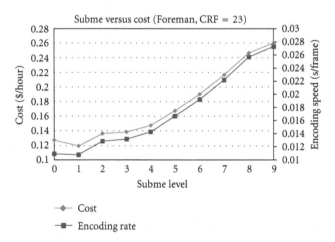

FIGURE 11: Encoding cost and rate with increasing Subme levels (Foreman, crf = 23).

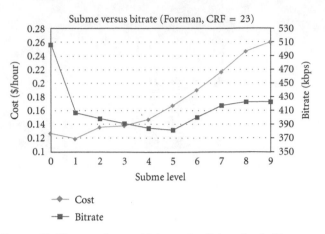

FIGURE 12: Bitrate and cost with increasing Subme levels (Foreman, crf = 23).

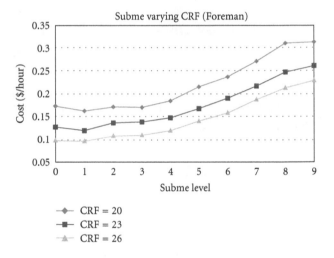

FIGURE 13: Encoding cost with increasing Subme levels under different CRF settings (Foreman).

it requires trellis option to be enabled, which only applies to extreme cases. Intuitively, higher Subme level leads to better compression efficiency at the price of encoding speed loss.

Figures 11 and 12 show the encoding cost, rate, and bitrate with increasing Subme levels. We can see that the encoding cost increases as Subme does, except a little decrease when the level goes from 0 to 1. However, in Figure 12, there is a valley at level 5 on the bitrate curve, suggesting that the application of SATD and RDO in fact increases the bitrate. This is mainly due to the rate control method (CRF) of our choice, which focuses on perceptual quality rather than the objective quality PSNR, which these two techniques target to improve. Similarly, Figure 13 shows the average encoding cost under different quality levels.

5.4. Trellis. Trellis quantization is used to optimize residual DCT coefficients by reducing the size of some coefficients while recovering others to take their place. This technique can effectively find the optimal quantization for each macroblock to optimize the PSNR relative to bitrate. There are three options in x264: level 1 applies conventional uniform

deadzone; level 2 uses trellis only on the final encode of macroblock, while level 3 does them all. In addition, trellis quantization in x264 requires CABAC (Context Adaptive Binary Arithmetic Coder), instead of the less-expensive and more-popular CAVLC (Context Adaptive Variable Length Coder). Thus, we introduce a level 0, which repeats level 1, only replacing CABAC with CAVLC.

Figures 14 and 15 show the encoding cost, rate, and bitrate with varying trellis levels. Trellis is similar to the case of Subme (Figures 11 and 12), in which the encoding cost grows as the level increases, but the bitrate fluctuates. Again, this suggests that the objective of trellis quantization (optimizing objective quality PSNR) does not always agree with the objective of the CRF method, which is the perceptual quality. This is further confirmed by our later observation on PSNR. We also see that CABAC does not cause additional speed loss while reducing bitrate by about 10%, which implies that CABAC should always be turned on. Not surprisingly, applying trellis quantization increases encoding time, especially for the level 3. In Figure 16, the encoding

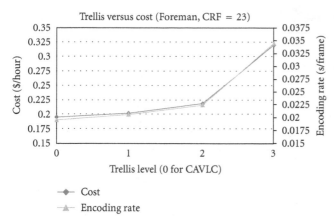

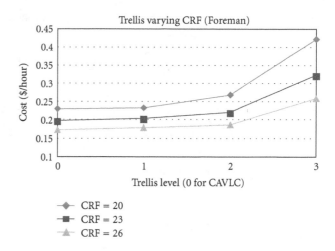

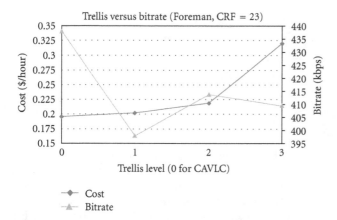

FIGURE 14: Encoding cost and rate with varying Trellis levels (Foreman, crf = 23).

FIGURE 16: Encoding cost with varying Trellis levels under different CRF settings (Foreman).

FIGURE 15: Bitrate and cost with varying Trellis levels (Foreman, crf = 23).

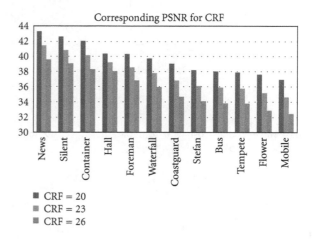

FIGURE 17: Correspondence between PSNR and CRF setting.

cost increases with the quality improvement, matching observations obtained from all previous experiments.

5.5. CRF versus PSNR. Although targeting at perceptual quality, CRF is known to be able to still achieve relatively constant objective quality level, that is, PSNR. To quantify the deviation, we observe PSNR in the above four parameter settings and obtain the following results in Table 1 (take Foreman, e.g.). The deviation is defined as the percentage of difference between lowest and highest PSNR to the highest value. We can see that during B-frame, Ref and Trellis tests, such change is within 1% range, while for Subme it is still around 3%. This makes us more confident to use CRF as the indication for quality level. Averaging all PSNR values from all tests gets us the correspondence between PSNR and CRF, as shown in Figure 17. The three quality levels show consistent rankings for all 12 videos, which implies that the encoding complexity varies with different videos.

5.6. Composite Effect of Multiple Parameters. In previous experiments, we only vary one parameter and leave all others default. Default setting uses 3 B-frames, 3 Refs, Subme level 7, and Trellis level 1. We plot the encoding costs from four parameters together in Figure 18. Approximately, the

same costs are achieved with their respective default values. Subme leads to relatively lower costs while Ref renders linearly increasing costs with Ref number. The encoding costs incurred by all the settings, except for the cases of Trellis level 2, more than 3 Refs and Subme level 8 and 9, are bounded by the costs in B-frame tests. We also test for CRF value of 20 and 26, which show similar patterns. Therefore, we can define the baseline cost for Foreman under different quality levels as the averaged encoding cost in the B-frame tests. By this definition, our B-frame test (Figure 3) actually shows the baseline costs for all videos.

The encoding cost is influenced by the comprehensive impacts of multiple parameters. In order to understand how separate parameters collaborate with each other, in one experiment we vary all the four parameters, that is, B-frame from 1 to 3, Ref from 3 to 12, Subme level from 5 to 7, and Trellis level 0 and 1. There are 180 test points in total. The results are shown in Figure 19. We can see that the encoding cost shows a recurring pattern, which implies that the aggregated cost can probably be decomposed into separate weighted factors attributable to specific parameters.

TABLE 1: PSNR versus CRF (foreman).

Foreman	crf = 20		crf = 23		crf = 26	
	PSNR mean	Deviation (%)	PSNR mean	Deviation (%)	PSRN mean	Deviation (%)
B-frame	40.38	0.51	38.60	0.09	36.88	0.33
Ref	40.45	0.79	38.73	1.08	37.03	1.21
Subme	40.05	2.6	38.25	3.01	36.49	3.26
Trellis	40.22	0.73	38.46	0.71	36.74	0.77

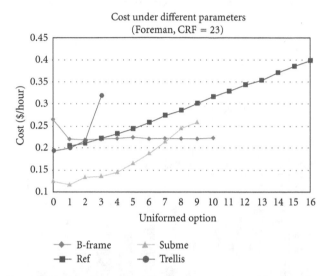

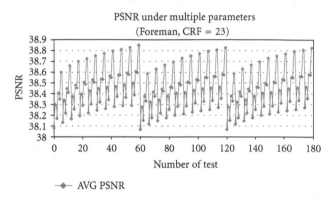

FIGURE 20: PSNR under combinations of four parameters (Foreman, crf = 23).

FIGURE 18: Encoding cost with four parameters setting together (Foreman, crf = 23).

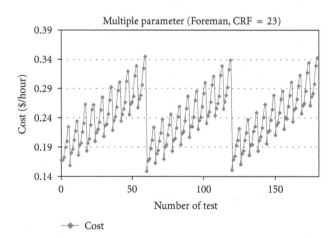

FIGURE 19: Encoding cost under combinations of four parameters (Foreman, crf = 23).

We also find that the average PSNR follows the similar pattern in Figure 20. PSNR ranges from 38.07 to 38.854, with the deviation of less than 2%. On a closer look, Trellis, Subme, and Ref consistently produce the expected impacts on PSNR.

5.7. Other Parameters. We have tested all major numerical parameters in x264, at least all that applicable to the CRF method. We here list other important parameters not included in our tests as below.

(i) ME determines the full-pixel motion estimation methods, and there are four choices in x264, namely, DIA (diamond), HEX (hexagon), UMH (Uneven Multi Hexagon), and ESA (Exhaustive Search). Generally, UMH provides good speed without sacrificing significant quality, while HEX is a better trade-off. We are using the default option HEX.

(ii) Partition controls the split up of 16×16 macroblock. Partitions are enabled per frame type and for intra- and interprediction, respectively. The default setting in x264 is "p8 $\times$ 8, b8 $\times$ 8, i8 $\times$ 8, i4 $\times$ 4." The p4 $\times$ 4 is not defaulted due to the high speed cost with respect to quality gain.

The above two parameters have also essential impacts on the encoding speed and quality. The reason why they do not fall into the scope of our consideration is that there is no apparent and absolute ranking among those options, which makes them hardly fit into our quantified parameter tuning framework. Besides, the empirical guidance about using the above two parameters are quite clear.

6. Discussion

Based on all the experiment results in the previous section, we claim the following observations.

(1) For all the tests conducted, if grouped by targeted CRF values, the resulting PSNR values in each group remain largely equal with a maximum deviation of 3% (Table 1).

(2) Each tested video, when trialed with different quality levels (CRFs), has its PSNR values shown with consistent ranking (Figure 17).

(3) Tests conducted regarding each parameter shows at least one period of asymptotic growth of encoding cost (e.g., when Ref ranges from 1 to 16), and one clear optimal point to minimize the cost (e.g., when Ref = 1). This observation also holds true across different quality levels tested.

The first two observations collectively confirm the effectiveness of CRF as a rate control method to accurately obtain consistent results on measurable and objective quality, that is, PSNR. Combined with the third observation, we can claim that our primary goal set at the end of Section 3 can be achieved. Conversely, with a clearly defined service model and desired quality level set by the user, our framework can find the optimal parameter setting to minimize the encoding cost.

However, this only works well in the best-effort way, that is, one can claim confidently that the encoding cost is indeed minimized, but never know how much the cost is until the job is done. This leads to the predictive power of the optimization framework, that is, can we predict the encoding cost of a video before it is encoded? This feature, if at all achievable, will be significantly valuable to the budget planning (hence projection of price and profit margin) for any service providers, especially appreciated when unclear service models are present, typically when it comes to the cloud-based distribution service whose storage and bandwidth costs are hard to determine. We further claim the following observations from our tests.

(4) By the functioning principles of block-based hybrid video coding, the tested parameters (e.g., Ref, Trellis, etc.) operate largely independent from each other. Our tests establish that, regarding each tested parameter, its asymptotic growth window (mentioned in claim (3)) is not affected by the changing of other parameters.

(5) Aside from independence, it is very likely that these parameters can be decomposed in a weighted sum fashion to qualify their contribution to the final encoding cost. Furthermore, such weights are not subject to the changing of the cost coefficients α and β.

(6) The B-frame test as the baseline cost (Figure 18) provides a worst-case envelope for the cost estimation if the prospect of claim (5) gets gloomy.

All these claims sound promising, even to a self-improving framework, which, with the growth of its sampling set, provides increasingly accurate weight estimation.

However, we must not ignore the elephant in the room. In Section 3, we mentioned the encoding complexity, which originates from the intrinsic characteristics of the video content itself. Evidently, Figure 21 shows the resulting bitrates of all 12 videos under the default setting (crf = 23) of x264, where the most complex video is encoded with

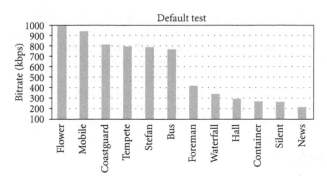

FIGURE 21: Resulting bitrates under the default setting of x264 for all videos.

bitrate 5 times the one of the lowest complexity. Figures 6 and 10 further confirm that this ranking holds across different quality levels, with the Hall as the only exception, indicating that the encoding complexity is largely rooted in the content itself.

There is no silver bullet to this problem. In order to learn the encoding complexity of a video, one has to encode it to know it, which paradoxically defeats the very propose of saving encoding cost. Fortunately, common practices of the modern encoding service largely alleviate this problem. First, most of the original content is already in the digital format (usually encoded by block-based hybrid video coding technology) awaiting transcoding to be suitable to play on the new platform. Second, the diversity of end-user terminals requires each video to be encoded multiple times to different qualities, resolutions, and formats. As such, we can easily obtain statistics from metadata of the originally encoded file to obtain the first-hand knowledge of the encoding complexity.

7. Conclusion

In this paper, we conduct an empirical study in the cloud-computing environment, targeting an optimization framework to save H.264 encoding cost by tuning the key parameters. Our study shows convincing results, in which the rate control method (CRF) demonstrates remarkable ability to precisely achieve the targeted quality level, and the tested parameters can be independently tuned to minimize the encoding cost. We have also discussed the encoding complexity as a major hurdle to the predictive power of our framework and how it can be alleviated by leveraging the diversity of end-user platforms.

Towards future study, the most urgent task is to quantify the contributing weight of key parameters to encoding cost, through more extensive experiments. Also we will incorporate important but nonnumerical parameters (such as motion estimation method) and examine its fitness to the current framework.

The final note is on the objective of our optimization framework, which is to minimize encoding cost, meanwhile maintaining certain quality level. It is not impossible for service providers to reverse the equation to give a cost budget, try to maximize the encoded quality. In light of such a change, we should switch to rate control methods best at controlling bitrate, that is, ABR and VBR. Study of this flavor will be especially valuable when distribution cost becomes the overwhelming concern. Whether a similar parameter-tuning framework could be established on this regard could be only answered by another empirical study.

References

[1] Amazon Web Services, http://aws.amazon.com/.

[2] Google Web Application Engine, http://code.google.com/appengine/.

[3] Microsoft Azure, http://www.microsoft.com/windowsazure/.

[4] http://www.youtube.com.

[5] http://www.youku.com.

[6] http://www.tudou.com.

[7] http://www.zencoder.com/flixcloud/.

[8] http://mewiki.project357.com/wiki/X264_Settings.

[9] A. Jagmohan and K. Ratakonda, "Time-efficient learning theoretic algorithms for H.264 mode selection," in *Proceedings of the International Conference on Image Processing*, pp. 749–752, October 2004.

[10] T. A. da Fonseca and R. L. de Queiroz, "Complexity-constrained H.264 HD video coding through mode ranking," in *Proceedings of the Picture Coding Symposium*, pp. 329–332, 2009.

[11] E. Akyol, D. Mukherjee, and Y. Liu, "Complexity control for real-time video coding," in *Proceedings of the IEEE International Conference on Image Processing*, pp. 177–180, September 2007.

[12] X. Li, M. Wien, and J.-R. Ohm, "Rate-complexity-distortion optimization for hybrid video coding," *IEEE Transactions on Circuits and Systems for Video Technology*, vol. 21, no. 7, pp. 957–970, 2011.

[13] L. Su, Y. Lu, F. Wu, S. Li, and W. Gao, "Complexity-constrained H.264 video encoding," *IEEE Transactions on Circuits and Systems for Video Technology*, vol. 19, no. 4, pp. 477–490, 2009.

[14] R. Vanam, E. A. Riskin, S. S. Hemami, and R. E. Ladner, "Distortion-complexity optimization of the H.264/MPEG-4 AVC encoder using the GBFOS algorithm," in *Proceedings of the Data Compression Conference*, pp. 303–312, March 2007.

[15] R. Vanam, E. A. Riskin, and R. E. Ladner, "H.264/MPEG-4 AVC encoder parameter selection algorithms for complexity distortion tradeoff," in *Proceedings of the Data Compression Conference*, pp. 372–381, March 2009.

[16] C.-E. Rhee, J.-S. Jung, and H.-J. Lee, "A real-time H.264/AVC encoder with complexity-aware time allocation," *IEEE Transactions on Circuits and Systems for Video Technology*, vol. 20, no. 12, pp. 1848–1862, 2010.

[17] http://www.mplayerhq.hu.

[18] http://www.zencoder.com/.

[19] http://www.videolan.org/developers/x264.html.

[20] MSU Graphics & Media Lab (Video Group), "Fourth annual msu mpeg-4 avc/h.264 video codec comparison," http://compression.ru/video/codec comparison/mpeg-4 avc h264 2007 en.html.

[21] http://www.ffmpeg.org/.

[22] YUV Soft Inc., http://www.yuvsoft.com.

[23] L. Merritt and R. Vanam, "Improved rate control and motion estimation for H.264 encoder," in *Proceedings of the International Conference on Image Processing*, vol. 5, pp. 309–312, 2007.

[24] http://media.xiph.org/video/derf/.

4

PAPR Reduction of OFDM Signals by Novel Global Harmony Search in PTS Scheme

Hojjat Salehinejad[1,2] and Siamak Talebi[1,2,3]

[1] Electrical Engineering Department, Shahid Bahonar University of Kerman, Kerman 76169-133, Iran
[2] International Center for Science, High Technology, and Environmental Sciences, Kerman, Iran
[3] Advanced Communications Research Institute, Sharif University of Technology, Tehran 11365-11155, Iran

Correspondence should be addressed to Hojjat Salehinejad, h.salehi@eng.uk.ac.ir

Academic Editor: Massimiliano Laddomada

The orthogonal frequency division multiplexing (OFDM) modulation technique is one of the key strategies for multiuser signal transmission especially in smart grids and wind farms. This paper introduces an approach for peak-to-average power ratio (PAPR) reduction of such signals based on novel global harmony search (NGHS) and partial transmit sequence (PTS) schemes. In PTS technique, the data block to be transmitted is partitioned into disjoint subblocks, which are combined using phase factors to minimize PAPR. The PTS requires an exhaustive search over all combinations of allowed phase factors. Therefore, with respect to the fast implementation and simplicity of NGHS technique, we could achieve significant reduction of PAPR.

1. Introduction

Orthogonal frequency division multiplexing (OFDM) is an attractive technology for high-bit-rate transmission in wireless communications and has been widely adopted in different communication applications such as smart grid communication systems and offshore wind farms (OWFs) for data transmission between wind turbines [1]. However, some challenging issues still remain unsolved in design of such systems. One critical problem is large peak-to-average power ratio (PAPR) of the transmitted signals, which requires power amplifiers with a large linear range. Therefore, the OFDM receiver's detection is very sensitive to the nonlinear devices [2].

Over the past decade, various PAPR reduction techniques have been proposed in the literature [2]. One type of PAPR reduction methods is the probabilistic scheme; such as partial transmit sequence (PTS) technique that is based on combining signal subblocks which are phase-shifted by constant phase factors [3]. Another probabilistic scheme is selective mapping (SLM) in which multiple sequences with the lowest PAPR are transmitted [2]. PTS technique can get

side information, which is needed to be sent at the same time and is able to achieve sufficient PAPR reduction [3]. However, the continuous search complexity of the optimal phase combination increases exponentially with the number of subblocks. Suboptimal PTS methods are of interest in the literature [4]. The iterative flipping PTS (IPTS) in [5] has linearly proportional computational complexity to the number of subblocks. A systematic procedure for the minimum error probability to look for and form the optimal precoding matrices is proposed in [6]. In exhaustive search of phase factors, the computational complexity increases exponentially with the number of the subblocks. Therefore, a scheme is proposed in [7] by utilizing the correlation among the candidate signals generated in PTS. In [8], two phase weighting methods with low computational complexity for PTS, namely grouping phase weighting (GPW) and recursive phase weighting (RPW), are proposed. These methods focus on simplifying the computation for candidate sequences.

The conventional PTS scheme requires an exhaustive searching over all combinations of allowed phase factors [7, 8]. Optimization algorithms, and particularly bioinspired approaches, due to their low computational complexities and fast implementation, have attracted many attentions in recent years in major OFDM drawbacks. Some examples are a suboptimal PTS algorithm based on particle swarm optimization (PSO) [9]; an intelligent genetic algorithm (GA) for PAPR reduction [10]; cross entropy (CE) approach for sign-selection in PAPR [11]; artificial bee colony (ABC) algorithm for larger PTS subblocks [12]; harmony search algorithm (HSA) in [13] that could reduce the PAPR simply and efficiently.

In this paper, we propose a suboptimal phase optimization scheme, which can efficiently reduce the PAPR of the OFDM signals, based on a modified global harmony search (GHS) algorithm [14], called novel global harmony search (NGHS) algorithm [14]. This algorithm is analogous with the music improvisation process, where a musician continue to polish the pitches in order to obtain better harmony. We show that this scheme can achieve a superb PAPR reduction performance, while keeping its efficient and simple structure.

This paper is organized as follows. In Section 2, we shortly review harmony search principals. In Section 3, the OFDM is briefly introduced and the PAPR problem is formulated. The proposed NGHS-PTS approach is then discussed in Section 4. In Section 5, performance of the proposed algorithm is evaluated and discussed. Finally, the paper is concluded in Section 6.

2. A Survey on Harmony Search and Further Developments

2.1. Harmony Search Algorithm. The musical process of searching for a perfect state of harmony has inspired researches to propose HSA as a metaheuristic optimization method [15]. An interesting analogous between the HSA and real musical instruments adjustment is the optimization solution vector and the harmony in music, respectively. Also the musician's improvisations are analogous to local and global search schemes in optimization methods. An advantage of HSA is the use of stochastic random search based on harmony memory considering and pitch adjustment rates, instead of the need for an initial value as well as few mathematical requirements. According to [14, 15], a typical HSA is consisted of 5 steps which are as follows.

Step 1 (initialization). This step consists of defining the objective function, system parameters, decision variables, and the corresponding boundaries. Typically, an optimization problem can be defined as minimizing $f(x)$ subject to $x_{iL} \leq x_i \leq x_{iU}$ for $i = 1, 2, \ldots, N$ where x_{iL} and x_{iU} are the lower and upper bounds for decision variables. The HSA parameters are the harmony memory size (HMS) or the number of solution vectors in harmony memory, harmony memory considering rate (HMCR), distance bandwidth (bw), pitch adjusting rate (PAR), and the number of improvisations K, or stopping criterion. Value of K is the same as the total number of function evaluations.

Step 2 (HM initialization). All the solution vectors (sets of decision variables) are stored in the harmony memory (HM).

Its initial HM is randomly selected in $[x_{iL}, x_{iU}]$ for $i = 1, 2, \ldots, N$ by

$$x_i^j = x_{iL} + (q \times (x_{iU} - x_{iL})), \quad j = 1, 2, \ldots, \text{HMS}, \quad (1)$$

where q is a random number with uniform distribution in $[0, 1]$.

Step 3 (new harmony improvisation). This step generates a new harmony x_i^{new}. To do so, a uniform random number r_1 is generated uniformly in $[0, 1]$. If r_1 is less than HMCR, x_i^{new} is generated by memory consideration and otherwise, x_i^{new} is achieved by a random selection. As an example, an HMCR of 0.75 designates that the HS algorithm will choose the decision variable value from the historically stored values in the HM with the probability of 75% or from the entire possible range with a 25% probability. If x_i^{new} is produced by the memory consideration, then it will undergo a pitch adjustment. The pitch adjustment rule is defined as

$$x_i^{\text{new}} = x_i^{\text{new}} \pm (r \times \text{bw}), \quad (2)$$

where r is a uniform random number in $[0, 1]$.

Step 4 (HM refreshing). The HM is updated after generation of x_i^{new}. If the fitness of the improvised harmony vector $x^{\text{new}} = (x_1^{\text{new}}, x_2^{\text{new}}, \ldots, x_N^{\text{new}})$ is better than that of the worst harmony, the worst harmony in the HM will be replaced with x^{new} and becomes a new member of the HM.

Step 5 (stop criterion). The *new harmony improvisation* and HM *refreshing* steps are repeated until the maximum number of improvisations, K, is met.

2.2. Improved Harmony Search Algorithm. After fundamental presentation of the HS in 2001, Mahdavi et al. proposed an improved version of the HSA, called improved harmony search (IHS) algorithm later in 2007, [16]. The key modifications of this improvement are regarding PAR and bw, which are updated dynamically as

$$\text{PAR}(k) = \text{PAR}_{\min} + \left(\frac{\text{PAR}_{\max} - \text{PAR}_{\min}}{K} \right) k,$$

$$\text{bw}(k) = \text{bw}_{\max} \exp \left(\frac{\ln(\text{bw}_{\min}/\text{bw}_{\max})}{K} \right) k, \quad (3)$$

where k and K are current number of improvisations and maximum number of improvisations, respectively. The key property of IHS is its approach for generating of new solution vectors that enhances accuracy and convergence rate of harmony search.

The key difference between IHS and traditional HS method is in the way of adjusting PAR and bw. To improve the performance of the HS algorithm and eliminate the drawbacks lies with fixed values of PAR and bw, IHS algorithm uses variables PAR and bw in improvisation step. The traditional HS algorithm employs a fixed value of PAR and bw for specific purposes. In the HS method PAR and bw values are adjusted in initialization step and are fixed throughout the algorithm. These parameters are

```
Initialize New Harmony Vector Generation
For each i ∈ [1, N]
    step_i = |x_i^best − x_i^wrost|
    x_i^new = x_i^best ± r × step_i
    If U(0, 1) ≤ p_m
        x_i^new = x_{iL} + ‖r‖ × (x_{iU} − x_{iL}), where r ∼ U(0, 1)
    End
End
End New Harmony Vector Generation
```

PSEUDOCODE 1: New harmony vector generation procedure of NGHS in pseudocode.

of great importance in optimum adjustment of optimized solution vectors and can be potentially useful in adjusting convergence rate of algorithm to optimal solution. Therefore, fine adjustment of these parameters is of great interest [14]. Combination of small PAR and large bw values results in low performance of the algorithm as well as more number of iterations to find optimum solution. Small values of bw in the final generations can adjust tuning of solution vectors. However, in beginning generations bw must have a large value to in order to have a rise in diversity of solution vectors. On the other side, large PAR values in combination with small bw values mostly result in best solutions in final generations, in which algorithm converged to optimal solution vector [14].

2.3. Novel Global Harmony Search Algorithm. In 2010, Zou et al. proposed the NGHS algorithm. In this approach, a genetic mutation probability p_m is considered, which modifies the *new harmony improvisation* step of the HS such that the new harmony mimics the global best harmony in the HM. In fact, it works instead of the HMCR and PAR as in Pseudocode 1. In this procedure, the terms "best" and "worst" are the indexes of the global best harmony and the worst harmony in HM, respectively. The parameters r and $rand()$ are all uniformly random generated numbers in $[0, 1]$. After improvisation, the NGHS replaces the worst harmony x^{worst} in HM with the new harmony x^{new} even if x^{new} is worse than x^{worst} [14].

3. OFDM System and PAPR Formulation

The OFDM input data block is denoted as the vector $[X_0, X_1, \ldots, X_{N-1}]$, where N is number of subcarriers. Each symbol in X is one subcarrier of $\{f_0, f_1, \ldots, f_{N-1}\}$. These subcarriers are orthogonal and independently modulated using quadrature phase-shift keying (QPSK) or quadrature amplitude modulation (QAM), that is, $f_n = n/NT$ for $n = 0, 1, \ldots, N - 1$, where T is the duration of a symbol X_n in X. The complex envelope of the transmitted OFDM signal in one symbol period is given by

$$x(t) = \frac{1}{\sqrt{N}} \sum_{n=0}^{N-1} X_n \cdot e^{j2\pi f_n t}, \quad 0 \le t \le NT. \quad (4)$$

However, most systems use discrete time signals in which the OFDM signal in expressed as

$$x(k) = \frac{1}{\sqrt{N}} \sum_{n=0}^{N-1} X_n \cdot e^{j2\pi nk/NL}, \quad k = 0, 1, \ldots, NL - 1, \quad (5)$$

where L is the oversampled factor. To capture the peaks, it is shown in [1] that the oversampled factor $L \ge 4$ is sufficient to get accurate PAPR results. The PAPR of the transmitted signal, $x(k)$, in (2) is defined as

$$\frac{\max |x(t)|^2}{E\big[|x(t)|^2\big]}, \quad k = 0, 1, \ldots, NL - 1, \quad (6)$$

where $E[\cdot]$ is the expected value operator.

It is known that the complementary cumulative distribution function (CCDF) of PAPR can be used to estimate the bounds for the minimum number of redundancy bits required to identify the PAPR sequences and evaluate the performance of any PAPR reduction schemes. The CCDF of the PAPR denotes the probability that the PAPR of a data block exceeds a given threshold and is denoted as

$$\text{PAPR} > \text{PAPR}_0, \quad (7)$$

where PAPR_0 is considered as the PAPR threshold.

4. NGHS-PTS Approach

The PTS is one of the most significant techniques due its worthy performance in terms of PAPR reduction [17]. The idea is to generate several alternative OFDM signals by multiplying every original data sub-block with different phase rotation vectors. In the next step, the generated signal based on the minimum PAPR is selected to be transmitted, and its corresponding phase rotation vectors for subblocks are denoted as optimal phase rotation combination [17]. Therefore, parts of subcarriers are occupied to transmit the optimal phase rotation combination as side information to recover the original data at the receiver [17].

The known sub-block partitioning methods for PTS scheme can be classified into three categories [3] which are adjacent partition, interleaved partition, and pseudorandom partition. The PTS technique that uses the pseudorandom partition has better PAPR performance than employing the other two partition methods [9].

4.1. Ordinary PTS Technique. In a typical OFDM system, with PTS approach for PAPR reduction, the input data block in X is partitioned into M disjoint subblocks. The subblocks are combined to minimize the PAPR in the time domain, which are represented by the vectors X_m for $m = 1, 2, \ldots, M$ as shown in Figure 1 [3]. Therefore, we can have

$$\mathbf{X} = \sum_{m=1}^{M} \mathbf{X}_m, \qquad (8)$$

where $\mathbf{X}_m = [X_{m,0}, X_{m,1}, \ldots, X_{m,N-1}]^T$ for $1 \le m \le M$.

The L-times oversampled time domain signal of $\mathbf{X}_m$ is denoted as $\mathbf{x}_m = [x_{m,0}, x_{m,1}, \ldots, x_{m,N-1}]^T$, where x_m for $m = 1, 2, \ldots, M$ is obtained by taking IDFT of length NL on $\mathbf{X}_m$, concatenated with $N(L-1)$ zeros. These are called the partial transmit sequences. These partial sequences are independently rotated by phase factors $b_m = e^{j\theta_m}$, where $\theta_m \in [0, 2\pi]$ for $m = 1, 2, \ldots, M$. The set of the phase factor is defined as a vector $\mathbf{b} = [b_1, b_2, \ldots, b_M]^T$. The time-domain of OFDM signal after combining is expressed as

$$x'(\mathbf{b}) = \sum_{i=1}^{M} b_i x_i, \qquad (9)$$

where $x'(\mathbf{b}) = [x_1'(\mathbf{b}), x_2'(\mathbf{b}), \ldots, x_{NL}'(\mathbf{b})]^T$. The PTS technique target is to find an optimal phase weighted combination to minimize the PAPR value. Minimization of PAPR is related to the minimization of

$$\text{Max} \left| x_k'(\mathbf{b}) \right|, \quad 0 \le k \le NL - 1. \qquad (10)$$

In general, the selection of phase factors is confined to a set with a finite number of elements to reduce the search complexity. The set of allowed phase factors is written as

$$P = \left\{ e^{j2\pi l/w} \mid l = 0, 1, \ldots, W - 1 \right\}, \qquad (11)$$

where W is the number of allowed phase factors. We can fix a phase factor without any performance loss. There are only $M - 1$ free variables to be optimized and hence W^{M-1} different phase vectors are searched to find the global optimal phase factor. The search complexity increases exponentially with the number of sub-blocks M.

4.2. NGHS in PTS. The minimum PAPR for PTS problem is stated as

$$f(\mathbf{b}) = \frac{\max |x'(\mathbf{b})|^2}{E\left[|x'(\mathbf{b})|^2 \right]}, \qquad (12)$$

where $f(\mathbf{b})$ must be minimized subject to

$$\mathbf{b} \in \left\{ e^{j\varphi_m} \right\}^M \qquad (13)$$

for $\varphi_m \in \{ 2\pi k/W \mid k = 0, 1, \ldots, W - 1 \}$.

To minimize (12), the NGHS approach works as follow.

Step 1 (parameters initialization). By considering $f(\mathbf{b})$ as the objective functions, NL is considered as the number of decision variables and K as the number of possible values for the discrete variables. The lower and upper bands of the discrete variables $[b_{iL}, b_{iU}]$ are considered as $[-1, 1]$ for $i = 1, \ldots, NL$. The HMS is considered as the number of solution vectors in the HM defined as

$$\text{HM} = \begin{bmatrix} b_1^1 & b_2^1 & \cdots & b_{NL}^1 \\ b_1^2 & b_2^2 & \cdots & b_{NL}^2 \\ \vdots & \vdots & \ddots & \vdots \\ b_1^{\text{HMS}} & b_2^{\text{HMS}} & \cdots & b_{NL}^{\text{HMS}} \end{bmatrix}. \qquad (14)$$

Each row of HM is a random solution for the optimization problem and then the value of the objective function $f(\mathbf{b})$ is computed for each harmony vector. The HMCR, PAR, and the maximum number of initialized searches (stopping criterion) are used to improve the solution vector. The HMCR and PAR parameters task is to help the algorithm find global and local enhanced solutions, respectively.

Step 2 (new harmony improvisation). The HM is improvised by generating a new harmony vector $\mathbf{b}' = (b_1', b_1', \ldots, b_{NL}')$ as in Pseudocode 2. In this procedure, the term $b_i^{\text{new}} = b_{iL} + \|r\| \times (b_{iU} - b_{iL})$, where $r \sim \text{U}(0, 1)$ is called the genetic mutation. In NGHS, the original structure of HS is changed by excluding the HMCR parameter and including a mutation probability p_m. The genetic mutation operation with a small probability is carried out for the worst harmony of HM after position updating. Therefore, it can enhance the capacity of escaping from the local optimum for the proposed algorithm. By a careful consideration, we can find that the role of p_m is the same as 1-HMCR. Therefore, in this paper HMCR is used to emphasize that the original structure of harmony search is held and the improvisation step becomes as follows. In NGHS, new harmony is inclined to mimic the global best harmony in HM. In our approach, 1-HMCR determines the randomness of new harmony. Therefore, large HMCR results in premature convergence. To maintain the diversity of HM, HMCR must be small. But small HMCR decreases convergence velocity and also results in producing new harmonies which are infeasible.

In this paper, HMCR is adjusted close to one to produce feasible solutions and to have a good exploitation. After some evaluations, the algorithm may reach to a local solution and the adaptive step $step_i$ goes to zero. At this step, the algorithm is stagnated. Therefore, to prevent the stagnation, we generate a few harmonies randomly and replace them by the worse harmonies in the HM. The number of new random harmonies depends on the problem and the size of the HM. The new random harmonies cause increase of $step_i$ and the algorithm starts new exploration to find a better solution.

Furthermore, after improvisation in the NGHS, the worst harmony b_i^{wrost} in HM will be replaced with the new harmony b_i^{new} even if b_i^{new} is worse than b_i^{wrost}. This replacement is not good and it does not make the algorithm to converge. Therefore, in this paper, the worst harmony

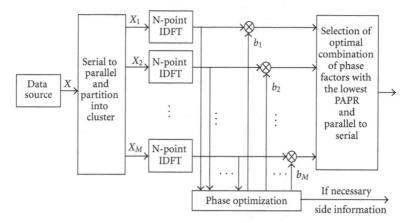

FIGURE 1: PTS techniques block diagram.

Initialize New Harmony Vector Generation Procedure
For each $i \in [1, \ NL]$
    If $U(0,1) \quad \leq \quad$ HMCR
        $step_i = |b_i^{\text{best}} - b_i^{\text{wrost}}|$
        $b_i^{\text{new}} = b_i^{\text{best}} \pm \|r\| \times step_i$, where $r \sim U(0,1)$
        $b_i^{\text{new}} = \max(b_{iL}, \min(b_{iU}, b_i^{\text{new}}))$
    else
        $b_i^{\text{new}} = b_{iL} + \|r\| \times (b_{iU} - b_{iL})$, where $r \sim U(0,1)$
    End
  End
End New Harmony Vector Generation Procedure

PSEUDOCODE 2: New harmony vector generation procedure of proposed NGHS-PTS in pseudocode.

b_i^{wrost} in HM will be replaced with the new harmony b_i^{new} if b_i^{new} is better than b_i^{wrost}.

The reasonable design for $step_i$ can guarantee that the algorithm has strong global search ability in the early stage of optimization and has strong local search ability in the late stage of optimization. Dynamically adjusted $step_i$ keeps a balance between the global search and the local search. The genetic mutation operation is carried out for the worst harmony of harmony memory after updating position to prevent the premature convergence of the NGHS.

In approaches using improved versions of harmony search such as IHS, the number of parameters is increased which is not good. It should be note that in order to get the optimum point by heuristic algorithms, the parameters of the algorithm must be tuned for the problem at hand. In NGHS the number of parameters is decreased, and our approach does not add any parameters to NGHS. Therefore it can be used for any problem easily.

Step 3 (Update HM). The newly generated harmony vector is evaluated in terms of the objective function value. If the objective function value for the new harmony vector is better than the objective function value for the worst harmony in the HM, then the new harmony is included in the HM and the existing worst harmony is excluded from the HM. In fact, the HM is sorted by the objective function value.

Step 4. Go to step two until termination criterion is satisfied. The current best solution is selected from the HM after the termination criterion is satisfied. This is the solution for the optimization problem formulated.

5. Simulation Results

In this section, performance of NGHS-PTS versus CE [11], ABC-PTS [12], and HSA-PTS [13] is evaluated. We assume an OFDM system with 256 subcarriers ($N = 256$) with 16-QAM modulation. The number of allowed phase factor is considered as $W = 2$, since by increasing the W similar simulation results can be obtained while the performance will be better [12]. The transmitted signal is oversampled by a factor of 4 ($L = 4$) and 100000 random OFDM symbols are generated to obtain the complementary cumulative density functions (CCDFs) of PAPR. The CCDF denotes the probability that the PAPR of a data block exceeds a given threshold and is expressed as

$$\text{CCDF}(\text{PAPR}_0) = \Pr\{\text{PAPR} > \text{PAPR}_0\}. \quad (15)$$

The HMS is selected to be 20 and HMCR and the number of evaluations is set to 0.9 and 1000, respectively. In the simulations, parameters are set by trial and error for optimum algorithm performance.

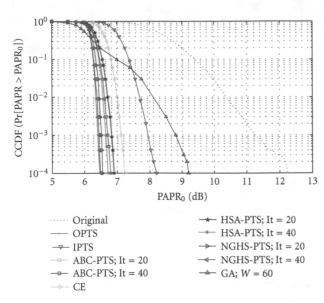

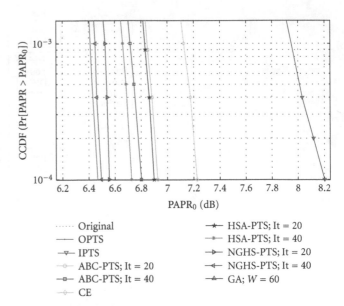

FIGURE 2: PAPR reduction comparison for iteration numbers 20 and 40.

FIGURE 3: Zoomed version of Figure 2 around CCDF = 10^{-4}.

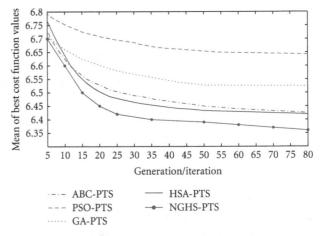

FIGURE 4: Mean of best cost function values.

Performances of the under study algorithms are compared for different iteration numbers: It = 20 and It = 40 in Figure 2. When Pr(PAPR > PAPR$_0$) = 10^{-3}, the PAPR of the original OFDM is 11.30 dB. The PAPR by the IPTS in [5] is 7.95 dB. The PAPR by the ABC-PTSs with iteration number 20 and 40 is approximately 6.847 dB and 6.717 dB and also the HSA-PTS provides approximately 6.828 dB and 6.66 dB for the iteration number 20 and 40 respectively. The GA-PTS with W = 60, which is reported as the best condition for the GA approach in [10], is not better than above approaches except for the original one with the PAPR of about 8.75 dB. This is while the NGHS-PTS provides approximately 6.526 dB and 6.412 dB PAPRs for the iteration number 20 and 40, respectively. A closer look at the performance of algorithms for Pr(PAPR > PAPR$_0$) = 10^{-4} is presented in Figure 3. As it is demonstrated that the proposed NGHS algorithm with iteration number of could achieve OPTS for less than 0.1 dB of PAPR.

To study performance of the approaches versus different number of iterations/generations, a simulation with 100 experiments is performed. This study compares PAPR convergence performance for an OFDM symbol, where M = 16 subblocks are generated by pseudorandom partition. Figure 4 shows simulation results of the under study methods on the mean of the best cost function values. As it is depicted in this figure, the NGHS-PTS has the least mean of best cost function value for all iterations. This is an advantage of this method versus other evolutionary approaches due to its less running cost.

6. Conclusion

The PAPR reduction problem for OFDM signals has received a great deal of attention recently, both in academia and industry. This issue attracted more attention after development of smart grid systems and the need for reliable multiuser communication. In the proposed NGHS-PTS algorithm, harmony search is performed to obtain better phase factor. Computer simulation shows that the algorithm offers improved performance in terms of complementary cumulative density function (CCDF) while reducing PAPR effectively. Compared to the existing PAPR reduction methods, the NGHS-PTS algorithm can get better PAPR reduction due to its simple structure and few parameters to adjust. Performance study of the proposed method demonstrates its feasibility and performance.

Acknowledgment

An earlier version of this paper is presented at 18th International Conference on Telecommunications (ICT2011), Cyprus, 2011.

References

[1] A. Maneerung, S. Sittichivapak, and K. Hongesombut, "Application of power line communication with OFDM to smart grid system," in *Proceedings of the 8th International Conference on Fuzzy Systems and Knowledge Discovery*, vol. 4, pp. 2239–2244, 2011.

[2] S. H. Han and J. H. Lee, "An overview of peak-to-average power ratio reduction techniques for multicarrier transmission," *IEEE Wireless Communications*, vol. 12, no. 2, pp. 56–65, 2005.

[3] S. H. Müller and J. B. Huber, "OFDM with reduced peak-to-average power ratio by optimum combination of partial transmit sequences," *Electronics Letters*, vol. 33, no. 5, pp. 368–369, 1997.

[4] S. H. Han and J. H. Lee, "PAPR reduction of OFDM signals using a reduced complexity PTS technique," *IEEE Signal Processing Letters*, vol. 11, no. 11, pp. 887–890, 2004.

[5] L. J. Cimini Jr. and N. R. Sollenberger, "Peak-to-average power ratio reduction of an OFDM signal using partial transmit sequences," *IEEE Communications Letters*, vol. 4, no. 3, pp. 86–88, 2000.

[6] M. J. Hao and C. H. Lai, "Precoding for PAPR reduction of OFDM signals with minimum error probability," *IEEE Transactions on Broadcasting*, vol. 56, no. 1, pp. 120–128, 2010.

[7] J. Hou, J. Ge, and J. Li, "Peak-to-average power ratio reduction of OFDM signals using PTS scheme with low computational complexity," *IEEE Transactions on Broadcasting*, vol. 57, no. 1, pp. 143–148, 2011.

[8] L. Wang and J. Liu, "PAPR reduction of OFDM signals by PTS with grouping and recursive phase weighting methods," *IEEE Transactions on Broadcasting*, vol. 57, no. 2, pp. 299–306, 2011.

[9] H. L. Hung, J. H. Wen, S. H. Lee, and Y. F. Huang, "A suboptimal PTS algorithm based on particle swarm optimization technique for PAPR reduction in OFDM systems," *Eurasip Journal on Wireless Communications and Networking*, vol. 2008, Article ID 601346, 2008.

[10] M. Lixia and M. Murroni, "Peak-to-average power ratio reduction in multi-carrier system using genetic algorithms," *IET Signal Processing*, vol. 5, no. 3, pp. 356–363, 2011.

[11] L. Wang and C. Tellambura, "Cross-entropy-based sign-selection algorithms for peak-to-average power ratio reduction of OFDM systems," *IEEE Transactions on Signal Processing*, vol. 56, no. 10 I, pp. 4990–4994, 2008.

[12] Y. Wang, W. Chen, and C. Tellambura, "A PAPR reduction method based on artificial bee colony algorithm for OFDM signals," *IEEE Transactions on Wireless Communications*, vol. 9, no. 10, pp. 2994–2999, 2010.

[13] E. M. Kermani, H. Salehinejad, and S. Talebi, "PAPR reduction of OFDM signals using harmony search algorithm," in *Proceedings of the 18th International Conference on Telecommunications, (ICT '11)*, pp. 90–94, May 2011.

[14] D. Zou, L. Gao, J. Wu, S. Li, and Y. Li, "A novel global harmony search algorithm for reliability problems," *Computers and Industrial Engineering*, vol. 58, no. 2, pp. 307–316, 2010.

[15] M. G. H. Omran and M. Mahdavi, "Global-best harmony search," *Applied Mathematics and Computation*, vol. 198, no. 2, pp. 643–656, 2008.

[16] M. Mahdavi, M. Fesanghary, and E. Damangir, "An improved harmony search algorithm for solving optimization problems," *Applied Mathematics and Computation*, vol. 188, no. 2, pp. 1567–1579, 2007.

[17] C. Li, T. Jiang, Y. Zhou, and H. Li, "A novel constellation reshaping method for PAPR reduction of OFDM signals," *IEEE Transactions on Signal Processing*, vol. 59, no. 6, pp. 2710–2719, 2011.

5

A Model for Video Quality Assessment Considering Packet Loss for Broadcast Digital Television Coded in H.264

Jose Joskowicz[1] and Rafael Sotelo[2]

[1] *Universidad de la República, 11300 Montevideo, Uruguay*
[2] *Universidad de Montevideo, 11600 Montevideo, Uruguay*

Correspondence should be addressed to Jose Joskowicz; josej@fing.edu.uy

Academic Editor: Fabrice Labeau

This paper presents a model to predict video quality perceived by the broadcast digital television (DTV) viewer. We present how noise on DTV can introduce individual transport stream (TS) packet losses at the receiver. The type of these errors is different than the produced on IP networks. Different scenarios of TS packet loss are analyzed, including uniform and burst distributions. The results show that there is a high variability on the perceived quality for a given percentage of packet loss and type of error. This implies that there is practically no correlation between the type of error or the percentage of packets loss and the perceived degradation. A new metric is introduced, the *weighted percentage* of slice loss, which takes into account the affected slice type in each lost TS packet. We show that this metric is correlated with the video quality degradation. A novel parametric model for video quality estimation is proposed, designed, and verified based on the results of subjective tests in SD and HD. The results were compared to a standard model used in IP transmission scenarios. The proposed model improves Pearson Correlation and root mean square error between the subjective and the predicted MOS.

1. Introduction

Television is by far the communications service with higher penetration in society. It reaches every household in many countries of the world. Broadband Internet access does not have such an extended penetration in some countries. While in developing countries 72.4% of households have a TV set, only 22.5% have a computer and only 15.8% have Internet access (compared to 98%, 71%, and 65.6%, resp., in developed countries) [1].

In order to care for bringing quality to the people through communications services it is essential to be concerned about the quality delivered by the TV services. Nowadays great attention is given to Digital Television (DTV). Many countries in the world have already made the so-called "analog switch-off" which means that all analog TV transmitters in a given country or city are finally switched off, paving the way to new usage of the spectrum. Some other countries are planning it for some time between 2015 and 2020.

The completion of the analog switch-off will imply the end of the migration from analog TV to DTV.

The above mentioned applies to Terrestrial Digital Television, that is, the traditional free-to-air TV service. However, there are also some other transmitting mediums used for TV services, mainly for Pay TV, which were digitalized many years ago. Those are the cases of satellite TV and cable TV. Besides, digitalization has enabled the emergence of TV services over IP networks, allowing new network and service operators to offer Pay TV.

Although nowadays DTV is a relatively novel topic for the public and for policy makers in many countries of the world, it has been among us over other mediums, different from terrestrial, from some time ago. We call the set of DTV standards used up to the moment as the First Generation DTV Standards. They allow us to watch television and to access complementary multimedia content or applications but with a limited scope.

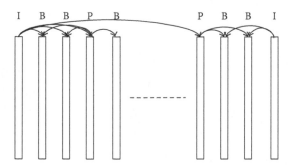

FIGURE 1: The MPEG-2 GoP and dependencies between I, P, and B frames.

In DTV, the video signal is coded in a certain codec, mainly MPEG-2 and H.264, and packetized in preparation for transmission. These Transport Stream packets (TS packets) are 188 bytes long. Its structure is defined in [2]. TS packets may be grouped and encapsulated in IP packets for streaming or IPTV services and are transmitted independently in terrestrial DTV.

DTV signal is subject to degradations in its path from the transmitter to the viewer. No matter which transmission medium is used (i.e., terrestrial, coaxial, fiber or satellite), noise is added to the original signal, leading to potential packet loss. Besides, when TV signals are transmitted over IP networks, packet loss may occur due to network issues, such as congestion. In order to control the quality of service the DTV operator offers to its audience, it is necessary to understand the way these packet losses affect the quality perceived by the TV viewer. Quality of experience (QoE) is a concept coined to represent how the viewer perceives not only the video or audio of a program but also the whole multimedia experience. Quality of service (QoS), a term commonly used in telecommunications, refers to many network-related parameters of a certain service that must be considered in order to fulfill a set of requirements that are related to quality. Beyond QoS, QoE evaluates the impact that different parameters affecting the joint transmission of audio, video, and associated data or applications have on the final audiovisual experience that the user has.

In this paper we present an approach to evaluate the impact of packet loss on video quality perceived by the user for broadcast television transmission environments. We will briefly describe video coding and transmission techniques in the current DTV standards in Section 2. Then in Section 3 we review the topic of packet loss impact on QoE. Firstly, we consider IP transmission and then Terrestrial DTV transmission. We show essential differences that must be taken into account between IP and Terrestrial DTV, when measuring impact of packet loss on video quality perceived. In Section 4 we present an overview of different techniques to achieve video quality evaluation. We performed some subjective tests that are presented on Section 5, along with the discussion of the results, where we report that the percentage of packet loss and its distribution are not sufficient to describe perceived quality. Section 6 introduces a new metric, representing the *weighted percentage* of slice loss, which is correlated with

the perceived degradation introduced by TS packet loss. Using this metric and a previously published model to predict video quality in the absence of packet loss, a new model is developed that estimates video quality for Terrestrial DTV coded in H.264. The verification of the model with a second round of subjective tests with clips obtained from actual DTV recordings is also presented in this section, along with a comparison to a standard model for video quality estimation. Finally, Section 7 has the conclusions and future planned work.

2. Video Coding and Transmission in Current DTV Standards

There are three main DTV families of standards that are being or have already been deployed all over the world:

(i) Advance Television System Committee (ATSC) [3];

(ii) Digital Video Broadcasting (DVB) [4];

(iii) Integrated Services Digital Broadcasting (ISDB) [5].

There are particular standards for different mediums for DTV transmissions, for example, DVB-S for Satellite TV, ATSC, DVB-T and ISDB-T for Terrestrial TV, and DVB-C for Cable Television. In these standards the video signal is typically coded in MPEG-2 or H.264 [6] and packetized in small packets prior to being transmitted. In MPEG-2 video frames are grouped into sequences, called "Groups of Pictures" (GoP). Each GoP can include three different types of frames (see Figure 1): I ("Intra"), P ("Predictive"), and B ("Bidirectional predictive"). Type I frames are encoded only with spatial compression techniques. They are used as reference frames for the prediction (forward or backward) of other P or B frames. P slices are coded using prior information from frames I and other P frames, based on motion estimation and compensation techniques. The B frames are predicted based on information from previous (past) and subsequent (future) frames. The size of a GoP is given by the number of frames existing between two I frames. H.264 provides better compression techniques than MPEG-2 and each frame can be divided into one or more slices. In this case the GoP structure is related to slices rather than frames, and the encoding process is different. Another difference is that while in MPEG-2 GoP structure is fixed, in H.264 it can vary during time. In both MPEG-2 and H.264, the coded video can then be packetized in small Transport Stream (TS) packets, 188 bytes long. As shown in Figure 2, they consist of a header of 4 bytes and 184 bytes of payload. The header contains different fields, including a Packet Identifier (PID), the Program Clock Reference (PCR), a Transport Error Indicator (TEI) flag, and a 4-bit Continuity Counter, among others.

All these DTV standards have differences between them, but they share some characteristics on the channel coding. They have an initial stage for data randomizing followed by another one with a Reed-Solomon Encoder, a data interleaver, and an inner code. These blocks are defined in order to reduce the impact of errors on transmission. A DTV receiver, once it has demodulated the transmitted signal, undoes the processes

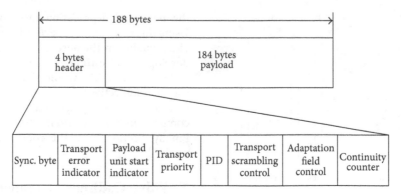

FIGURE 2: Structure of the MPEG-2 Transport Stream packet.

of channel coding achieved at the transmitter. The last stage in a DTV receiver is the Reed-Solomon (RS) decoder. In the case of ISDB-T, DVB-T, DVB-S, or DVB-C, the Reed-Solomon Code is (204, 188) and can correct errors in up to 8 bytes. On the other hand, ATSC uses a Reed-Solomon Code of (207, 187) capable of correcting errors in up to 10 bytes. Thus, some kind of bit errors in the TS packets at the initial stage of the decoder can eventually be corrected, and a valid TS packet can be presented to the video decoder, even if the packet had some errors at the front end of the decoder.

3. Packet Loss Impact on QoE

There has been considerable work published regarding the QoE impact of packet loss in video transmission over IP networks. Most of the published papers consider the effect on video quality with respect to the percentage of IP packet losses. There are different possible patterns for packet losses studied in the literature, both with a random distribution and with taking into account the effect of bursts [7, 8]. It is known that even small percentages of IP packets loss with uniform distribution can produce high effects in the perceived video quality. Reference [9] describes a test performed transmitting H.264 streams over IP networks with 0.02% random packet loss rate. The authors report that higher levels of packet loss severely damage the user experience by freezing the receiver for long periods of time. Authors of [10] have verified that noise structure affects perceived quality for a given packet loss rate. They experimented with 0.375% and 2% of packet loss rate with different burst densities (5%, 20%, 45%, 75%, and 100%). Reference [11] while studying how to assess quality of experience for high definition video streaming under diverse packet loss patterns it concludes that the perceived quality of HD video streaming is prone not only to packet losses but also to patterns of losses.

In IP networks, multimedia transport can be performed by encapsulation of TS packets in User Datagram Packets (UDP) or in Real Time Protocol (RTP) [12] over UDP. In any case up to seven TS packets of 188 bytes can be carried in a single 1500 bytes IP packet, in order to improve efficiency. Thus, in an IP transmission environment, a lost IP packet produces a burst of seven lost TS packets.

On the other hand, the common approach in DTV is to use the Bit Error Rate (BER) as a parameter related to the capability of the receiver to reconstruct the transmitted signal. For example, DVB-T [13] defines Quasierror Free (QEF) reception as less than one uncorrected error event per hour, corresponding to BER = 10^{-11} at the input of the MPEG-2 demultiplexer or a BER = 2×10^{-4} after Viterbi. The common approach is that if Carrier to Noise relation (C/N) is below a certain value, there will be a cliff effect (also called brick effect or "brick wall" effect or "fall off the cliff") that will cause an immediate degradation of the signal [14–16].

Another concept called the Correct Reception Rate (CRR) has been used in [17, 18], but it also is used as a threshold (good/bad reception) and does not enable making any analysis of the perceived video quality as a function of this parameter. Other works have partially analyzed the effect of the signal fading in the video quality [19]. However this parameter is very difficult to measure at the receiver and cannot be included in a video quality estimation model.

Although the quality of the radio frequency transmission link is usually characterized by the BER, this approach is not sufficient to study the problem on how transmission link noise affects QoE from the user's perspective in DTV. A decrease in received C/N will make the DTV receiver go from a clear and no error picture to a "picture freeze" (the so-called cliff effect). However, this transition is not extremely abrupt, and as C/N decreases from perfect reception, received picture experiences different kinds of degradations before reaching a complete "blockiness." According to some literature [20, 21] this transition from no degradation to full degradation takes place in a received C/N fall of 1 to 3 dB. Reference [22] evaluates theoretically and practically the performance of DTV signals over Gaussian, Rician, and Rayleigh channels. It also evaluates video quality with a metric called DVQL-W. Their results for the Rician channel are that the evaluated picture quality indicates visible errors in the picture with the C/N equal to 22 dB or lower, while the "cliff-off" effect comes with the C/N equal to 20 dB or less in the transmission channel. That means that for this case there is an interval in which, while C/N varies between 22 and 20 dB, the quality perceived varies from acceptable to bad. On the other hand, for a Rayleigh channel, the evaluated picture quality based on DVQL-W metric indicates visible errors in the picture with the C/N equal to 28 dB or lower. The "cliff-off" effect comes with the C/N equal to 23 dB or less in the transmission channel. That is, in this case, the transition from a good quality to a completely bad quality is a 5 dB fall in the C/N of the received signal. This range may include many households in a normal coverage area of a DTV station. C/N varies with environment conditions and varies with time. That increases the number of receivers that can be on the edge of this "cliff effect" in different periods of time. Besides, noise intensity may have different structures during time, depending on its origin (i.e., homogeneous or bursts). When the signal intensity decreases, some errors may be present in the TS packets. The error correction techniques provided by the standards (RS Codes) can eventually correct the errors, but the RS decoding algorithm may be overloaded and be unable to correct the packet. In this case the transport_error_indicator bit in the TSP header shall be set [23]. The decoder can decide what to do with the missing information. As for our experience, we have analyzed three different consumer type receivers that when recording a Transport Stream file and when an error occurs, they simply drop the TSPs marked as having had a transport error. That is, by checking the continuity counter of the header of the TSP of the TS file recorded, some missing TS may be found.

Taking into consideration the previous paragraphs, it is important to point out that, when studying losses related to DTV which have origin in channel noise, it is necessary to focus on degradations experienced by packet loss due to digital broadcasting transmission. Particularly, the problem of the video quality assessment in the transition from completely good reception (no packet loss after error correction) to completely bad reception (totally degraded picture) must be studied. Channel noise leads to errors in bits at the receiver front end; but since the Reed-Solomon Code can correct errors in packets, either bit errors are corrected or there are errors in TS packets at the output of the Reed-Solomon decoder, previous to the video decoder. This will affect each TS packet independently, leading to individual TS packet loss patterns, as opposed to what happens in IP networks, where the loss of an IP packet produces seven consecutive lost TS packets.

The distribution pattern of the packets loss at the output of the RS decoder may also be different with respect to the IP networks loss patterns. In IP networks, packets loss can be produced by network congestion or jitter-buffer overflow, with patterns distributions such as the Gilbert-Elliot or similar variants. This kind of packet loss distributions has been analyzed for multimedia services over IP [24, 25]. Nevertheless, in Terrestrial DTV scenarios, the packet loss is produced by a completely different cause than in IP networks, that is, low signal to noise ratio at the front end of the receiver, which is followed by the Viterbi decoder and followed by the Reed-Solomon decoder. Besides, in DTV systems, many other error prevention mechanisms are used, such as byte or bit interleaving before modulation and time interleaving or frequency interleaving while preparing the OFDM-frame structure (for systems using OFDM). Thus, it is not evident that the same typical loss patterns model can be applied in this case. In order to explore the type of degradations we need

to set up our base of video clips for the subjective tests; we have recorded many different intervals from free-to-air DTV from two different broadcasters from Montevideo, Uruguay, with low reception at the front of the receiver. The video clips used for subjective tests are usually 10 seconds long, so we the recordings we made from the free-to-air DTV have that exact duration. Analyzing the decoded TS packets, we have found the following characteristics.

(i) There are periods with homogeneous losses, presumably corresponding to signal fading. These periods have a length higher than the 10 seconds used.

(ii) There are periods without any lost packet and periods with many losses (bursts). In most cases, the periods with losses (bursts) are less than one second, followed by periods of more than one second without losses.

(iii) Nearly, the 50% of the losses consist of individual TS packets (i.e., the continuity counter of the header of the TSP reports only one missing TS packet).

Each lost TS packet can carry video coded information related to a specific frame or slice type, that is, I, P, or B. Although it seems intuitive that the impact of the loss would be very different depending on the type of frame it corresponds to, there are few papers that take this approach. In [26] it is shown that "not all packets are equal." Loss or damaged I frames affect much more than P or B frames, because the information of I frames is used to decode P and B frames of the entire GoP, so the effect is propagated to more frames. Loss of P frames affect more than B frames, because its information is used to decode other P and B frames, from the lost P frame until the next I frame. Finally, a lost or damaged B frame does not affect any other frames, just itself. Reference [27] studies QoE in DVB-H networks using frame loss pattern and video encoding characteristics. They define and use a parameter called the "loss rank" that weighs the impact of a lost frame on the perceived quality by counting how many other frames the error propagates.

4. Video Quality Evaluation

Audiovisual content producers and TV operators try to offer the best possible video quality to their viewers. Better video quality has been one of the driving forces for the advent of DTV. However, some processes involved in DTV, such as digital video encoding and transmission systems, introduce degradations that may result in unsatisfactory perceived quality. Video quality depends on many aspects related to the encoding process, the transmission stage, the receiver, or even to the content itself.

TV operators can define an upper limit to the video quality by setting the bit rate assigned to each signal, the GoP structure and size, and other parameters, while controlling the encoding process. Besides, the selection of the transmission parameters can affect the way the signal is propagated and received, particularly, in relation to the robustness to noise, thus affecting the degradation introduced during the transmission stage. These configurable parameters such as the modulation used, the FEC, or the guard interval have incidence on the signal to noise required for proper reception. The perceived quality can also be affected by the receiver. Different display sizes, display technologies (CRT, LCD, or LED), and error concealment strategies applied at the receivers can affect the perceived quality as experienced by the end user. Finally, given the encoding and transmission parameters and the receiver settings, different video contents can be perceived with different quality, depending on the amount of spatial and temporal activity of the sequence.

The most accurate methods for measuring the perceived video quality of a video clip are the subjective tests, where the video sequences are presented to different viewers and opinions are averaged. The Mean Opinion Score (MOS) or the Difference Mean Opinion Scores (DMOS) are the metrics typically used in these tests. Different kinds of subjective tests can be performed, based on recommendations ITU-R BT.500-13 [28], ITU-R BT.710-4 [29], and ITU-T P.910 [30]. These recommendations describe the methodology, environment, scales, and number of observers and conditions, among other aspects of the tests. In all cases, the tests are conducted in laboratories, using controlled environments, and with video sequences specially selected and prepared for this purpose. MOS varies from 1 ("bad" quality) to 5 ("excellent" quality).

5. Subjective Tests Performed and Analysis of Results

We performed subjective tests to verify the effect of packet loss on DTV signals. Five different video clips were used: "Fox & Bird", "Football", "Concert", "Voile", and "Golf," obtained from [31]. These video clips span over a wide range of different spatial and temporal activity. Each clip's length is ten seconds. The video clips were coded in H.264/AVC, High Profile, Level 4.1 for HD and Main Profile, Level 3.1 for SD, with no more than two consecutive B frames and key interval of 33 frames. One hundred different degraded video clips were generated in HD and one hundred in SD, varying the bit rate and the percentage of packet loss with different distribution patterns, including uniform distribution and different number of bursts, as detailed in Table 1.

Burst intervals were less than one second long, according to the observed bursts duration in real broadcasting signals, as described in the previous section. During the burst interval, we have decided to use a uniform distribution loss pattern for this study, because we have observed many individual TS lost packets inside the burst interval in real signal recording, as described in the previous section. The different percentages of packet loss inside each burst (0.1% and 10%) were selected in order to simulate scenarios with very different number of losses. The case of 0.1% simulates that most of the error can be corrected by the RS decoder. On the other hand 10% of loss simulates that most of the errors cannot be corrected by the RS decoder.

The subjective tests were performed according to the general guidelines of Recommendation ITU-R BT.500-13, using the five points Absolute Category Rating with Hidden Reference (ACR-HR) scale, as defined in Recommendation

TABLE 1: Packet loss patterns tested.

	Percentage of packet loss
No packet loss	0% along all the video clips
Uniform	0.3% along all the video clips
One burst	0.1% inside the burst; 0% outside the burst
One burst	10% inside the burst; 0% outside the burst
Two bursts	0.1% inside the burst; 0% outside the burst
Two bursts	10% inside the burst; 0% outside the burst
Three bursts	0.1% inside the burst; 0% outside the burst
Three bursts	10% inside the burst; 0% outside the burst

ITU-T P.910. A 42″ Led TV was used, without any kind of postprocessing techniques. The test room allows up to four simultaneous people watching the video clips and voting. A special voting system was developed, allowing the evaluators to use a smart phone application, synchronized with the clip sequences, to enter each score. The voted scores are automatically stored in a database, associated with the test session, the specific video clip, and the user. The system is depicted in Figure 3. This application can be downloaded from [32].

Nineteen nonexpert viewers from 21 to 55 years old performed the evaluation for the SD clips. Three of them were identified as "outliers," as the Pearson Correlation of their ratings compared to the average was below the threshold established in 0.75 in the test plan. Twenty-five viewers from 21 to 42 years old performed the evaluation for the HD clips. Four of them did not pass the normal vision tests. From the twenty-one remainders, one of them was identified as "outlier." The data collected from the remainder viewers in the SD and HD tests was used to compute the MOS values. The tests are considered "formal" according to the definition of ITU-R BT.500.

Video quality is often evaluated according to [33]

$$V_q = 1 + I_c I_p, \qquad (1)$$

where V_q is the predicted MOS (or MOSp), I_c is the video quality determined by the encoding process, and I_p is the video quality degradation introduced by the packet losses in the transmission process. I_c can vary from 0 to 4 and I_p from 0 to 1. When there is no packet loss, I_p equals 1, leading to a V_q dependence on I_c exclusively (determined by the encoding process). On the other hand, when packet loss extremely affects video quality, I_p equals 0, resulting in the worst possible value for V_q, 1. Thus, I_p reduces I_c by a factor related to the degradations introduced by packet loss in the transmission stage. Resulting values for MOS are appropriately from 1 to 5.

Using the data obtained from the subjective tests, we compute I_c and I_p for each coded clip ("Fox," "Voile"...) in each degraded condition. Subjective tests produced a MOS value for each of the two hundred coded clips (including HD and SD). Since when there is no packet loss, I_p equals 1, I_c was obtained for each combination of bit rate and clip, using the degraded video clips without packet loss (i.e., the clips degraded according to the first row of Table 1). Then, for each

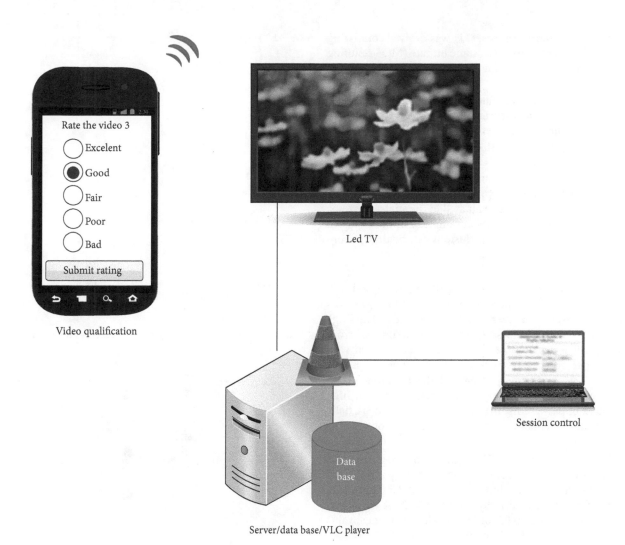

FIGURE 3: Automatic rating system for subjective tests.

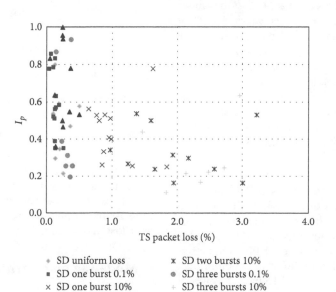

FIGURE 4: I_p versus percentage of TS packet loss for SD resolution.

other clip, where there are losses, I_p was derived comparing the MOS of the same clip at the same bit rate (MOS resulting from subjective tests), but with the corresponding packet loss degradation.

Packet losses were generated on individual TS packets. This represents a broadcast transmission scenario, not an IP transmission (where TS packets are lost in blocks of seven).

Figures 4 and 5 present the results of I_p with respect to the percentage of TS packet loss, for SD and HD, respectively, and in different conditions (random and burst distribution). Each point in the graphs represents a particular degraded video from the two hundred evaluated in the subjective tests. Video clips without packet loss are omitted in both graphs, for better readability. Many conclusions can be drawn from these charts.

5.1. General Considerations. Looking at Figures 4 and 5, it can be seen that, given a percentage of packet loss, I_p shows a very high dispersion, even for the same video clip (e.g., for 1.5% of TS packet loss, I_p varies approximately from 0.2 to 0.8). It is remarkable that, in some cases, even with very low percentages of packet loss, the video is highly degraded. This is expected as part of the mentioned "cliff effect." Nevertheless, in many other cases, even with high percentages of packet loss, the video quality is only partially degraded, and acceptable values for the MOS are obtained.

5.2. Uniform Loss Pattern. With uniform TS packet loss (green squares in both graphs), the video quality is degraded (I_p is low) even with very low percentage of TS packet loss. The case of HD is especially illustrative: at 0.3% of TS packets loss, I_p varies between 0.03 and 0.56, with an average value of 0.14, as can be seen in Figure 6. This means that, even for "perfect" encoded videos (MOS = 5), at 0.3% of TS packet loss, the MOS drops in average to 1.6.

A ten seconds HD video clip, coded at 14 Mb/s, has about 15 000 TS packets, distributed in 600 video slices. A 0.3% of packet loss means 45 individual TS lost packets, randomly distributed along the entire video clip. These 45 lost packets can impact in up to 45 different slices, leading up to 45/600 = 7.5% of lost slices. In our tests, using 5 different degraded HD video clips coded at 14 Mb/s with 0.3% of TS packet loss, a minimum of 22 slices, and a maximum of 35 slices was affected, corresponding to 4.5% and 5.8% of lost slices. This explains the huge effect that random packet loss can have in the perceived video quality.

5.3. Burst Loss Patterns. With burst losses, as shown in Figures 4 and 5, I_p decays much slower than with a uniform loss pattern, even with much higher percentages of lost TS packets. As stated before, a ten seconds HD video clip, coded at 14 Mb/s, can have the order of 15.000 TS packets distributed in 600 video slices. One burst of no more than one second can contain the order of 1500 TS packet. A 10% of packet loss means 150 individual TS lost packets, randomly distributed inside the burst. The total number of affected TS packets in this case is higher than the obtained with 0.3% of uniform distribution loss. Nevertheless, this kind of

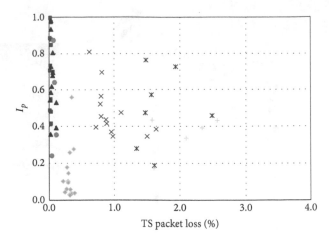

◆ HD uniform loss	✕ HD two bursts 10%
■ HD one burst 0.1%	● HD three bursts 0.1%
✕ HD one burst 10%	+ HD three bursts 10%
▲ HD two bursts 0.1%	

FIGURE 5: I_p versus percentage of TS packet loss for HD resolution.

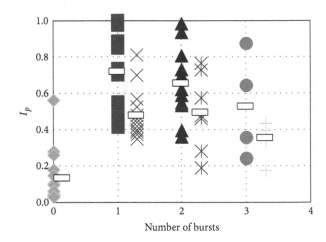

◆ HD uniform loss	✕ HD two bursts 10%
■ HD one burst 0.1%	● HD three bursts 0.1%
✕ HD one burst 10%	+ HD three bursts 10%
▲ HD two bursts 0.1%	▭ Average

FIGURE 6: I_p versus number of bursts in HD video clips.

degradation affects much less the video quality, as can be seen in the average I_p values in Figure 6. This can be explained by the fact that many lost TS packets can be related to the same slice, because the lost packets are very close between them in time. As an example, in a particular video clip, 106 TS packets were lost in one burst, but only two slices were affected.

6. Modeling and Verification

Different models for video quality estimation were presented by different authors in recent years. Some of them include the video quality estimation in the presence of lost packets, but in an IP data network scenario. In a previous work [33] we have made a comparison of ten of such models. Within the models that take into account packet loss, the one with the best performance was the proposed in Recommendation ITU-T G.1070 [34]. This model was developed for small display sizes, but a similar model for HDTV was proposed in [35]. In the ITU-T G.1070 model, I_p is expressed as

$$I_p = e^{-p/D_{Pplv}},$$

$$D_{Pplv} = v_{10} + v_{11}e^{-f/v_8} + v_{12}e^{-b/v_9}, \tag{2}$$

where b is the bit rate, f is the frame rate, p is the percentage of IP packet loss, and v_8 to v_{12} are coefficients that must be calculated for each codec and display size (coefficients' names are presented as in the recommendation). In our work, the frame rate was fixed at 25 fps in all cases, so the number of coefficients can be reduced to three, defining $v = v_{10} + v_{11}e^{-(25/v_8)}$, and I_p can be expressed as

$$I_p = e^{-p/(v+v_{12}e^{-b/v_9})}. \tag{3}$$

We have tested this model in the Terrestrial DTV scenario, using p as the percentage of lost TS packets (instead of the percentage of lost IP packets). We have calculated the values of v, v_9, and v_{12} that minimize the Root Mean Square Error (RMSE) between the actual I_p values (derived from the subjective tests) and the values derived from (3). With these values, the obtained Pearson Correlation was 0.60 and the RMSE 0.30 (in the 0-1 scale), which are not good results. These poor results were in some way expected. Figures 4 to 6 show that there are great variations in the I_p value for the same percentage of packet loss and even for the same number of bursts. Based on these observations, we can conclude that video quality cannot be properly estimated by any model that takes into account just the percentage of packet loss and number of bursts, as most of the published papers consider.

Taking into account the previous considerations, we can conclude that the impact of a particular loss has a great variance depending on the impacted slice (I, P, or B) and probably on the video content. As stated in Section 2, since B and P slices depend on information from I ones, loss of I slices affect much more than P or B ones, and, analogously, loss of P slices affect more than B slices. With these considerations, a new metric representing the *weighted percentage* of slice loss p_w can be defined, as detailed in

$$p_w = x_1 I + x_2 P + B, \tag{4}$$

where I is the percentage of affected I slices (i.e., the number of affected I slices with respect to the total number of slices in the video clip), P is the percentage of affected P slices, B is the percentage of affected B slices, and x_1, x_2 are two coefficients. The coefficient x_1 can be interpreted as the average number of affected slices when there is an error in a I slice. Analogously, x_2 can be interpreted as the average number of affected slices when there is an error in a P slice. There is no coefficient in B because the errors in affected B slices are not propagated.

We have found that I_p can be correlated with p_w, selecting the appropriate values for x_1, x_2. This is depicted in Figure 7,

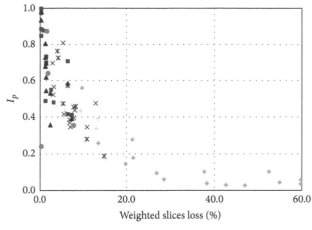

⬩ HD uniform loss	✕ HD two bursts 10%
■ HD one burst 0.1%	● HD three bursts 0.1%
✕ HD one burst 10%	+ HD three bursts 10%
▲ HD two bursts 0.1%	

FIGURE 7: I_p versus p_w (*weighted percentage* of I, P, and B lost slices).

TABLE 2: Best values for k, x_1, x_2.

x_1	21.5
x_2	5.7
k	26.9

where I_p is plotted against p_w (for the case of HD video clips). The relation between I_p and p_w can be expressed as

$$I_p = \frac{1}{1 + kp_w}, \tag{5}$$

where k is a constant. We have calculated the values of k, x_1, x_2 that minimize the RMSE between the actual I_p values (derived from the subjective tests) and the values derived from (5). The resulting values are presented in Table 2. With these values, the obtained Pearson Correlation (PC) is 0.84 and the Root Mean Square Error (RMSE) between the actual and the derived I_p values is 0.16. These values are much better than the obtained using the G.1070 model and that were mentioned above.

This corroborates the fact that the influence of a lost packet depends on which type of slice was impacted and gives some insights into the relative weights of the impact in the degradation perceived for each slice type.

In order to obtain an estimation of the MOS (MOSp or V_q) for each clip using (1), I_c must also be evaluated. We have calculated I_c according to the formula and coefficient values previously presented in [36], showed in

$$I_c = 4\left(1 - \frac{1}{1 + (ab/v_4)^{v_5}}\right), \tag{6}$$

where I_c is the video quality due to the encoding process, a depends on display size, b is the bit rate, and v_4 and v_5

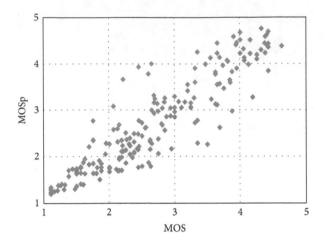

FIGURE 8: MOSp (V_q) versus MOS for the first set of measurements.

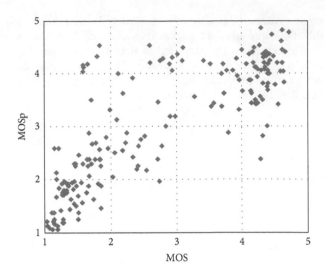

FIGURE 9: MOSp (V_q) versus MOS for model validation.

are coefficients that depend on video content, according to (coefficient's name are presented as in [36])

$$v_4 = c_1 s^{c_2} + c_3$$
$$v_5 = c_4 s^{c_5} + c_6, \tag{7}$$

where the parameter s depends on video content and is the average Sum of Absolute Differences (SAD) of the video and $c_1, \ldots, c_6$ are fixed coefficients.

Figure 8 shows the MOSp (V_q, obtained using (1), (4), (5), and (6)) for each clip against the actual MOS obtained with the subjective tests. The overall Pearson Correlation (PC) is 0.91 and the RMSE is 0.42. Using the same values estimation for I_c according to (6), but the standard G.1070 estimation according to (3) for I_p, then the overall PC falls to 0.75 and the RMSE raises to 0.80. As can be seen, using the model for I_c presented in [36] and the model for I_p detailed in this paper, a good prediction of the MOS (and better than G.1070) can be obtained.

In order to validate the model, a second set of tests was achieved with actual video clips recorded from free-to-air DTV from two different broadcasters from Montevideo, Uruguay. The recorded clips selected had the following conditions.

(i) Some of the signals were recorded in good reception conditions, without packet loss; some of the signals were recorded with low reception conditions, thus obtaining "real world" packet loss.

(ii) It can be inferred that the original signal is of "excellent quality."

(iii) They are representative of various types of content, including movies, sports, music, advertising, cartoons, news, and documentaries.

(iv) As far as possible, the selected clips cover different ranges of spatial and temporal activity.

(v) Scene changes rates are typical from actual TV.

One hundred clips in HD format and one hundred clips in SD format, with 10 seconds of duration, were recorded. These recorded clips had differences with respect to the specially prepared ones for the first training phase of the model. The first difference is that one broadcaster used six slices per frame, and the other used one slice per frame (in the first sets of clips, all of them had one slice per frame). The second one is that one broadcaster had dynamic GoP structure, compared to the static GoP structure used in the first set of clips.

The subjective tests were performed in the same conditions as the first ones, according to ITU-R BT.500. The five points Absolute Category Rating method was used. Eighteen nonexpert viewers from 18 to 55 years old performed the evaluation for the SD clips. Two of them were identified as outliers, leaving sixteen evaluations for the MOS calculation. Twenty-seven viewers from 17 to 68 years old performed the evaluation for the HD clips, but three of them did not pass the vision test. There were not outliers in the remaining twenty-four evaluations. This second test is also "formal" according to ITU-R BT.500.

The dispersion between the subjective scores and the obtained with (1), (4), (5), and (6) was calculated, maintaining the same coefficient values used for the first set of clips, as shown in Figure 9. The PC was 0.81 and the RMSE was 0.80. Although these values are worse than the obtained using the "training" data, they are good enough to support the fact that the proposed model can be applied for real DTV signals, where many packet loss patterns may be present.

7. Conclusions and Future Work

This paper describes a model to assess video quality in Terrestrial Digital Television when packet loss is present. We justify that the correct approach in the case of DTV is losses of individual TS packets in contrast to the case of IP transmission, where seven TS packets are lost with each IP packet.

Results of subjective tests performed with two hundred video clips in HD and SD resolution are presented that show a different incidence of the packet loss when it is present randomly than when in bursts. The results also show that there is a high variability on how quality is described by end users for a given type of error (i.e., a great variation in the final MOS values can be seen for the same number of bursts and with the same loss distribution pattern). This fact implies that there is practically no correlation with the type of error or the percentage of TS packets loss and the perceived degradation. This implies that none of the models based only on these parameters (percentage of lost packets and number of bursts) can produce appropriate results. A deeper inspection must be performed in the lost TS packet in order to understand the impact on video quality.

We have introduced a new metric, the *weighted percentage of slice loss*, which takes into account the affected slice type (I, P, or B) for each TS packet. This metric is correlated with the video quality degradation introduced by the packet losses in the transmission process of Terrestrial DTV. Using this metric and a previously published model to predict video quality in the absence of transmission degradations, a novel parametric model for video quality estimation in Terrestrial DTV was proposed. The results were compared to a standard model used in IP transmission scenarios, obtaining much better Pearson Correlation and RMSE between the subjective MOS and the predicted MOS using the proposed model. The model was also verified using actual video clips recorded from free-to-air DTV from two different broadcasters, obtaining satisfactory results. We conclude that the proposed model can be applied in real DTV environments.

Future planned work will improve the model, including the ability to explicitly take into account dynamic GoP structures and different number of slices per frame.

Conflict of Interests

The authors declare that there is no conflict of interests regarding the publication of this paper.

Acknowledgment

This work was supported by ANII-MIEM/Dinatel, FST_1_-2012_1_8147.

References

[1] ITU, "The World in 2010: ICT Facts and Figures," 2010, http://www.itu.int/ITU-D/ict/material/FactsFigures2010.pdf.

[2] ISO/IEC, "ISO/IEC, 13818-1: MPEG-2 Part1. Information technology— generic coding of moving pictures and associated audio information: systems".

[3] ATSC, http://www.atsc.org/.

[4] DVB, http://www.dvb.org/.

[5] ARIB, http://www.arib.or.jp/english/.

[6] G. J. Sullivan and T. Wiegand, "Video compression-from concepts to the H.264/AVC standard," *Proceedings of the IEEE*, vol. 93, no. 1, pp. 18–31, 2005.

[7] Y. J. Liang, J. G. Apostolopoulos, and B. Girod, "Analysis of packet loss for compressed video: effect of burst losses and correlation between error frames," *IEEE Transactions on Circuits and Systems for Video Technology*, vol. 18, no. 7, pp. 861–874, 2008.

[8] F. You, W. Zhang, and J. Xiao, "Packet loss pattern and parametric video quality model for IPTV," in *Proceedings of the 8th IEEE/ACIS International Conference on Computer and Information Science (ICIS '09)*, pp. 824–828, June 2009.

[9] M. H. Pinson, S. Wolf, and G. Cermak, "HDTV subjective quality of H.264 vs. MPEG-2, with and without packet loss," *IEEE Transactions on Broadcasting*, vol. 56, no. 1, pp. 86–91, 2010.

[10] N. Chen, X. Jiang, and C. Wang, "Impact of packet loss distribution on the perceived IPTV video quality," in *Proceedings of the 5th International Congress on Image and Signal Processing (CISP '12)*, pp. 38–42, 2012.

[11] M. Leszczuk, L. Janowski, P. Romaniak, and Z. Papir, "Assessing quality of experience for high definition video streaming under diverse packet loss patterns," *Signal Processing: Image Communication*, vol. 28, no. 8, pp. 903–916, 2013.

[12] H. Schulzrinne, S. Casner, R. Frederick, and V. Jacobson, "RFC, 3550 RTP: A Transport Protocol for Real-Time Applications," 2003.

[13] ETSI, "300 744 V1. 6. 1 (2009-01): Digital video broadcasting (DVB), framing structure, channel coding and modulation for digital terrestrial television," 2009.

[14] F. C. C. De Castro, M. C. F. De Castro, M. A. C. Fernandes, and D. S. Arantes, "8-VSB channel coding analysis for DTV broadcast," *IEEE Transactions on Consumer Electronics*, vol. 46, no. 3, pp. 539–547, 2000.

[15] W. Fischer, *Digital Video and Audio Broadcasting Technology*, Chapter 12, Springer, Berlin, Germany, 2010.

[16] T. Kratochvil and V. Ricny, "Simulation and experimental testing of the DVB-T broadcasting in the SFN networks," in *Proceedings of the 18th International Conference Radioelektronika*, April 2008.

[17] G. Bedicks, F. Sukys, E. L. Horta et al., "Field measurements for ISDB-TB in the VHF band," in *Proceedings of the IEEE International Symposium on Broadband Multimedia Systems and Broadcasting (BMSB '11)*, June 2011.

[18] C. Akamine, F. Yamada, G. Bedicks Jr. et al., "Field trial for Brazilian DTV using space diversity," in *Proceedings of the IEEE International Symposium on Broadband Multimedia Systems and Broadcasting (BMSB '10)*, March 2010.

[19] D. Zegarra Rodriguez and G. Bressan, "Video quality assessments on digital TV and video streaming services using objective metrics," *IEEE Latin America Transactions*, vol. 10, no. 1, pp. 1184–1189, 2012.

[20] S. R. Martin, "RF performance of DTV converter boxes-an overview of FCC measurements," *IEEE Transactions on Broadcasting*, vol. 56, no. 4, pp. 441–451, 2010.

[21] T. S. Bonfim and M. M. Carvalho, "Video Quality Evaluation for a Digital Television Broadcasting Scenario," http://enpub.fulton.asu.edu/resp/vpqm/vpqm10/proceedings_vpqm2010/vpqm_p41.pdf.

[22] T. Kratochvíl and R. Štukavec, "DVB-T digital terrestrial television transmission over fading channels," *Radioengineering*, vol. 17, no. 3, pp. 96–102, 2008.

[23] DVB, "ETSI TR 101 290, Measurement guidelines for DVB systems," Digital Video Broadcasting.

[24] G. Hasslinger and O. Hohlfeld, "The Gilbert-Elliott model for packet loss in real time services on the Internet," in *Proceedings of the 14th GI/ITG Conference on Measuring, Modelling and

Evaluation of Computer and Communication Systems (MMB '08), 2008.

[25] N. B. Yoma, C. Busso, and I. Soto, "Packet-loss modelling in IP networks with state-duration constraints," *IEE Proceedings on Communications*, vol. 152, no. 1, pp. 1–5, 2005.

[26] J. Greengrass, J. Evans, and A. C. Begen, "Not all packets are equal, Part 2: the impact of network packet loss on video quality," *IEEE Internet Computing*, vol. 13, no. 2, pp. 74–82, 2009.

[27] K. D. Singh and G. Rubino, "Quality of experience estimation using frame loss pattern and video encoding characteristics in DVB-H networks," in *Proceedings of the 18th International Packet Video Workshop (PV '10)*, pp. 150–157, December 2010.

[28] ITU, "Recommendation ITU-R BT. 500-13, Methodology for the subjective assessment of the quality of television pictures," January 2012.

[29] ITU, "Recommnedation ITU-R BT. 710-4 Subjective Assessment Methods for Image Quality in High Definition Television," November 1998.

[30] ITU, "Recommendation ITU-T P. 910 Subjective video quality assessment methods," April 2008.

[31] The Consumer Digital Video Library, http://www.cdvl.org.

[32] http://www2.um.edu.uy/ingenieria/vqi/subjectivetests.htm.

[33] J. Joskowicz, R. Sotelo, and J. C. L. Ardao, "Comparison of parametric models for video quality estimation: towards a general model," in *Proceedings of the IEEE International Symposium on Broadband Multimedia Systems and Broadcasting (BMSB '12)*, Seoul, Republic of Korea, 2012.

[34] ITU-T, "Recommendation ITU-T G. 1070: opinion model for video-telephony applications," July 2012.

[35] K. Yamagishi and T. Hayashi, "Parametric packet-layer model for monitoring video quality of IPTV services," in *Proceedings of the IEEE International Conference on Communications (ICC '08)*, pp. 110–114, May 2008.

[36] J. Joskowicz and J. C. L. Ardao, "Combining the effects of frame rate, bit rate, display size and video content in a parametric video quality model," in *Proceedings of the 6th IFIP/ACM Latin America Networking Conference (LANC '11)*, pp. 4–11, October 2011.

6

M2M Communications in the Smart Grid: Applications, Standards, Enabling Technologies, and Research Challenges

Siok Kheng Tan, Mahesh Sooriyabandara, and Zhong Fan

Telecommunications Research Laboratory, Toshiba Research Europe Ltd., 32 Queen Square, Bristol BS1 4ND, UK

Correspondence should be addressed to Zhong Fan, zhong.fan@toshiba-trel.com

Academic Editor: Chi Zhou

We present some of the ongoing standardisation work in M2M communications followed by the application of machine-to-machine (M2M) communications to smart grid. We analyse and discuss the enabling technologies in M2M and present an overview of the communications challenges and research opportunities with a focus on wireless sensor networks and their applications in a smart grid environment.

1. Introduction

Smart grid (SG) networks will be characterised by the tight integration of a flexible and secure communications network with novel energy management techniques requiring a very large number of sensor and actuator nodes. The communications network will not only facilitate advanced control and monitoring, but also support extension of participation of generation, transmission, marketing, and service provision to new interested parties.

In order to realise the intelligent electricity network, machine-to-machine (M2M) communication is considered as a building block for SG as a means to deploy a wide-scale monitoring and control infrastructure, thus bringing big opportunities for the information and communication technology (ICT) industry. For example, smart metering in M2M can facilitate flexible demand management where a smart meter (SM) is a two-way communicating device that measures energy (electricity, gas, water, or heat) consumption and communicates that information via some communications means back to the local utility. With near realtime information available for example based on the flow of energy in the grid, different levels of tariff can be calculated and made available for the consumer, the consumer can make a smarter and more responsible choice. The information generated by SM therefore acts like "glue" allowing various components of SG to work together efficiently. There are also various large-scale wireless sensor and actuator networks (WSAN) deployed in SG (such as the electric power system generation, or home applications) in order to carry out the monitoring task, for example [1]. These WSANs with the collaborative and self-healing nature have an important role to play in realising some of the functionalities needed in SG. On the other hand, there is also cellular M2M where cellular technology plays an important role in M2M communications due to its good coverage, promising data rates for many applications, and so forth. However, in this paper, we mainly focus on WSAN where various short-range wireless technologies are used to support various M2M applications.

There are currently various standardisation activities in M2M communications with a conscious effort to deliver a harmonised set of European standards. The challenges and opportunities that smart metering and smart grids present to communications networks are significant and include interoperability, scalable internetworking, scalable overlay networks, and home networking with potentially much larger numbers of devices and appliances. The security and privacy aspects are also extremely important given the large amount of private data that can be exposed by smart metering alone.

In this paper, we discuss the applications of M2M communications to SG. We present a brief introduction

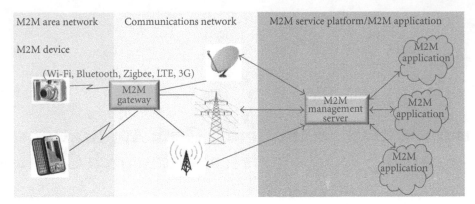

FIGURE 1: Architecture of M2M networks.

on M2M standardisation work in Section 2, and M2M scenarios and requirements in SG in Section 3. Further we discuss the enabling technologies in Section 4 and provide an overview of the communications challenges and research opportunities in Section 5, with a focus on WSAN and its applications in an SG environment. Section 6 is devoted to the conclusion of this paper.

2. M2M Standardisation Activities

2.1. M2M Architecture and Topology. M2M is unarguably a combination of various heterogeneous electronic, communication, and software technologies. The general architecture of M2M networks such as those being specified in ETSI TC (technical committee) M2M is shown in Figure 1. Other more detailed information of the M2M architecture can be derived from the on-going work in ETSI TC M2M. In reference to this architecture, M2M devices (intelligent and communication enabled) form an M2M area network; this could be from a small-scale home environment to a bigger environment such as a factory. The M2M area network is connected to the communication network such as satellite, power line, or mobile base stations through the M2M gateway. Through the communication networks, they are connected to the M2M management server on the M2M service platform and subsequently reaching the M2M applications (video for monitoring, online social networking, etc.) on the other side of the M2M management server.

2.2. ETSI M2M. The European Telecommunications Standards Institute (ETSI) Technical Committee is developing standards for M2M communications. The group aims to provide an end-to-end view of M2M standardisation, and will cooperate closely with ETSI's activities on next generation networks, and also with the work of the 3GPP standards initiative for mobile communication technologies. ETSI TC M2M is among one of the three European Standardisation Organisations which have been issued a mandate by the European Commission on Smart Metering (M/441). The TC M2M domain of coordination to answer M/441 includes providing access to the meter databases through the best network infrastructure (cellular or fixed) and providing end-to-end service capabilities, with three targets: the end device

(smart meter), the concentrator/gateway, and the service platform. Further, smart metering application profiles will be specified including service functionalities. Figure 2 shows the responsibility area among CEN (European Committee for Standardisation), CENELEC (European Committee for Electrotechnical Standardisation), and ETSI on the M/441 mandate work.

A number of liaisons have also been established with other standardisation bodies, for example, CEN, CENELEC, DLMS UA, ZigBee Alliance, and other ETSI TCs.

2.3. 3GPP. Apart from ETSI, 3GPP is also active in M2M technology-related activities. In 3GPP M2M is also called machine-type communications (MTC) where work has been carried out on the optimisation of access and core network infrastructure, allowing efficient delivery of M2M services. 3GPP SA1 has already completed a technical report TR 22.868 in 2008 on "Facilitating M2M Communications in GSM and UMTS." They have now started a new work item on network improvement for MTC, in order to gather requirements to reduce the operational costs of supporting M2M services. 3GPP SA1 Services is working on the services and features for 3G systems. In release 10, they have produced "Service Requirements for Machine Type Communications (MTC) Stage 1." 3GPP SA 3 has started looking into the security aspects of MTCs.

2.4. IETF ROLL—Wireless Sensor Networks (WSN) and Internet of Things. IETF has created a set of activities related to sensor technologies and smart objects such as 6Lowpan and ROLL (routing over low-power and lossy networks). These efforts are aiming at bringing the Internet Protocol to sensors and M2M devices needed for building a monitoring infrastructure for SG. Working Group ROLL is focusing on RPL (routing protocol for LLNs) for low-power and lossy networks (LLNs) where the nodes in the networks are many embedded devices with limited power, memory, and processing resources. These nodes are interconnected by various wireless technologies such as IEEE 802.15.4, Bluetooth, low-power WiFi, and power line communication links. The emphasis of the work is on providing an end-to-end IP-based solution in order to avoid the non-interoperable networks problem.

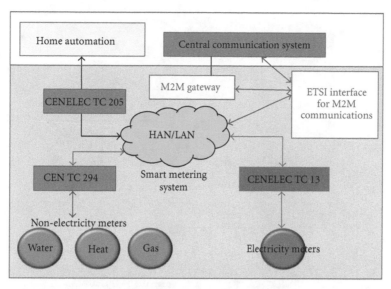

FIGURE 2: M441 responsibility split among CEN/CENELEC/ETSI.

3. M2M in Smart Grid:M2M Scenarios and Requirements in SG

With the various functionalities that an M2M system could offer, it has been considered as one of the foundation ICT solutions on realising SG. In this section, first of all, we look into the basic architecture for SG and how the M2M architecture relates to this. This is followed by discussing two important M2M scenarios and exploring the related applications with WSAN in mind. Such understanding is essential when more detailed functional and technical requirements need to be developed. In particular, we look into how WSAN play a key part in delivering M2M applications in an SG context.

Figure 3 [2] shows the ETSI board of director architecture for SG which is formed by three main planes: Layer 1, the energy plane handles the energy related to production, distribution, transmission, and consumption, therefore includes a large amount of sensors, electricity storage systems, transmission, and distribution systems. This layer corresponds to the M2M area (device) network in M2M networks. Layer 2 is the control and connectivity layer which connects the energy plane to the service plane. This relates to the M2M communications network layer. Layer 3 is the service layer which provides all the SG-related services. This is related to the M2M service layer in the M2M network architecture. How to apply M2M architecture to SG networks will need to be further studied or standardised.

More recently, WSAN has been gaining popularity on becoming a promising technology that can enhance various aspects of today's electric power systems, including generation, delivery, and utilisation. This is due to the collaborative and low-cost nature of the networks (also without the need to construct a complex and expensive infrastructure). At the same time WSAN also has some intrinsic advantages over other conventional communication technologies, such as wide area coverage and adaptability to changing network conditions. However, different environments pose different challenges to a WSAN; for example in a harsh and complex electric power system environment, WSAN communication in SG applications faces significant challenges on its communications reliability, robustness, and fault tolerance. In this section, we study the role of WSAN in different M2M applications/scenarios in SG and discuss the different characteristics and challenges.

3.1. Home Applications and Smart Buildings. Wireless home networks (or home area networks (HANs)) are now becoming increasingly popular and have evolved from just computers to including all different types of electronic devices including home appliances and home entertainment systems such as TVs and audio. General applications include that of lighting control, heating, ventilation, and air conditioning control (HVAC) which requires WSAN in place to support the monitoring and also act as the wireless communication infrastructure. Further, they also provide a way to detect fluctuations and power outages. It also allows customers to control remotely the meter (such as switching on and off) enabling cost savings, and to prevent electricity theft. Other applications include demand response and electric vehicle charging.

Smart buildings such as offices rely on a set of technologies to enhance energy-efficiency and user comfort as well as for monitoring and safety of the building. The M2M technology and WSAN are used in building management system for lighting, HVAC, detecting empty offices and then switching off devices such as monitors, and for security and access systems.

The main requirement of the M2M devices in a home and office environment is their very low power consumption so that many devices can last years without requiring battery replacement. With the wide range of home/office devices that need to be networked, there is a need to support several different physical links. Among all the different networking

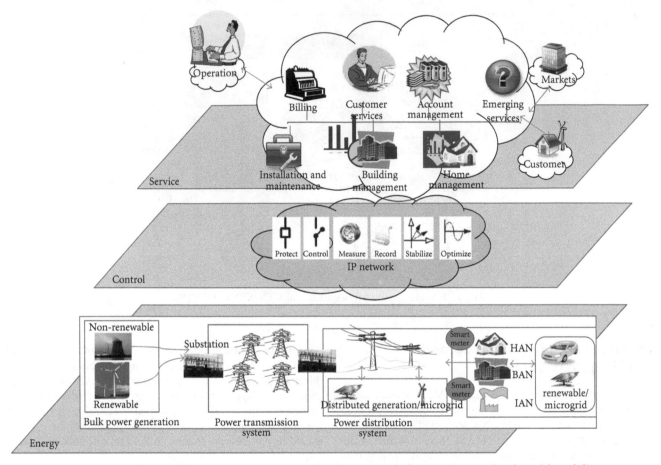

FIGURE 3: ETSI board of directors view on smart grid architecture including M2M network (adapted from [2]).

technologies, Ethernet, 802.15.4, Wi-Fi, Bluetooth, power line communications, and cellular all have a place in the home networking environment. The home M2M network will have to support all the different physical links and protocol stacks through the M2M gateway. The gateway also needs to be able to gather information on what processing and energy resources are available in the M2M devices (which are usually equipped with limited resources) and decide on how to disseminate data in a way that can optimise the resources. In general, the gateway capabilities include that of routing, network address translation (NAT), authentication, resource allocation, and so forth. Other more elaborate services or capabilities of the M2M gateway are on-going work in TC M2M dealing with gateway reachability, addressing and repository, communication, remote entity management, security, history and data retention, transaction management, interworking proxy, and compensation brokerage. Smart building systems with WSAN are also expected to learn from the building environment and adapt the monitoring and control functions accordingly.

3.2. Power Distribution Systems. An SG being the emerging next-generation electric power system, offers improved efficiency, reliability, and safety by allowing smooth integration of alternative energy source as well as automated control

and modern communication technologies [3]. Traditional electric power systems rely on wired communication for monitoring and diagnostic purposes. However, these systems require expensive cables to be installed and maintained on a regular basis. Therefore, there is a need for a cost-effective solution that would enhance the management process of the electric power systems.

WSAN has an important role to play in this area due to its low cost, flexible, and collaborative nature for aggregated intelligence. They are capable of monitoring the critical parameters of the equipments in SG and provide a timely feedback to enable the SG system to respond to the changing conditions. This enables SG to function in a reliable way with self-healing capability. The role of sensors in various parts of the SG power distribution system cover a wide range of transmission systems, substations and distribution systems. A WSAN-based wide area network (WAN) electric energy substation monitoring system plays an important role in ensuring the health of the power subsystems (transformers, circuit breakers, etc.) and transmission lines, and improving the observability and reliability of power systems [1].

WSN provides the capability for wireless automatic meter reading (WAMR) for electric power distribution systems with the benefit of reduced operational cost, online pricing, and remote monitoring for asset protection. The challenge in WAMR is reliable two-way communications between the electric utilities and customer's smart metering devices.

One of the major roles of the WSAN in a power distribution system is voltage quality management (VQM). With the growth of nonlinear time variant loads due to various existing and new applications, the distortion and disturbances on the voltage signal have become increasingly a significant problem. In a VQM WSAN, ideally each node can assess the information of performance of the monitored site, by using local information for computation, also the global performance of the monitored grid section by using local information exchanges between its neighbour nodes. With these features, the node could detect local voltage quality anomalies [4].

Some of the requirements of WSAN solutions in SG in a power distribution system are as follows. Highly scalable: the network should be able to scale to hundreds and thousands of devices and many could be communicating at the same time. High reliability: many of these power automation systems are expected to maintain good reliability that will last at least 20–30 years once installed. Other requirements include being able to handle range and obstruction issues as the harsh environment in a power distribution system could affect the link quality and range. Further, there could be various hardware and infrastructure obstructing the communication of the WSAN.

3.3. Other Applications. Other M2M applications cover a wide variety of domains from sales and payment, fleet management, telemetry, e-health applications, to security and surveillance.

4. Enabling Technologies

4.1. Short-Range Wireless Technology. Short-range wireless technology (SRWT) is becoming increasingly popular for ubiquitous WSAN connectivity in various instrumentation, monitoring, and measurement systems. In the context of M2M communications, SRWT plays a crucial role in terms of communication of the M2M devices with little or no human intervention. Such devices will proliferate in various environments with different applications up and running such as home security sensing, lighting control, and health monitoring. There are many challenges in designing such M2M networks which will be described in the later section. In this section, we survey the various potential SRWT for M2M networks and their respective features. In summary as shown in Table 1 (adapted from [5]), IEEE 802.15.4-based protocols such as 6LowPAN and ZigBee are suitable for low power and low data rate applications, also with less stringent range requirements such as sensor networks applications, whereas the IEEE 802.11 (Wi-Fi) protocol is well suited for higher data rate applications (also supporting longer range) including audio and video streaming-related applications. Bluetooth, on the other hand, is suitable for short-range and low-data-rate peer-to-peer communications.

4.2. Networks and Protocols. An efficient routing mechanism in the M2M networks decides how efficient the data can be

transported from one end to the other. There are various challenges on applying existing routing protocols to these M2M networks due to some inherent characteristics of the networks such as

(i) Long sleep cycles

(ii) Low power nodes

(iii) Changes to the radio propagation environment

(iv) Changes of topology (mobility of nodes, nodes in sleep mode).

Many low-power protocols such as Zigbee uses the AODV protocol from RFC 3561 [7] as its routing protocol. Under the AODV protocol method, nodes in the network that are not part of an active communication do not maintain any routing information or participate in the periodic routing table exchanges as required in the algorithm. The routing paths are established on an on-demand basis, so only nodes that are awake will be involved in the process. The node that initiates the process will be responsible for most of the computational work in the routing protocol, which includes collecting and evaluating the responses to the route request sent and making decisions on the route with the lowest network cost which could be the path with the smallest number of hop counts or the path with the largest remaining battery power of the nodes.

Another solution proposed in the literature is [6] which is suitable for a long-term environment monitoring network with low duty cycles. The routing is done by allowing the network nodes to sleep most of the time and reviving them whenever the gateway is performing a bulk data download. The low-power node upon waking up would send a probe message to its neighbour to check for any potential communication and the gateway would calculate the network paths using the reachability information collected.

The IETF RPL protocol will enhance the advanced metering infrastructure (a network of smart meters) with IP routing characteristics such as dynamic discovery of network paths and destination, ability to adapt to logical network topology changes, equipment failures or network outages, independence from data link layer technologies, and support for high availability and load balancing. In [8], an RPL-based routing protocol for advanced metering infrastructure (AMI) in SG has been proposed, aiming to enable realtime automated meter reading and realtime remote utility management in the AMI.

5. Challenges and Research Opportunities

Having discussed the various scenarios and its challenges of WSAN in SG, in this section, we elaborate on the various topics of research interests that demonstrate great potential for further studies.

(1) *Gateway Design.* The gateway plays an important role in interconnecting various network devices and sensors in an application scenario. There is a need to cater for the different characteristics of the devices in the gateway. For example

TABLE 1: M2M short range wireless technology (adapted from [6]).

	802.15.4 (ZigBee/6LoWPAN)	Bluetooth/Bluetooth low energy (LE)	802.11 (Wi-Fi)
Max data rate	250 kb/s	3 Mb/s (enhanced) 1 Mb/s (basic or LE)	22 Mb/s (802.11 g) 144 Mb/2 (802.11 n)
Indoor range	10 m–20 m	1 m, 10 m and 100 m classes, 5–15 m (LE)	45 m
Power	Low	Medium low (LE)	High
Battery life	Years	Days years (LE)	Hours
Frequency band	2.4 GHz 868 MHz and 915 MHz	2.4 GHz	2.4 GHz, 3.6 GHz, and 5 GHz
Channel access	CSMA/CA (non-beacon based) or superframe structure (beacon based, non-contention)	Frequency hopping or CSMA/CA	CSMA/CA
Applications	Smart appliances Smart meters Lighting control Home security Office automation	Voice Smart meters Data transfer Game control Health monitoring (LE) Computer peripheral (LE)	Networking between WAN and customer premises (M2M area networks) Digital audio/voice

in a home environment, there will be devices that have different requirements on power, distance, data rate, and are running different communication protocols. Other issues are security capability, communication selection capability, and so forth. Software-defined radio technologies have been proposed in [5] as a solution to the home M2M gateway architecture enabling the gateway to function at multicarriers and multibands which can communicate simultaneously with different protocols, on different frequencies and in different frequency bands.

(2) *Harsh Environment.* This is a common problem for certain WSANs in SG such as those operating in the power system environment. The WSAN may be subject to strong RF interference, and also harsh physical environment such as corrosion and high humidity. These may cause the network topology and wireless connectivity to change when certain nodes fail or the measurements are not suitable for drawing good conclusions. Wireless channel modelling and link quality characterisation are some of the important work [9] when designing a reliable WSAN in the smart grid in such harsh environment as the power system designers can make use of such model to predict the performance of the network.

(3) *Service Differentiation.* In order to enable efficient prioritisation of certain applications that have some critical requirements to meet such as those belonging to protection and control functions, the WSAN must be able to support quality of service (QoS). For example, an alarm notification for the electric power systems will require immediate attention hence requires a realtime communication; other periodic reporting activities would require reliable communications.

(4) *Packet Loss or Errors and Variable Link Capacity.* In WSAN, the perceived level of interference and bit error rates affects the attainable capacity of each wireless link [9]. Also, the wireless links exhibit a varying characteristic over time and space due to various reasons such as obstructions and noisy environment in an electric power system. Therefore the capacity and delay at each link vary from location to location and could be bursty in nature. This poses a serious challenge to providing QoS in the system. There have been a wide range of methods proposed in the literature based on MIMO (multiple-input and multiple-output) communication and smart antennas that can be exploited to improve the network capacity in a noisy environment.

(5) *Resource Constraint.* The resources required in a sensor node can vary from application to application in terms of energy, memory, as well as processing power. In general, limited battery power is the main resource constraint that requires various communication protocols for WSAN to provide high energy efficiency. Energy efficient protocols such as routing solutions are needed where WSAN are usually expected to function over years without having to change the battery. The routing technique also has to take into account the long sleep cycles, changing radio environment, change of topology, and the limited processing power.

(6) *Security.* Security for WSAN in SG is an essential requirement in order to ensure that the whole system functions smoothly and safe from any sorts of attack and intrusion. This covers a wide range of solutions targeting threats such as denial-of-service, eavesdropping on transmission, routing attacks, flooding for generation plant security, data centre security, WAN security, identity management, access control,

and so forth. Conventional centralised IT network security models are not directly applicable to the highly distributed and low-cost devices in M2M communications networks due to the need for dispersed and decentralized methods.

(7) *Self-Configuration and Self-Organisation.* As the topology of the sensor nodes in a WSAN changes due to sleep mode schedule, mobility or node failure, there is a need for self-configuration and self-organisation to make sure that the network functions as normal. Therefore, fault diagnosis is essential for the hardware as well as software in the infrastructure. Failure analysis or predictive maintenance makes sure that the system has the ability to identify failure (assisting quick failure remedy), predict failure and recover from fault/failure. Intelligent diagnosis methods such as those that filter and reason the mass information related to an alarm, helps quick understanding of the nature of the fault and localised the fault. Various machine learning techniques such as artificial neural network have been proposed in [10, 11] for power system fault diagnosis and alarm information processing.

(8) *Data Processing.* With the large scale development of WSAN in SG, there are a large amount of information collected over time. There is a need to intelligently combine or aggregate, fuse or infer these data in order to draw conclusion on what action is needed or how to configure the parameters in the system for optimum functionality. The other benefit is for increased energy efficiency by better match of supply and demand. For example, the authors [12, 13] proposed using artificial neural network for load forecasting which is important for demand response. Data processing can also help achieve improved security and reliability by fast response to unusual events and in the case of energy shortage. For example, methods for traceback and traceability for malicious activities in critical information such as methods proposed in [14] to examine relevant attributes features at intermediary stages of data transaction in the infrastructure. This is followed by finding the maximum occurrence features pertaining to characteristics of normal and abnormal transactions. These attributes are mined using hybrid data mining algorithms in order to identify unique classes in the traceability matrix for security and privacy.

(9) *Reliability.* Reliability can be tackled from multiple levels such as the communication link level and the system level. The system needs to be able to cope with the harsh environment and adaptively work out the best way to cope with node failure and link variability.

(10) *Middleware and APIs.* Advanced application programming interfaces (APIs) help to enable implementation of optimisation algorithms and efficient management and configuration of networks, open interfaces to enable independent software vendor, device manufactures, and telecoms operators to implement their services. Open APIs provide the means for third parties not directly associated with the original equipment manufacturers to develop a software component which could add functionality or enhancements

to the system. On the other hand, smart energy management solutions require access to more information ideally from different service providers and devices implemented by different vendors. Such information should be available and presented in a usable format to interested parties. Further, timing and specific configuration of measurements and controls are also critical for dynamic scenarios. Since support for different technologies and some level of cooperation over administrative boundaries are required, proprietary or widely simplified interfaces will not be sufficient in these scenarios. This situation can be improved by standard generic API definitions covering methods and attributes related to capability, measurement, and configurations. The design of such APIs should be technology agnostic, lightweight and future-proof.

(11) *M2M Computing Platform.* With the deployment of large-scale M2M networks and its various applications to be provided, there needs to be a way to control and manage these devices as well as to work on the data or make the data available efficiently for a different purpose. Cloud computing has been regarded as one of the potential technology to be leveraged for M2M computing. The cloud, a combination of IT virtualisation by combining Internet, information and communication technology, and various resources (hardware, development platforms), makes it easier to deliver the M2M applications as services (through the Cloud) virtually. This allows flexible IT management and data sharing across the platform and resources can be dynamically reconfigured according to the variable load allowing optimum resource utilisation. For example, a commercially available cloud platform for M2M applications is Sierra Wireless AirVantage Cloud Platform [15] which enables M2M solution providers, system integrators and network operators to rapidly develop, is deploy and operate M2M applications and services.

(12) *Multi-Radio Support and Spectrum Efficiency.* Multiple communication technologies and standards are being deployed to support communications in different parts of SG. For example, Bluetooth could be used for the communications between meter and end customer devices. On the other hands, ZigBee and IEEE 802.11 could be used for smart meter interfaces in the home and local area network. In order to manage and support all these different communications, there needs to be multi-radio support functionality in the SG. Also, radio spectrum scarcity is an increasingly important problem due to the rapid growth in the telecommunication service industry. One of the proposed ways of managing the spectrum efficiently is a solution such as using the unoccupied television spectrum, also known as the white space, has been proposed by the Federal Communications Commission (FCC). As this is no longer the static spectrum allocation case in the conventional way, there needs to be an efficient secondary spectrum management strategy. Company such as NEUL [16] has developed M2M communications network solutions which operate in TV white spaces.

(13) *M2M Protocols.* There are various scopes for M2M protocols research such as reliable (i.e. delivery-guaranteed),

delay-guaranteed, rate-efficient, and energy-efficient protocols design. Energy-efficient protocols such as routing and transmission protocols are needed where WSAN are usually expected to function over years without having to change the battery. The routing technique also has to take into account the long sleep cycles, the changing radio environment, changes of topology, and also the limited processing power. The existing leading transmission protocol, that is, TCP/IP is known to be inefficient for M2M traffic with low data volume as there are redundant and overhead which therefore is not energy efficient for M2M communications. Therefore, protocols redesign for M2M communications needs to be explored.

(14) *Optimal Network Design.* As an M2M network consists of an interconnection of a number of devices and systems together, there is a need to design the network to minimise the cost of M2M communications while still meeting the QoS requirements. Placement of gateway, number of M2M devices supported in a clusters, and so forth are some of the related topics [17].

6. Conclusion

There has been no doubt that M2M communication plays an important role in realising the next-generation smart electrical system, SG. In this paper, we have looked into various on-going M2M standardisations-related activities which have shown the growing momentum of M2M in becoming the one of the important ICT solution for SG. We highlighted the work carried out in organisations such as ETSI M2M, 3GPP, and IETF ROLL to draw attention on the set of topics of interest among various stakeholders on M2M in SG picture. Next, we studied a selection of challenges and requirements of M2M application/scenario and WSAN in SG. We then focused on the technical details of M2M communications, which covered a wide range of topics, M2M architecture and topology, various short-range wireless technology, and networks and protocols. Having extensively discussed the above topics, we provided our view on various research opportunities in this topic. We believe that data processing, security, reliability, middleware and APIs, M2M computing platform, multiradio support and spectrum efficiency, M2M protocols and optimal network design are some important and interesting topics that can be looked into in the future work.

Although the roadmap of worldwide smart grid deployment is still not clear, it is almost certain that the future intelligent energy network empowered by advanced ICT technology will not only be as big as the current Internet, but also change people's lives in a fundamental way similar to the Internet. On an even larger scale, the notion of Internet of things will connect trillions of objects and the whole world will become an extremely large-scale wireless sensor network. As M2M communications is an underpinning technology for this vision, we therefore envisage that M2M will be an exciting research area for communication engineers for many years to come.

References

[1] R. A. León, V. Vittal, and G. Manimaran, "Application of sensor network for secure electric energy infrastructure," *IEEE Transactions on Power Delivery*, vol. 22, no. 2, pp. 1021–1028, 2007.

[2] O. Elloumi, J. M. Ballot, and D. Boswarthick, "Smart Grid- an introduction," presentation slides, TCM2M #9, 2010.

[3] U.S. Department of Energy, "The SG: An Introduction," September 2008.

[4] M. di Bisceglie, C. Galdi, A. Vaccaro, and D. Villacci, "Cooperative sensor networks for voltage quality monitoring in SGs," in *Proceedings of the IEEE Bucharest PowerTech Conference*, 2009.

[5] M. Starsinic, "System architecture challenges in the home M2M network," in *Proceedings of the Applications and Technology Conference, (LISAT '10)*, pp. 1–7, 2010.

[6] R. Musaloiu-E, C. J. M. Liang, and A. Terzis, "Koala: ultra-low power data retrieval in wireless sensor networks," *Information Processing in Sensor Networks*, pp. 421–432, 2008.

[7] RFC 3561, http://www.ietf.org/rfc/rfc3561.txt.

[8] D. Wang, Z. Tao, J. Zhang, and A. Abouzeid, "RPL based routing for advanced metering infrastructure in smart grid," in *Proceedings of the ICC*, pp. 1–6, 2010.

[9] V. C. Gungor, B. Lu, and G. P. Hancke, "Opportunities and challenges of wireless sensor networks in smart grid—a case study of link quality assessments in power distribution systems," *IEEE Transactions on Industrial Electronics*, vol. 57, no. 99, pp. 3557–3564, 2010.

[10] M. A. H. El-Sayed and A. S. Alfuhaid, "ANN-based approach for fast fault diagnosis and alarm handling of power systems," in *Proceedings of the 5th International Conference on Advances in Power System Control, Operation and Management (APSCOM '00)*, pp. 54–58, October, 2000.

[11] M. Ma, D. Zhao, X. Zhang, and D. Liu, "China's research status quo and development trend of power grid fault diagnosis," in *Proceedings of the Asia-Pacific Power and Energy Engineering Conference (APPEEC '10)*, pp. 1–4, 2010.

[12] H. T. Zhang, F. Y. Xu, and L. Zhou, "Artificial Neural Network for load forecasting in smart grid," in *Proceedings of the International Conference on Machine Learning and Cybernetics (ICMLC '10)*, vol. 6, pp. 3200–3205, 2010.

[13] F. Y. Xu, M. C. Leung, and L. Zhou, "A RBF network for short-term load forecast on microgrid," in *Proceedings of the International Conference on Machine Learning and Cybernetics (ICMLC '10)*, vol. 6, pp. 3195–3199, 2010.

[14] E. Hooper, "Strategic and intelligent smart grid systems engineering," in *Proceedings of the International Conference for Internet Technology and Secured Transactions (ICITST '10)*, 2010.

[15] http://www.sierrawireless.com/productsandservices/AirVantage.

[16] NEUL, http://www.neul.com/.

[17] D. Niyato, L. Xiao, and P. Wang, "Machine-to-machine communications for home energy management system in smart grid," *IEEE Communications Magazine*, vol. 49, no. 4, pp. 53–59, 2011.

7

The Exploration of Network Coding in IEEE 802.15.4 Networks

Deze Zeng,[1] Song Guo,[1] Victor Leung,[2] and Jiankun Hu[3]

[1] School of Computer Science and Engineering, The University of Aizu, Fukushima-Ken 965-8580, Japan
[2] Electrical and Computer Engineering Department, The University of British Columbia, Vancouver, BC, Canada V6T 1Z4
[3] School of Engineering and Information Technology, The University of New South Wales at the Australia Defence Force Academy, Canberra, ACT 2600, Australia

Correspondence should be addressed to Song Guo, sguo@u-aizu.ac.jp

Academic Editor: Ning Chen

Wireless personal area networks (WPANs) are getting popular in a variety of fields such as smart home, office automation, and e-healthcare. In WPANs, most devices are considerably energy constrained, so the communication protocol should be energy efficient. The IEEE 802.15.4 is designed as a standard protocol for low power, low data rate, low complexity, and short range connections in WPANs. The standard supports allocating several numbers of collision-free guarantee time slots (GTSs) within a superframe for some time-critical transmissions. Recently, COPE was proposed as a promising network coding architecture to essentially improve the throughput of wireless networks. In this paper, we exploit the network coding technique at coordinators to improve energy efficiency of the WPAN. Some related practical issues, such as GTS allocation and multicast, are also discussed in order to exploit the network coding opportunities efficiently. Since the coding opportunities are mostly exploited, our proposal achieves both higher energy efficiency and throughput performance than the original IEEE 802.15.4.

1. Introduction

Wireless sensor network (WSN) is a kind of network consisting of a collective of sensor nodes systematically connected by wireless radio. A sensor node may be equipped with one or several different sensors with different sensing abilities, for example, temperature sensing, light sensing, and pressure sensing. WSNs show great potential to and have been widely deployed for many applications involving monitoring, tracking, and controlling, such as home automation, environment monitoring, industrial and agricultural monitoring and controlling, and wild animal tracking. Yet there are still many challenge issues hindering the further development of WSNs. This is because most sensor nodes are constrained by their low processing capability, low memory spaces, and limited power supply. In addition, wireless sensor nodes are usually attached with radio transceiver with short-range communication capabilities. The transceiver is one of the most energy consumable parts. Hence, one key issue to tackle the challenge is to design a suite of communication protocols in a low complexity and enabling low-power connections between sensor nodes in WSN.

Wireless personal area network (WPAN) is a kind of WSN, which has also been widely deployed in various automation systems, such as home/office automation systems and e-healthcare systems. WPANs have also drawn a lot of attention from both academia and industry. The IEEE 802.15.4 is a standard formed by the WPAN working group, which specifies the physical layer and medium access control (MAC) layer protocols for low-rate WPANs (LR-WPANs). Above IEEE 802.15.4, an association of industrial companies formed ZigBee Alliance [1] and published ZigBee standard which specifies a suite of high level communication protocols, for example, network layer protocol and security specifications, targeting simpler and less expensive solutions for LR-WPANs.

The IEEE 802.15.4 physical layer specifies the possible operation frequency bands as well as the modulation techniques. Recently, the work group is planning to expand the available frequency bands. Depending on whether a beacon frame is used or not, the IEEE 802.15.4 MAC layer specification defines two transmission modes, non-beacon-enabled and beacon-enabled mode. In the non-beacon-enabled mode, it simply makes use of unslotted carrier sense multiple access with collision avoidance (CSMA/CA) to control the medium access distributively. While in the beacon-enabled mode, besides the contention-based slotted CSMA/CA access control in the contention access period (CAP), the protocol also defines contention free period (CFP) for devices that require dedicated bandwidth or low-latency transmission. The IEEE 802.15.4 also defines two kinds of devices probably used in the LR-WPANs, the full function device (FFD) with all the IEEE 802.15.4 functions and features specified by the standard and the reduced function device (RFD) with only limited functionality to lower cost and complexity. A FFD can take the role as the PAN coordinator while a RFD can only talk to the FFD.

The IEEE 802.15.4 network can be built as star topology (Figure 1(a)), peer-to-peer topology (Figure 1(b)), and cluster tree (Figure 1(c)). In each topology, at least one FFD is required to serve as the coordinator of the network. In the star topology, all communications, including the transmissions between the devices, must go through the coordinator. Although in peer-to-peer topology the devices can communicate directly with each other, the coordinator is still required. In this paper, we mainly consider the LR-WPANs in home areas where star topology is widely adopted because of its simplicity and effectiveness. A star topology consists of one coordinator and several devices, as shown in Figure 1(a). The coordinator is responsible for management of an LR-WPAN, such as association/disassociation of the devices and medium access coordination of the devices in the LR-WPAN. It also relays packets for the devices who need to talk with each other since they cannot communicate directly according to the IEEE 802.15.4 specification.

The special scenario exhibits a good network coding opportunity. Network coding [2, 3] is an emerging technique that has been proposed as a promising method to improve the throughput via encoding the packets at the intermediate routers/relays. In particular, by exploring the broadcast nature of wireless communication medium, COPE [3] has been proved by a practical implementation in IEEE 802.11 network as an efficient network coding architecture that can substantially increase the throughput of wireless networks.

While, in IEEE 802.15.4 networks, the coordinator can also exploit network coding for the traffic between devices other than simply relaying them directly, the way should be in a lower complexity with lower energy consumption as lower power is an important requirement of LR-WPAN compared to IEEE 802.11 WLAN. Therefore, several issues such as how to apply network coding in LR-WPANs and how the network coding performs in LR-WPANs still need to be studied. We first consider the communication pattern in LR-WPANs and try to discover the network coding opportunities. Then, some practical issues, such as GTS allocation and multicast, are also considered in order to exploit the network coding opportunities efficiently. Simulation studies provide a deep insight to how the network coding performs in LR-WPANs. Our experimental results indicate that network coding provides a good alternative to improve the performance of wireless networks in terms of both throughput and energy consumption.

The rest of this paper is organized as follows. The background and related work are presented in Section 2. Section 3 describes how to integrate network coding into IEEE 802.15.4 protocols in detail. Section 4 presents the experimental results. Section 5 concludes the paper.

2. Background and Related Work

In this section, we first briefly introduce the IEEE 802.15.4 beacon-enabled transmission as the background of this paper. Then we show some related research results in the literatures.

2.1. Overview of the IEEE 802.15.4 Beacon-Enabled Transmission. In beacon-enabled mode, the channel time is divided into superframes bounded by the beacon frames transmitted from the coordinator, as shown in Figure 2. The time between two consecutive beacon frames is defined as the beacon interval (BI). BI is further divided into two periods, active period and inactive period. All the transmissions happen in and only in the active period, while, in the inactive period, all the devices in the network go into a low-power mode or sleep mode for energy saving. The active period is also referred to as superframe duration (SD). The inactive period is optional according to the requirement of the applications.

By default, the nodes compete for medium access using slotted CSMA/CA within the contention access period (CAP) during SD. The IEEE 802.15.4 protocol also offers the possibility of having a contention-free period (CFP) within the SD. The CFP is optionally activated upon request from a node. It consists of several numbers of guaranteed time slots (GTSs). The device, which needs dedicated bandwidth to transmit to or receive from the coordinator, can transmit a GTS request command to the coordinator. Upon reception of this request, the coordinator checks whether there are sufficient resources and, if possible, allocates the requested GTSs such that the device can communicate with the coordinator in the reserved GTS in a collision-free way. There are up to seven GTSs that can be allocated provided that there are sufficient capacity available. If the available resources are not sufficient, the GTS allocation request fails and the corresponding node then has to send its data frames during the CAP. A detailed description of the GTS management and the slotted CSMA/CA mechanism is presented in [4].

2.2. Related Work. Since the IEEE 802.15.4 was proposed, a lot of work has been done focusing on how to optimize its performance [5–10]. Compared to other wireless techniques, a key difference is the introduction of GTS in IEEE 802.15.4. As a result, the GTS optimization has received particular attentions to improve IEEE 802.15.4 performance.

In [5], the authors propose an implicit GTS allocation mechanism (i-Game) to improve bandwidth utilization, by allocating GTS to devices implicitly based not only on the remaining time slots but also on the traffic specifications of the flows, their delay requirements, and the available bandwidth resources. An adaptive GTS allocation (AGA) scheme is proposed in [6]. It uses dynamic priority control

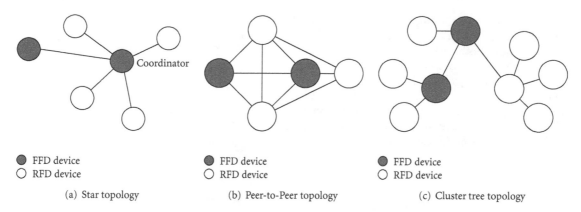

(a) Star topology   (b) Peer-to-Peer topology   (c) Cluster tree topology

FIGURE 1: Various topologies in IEEE 802.15.4 networks.

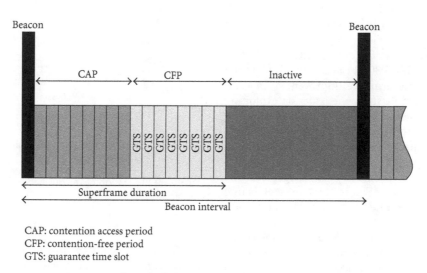

CAP: contention access period
CFP: contention-free period
GTS: guarantee time slot

FIGURE 2: The superframe structure defined in IEEE 802.15.4.

to allocate GTS to devices, in which GTSs are allocated in a nondecreasing order of the devices' priorities, and a starvation avoidance mechanism is also presented. Bhatti et al. propose a set of new MAC superframes with an aim to lower the response latency and to enhance the reliability in [11]. They swap the position of CFP and CAP in the superframe such that a failed GTS transmission can be retransmitted immediately in the CAP, and as a result the delay can be reduced. Because the FCFS GTS allocation scheme does not meet the requirement of some delay-sensitive or time-critical applications, an optimal work-conserving scheduling algorithm is designed in [7] to meet the delay constraints of time-sensitive transactions. Shrestha et al. formulate the GTS allocation problem as a knapsack problem and provide an optimal GTS allocation scheme to wireless body-area sensor networks such that a minimum bandwidth requirement is satisfied for on-body sensor devices [8]. In [10], the whole wireless sensor network is formulated as a multilevel tree and a framework is devised to construct a flow-balance TDMA schedules for solving the underlying rate differentiation problem using the GTS facility of the standard. A backward compatible energy efficient 802.15.4 MAC protocol for beacon-enabled sensor

networks called Deployable Energy Efficient MAC Protocol (DEEP) is proposed in [9]. DEEP modifies the IEEE 802.15.4 beacon frame structure by removing GTS descriptors from the beacons when requested. Therefore, the beacon frame is shortened and the energy consumption can be reduced.

Network coding origins from the seminal work [2] and has been proposed as a promising technique to improve the throughput via encoding the packets at the intermediate relay. Later, Katti et al. [3] first derive that the network coding gain is at most 2, which is also validated by their proposed practical COPE system. Liu and Xue [12] characterize the achievable rate regions and find the theoretical optimal sum rates for a basic 3-node topology. Liu et al. [13] show the benefit of network coding for 1D and 2D networks. Keshavarz-Haddad and Riedi [14] prove that the gain of network coding in terms of transport capacity is bounded by a constant factor in an arbitrary wireless network under traditional channel models. Le et al. [15] derive an upper bound of the throughput gain as $n/(n + 1)$ in an n-node network based on the encoding number. Iraji et al. [16] propose a new analytical model for throughput evaluation of a wireless tandem network coding based on a multiclass open queueing network. More recently, Umehara et al. [17]

provide explicit expressions of the throughput for a single-relay two-hop wireless CSMA system. Seferoglu et al. [18] take into consideration both network coded flows and induced conflicts between nodes in the optimization of intersession wireless network coding. Khreishah et al. [19] propose a joint optimal coding, scheduling, and rate-control scheme using pairwise intersession coding for wireless multihop networks. Nevertheless, little work focuses on applying and exploiting the recent advanced results in network coding into IEEE 802.15.4 networks.

3. Network Coding-Aware Bidirectional Communications

3.1. Motivation. The performance gain can be achieved by network coding under both GTS in CFP and CSMA in CAP, or even under the beacon-disable transmission model where only CSMA is possible. Most existing network coding strategies focus on the CSMA case, for example, COPE [3] and its variants proposed for IEEE 802.11 networks. To fill in the vacancy of research on performance improvement in IEEE 802.15.4 networks, we mainly study the issues on exploiting the network coding opportunities via GTS in this paper.

Figure 3 shows two network coding examples in which the relay node XORs packets from the transmitters and broadcasts the XORed packet to the receivers. The receivers can decode the XORed packet by XORing with the packets they have overheard (Figure 3(a)) or sent before (Figure 3(b)). The former one is known as intersession network coding, in which the receivers must overhear and buffer the packets that may help the decoding of the coded packet. The overhearing takes advantage of the broadcast nature of the wireless communication. The scenario in Figure 3(b) is called intrasession network coding, where the receivers do not need to overhear any packets but have to preserve the packets they have sent in their local buffer for the decoding of the coded packet.

It has been proved that network coding can significantly improve the throughput of the network. Now, let us first investigate whether the network coding is beneficial to energy saving by the example shown in Figure 3(b). Considering the scenario shown in Figure 3(b), there is a traffic from *Alice* to *Bob* and vice versa. The coordinator (*PANC*) controls the medium access of the two devices and also relays the data stream between them. Without network coding, the transmissions may be scheduled in the following way:

(1) *Alice* → *PANC*,

(2) *PANC* → *Bob*,

(3) *Bob* → *PANC*,

(4) *PANC* → *Alice*.

We need 4 transmissions and 4 receptions to complete one transaction without network coding. However, if network coding is considered, the scheduling may go as

(1) *Alice* → *PANC*,

(2) *Bob* → *PANC*,

(3) *Alice* ← *PANC* → *Bob*.

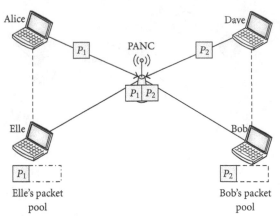

(a) In X topology using intersession network coding, overhearing is required

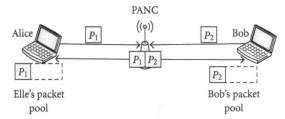

(b) In chain topology using intrasession network coding, overhearing is not required

FIGURE 3: Illustration of various network coding strategies in wireless networks.

Obviously, one transmission can be saved in one transaction compared to the case without network coding. Since the transmission dominates the energy consumption, saving transmissions is of great benefits to the energy efficiency. For more complicated situations from a practical point of view, several technical issues should be still carefully studied to exploit network coding opportunities in IEEE 802.15.4 networks in the following sections.

3.2. Network Coding Opportunities. Recalling the COPE built on the IEEE 802.11 networks, where the energy efficiency is not the major concern, we notice that the coordinator can discover the network coding opportunities by letting all the devices report the list of possessed packets. For example, *Alice* in Figure 3(a) shall tell the coordinator first that it has packet P_1. Then, the coordinator can make a decision whether it can encode packet P_1 with P_2 or not. We think it not efficient for the IEEE 802.15.4 devices to report the packets they are possessing. Instead, we exploit the features of communications in WPANs. The communications in WPANs are usually stable and regular compared to the IEEE 802.11 networks. Furthermore, the overhearing in WPANs should be disabled since it consumes additional energy. As a result, we only focus on intrasession network coding.

For intrasession network coding, the first thing to discover the network coding opportunity is to recognize the communication patterns. Whenever there is a relay request, the coordinator registers the source address and

```
(1) receive a packet p
(2) if
(3) p's destination address or source address = the coordinator's address then
(4)     ignore
(5) else
(6)     update the superframe window with the number of slots for the reception p
(7)     lookup the communication pattern table and check the superframe utilization window
(8)     if there is a communication in reverse direction and the slot utilization difference is less than
        the predetermined threshold then
(9)         discover a coding opportunity
(10)    end if
(11) end if
```

ALGORITHM 1: Algorithm to discover the intrasession network coding opportunities.

TABLE 1: An example of communication pattern table.

Transmitter	Receiver	Slide window				
Alice	Bob	4	4	4	4	4
Bob	Alice	4	4	4	4	0

the destination address in a communication pattern table. When the coordinator has a packet to relay, it first looks up the table to check whether there is any traffic in the reverse direction. If there is, the communication can be viewed as bidirectional; otherwise it is unidirectional. Since there is no intrasession network coding opportunity in the unidirectional session, either between two devices or between a device and the coordinator, the coordinator simply ignores the unidirectional communication and makes efforts to discover the bidirectional communication first. For bidirectional communications in WPANs, we consider two typical traffic categories: irregular data (e.g., periodical or occasional data exchange) and regular stream (e.g., interactive multimedia applications).

Only the information of traffic direction is not enough to define a network coding opportunity. If the communication rates in the two directions do not match well, network coding may degrade the performance as shown in [20]. So the transmission rate should also be taken into consideration. To measure the transmission rate, that is, the utilization of superframe slots, the coordinator maintains a superframe slide window to hold certain past superframes. We view the traffic with similar superframe slot utilization in both sides as the communication pattern with network coding opportunities. The process to identify the network coding opportunity is shown in Algorithm 1.

We use an example to illustrate the algorithm with window size = 5 and threshold = 5. The coordinator first discovers that there is a bidirectional communication between Alice and Bob. It creates two communication pattern entries and also monitors the superframe slot utilization of both sides in the past 5 superframes. As shown in Table 1, the coordinator used 20 slots to receive packets from Alice while 16 slots from Bob. The transmission rates of both sides are similar to each other since their utilization difference is less

than the threshold. Henceforth, the coordinator discovers a network coding opportunity between Alice and Bob and shall try to exploit the network coding opportunity.

3.3. Network Coding-Aware Session-Based GTS Allocation. Now the problem comes to how to exploit the discovered network coding opportunity. Intuitively the process should go this way: the coordinator shall first buffer a received packet and wait for the arrival of another packet from the network coding counterpart, then encode the two native packets into a coded packet, and finally multicast it to the two corresponding receivers. This shall work fine during the CAP using slotted CSMA/CA, provided that there is sufficient capacity available to satisfy the transmission requirements for both sides. However, when the bidirectional transmissions happen during the CFP, the GTS allocation shall be taken into account.

Consider the scenario where Alice and Bob have a video conversation on the visual doorbell. A comparatively large amount of streaming data will be transferred between them. Both of them may request a dedicated bandwidth for real-time communication. Suppose both request an 8-slot GTS in every two beacons as required by the application and the request from Alice comes first. Upon the reception of Alice's request, the coordinator may allocate an 8-slot GTS in the next superframe. After that, there may be no sufficient capacity to allocate additional 8-slot GTS to Bob since a minimum CAP duration must be reserved. If the GTS to Alice is not deallocated explicitly by Alice, Bob will continue tracking beacons and wait for aGTSDescPersistenceTime superframes as defined in the IEEE 802.15.4 [4]. In such case, Bob and other devices probably suffer starvation. According to the IEEE 802.15.4, the coordinator assumes that a device has stopped using its transmit-GTS [4] if a data frame is not received in the GTS from the device over at least $2 * n$ superframes, where n is defined as follows:

$$n = \begin{cases} 2^{8-\text{macBeaconOrder}} & 0 \leq \text{macBeaconOrder} \leq 8, \\ 1 & 9 \leq \text{macBeaconOrder} \leq 14. \end{cases} \quad (1)$$

As a result, a GTS shall be deallocated by the coordinator only when it has not been used for at least 2 superframes.

Alice may not lose the GTS privilege and continue to use the GTS every 2 superframes. In home area WPAN, a lower *mabBeaconOrder* is preferred as it ensures quick response to emergency alert, such as firm alarm. In this case, the network coding opportunity may be lost. This is not acceptable even without the consideration of network coding as this will lead to a low utilization of the GTS. To tackle this issue, we propose a network coding-aware session-based (NCAS) GTS allocation scheme.

At first, the coordinator allocates GTS by a device-based GTS allocation scheme same as the IEEE 802.15.4. The coordinator shall then track the GTS allocation and utilization of all the devices. Whenever the coordinator detects a network coding opportunity, it turns on the session-based allocation scheme for the two devices. It takes the traffic requirement as well as the GTS request into consideration. As presented before, the two devices usually share the same traffic requirement and the same GTS request. The coordinator shall allocate GTSs for both devices in every superframe and satisfy their traffic requirement at the same time. For the example above, the coordinator shall allocate 4-slot GTS for both devices in every superframe and a virtual link between the two device is created.

Although we mainly concern the transmit-GTS, the two devices may also request the receive-GTS to obtain data from the coordinator. In such case, there are two transmit-GTS requests and two receive-GTS requests for each session. In NCAS-based GTS allocation scheme, all of them are considered as a whole and treated as two transmit-GTS requests and one receive-GTS request. As a result, the coordinator shall allocate three GTSs within one superframe so as to complete the network coding-based communication transaction within one superframe.

As session-based GTS allocation scheme is incorporated, one may be concerned that whether it influences the communication of other devices because the session-based allocation violates the FCFS basis. For GTS requests from two devices within one session, the coordinator combines the two requests and treats it as the last-come. By such means, no negative impact will occur for the requests in between. For the subsequent requests, they are handled the same as in the IEEE 802.15.4.

3.4. Pseudo-Multicast for Intrasession Network Coding. The coded packet shall be relayed to both receivers simultaneously. It is straightforward and reasonable to broadcast the coded packet directly in the IEEE 802.11 networks when the energy is not a major concern. When it comes to the IEEE 802.15.4 networks, on the other hand, the broadcast is not energy efficient if irrelevant devices are involved. Therefore, a careful design of scheduling is required to make sure that both devices can receive the coded packet simultaneously. Otherwise, we may lose the benefit of network coding. To tackle these issues, we propose a Pseudo-Multicast for intrasession network coding in the IEEE 802.15.4 WPANs.

A device on a beacon-enabled WPAN can determine whether any data are pending for it by examining the *pending address information* field [4] of the received beacon frame. As a result, if there is coded packet pending for two devices,

the coordinator adds both corresponding addresses into the pending address information field to notify both sides. Upon reception of the beacon frames, both devices will transmit a MAC command requesting the data, using slotted CSMA/CA. The coordinator acknowledges the successful reception of the data request by transmitting an acknowledgment frame. However, the pending coded packet can not be sent immediately after one request. The coordinator shall wait until both requests are received. Due to the different duty cycle or some other reason, the two requests may not arrive within one superframe. Thus, the device who sends the request early shall wait for some time to get the coded packet. According to the IEEE 802.15.4, a device shall enable its receiver for at most *macMaxFrameTotalWaitTime* CAP symbols and then it may conclude that there are no data pending at the coordinator. To prevent this case, the coordinator shall relay the native packet to that device if the data request from the other side is not received within the *macMaxFrameTotalWaitTime* CAP symbols. Upon reception of both requests before the *macMaxFrameTotalWaitTime* CAP symbols, the coordinator sends the coded packet in a Pseudo-Multicast way.

As we have known, it is not energy efficient to send the coded packet with broadcast address (0xffff). Instead of using broadcast, we advocate a Pseudo-Multicast to enable the simultaneous reception of both packets without negative impact on other devices. The Pseudo-Multicast actually is a unicast. The coordinator chooses address of the receiver which requested its pending data earlier as the destination address and sends the coded packet out. The device with the specified destination address receives the coded packet directly, while the other device should also take it as desired by recognizing the address of its network coding counterpart in the coded packet. When both devices successfully receive the coded packet, each device should acknowledge the successful reception by an acknowledgement frame, which is the same as specified in the IEEE 802.15.4.

If the devices prefer to receive from the coordinator in the GTSs, as presented in last section, the coordinator may allocate a receive-GTS for both devices in the session. Thus, from the starting slot of the allocated GTS, both devices just turn on their receivers and wait for the pending coded packet.

4. Performance Evaluation

To investigate how network coding performs in the beacon-enabled IEEE 802.15.4 WPANs, we have developed a Java-based simulator. It simulates the network topology shown in Figure 3(a) where there are two devices communicating with each other via a single relay. The connections between the device and the relay are assumed as packetloss-free half-duplex channel. Each superframe consists of up to 16 time slots, and one traffic unit can be transmitted within a time slot.

Two bidirectional traffic models are considered in our experiments. For the irregular traffic, data generation with a Poisson distribution is simulated. We investigate the performance of XOR-based network coding under various traffic loads (4 and 5) and mean packet arrival rates

(0.2, 0.5, 0.8, and 1.0), which are defined as the number of traffic units per packet and the number of packets per superframe, respectively. For regular traffic with streaming data, packets are uniformly generated within each superframe with various loads from 1 to 5 traffic units per packet, below the network capacity with network coding. To study the energy consumption of the proposed scheme in our experiments, we follow the power model on the energy measurements for the CC1000 radio on Mica2 motes [21], which is a third generation mote module used for low-power WSNs. The parameters used in our simulations are summarized in Table 2.

To investigate the benefit of network coding in IEEE 802.15.4 network, we assume that all transmissions happen during the CFP since a key difference between IEEE 802.11 network and IEEE 802.15.4 network is the CFP. We consider an extreme condition that the whole superframes are statically allocated as GTSs to each device. The allocation remains unchanged for duration of the simulation. For network coding-aware allocation, we follow the session-based GTS allocation presented in Section 3.3, while for conventional way, we adopt FIFO policy as described in [4].

4.1. Power Efficiency. In the first set of experiments, we evaluate and compare the power consumption for the schemes with and without network coding under different traffic scenarios. For streaming traffic, the packets arrive at every superframe with different traffic units, for example, 1, 2, 3, 4, or 5. For Poisson traffic, the mean packet arrival rates are 0.2, 0.5, 0.8, and 1.0 packet per superframe, and each packet has 4 or 5 traffic units. Recall that one traffic unit can be transmitted within one GTS, leading to 4 or 5 GTSs required by each device.

The simulation results for the streaming traffic case are illustrated in Figure 4(a). We notice that the energy consumptions of each device (Alice or Bob) are almost the same when the traffic load is between 1 and 4, no matter whether network coding is applied or not. Recall that one bidirectional communication can be completed within one superframe in either case, where 4-slot transmissions and 4-slot receptions are required for each device. As a result, each device consumes almost the same energy within a superframe no matter network coding is applied or not. The same observation can be made for Poisson traffic with traffic load of 4 traffic units per packet, as shown in Figure 4(b), indicating that intrasession XORed based network coding is not beneficial to power efficiency of the devices. On the other hand, we may also say that it does not introduce any additional energy overhead to the devices either.

When the traffic load is 5, less energy is consumed without network coding at each device for both streaming traffic in Figure 4(a) and Poisson traffic in Figure 4(c). This is because one bidirectional communication can be completed and either device transmits in 5 slots and receives in other 5 slots in a superframe if network coding is exploited. In contrast, one bidirectional communication is across at least two superframes without using network coding. Within one of the frames, a device may switch into idle state if no packets are intended. In conclusion, both devices keep busy during

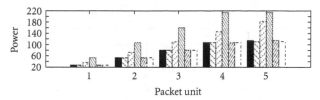

(a) Power consumption when both devices have streaming data with different traffic units GTS

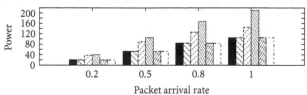

(b) Power consumption when both devices have Poisson traffic with different packet arrival rates (Packet size = 4)

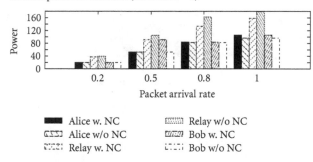

■ Alice w. NC	▨ Relay w/o NC
▧ Alice w/o NC	▨ Bob w. NC
▨ Relay w. NC	▨ Bob w/o NC

(c) Power consumption when both devices have Poisson traffic with different packet arrival rates (Packet size = 5)

FIGURE 4: Power consumption comparison.

almost every superframe if network coding is exploited, while one device may switch into low-power state during some superframes if network coding is not exploited.

We then study the power consumption of the relay node. From Figure 4, we can see that network coding can always save power in all cases. For example, when the packet size is 4 in Poisson traffic, the relay needs 4 slots to transmit the encoded packets if the network coding is applied and 8 slots to relay the native ones if the network coding is not exploited. Therefore, 4 slots can be saved for the relay to complete one communication between the two nodes by exploiting the network coding opportunities. Similar observations apply to the packet size of 5 traffic units.

One may also notice that the power saving of the relay with network coding is an increasing function of the packet size in streaming traffic in Figure 4(a) or an increasing function of the packet arrival rate in Poisson traffic in both Figures 4(b) and 4(c). For example by exploiting network coding in Figure 4(b), the power is saved around 6% when the mean packet arrival rate is 0.2 and up to 45% when the mean rate is 1.0. This is because the higher the packet arrival rate is, the more network coding opportunities are possible to be exploited.

Figure 5 compares the number of packets directly relayed as native ones and the number of XORed packets under

TABLE 2: Simulation parameters and power model.

Simulation parameters		
Traffic model	Poisson traffic	Streaming traffic
Traffic load (traffic units/packet)	4 and 5	1, 2, 3, 4, 5
Data arrival rate (packet/superframe)	0.2, 0.5, 0.8, 1.0	N/A
Superframe length (slots)	16	
Power model		
Radio power in idle (mW)	1.38	
Radio power in receiving (mW)	9.6	
Radio power in transmitting (mW)	17	

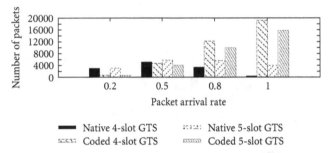

FIGURE 5: The number of packets directly relayed or XORed under different data rates.

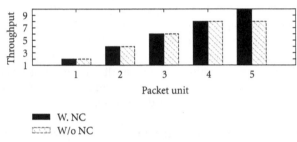

(a) Throughput of streaming traffic with different traffic units

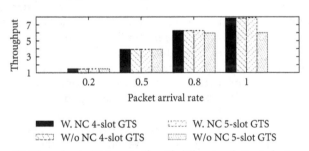

(b) Throughput of Poisson traffic with different packet arrival rates

FIGURE 6: Throughput comparison.

different packet arrival rates. No matter the packet size is 4 or 5, it can be always observed that higher rate exhibits more network coding opportunities. In the case when the packet size is 4 and the mean data rate is 0.2, most packets, around 3032, are relayed directly while only 664 packets are relayed as coded ones. When the packet arrival rate rises to 1.0, 19176 packets are relayed as coded ones while only 388 packets are directly relayed.

4.2. Throughput. The throughput for streaming traffic with various packet sizes and for Poisson traffic with various packet arrival rates, with/without network coding, is shown in Figure 6. One may first notice that the same throughput is achieved when the packet sizes are less than 5, as shown in Figure 6(a). This is because, under these situations, a superframe with 16 time slots is enough for one bidirectional communication no matter network coding is used or not. Same phenomena can be also observed in Figure 6(b) when the packet size is 4. We may also note that the saved slots in each superframe by exploiting network coding could be utilized by other communication sessions if possible, resulting in an improved throughput.

The throughput improvement by network coding is significant when each packet has a length of 5 traffic units. To complete a whole bidirectional communication session, 20 slots are required if direct relay is used, while only 15 slots are required if network coding is applied. For example, the throughput is 7.90 with network coding but only 5.99

without network coding when the packet arrival rate is 1.0 as shown in Figure 6(b).

5. Conclusion

In this paper, we have studied how to exploit network coding in the beacon-enabled IEEE 802.15.4 LR-WPAN and how it benefits the performance of the network in terms of power saving and throughput. Several important practical issues are studied, such as the discovery of network coding opportunities, GTS allocation for network coded transmissions in GTS during the CFP, and pseudo-multicast for simultaneous reception of coded packets without negative impact on other devices. All these concerns enable a realistic and efficient network coding paradigm in the IEEE 802.15.4 LR-WPAN. The simulation results further provide an insight to the understanding that network coding can improve the performance of IEEE 802.15.4 LR-WPAN in terms of both throughput and power efficiency.

References

[1] Z. Alliance, "Zigbee alliance," 2010, http://www.zigbee.org/.

[2] R. Ahlswede, N. Cai, S. Y. R. Li, and R. W. Yeung, "Network information flow," *IEEE Transactions on Information Theory*, vol. 46, no. 4, pp. 1204–1216, 2000.

[3] S. Katti, H. Rahul, W. Hu, D. Katabi, M. Médard, and J. Crowcroft, "Xors in the air: practical wireless network coding," in *Proceedings of the 2006 Conference on Applications, Technologies, Architectures, and Protocols for Computer Communications (SIGCOMM '06)*, no. 4, pp. 243–254, ACM, New York, NY, USA, October 2006.

[4] *IEEE Standard for Information Technology Part 15.4: Wireless Medium Access Control (MAC) and Physical Layer (PHY) Specifications for Low-Rate Wireless Personal Area Networks (LR-WPANs)*, IEEE Standard 802.15.4 x Working Group Std. Std., 2003.

[5] A. Koubâa, M. Alves, E. Tovar, and A. Cunha, "An implicit GTS allocation mechanism in IEEE 802.15.4 for time-sensitive wireless sensor networks: theory and practice," *Real-Time Systems*, vol. 39, no. 1–3, pp. 169–204, 2008.

[6] Y. K. Huang, A. C. Pang, and H. N. Hung, "An adaptive GTS allocation scheme for IEEE 802.15.4," *IEEE Transactions on Parallel and Distributed Systems*, vol. 19, no. 5, pp. 641–651, 2008.

[7] C. Na, Y. Yang, and A. Mishra, "An optimal GTS scheduling algorithm for time-sensitive transactions in IEEE 802.15.4 networks," *Computer Networks*, vol. 52, no. 13, pp. 2543–2557, 2008.

[8] B. Shrestha, E. Hossain, S. Camorlinga, R. Krishnamoorthy, and D. Niyato, "An optimizationbased GTS allocation scheme for IEEE 802.15.4 MAC with application to wireless body-area sensor networks," in *Proceedings of the IEEE International Communications Conference (IEEE ICC '10)*, May 2010.

[9] M. Valero, A. Bourgeois, and R. Beyah, "DEEP: a deployable energy efficient 802.15.4 MAC protocol for sensor networks," in *Proceedings of the IEEE International Communications Conference (IEEE ICC '10)*, 2010.

[10] M. Takaffoli and W. Moussa, "Scheduled access using the IEEE 802.15.4 guaranteed time slots," in *Proceedings of the IEEE International Communications Conference (IEEE ICC '10)*, May 2010.

[11] G. Bhatti, A. Mehta, Z. Sahinoglu, J. Zhang, and R. Viswanathan, "Modified beacon-enabled IEEE 802.15.4 MAC for lower latency," in *Proceedings of the 2008 IEEE Global Telecommunications Conference (IEEE GLOBECOM '08)*, IEEE, 2008.

[12] C. H. Liu and F. Xue, "Network coding for two-way relaying: rate region, sum rate and opportunistic scheduling," in *Proceedings of the International Conference on Communications, (ICC '08)*, pp. 1044–1049, IEEE, Beijing, China, May 2008.

[13] J. Liu, D. Goeckel, and D. Towsley, "Bounds on the gain of network coding and broadcasting in wireless networks," in *Proceedings of the 26th Conference on Computer Communications (INFOCOM '07)*, pp. 724–732, IEEE, Anchorage, Alaska, USA, May 2007.

[14] A. Keshavarz-Haddad and R. Riedi, "Bounds on the benefit of network coding: throughput and energy saving in wireless networks," in *Proceedings of the 27th Conference on Computer Communications (INFOCOM '08)*, pp. 376–384, IEEE, April 2008.

[15] J. Le, J. Lui, and D. Chiu, "How many packets can we encode?—An analysis of practical wireless network coding," in *Proceedings of the 27th Conference on Computer Communications (INFOCOM '08)*, pp. 371–375, IEEE, Phoenix, Ariz, USA, April 2008.

[16] M. B. Iraji, M. H. Amerimehr, and F. Ashtiani, "A Queueing Model for Wireless Tandem Network Coding," in *Proceedings of the 2010 IEEE Wireless Communication and Network Conference (WCNC '09)*, 2009.

[17] D. Umehara, S. Denno, M. Morikura, and T. Sugiyama, "Throughput analysis of two-hop wireless CSMA network coding," in *Proceedings of the 2010 IEEE International Conference on Communications (ICC '10)*, pp. 1–6, IEEE, 2010.

[18] H. Seferoglu, A. Markopoulou, and U. Kozat, "Network coding-aware rate control and scheduling in wireless networks," in *Proceedings of the 2009 IEEE International Conference on Multimedia and Expo (ICME '09)*, pp. 1496–1499, IEEE, Piscataway, NJ, USA, 2009.

[19] A. Khreishah, C. C. Wang, and N. B. Shroff, "Cross-layer optimization for wireless multihop networks with pairwise intersession network coding," *IEEE Journal on Selected Areas in Communications*, vol. 27, no. 5, pp. 606–621, 2009.

[20] T. S. Kim, S. Vural, I. Broustis, D. Syrivelis, S. V. Krishnamurthy, and T. F. La Porta, "A framework for joint network coding and transmission rate control in wireless networks," in *Proceedings of the 29th Conference on Information Communications (INFOCOM '10)*, pp. 2937–2945, IEEE, Piscataway, NJ, USA, 2010.

[21] O. Landsiedel, K. Wehrle, and S. Götz, "Accurate prediction of power consumption in sensor networks," in *Proceedings of the 2nd IEEE workshop on Embedded Networked Sensors (EmNet '05)*, vol. 2005, pp. 37–44, IEEE Computer Society, Washington, DC, USA, 2005.

8

PAPR Reduction Approach Based on Channel Estimation Pilots for Next Generations Broadcasting Systems

Anh-Tai Ho,[1] Jean-François Helard,[1] Youssef Nasser,[2] and Yves Louet[3]

[1] IETR UMR 6164, INSA, Université Européenne de Bretagne, 35708 Rennes, France
[2] American University of Beirut, Bliss Street, Beirut 11-0236, Lebanon
[3] SCEE Team, Supelec, avenue de la Boulaie, 35576 Cesson-Sévigné, France

Correspondence should be addressed to Youssef Nasser, youssef.nasser@aub.edu.lb

Academic Editor: Massimiliano Laddomada

A novel peak-to-average power ratio (PAPR) reduction technique for orthogonal frequency division multiplexing (OFDM) systems is addressed. Instead of using dedicated pilots for PAPR reduction as with tone reservation (TR) method selected by the DVB-T2 standard, we propose to use existing pilots used for channel estimation. In this way, we avoid the use of reserved tone pilots and then improve the spectral efficiency of the system. In order to allow their recovery at the receiver, these pilots have to follow particular laws which permit their blind detection and avoid sending side information. In this work, we propose and investigate a multiplicative law operating in discrete frequency domain. The operation in discrete domain aims at reducing degradation due to detection and estimation error in continuous domain. Simulation results are performed using the new DVB-T2 standard parameters. Its performance is compared to the DVB-T2 PAPR gradient algorithm and to the second-order cone programming (SOCP) competitive technique proposed in the literature. We show that the proposed technique is efficient in terms of PAPR reduction value and of spectral efficiency while the channel estimation performance is maintained.

1. Introduction

orthogonal frequency division multiplexing (OFDM) technology has been the subject of numerous dissertations in recent years, mainly due to its several advantages for mobile wireless communications. It has been adopted in several systems mainly in digital video broadcasting (DVB) standards [1–3].

However, a main drawback of OFDM technique is the high peak-to-average power ratio (PAPR) of the transmitted signal. High PAPR value implies sophisticated and, thus, expensive radio transmitters with high-power amplifiers (HPAs) operating on a very large linear range at the transmitter side. Moreover, the nonlinearity of the HPA leads to in-band distortion, which increases the bit error rate (BER) of the system, and to out-of-band (OOB) distortion, which introduces high adjacent channel interference.

Various approaches have been proposed as summarized in [4, 5] to mitigate the PAPR of an OFDM signal. Among them, clipping and filtering technique is easy to implement.

However, these schemes yield a broken system performance since clipping is a nonlinear process [6] leading to a signal distortion. An alternative method based on coding was proposed in [7], in which a data sequence is embedded in a longer sequence, and only a subset of all these possible sequences is used to exclude patterns generating high PAPR. Moreover, other methods such as partial transmit sequence [8], selected mapping [9], and interleaving [10] are also proposed. The main drawback of these methods is the necessity to transmit side information (SI) to the receiver, resulting in some loss of throughput efficiency.

Some methods recently proposed do not need this SI transmission [11, 12]. Indeed, the active constellation extension (ACE) method proposed in [12] reduces the PAPR by changing the constellation of the signal without modifying the minimum distance. However, this technique has some gain limits when the constellation size of the signal increases. Moreover, this technique is not suited for rotated constellation schemes, which have been selected for the second generation digital terrestrial television broadcasting system

(DVB-T2). The tone reservation (TR) method, proposed by Tellado and Tellambura [10] and adopted in DVB-T2 also, uses allocated subcarriers to generate additional signal that minimizes the PAPR value. However, TR technique reduces the spectrum efficiency since it requires some dedicated pilots for PAPR reduction issues. In DVB-T2, 1% of the subcarriers are dedicated for PAPR. Moreover, an iterative process should be implemented at the transmitter with a special need for a smooth control of the transmitted power on the dedicated subcarriers in order to respect the DVB-T2 spectrum mask requirements (the dedicated pilots should be at a power level less than 10 dB with respect to the data subcarriers power).

With the limitations of ACE technique for rotated constellation schemes and those of TR by spectral efficiency loss, an innovative technique which could be implemented for rotated constellation and without efficiency loss is clearly needed. In this paper, we adopt, as in [4], the TR technique by using the pilots of channel estimation for both PAPR reduction and channel estimation issues. The novelty of our proposition is based on the optimization of the phase and amplitude of the channel estimation pilots, used jointly for PAPR reduction process. Indeed, instead of using orthogonal pilots sequences (OPSs), we optimize the transmitted sequence for PAPR issue in terms of phase and amplitude. Using a predefined law between different sequences, the receiver could easily utilize a blind detection of the transmitted sequences.

The proposition of this work is multifold. First, instead of using dedicated pilots for PAPR reduction, we expend the idea of [4] which consists in utilizing existing pilots dedicated for channel estimation for both channel estimation and PAPR reduction issues. In this way, we avoid the use of reserved pilots as proposed in DVB-T2 standard improving thus the spectral efficiency of the system. Second, in order to allow their recovery serving for channel estimation process at the receiver, these pilots have to follow particular laws. Multiplicative law in frequency domain is then proposed and investigated in this work. At the receiver, this law is applied to detect and estimate transmitted pilots in frequency domain. As the detection and estimation of multiplicative law's parameters in continuous frequency domain, that is, in real space, cause degradations, we propose to operate this law in the discrete frequency domain, that is, in a predefined discrete set. Third, we show by simulations the validity of our technique using DVB-T2 standard [1] parameters. Its performance is compared to the DVB-T2 PAPR gradient algorithm and to the second-order cone programming (SOCP) technique proposed in [13–15].

The remainder of this paper is organized as follows. Section 2 briefly presents the OFDM system model and the PAPR statistics. Then, in order to have a clear overview about the benefits of our proposed technique, we will first explain the general principle of the TR-based techniques in Section 3. In Section 4, we describe our proposed pilot-aided PAPR reduction technique. In Section 5, blind pilot sequence detection and channel estimation are introduced. Section 6 presents the performance of the proposed method as well as a summary of the obtained results. Finally, conclusions are drawn in Section 7.

2. OFDM Signal and PAPR Value

Let $\mathbf{X} = [X_0, \ldots, X_{N-1}]$ be a sequence of complex symbols and $\mathbf{x} = [x_0, \ldots, x_{N-1}]$ be its discrete inverse Fourier transform. The OFDM baseband signal in continuous time domain, is expressed as,

$$x(t) = \frac{1}{\sqrt{N}} \sum_{k=0}^{N-1} X_k e^{j2\pi kt/TN}, \quad 0 \le t < NT, \quad (1)$$

where $j = \sqrt{-1}$, N denotes the number of subcarriers and T is the original complex signal duration. In practice, only NL equidistant samples of $x(t)$ are considered, where L represents the oversampling factor [13] used to make the signal as close as possible to the continuous signal. The oversampled signal is then given by

$$x_{[n/L]} = \frac{1}{\sqrt{N}} \sum_{k=0}^{N-1} X_k e^{j2\pi kn/LN}, \quad \forall n \in [0 \cdots NL - 1]. \quad (2)$$

When the oversampling factor L is large enough, the PAPR value of the OFDM signal is defined as the ratio of its maximum power divided by its average power. It is expressed as [16]

$$\text{PAPR}\{x(t)\} \approx \text{PAPR}(\mathbf{x}_L) = \frac{\max_n |x_{n/L}|^2}{E\left\{|x_{n/L}|^2\right\}}, \quad (3)$$

where $\mathbf{x}_L = \mathbf{Q}_L \mathbf{X}_L$, $\mathbf{X}_L$ is the zero-padded oversampled vector of $\mathbf{X}$, $E\{\}$ denotes expectation operation, and $\mathbf{Q}_L$ is the inverse discrete Fourier transform matrix of size NL. $\mathbf{Q}_L$ is given by

$$\mathbf{Q}_L = \frac{1}{\sqrt{N}} \begin{bmatrix} 1 & 1 & \cdots & 1 \\ 1 & e^{(\mathcal{A})1 \cdot 1} & & e^{(\mathcal{A})1 \cdot (NL-1)} \\ \vdots & & \ddots & \vdots \\ 1 & e^{(\mathcal{A})(NL-1) \cdot 1} & \cdots & e^{(\mathcal{A})(NL-1) \cdot (NL-1)} \end{bmatrix}, \quad (4)$$

where $\mathcal{A}$ denotes $j2\pi/NL$.

In this study, the PAPR performance is evaluated using the complementary cumulative distribution function (CCDF). It is defined by the probability that the PAPR value exceeds a given threshold γ. For $L = 1$, it can be expressed as [17]

$$\text{CCDF}_{\text{PAPR}} = \Pr[\text{PAPR}(\mathbf{x}_L) > \gamma, \ L = 1]$$
$$\approx 1 - (1 - e^{-\gamma})^N. \quad (5)$$

It is also demonstrated in [17] that the real PAPR value can be approximated independently of L when $L \ge 4$ by

$$\text{CCDF}_{\text{PAPR}\{x(t)\}} = \Pr[\text{PAPR}(\mathbf{x}_L) > \gamma, \ L \ge 4]$$
$$\approx 1 - (1 - e^{-\gamma})^{2.8 N}. \quad (6)$$

In this paper, we consider $L = 4$ and use this expression as a theoretical PAPR reference value of the original OFDM signal.

3. Existing TR-PAPR Reduction Methods

3.1. General Principle. In an OFDM0-based system (like DVB standards), the main idea of the TR technique is to use reserved pilots in order to reduce the PAPR value at the input of the power amplifier of the time domain transmitted signal.

Let us consider M as the number of channel estimation pilots used for PAPR reduction issue and $\mathbf{P} = [P_0, \ldots, P_{M-1}]$ as the M pilot positions dedicated for PAPR reduction, and let $\mathbf{C} = [C_0, \ldots, C_{M-1}]$ be the set of M pilots transmitted on these positions, as shown in Figure 1. Then, the N modulated symbols $\{X_k\}_{k=0\cdots N-1}$ of the OFDM symbol in frequency domain are expressed as:

$$X_k = \begin{cases} C_k & \text{if } k \in \mathbf{P}, \\ S_k & \text{if not,} \end{cases} \tag{7}$$

where S_k is the data symbol transmitted on subcarrier k and C_k is a pilot symbol used for PAPR reduction.

The OFDM baseband signal in time domain, after pilot insertion, becomes

$$\mathbf{x}_L = \mathbf{Q}_L \mathbf{X}_L = \mathbf{Q}_L (\mathbf{C} + \mathbf{S}_L) = \mathbf{Z}_L \mathbf{C} + \mathbf{s}_L, \tag{8}$$

where $\mathbf{S}_L$ is the data vector represented in frequency domain of size N (where the values at the pilots positions are set to 0), and $\mathbf{s}_L$ is its time domain representation. $\mathbf{Z}_L$ is given by

$$\mathbf{Z}_L = \frac{1}{\sqrt{N}} \begin{bmatrix} 1 & 1 & \cdots & 1 \\ e^{(\mathcal{A})1 \cdot p_1} & e^{(\mathcal{A})1 \cdot p_2} & & e^{(\mathcal{A})1 \cdot p_M} \\ \vdots & & \ddots & \vdots \\ e^{(\mathcal{A})(NL-1) \cdot p_1} & e^{(\mathcal{A})(NL-1) \cdot p_2} & \cdots & e^{(\mathcal{A})(NL-1) \cdot p_M} \end{bmatrix}, \tag{9}$$

and L holds for oversampling factor.

The added that signal $\mathbf{c}_L = \mathbf{Z}_L \mathbf{C}$ has to cope with PAPR values. In literature, different techniques have been proposed to optimize this signal. Among them, the SOCP and the gradient solutions are two of the most promising keys which have been extensively studied for optimization purposes. In the next section, we will give a general overview about these techniques. Performance of these techniques will be used as reference in comparison with our proposed technique.

3.2. SOCP Solution. The PAPR reduction problem can be formulated as follows: reducing PAPR value leads to the minimization of the maximum peak value of the combined signal $(\mathbf{s}_L + \mathbf{Z}_L \mathbf{C})$ while keeping the average power constant [12]. Mathematically speaking, this problem can be written as

$$\min_{\mathbf{C}} \max_n \left| \mathbf{s}_L + \mathbf{Z}_{n,L}^{\text{row}} \mathbf{C} \right|, \tag{10}$$

where $\mathbf{Z}_{n,L}^{\text{row}}$ denotes the nth row of $\mathbf{Z}_L$.

Equation (10) can be also rewritten as

$$\min_{\mathbf{C}} \left\| \mathbf{s}_L + \mathbf{Z}_{n,L}^{\text{row}} \mathbf{C} \right\|_\infty, \tag{11}$$

where $\| \cdot \|$ denotes the standard uniform norm.

Since the set $\mathbf{C}$ of pilots is used for PAPR reduction, the problem turns out now to find $\mathbf{C}$ which minimizes the PAPR of the current transmitted OFDM symbol. In the continuous domain, that is, for $\mathbf{C} \subset \mathbb{C}^M$, this search is formulated as a convex optimization problem and solved using SOCP problem [13–15]. The optimization process can take the form of

$$\begin{aligned} \text{Minimize} \quad & \beta \\ \text{subject to} \quad & \left\| \mathbf{s}_L + \mathbf{Z}_{n,L}^{\text{row}} \mathbf{C} \right\| \leq \beta \qquad (12) \\ & \forall 0 \leq n \leq NL - 1. \end{aligned}$$

It has been shown that this technique provides the optimized value in terms of PAPR reduction, but it presents a high calculation complexity [13–15]. In our study, we will use this technique as a comparison term with other techniques mainly with the proposed joint PAPR reduction and channel estimation scheme.

3.3. Gradient Iterative-Based Method. This method, adopted in DVB-T2 standard, is a suboptimal solution of the SOCP method. It is based on the gradient iterative method using the clipping process. In order to apply this technique, the technical specifications of DVB-T2 allowed 1% of active subcarriers for PAPR reduction issues. The pilots signal used for PAPR, defined as a reference kernel signal, is given by

$$p = \frac{N}{N_{\text{TR}}} \mathbf{Q}_L [1_{\text{TR}}], \tag{13}$$

where N_{TR} denotes the number of reserved subcarriers, $[1_{\text{TR}}]$ denotes the $(N, 1)$ vector having N_{TR} elements of ones at the positions corresponding to the reserved carriers and $(N - N_{\text{TR}})$ elements of zeros at the others. This reference signal presents a peak at the position 0.

For each iteration, the peak position k of the initial signal is detected. Reference signal is shifted of k positions in order to allow the reduction of peak signal to a predefined clipping value V_{clip}. The reduction principle is described in Figure 2.

The procedure of the PAPR reduction algorithm is given as follows.

Initialization. the initial values for peak reduction signal in time domain are set to zero:
$\mathbf{c}^{(0)} = [0 \cdots 0]^T$, where $\mathbf{c}^{(i)}$ denotes the vector of the peak reduction signal computed at ith iteration.

Iterations.

(1) i starts from 1;

(2) find the maximum magnitude of $(x + \mathbf{c}^{(i-1)})$, noted y_i, and the corresponding sample index k_i;

(3) if $y_i < V_{\text{clip}}$, go to step (5);

   if $y_i > V_{\text{clip}}$, clip the signal peak to this value;

   update the vector of peak reduction signal $\mathbf{c}^{(i)}$;

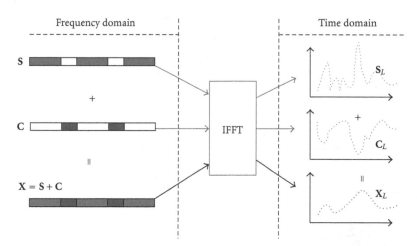

FIGURE 1: Pilots insertion scheme.

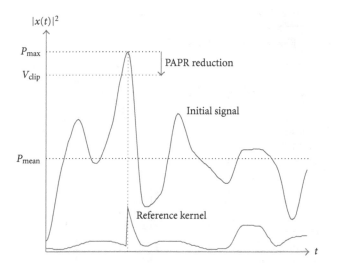

FIGURE 2: Principle of peak suppression by reference kernel signal.

(4) if $i < i_{\max}$, the maximum iteration number, increase i by one and return to step (2);

(5) terminate the iteration. The transmitted signal is obtained by: $x' = x + \mathbf{c}^{(i)}$.

The overall process of the gradient iterative-based method is summarized in Figure 3.

4. Proposed Pilot-Aided PAPR Reduction Method

The conventional TR method uses dedicated pilots for PAPR reduction issue leading to a spectral efficiency loss. In this proposition, we use some of the scattered pilots dedicated to channel estimation for both PAPR reduction and channel estimation purposes. The main problem turns out then to find the pilot symbols at the transmitter which minimizes the PAPR value but also to find these pilot symbols at the receiver in order to achieve channel estimation.

That is, in order to achieve both operations, that is, PAPR reduction and channel estimation, the set $\mathbf{c}$ chosen for PAPR reduction has to undergo some particular laws known at the receiver. Figure 4 shows the general principle of the proposed method. In this scheme, the function $f(\cdot)$ reflects the particular law known at both the transmitter and receiver. In our proposition, we consider a simple multiplicative law given by

$$C_{k+1} = C_k \times \Omega \quad \forall k \in [0, \dots, M-2] \text{ or equivalently}$$

$$C_k = \Omega^k C_0,$$
(14)

where Ω denotes the step between two consecutive pilots and C_0 is the first pilot symbol.

The choice of C_k and Ω could be either in continuous domain, that is, the pilots, could take any continuous value in $\mathbb{C}$, or they could take any discrete value from a discrete predefined set in discrete domain with a discrete value Ω. Since the estimation of the pilots and Ω at the receiver in continuous domain could yield to a residual estimation error, and then to a slight system performance degradation, we propose to perform research in a discrete subset of $\mathbb{C}$. Equation (14) becomes

$$C_0 = \lambda e^{j\phi},$$

$$\Omega = e^{j\Delta},$$
(15)

$$C_k = \lambda e^{j(\phi + k\Delta)},$$

where λ, ϕ, and Δ take values from a predefined set of discrete values. λ is the boost factor applied to the dedicated subcarriers, ϕ is the initial phase value of the first pilot symbol, and Δ is the phase increment. The main reason to select a multiplicative law is due to simplicity issues and boost factor control, that is, power control of the transmitted sequences. Indeed, using (15), we can equivalently control the boost factor of all pilots (joint PAPR and channel estimation pilots). Again, we recall that the "discrete domain" means that instead of searching SOCP solution in $\mathbb{C}$, we

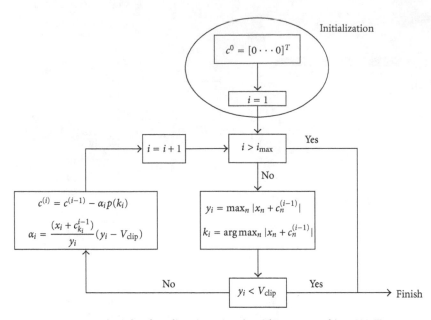

FIGURE 3: Principle of gradient iterative algorithm proposed in DVB-T2.

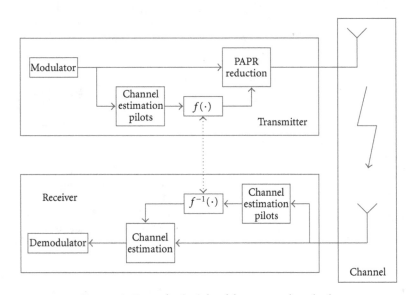

FIGURE 4: General principle of the proposed method.

search it in a predefined discrete set with a different discrete step for ϕ and Δ, called $\mu(\phi)$, and $\mu(\Delta)$, respectively. Figure 5 shows the multiplicative law scheme and the evolution of the pilots from one index to another. λ, ϕ, and Δ have to be selected in such a way to optimize the PAPR reduction gain and to limit channel estimation errors. This compromise will be detailed in next sections.

5. Pilots Recovery and Channel Estimation

In order to describe the channel estimation scheme and pilots recovery, frequency nonselective fading per subcarrier and time invariance during one OFDM symbol are assumed. Furthermore, the absence of intersymbol interference and intercarrier interference is guaranteed by the use of a guard interval longer than the maximum excess delay of the impulse response of the channel. In conventional OFDM schemes and under these assumptions, the received signal at the output of the FFT operation could be written as

$$\mathbf{R} = \mathbf{HS} + \mathbf{W}, \qquad (16)$$

where $\mathbf{H}$ denotes the $N \times N$ matrix which contains the complex channel coefficients, and $\mathbf{W}$ is the additive white Gaussian noise vector.

In conventional OFDM systems, the channel estimation is done by estimating the pilot channel coefficients $\hat{H}_p$ first and then by filtering the obtained coefficients using some conventional filters (the Wiener filter is widely used). The conventional OFDM channel estimation scheme is represented in Figure 6. Figure 7 shows the proposed channel

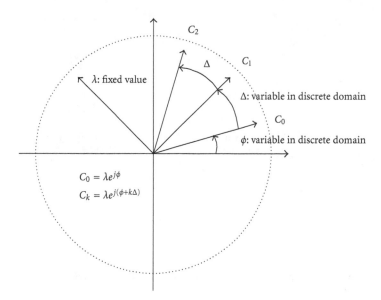

FIGURE 5: Multiplicative law scheme.

estimation scheme when some pilots are dedicated for PAPR issues. It is clear that there is a slight difference with the conventional estimation scheme shown in Figure 6. In our scheme, the pilot symbols C_p used for PAPR reduction are not known a priori at the receiver. Therefore, the pilots' recovery and channel estimation procedure is performed in two steps. First, we determine the transmitted sequence $\hat{C}_p$ used for PAPR reduction. In the second step, we determine the actual channel coefficients $\hat{H}_k$.

In order to accomplish the first step, we assume that the channel is almost constant between two successive OFDM symbols, that is, we assume that $\hat{\mathbf{H}}^{(l)} \approx \hat{\mathbf{H}}^{(l-1)}$, where l denotes the OFDM symbol index in time domain. Then, the pilot symbol used for PAPR reduction could be deduced by

$$\overline{C}_p^l = \frac{R_p}{\hat{H}_p^{(l-1)}} \quad \forall p \in P. \tag{17}$$

By considering multiplicative law in discrete domain, received symbols at pilot positions are expressed as

$$\overline{C}_p^l = \frac{H_p^l C_p^l + W_p^l}{\hat{H}_k^{(l-1)}} \approx C_p^l + \frac{W_p^l}{H_p^l} \quad \forall p \in P. \tag{18}$$

By combining (18) with (15), we have

$$\overline{C}_p^l = \lambda e^{j(\phi + p\Delta)} + \frac{W_p^l}{H_p^l} \quad \forall p \in P. \tag{19}$$

Since $\mathbf{C}$ is in discrete frequency domain, the estimate, $\hat{C}_p^l$, of C_p^l can be obtained from $\overline{C}_p^l$ by a simple quantization operation. As we consider that the boost factor λ is known at the receiver, the set $\mathbf{C}$ is characterized by two unknown variables of ϕ and Δ. Considering $\mu(\phi)$ and $\mu(\Delta)$ the elementary steps of ϕ and Δ in discrete domain, ϕ and Δ can be estimated as follows:

(i) estimation and decision of Δ:

$$\hat{\Delta} = \text{angle}\left[\sum_{p=1}^{M-1} \overline{C}_p^l \left(\overline{C}_{p-1}^l\right)^*\right],$$
$$\overline{\Delta} = D\left[\hat{\Delta}\Big|_{\mu(\Delta)}\right], \tag{20}$$

where $D[X|_\alpha]$ denotes decision function of X in discrete domain with a step α;

(ii) estimation and decision of ϕ:

$$\hat{\phi} = \text{angle}\left[\sum_{p=0}^{M-1} \overline{C}_p^l e^{-jp\Delta}\right],$$
$$\overline{\phi} = D\left[\hat{\phi}\Big|_{\mu(\phi)}\right]. \tag{21}$$

In order to evaluate our detection algorithm, we define the error detection probability (EDP) of ϕ and Δ as

$$\text{Pr}(\Delta) = \text{Pr}\left\{\left|\overline{\Delta} - \Delta\right| > \frac{\mu(\Delta)}{2}\right\},$$
$$\text{Pr}(\phi) = \text{Pr}\left\{\left|\overline{\phi} - \phi\right| > \frac{\mu(\phi)}{2}\right\}, \tag{22}$$

where $\text{Pr}\{|x| > \alpha\}$ denotes the probability that the absolute value of x is greater than α.

In the appendix, these probabilities are calculated in the case of AWGN channel. We obtain

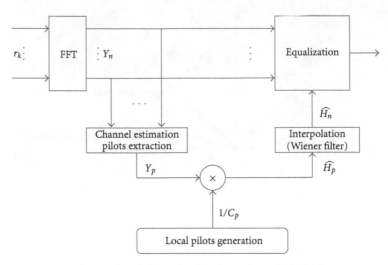

FIGURE 6: Conventional channel estimation scheme in OFDM systems.

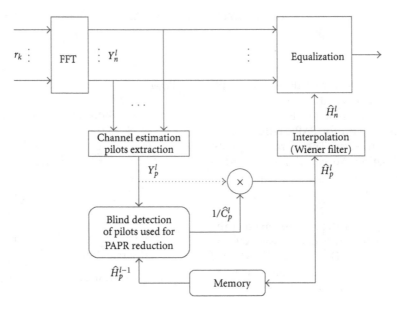

FIGURE 7: Modified channel estimation scheme.

$$\Pr(\Delta) = 1 - \mathrm{erf}\left(\frac{\mu(\Delta)/2}{\sqrt{2\left(\sigma^2/(M-1)^2\lambda^2 + 2(M-1)\sigma^4/(M-1)^2\lambda^4\right)}}\right),$$

(23)

$$\Pr(\phi) = 1 - \mathrm{erf}\left(\frac{\mu(\phi)/2}{\sqrt{\sigma^2/M\lambda^2}}\right).$$

The results of this computation are analyzed in the next section.

The estimation and detection of ϕ and Δ allow us to compute the transmitted pilot sequence. Once the transmitted pilot sequence is obtained, the second step consists of estimating the channel coefficients in the frequency domain. They could be obtained by the simple relationship

$$\widehat{H}_k^l = \frac{R_k}{\widehat{C}_k^l} \quad \forall k \in P.$$

(24)

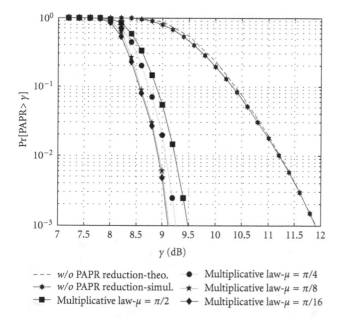

FIGURE 8: CCDF performance of multiplicative law using SOCP solution, continuous λ, 16-QAM, and 2 k mode.

Once the channel coefficients are computed on the pilot positions, the overall frequency channel response can be obtained by a simple Wiener filtering like in conventional channel estimation procedure. Both procedures are shown in Figures 6 and 7, respectively.

6. Simulation Results and Discussion

Simulation results are performed using DVB-T2 parameters. Some of the main parameters are summarized in Table 1. The PAPR parameters of the proposed method, that is, λ, Δ, and ϕ, are variable parameters which allow an optimization of both PAPR reduction and channel estimation processes. They will be specified in each simulation scenario.

Let us consider SOCP solution with a number of pilot tones M equal to 8. In fact, the SOCP solution is not possible using multiplicative law in continuous domain since the problem is not convex. In order to solve the problem, we consider discrete values of ϕ and Δ while maintaining λ in continuous domain. More precisely, we consider λ in continuous domain, and we change the values of ϕ from 0 to 2π with a step of $\pi/8$, while Δ varies from 0 to 2π with variable step μ, of $\pi/2$, $\pi/4$, $\pi/8$, and $\pi/16$. The results are presented in Figure 8 in terms of CCDF as declared in Section 2.

Figure 8 shows the CCDF of the multiplicative law using SOCP solution with respect to the continuous λ value and different step values μ. The PAPR gain increases when the step value μ decreases since the solution is approaching the continuous domain. Moreover, the solution converges when the step value μ reaches a limit value $\mu_{\text{lim}} = \pi/8$. In other words, the PAPR gain increases when the pilots' values are optimized in continuous domain. The results obtained in Figure 8 show first that CCDF simulation results

are close to theoretical value given in (6). Moreover, this figure shows that with a continuous λ value, a phase discretization using a step $\mu = \pi/8$ is enough to converge to the maximum PAPR reduction gain in the continuous domain.

6.1. Multiplicative Law Performance in Discrete Domain. We consider now the multiplicative law with ϕ and Δ in the discrete domain while λ takes a value from a predefined set. Firstly, we present CCDF performance for a fixed λ value and for ϕ and Δ varying from 0 to 2π with a step of $\pi/8$. The number of subcarriers used for PAPR reduction is always $M = 8$. In this case, reducing PAPR is not aN SOCP problem any more but becomes a search of the optimum combination minimizing PAPR. At the receiver, pilots are recovered by a detection and estimation algorithm. Figure 9 gives a comparison between different PAPR reduction techniques, namely, SOCP solution, gradient technique, and our proposed technique with a predefined power value $\lambda = 20$ dB. This figure shows that using our solution and this λ value, we obtain slightly better results than in DVB-T2 gradient solution. However, the gradient solution requires an iterative complex implementation. Again, we recall that this method avoids the use of dedicated pilots for PAPR reduction issue, improving also spectral efficiency of the system (1% in case of DVB-T2 specification).

In Figure 10, we present the PAPR gain in terms of CCDF, in comparison with the curve obtained without PAPR reduction technique, as a function of λ. We assume that ϕ and Δ change from 0 to 2π with a step of $\pi/8$, $\pi/16$, and $\pi/32$. This gain is evaluated at a CCDF = 10^{-3}. It is also compared with the SOCP solution for multiplicative law (λ continuous). Figure 10 shows that the system performance is improved when the step of ϕ and Δ becomes smaller. This is because the number of pilot combinations increases when the step decreases. For each value of this step, there exists one optimum value of λ for which the PAPR gain in terms of CCDF reaches the maximum.

Now, considering a discrete λ value, we compare the performance of the proposed method, for a step of ϕ and Δ of $\pi/8$, when $\lambda = 20$ dB which is the one maximizing the PAPR gain at CCDF = 10^{-3} and when λ is discrete, varying from 5 dB to 25 dB with a step of 3 dB. The results are presented in Figure 11. For a CCDF = 10^{-3}, the performance in terms of PAPR when $\lambda = 20$ dB is about 0.35 dB worse than the one of SOCP solution. It is about 0.17 dB worse than the case when λ is discrete. In other words, we lose only 0.17 dB when a predefined value of λ is selected instead of using a predefined set of discrete values.

In terms of complexity, the discrete solution is less complex than the SOCP solution (optimal solution). Indeed, our proposed PAPR reduction technique aims at searching the optimal solution in terms of λ, ϕ, and Δ in a predefined discrete set of values while SOCP solution applies a search in continuous domain. Moreover, setting a predefined value of λ yields to a reduced complexity implementation in comparison with the discrete λ solution, however, with a 0.17 dB PAPR loss. On the other hand, in terms of

TABLE 1: Simulation parameters, extracted from DVB-T2 standard.

Mode (OFDM size)	2 K
Number of subcarriers	$N_{FFT} = 2048$
Guard interval length	GI = 1/8
Modulation	16-QAM, 64-QAM
Coding rate	$R = 1/2$
Oversampling factor	$L = 4$
Number of subcarriers used for PAPR reduction	$M = 8, 16, 32$

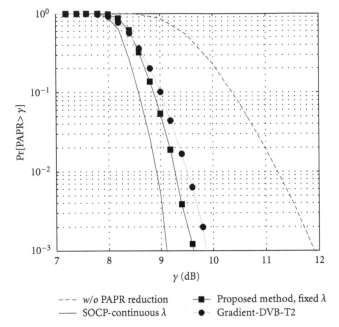

FIGURE 9: CCDF performance of multiplicative law in discrete domain, 16-QAM, $\lambda = 20$ dB.

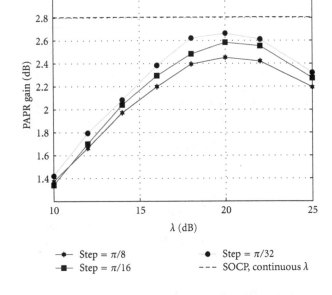

FIGURE 10: PAPR gain at a CCDF = 10^{-3} as a function of λ, $M = 8$, 16-QAM.

channel estimation, setting a predefined value of λ implies an improved performance in comparison with the discrete case since we avoid quantization at the receiver. So, the proposed method with a predefined value of λ presents a good tradeoff between channel estimation performance and PAPR gain.

In [4], OPS technique using Walsh-Hadamard sequences is chosen in order to make a blind detection of the transmitted sequence at the receiver side. In Figure 11, performance of this technique is given for WH sequences with length N_c = 32 chips. We can easily see that the performance of our proposed method is much better than the one proposed in [4]. A gain from 1.2 dB to 1.6 dB in terms of PAPR reduction is obtained in this case.

Finally, the performance in terms of PAPR gain is presented in Figure 12 for $M = 8$, 16, and 32 as a function of λ. Figure 12 shows that the PAPR gain performance slightly decreases when M increases, but we note that the optimum value of λ also decreases when M increases. This is important because it means that we can reduce the pilot's power when increasing the number of subcarriers used for PAPR reduction.

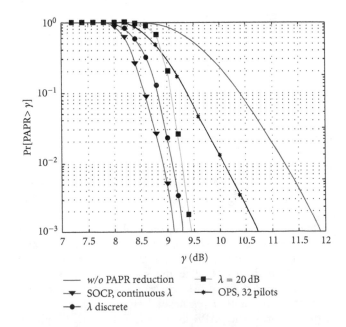

FIGURE 11: CCDF comparison in two cases: λ = 20 dB and discrete λ, with OPS technique [4], 16-QAM.

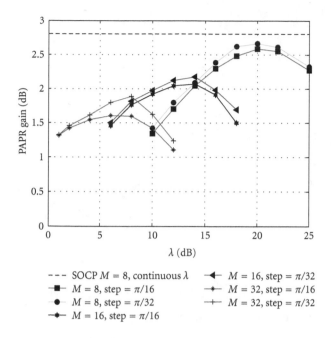

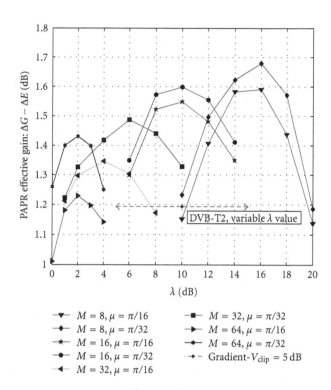

FIGURE 12: CCDF performance as a function of λ and M, 16-QAM.

FIGURE 14: PAPR effective gain: comparison between proposed and DVB-T2 TR techniques, 16-QAM.

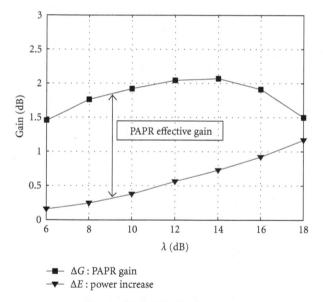

FIGURE 13: PAPR effective gain.

6.2. Comparison with DVB-T2 PAPR Techniques. First of all, one of the main advantages of this technique is that it could be used with rotated constellation schemes of DVB-T2 standard. This is not the case for ACE technique adopted in DVB-T2, where there is a restriction on rotated constellations. On the other hand, when the pilots are boosted by a factor λ, the transmitted power increases also. So, in order to have a fair comparison, we define the PAPR effective gain as the difference in dB between the PAPR gain ΔG and the power increase ΔE due to the use of boosted pilots (in both techniques), that is, PAPR$_{\text{eff}}$ = $\Delta G - \Delta E$ (Figure 13).

We evaluate in Figure 14 the PAPR effective gain of the proposed method as a function of the pilot power λ, which represents as previously the boost factor of the used pilots for different values of M, and of the elementary step μ. We plot in the same figure the results obtained with the gradient-based method proposed in DVB-T2. We note that the gradient solution proposed in DVB-T2 does not specify the boost factor of each dedicated pilot but specifies the maximum permitted power of these pilots. Hence, the boost factor of these pilots in DVB-T2 could change from one symbol to another. In other words, the PAPR gain in gradient-based solution of DVB-T2 depends on a variable λ value. The obtained results show that the performance of the proposed method is better than the one of the gradient-based method (TR technique) proposed in DVB-T2.

We also note that the optimal boost factor decreases when the number M of channel estimation pilots used for PAPR reduction increases. In DVB-T2 standard, it is specified that the boost factor of the channel estimation pilots could take values between 2 and 7 dB. Then, an optimal tradeoff should be found in terms of number of used pilots for PAPR reduction, PAPR effective gain, and channel estimation specifications. The same kind of results and conclusions could be given from Figure 15 for a 64-QAM constellation. In Figures 14 and 15, the performance of the DVB-T2 gradient algorithm is given as a reference result with a clipping value V_{clip} = 5 dB. We note, however, that the gradient algorithm needs a smooth control of the transmitted powers of the PAPR pilots. Moreover, using the Gradient algorithm, the allocated powers are varying from one pilot to another.

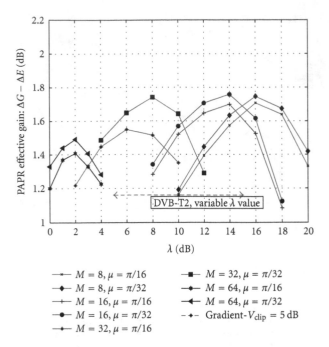

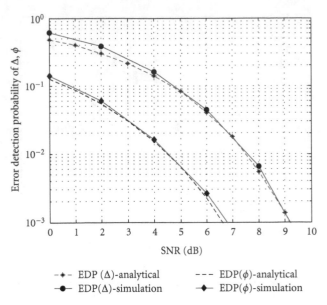

FIGURE 16: Analytical and simulated error detection probability.

FIGURE 15: PAPR effective gain: comparison between proposed and DVB-T2 TR techniques, 64-QAM.

6.3. Channel Estimation Results. The goal of this section is to show how the system performance is affected by the use of dedicated channel estimation for both PAPR reduction and channel estimation issues.

In order to give more insights about the proposed technique, the error detection probability (EDP) of a sequence used for PAPR and channel estimation is first evaluated. Then, the mean square error (MSE) of channel estimation is performed with respect to the signal to noise ratio (SNR) of the system. The simulation results obtained hereafter are achieved at the output of the Wiener filter. The latter is a 1D filter applied in the frequency domain only. An improvement of the results could be obtained by filtering in 2D, that is, frequency and time domain.

First, we verify the analytical performance evaluated in expressions (23). In order to evaluate the EDP values of Δ and ϕ, we consider appropriated elementary step such as for each evaluation, EDP of the other parameter is negligible. For instance, we choose $\mu(\Delta) = \pi/64$ and $\mu(\phi) = \pi/4$ in order to evaluate the EDP of Δ; $\mu(\Delta) = \pi/2$ and $\mu(\phi) = \pi/16$ in order to evaluate the EDP of ϕ. Figure 16 illustrates the comparison between analytical and simulated EDPs for different SNR values. It shows that our theoretical analysis matches perfectly with simulations.

Figure 17 shows the EDP obtained by simulations of the pilot sequence at the receiver as a function of SNR for different values of the elementary steps $\mu(\phi)$ and $\mu(\Delta)$. This figure shows that it is better to quantify the phase difference between two successive pilot symbols with small quantifications steps $\mu(\Delta)$ than quantifying with small steps the possible initial phase value of the first pilot, that is, $\mu(\phi)$.

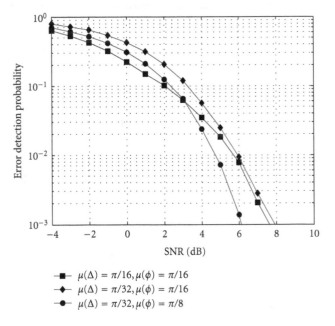

FIGURE 17: Error detection probability as a function of elementary steps.

In other words, it is more efficient to quantify more precisely Δ than the value of ϕ.

Figure 18 presents the MSE of the channel coefficients estimation scheme using an F1 channel proposed in DVB-T2 [1] using the conventional channel estimation scheme presented in DVB-T2 and the proposed channel estimation scheme. The conventional channel estimation relies on a traditional Wiener interpolation based on received channel estimation on pilot positions at the receiver. For the proposed method, as explained in Section 5, channel response on pilot positions used for PAPR reduction issue is recovered first by using channel response of the previous OFDM symbol.

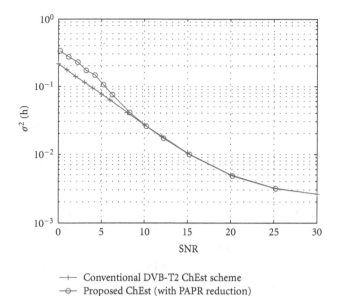

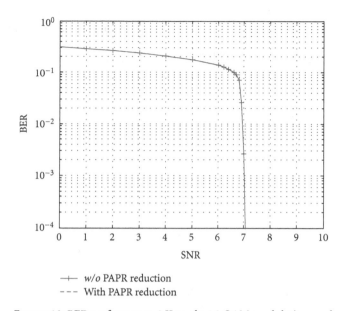

FIGURE 18: MSE of channel coefficients estimation, 2 K mode, 16-QAM modulation, and F1 channel [1].

FIGURE 19: BER performance, 2 K mode, 16-QAM modulation, and F1 channel.

Then channel estimation on all subcarriers is performed using traditional Wiener interpolation. This figure shows that the MSE of the channel coefficients estimated using our method is negligible for an SNR value greater than 6 dB. It is slightly higher than the conventional scheme for smaller SNR values. We recall that, for F1 channel and 16-QAM constellation, the required SNR value to obtain a BER = 10^{-7} at the output of the channel decoder is equal to 6.2 dB at a coding rate $R = 1/2$ [1]. The simulation results of this transmission scenario which is the most robust for a 16-QAM constellation are very important. Indeed, since the MSE is independent of the coding rate and, for higher coding rates the DVB-T2 requirements specify higher SNR values to make the system work properly, the proposed joint channel estimation scheme and PAPR reduction scheme will be always effective for these high SNR values.

We also evaluate the bit error rate (BER) of the overall DVB-T2 system. The F1 channel coefficients are estimated through dedicated pilots and then by applying a 2D Wiener filtering. Figure 19 shows the obtained BER performance using the conventional estimation scheme (Figure 6) and the proposed estimation scheme (Figure 7). As expected, the pilot sequence dedicated for channel estimation and used for PAPR reduction is well estimated at the receiver. Hence, the BER performance is not degraded.

Now, we consider a time-varying TU6 channel model given in [18]. The Doppler frequency f_d is equal to 33 Hz. Figure 20 gives the BER performance for a perfect channel estimation and a Wiener channel estimation without/with proposed PAPR reduction method. The obtained results show that the proposed scheme is efficient with high Doppler frequency scenario. We show in this figure that the overall degradation in comparison with perfect channel estimation is less than 1 dB where only 0.1 dB of SNR loss is due to the

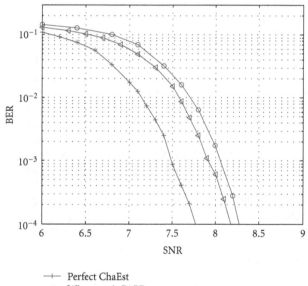

FIGURE 20: BER performance, 2 K mode, 16-QAM modulation, and TU6 channel.

joint application of PAPR reduction and channel estimation scheme.

6.4. Results Summary. Based on the conclusions given in previous sections, this section summarizes optimal parameters and the corresponding PAPR effective gains using the proposed technique. The different results previously presented have been obtained in the 2 k mode. The same analysis has been done in the 8 k mode. Tables 2 and 3 summarize the main parameters chosen as a good tradeoff between PAPR gain, channel estimation performance, and

TABLE 2: Optimal parameters using the proposed technique, 2 K mode.

Modulation	Number of pilots: PP2	M	Elementary steps of ϕ and Δ	λ_{opt}	PAPR effective gain
16-QAM	143	32	$\mu(\Delta) = \pi/32, \mu(\phi) = \pi/8$	5 dB	1.49 dB
	143		DVB-T2 ($V_{\text{clip}} = 5$ dB $-$ 18 pilots)		1.19 dB
64-QAM	143	32	$\mu(\Delta) = \pi/64, \mu(\phi) = \pi/16$	7 dB	1.80 dB
	143		DVB-T2 ($V_{\text{clip}} = 5$ dB $-$ 18 pilots)		1.16 dB

TABLE 3: Optimal parameters using the proposed technique, 8 K mode.

Modulation	Number of pilots: PP2	M	Elementary steps of ϕ and Δ	λ_{opt}	PAPR effective gain
16-QAM	569	128	$\mu(\Delta) = \pi/64, \mu(\phi) = \pi/16$	5 dB	1.47 dB
	569		DVB-T2 ($V_{\text{clip}} = 5$ dB $-$ 72 pilots)		1.39 dB
64-QAM	569	128	$\mu(\Delta) = \pi/128, \mu(\phi) = \pi/32$	5 dB	1.48 dB
	569		DVB-T2 ($V_{\text{clip}} = 5$ dB $-$ 72 pilots)		1.38 dB

optimal transmitted power in the 2 k and 8 k modes for 16-QAM and 64-QAM modulations. In all cases, the proposed technique presents better PAPR gain than the DVB-T2 TR technique, which requires less transmitted power on pilot symbols (the maximum value of the boost factor λ of the PAPR pilots in DVB-T2 is equal to 10 dB) but also a spectral efficiency increase of 1% when it is compared with the actual DVB-T2 standard. It could be also applied using the rotated constellation adopted in DVB-T2. We should note that these parameters, that is, M, λ, Δ, and ϕ, are applicable to the context of DVB-T2. However, they should be optimized to other contexts especially when the system parameters like the number of subcarriers and the constellation size change. Nevertheless, the optimization process remains unchanged.

7. Conclusion

A novel PAPR reduction method based on channel estimation pilots is addressed in this paper. By using channel estimation pilots to reduce PAPR value, dedicated pilots for PAPR reduction purpose are avoided improving the spectral efficiency of the system. These pilots have to be related by a particular law in order to allow their detection at the receiver side. Multiplicative law in discrete frequency domain is then investigated. Simulations, using the new DVB-T2 standard chain, showed that with appropriate parameters, the proposed method can achieve up to 1.80 dB in terms of PAPR effective gain. In comparison with the gradient-based method initially proposed in DVB-T2, the proposed method presents better performance in terms of PAPR reduction while avoiding the use of dedicated pilots. As a consequence, it allows achieving 1% of spectral efficiency gain. At the receiver side, only a slight modification is required. Simulations have shown that no degradation is caused by this additional function. The obtained results demonstrate the relevance of this method for future broadcasting of OFDM-based systems.

Appendix

This section aims to compute the error detection probability of the pilot sequence. It involves the computation of the error detection probability of Δ and ϕ in a Gaussian channel.

A. Error Detection Probability of Δ

From (20), we have

$$\hat{\Delta} = \text{angle}\left[\sum_{p=1}^{M-1} \overline{C}_p^l \left(\overline{C}_{p-1}^l\right)^*\right],$$

$$\overline{C}_p^l = \lambda e^{j(\phi+p\Delta)} + \frac{W_p^l}{H_p^l} \quad \forall p \in P. \tag{A.1}$$

Since we assume a Gaussian channel, received pilots can be expressed as

$$\overline{C}_p^l = \lambda e^{j(\phi+p\Delta)} + n_p \quad \forall p \in P, \tag{A.2}$$

where n_p denotes complex additive white gaussian noise (AWGN), at the pilot position p, of zero mean and of standard deviation σ, noted $\mathbf{N}(0, \sigma^2)$. It can be decomposed as follows: $n_p = n_{p,R} + jn_{p,I}$ where $n_{p,R}$ and $n_{p,I}$ denote real and imaginary parts of the complex noise n_p which are AWGN of zero mean and with standard deviation $\sigma/\sqrt{2}$.

Equation (A.1) becomes

$$\hat{\Delta} = \text{angle}\left[\sum_{p=1}^{M-1}\left(\lambda e^{j(\phi+p\Delta)} + n_p\right)\left(\lambda e^{j(\phi+(p-1)\Delta)} + n_{p-1}\right)^*\right],$$

$$\hat{\Delta} = \text{angle}\left[(M-1)\lambda^2 e^{j\Delta} + \sum_{p=1}^{M-1}\left(\lambda e^{j(\phi+p\Delta)}n_{p-1}^* + \lambda e^{-j(\phi+(p-1)\Delta)}n_p + n_p n_{p-1}^*\right)\right], \quad (A.3)$$

$$\hat{\Delta} = \text{angle}\left[(M-1)\lambda^2 e^{j\Delta}\left(1 + \frac{e^{-j\Delta}}{(M-1)\lambda^2}\sum_{p=1}^{M-1}\left(\lambda e^{j(\phi+p\Delta)}n_{p-1}^* + \lambda e^{-j(\phi+(p-1)\Delta)}n_p + n_p n_{p-1}^*\right)\right)\right].$$

Then, we have

$$\hat{\Delta} - \Delta = \text{angle}\left[1 + \frac{1}{(M-1)\lambda^2}\sum_{p=1}^{M-1}\left(\lambda e^{j(\phi+(p-1)\Delta)}n_{p-1}^* + \lambda e^{-j(\phi+p\Delta)}n_p + n_p n_{p-1}^*\right)\right], \quad (A.4)$$

$$\hat{\Delta} - \Delta = \text{angle}\left[1 + \underbrace{\frac{1}{(M-1)\lambda}\sum_{p=1}^{M-1}\left(e^{j(\phi+(p-1)\Delta)}n_{p-1}^* + e^{-j(\phi+p\Delta)}n_p\right)}_{A} + \underbrace{\frac{1}{(M-1)\lambda^2}\sum_{p=1}^{M-1}\left(n_p n_{p-1}^*\right)}_{B}\right]. \quad (A.5)$$

By substituting $n_p = n_{p,R} + jn_{p,I}$ in (A.5), the sum A becomes

$$A = \frac{1}{(M-1)\lambda}\sum_{p=1}^{M-1}\left(e^{j(\phi+(p-1)\Delta)}n_{p-1}^* + e^{-j(\phi+p\Delta)}n_p\right) = \frac{1}{(M-1)\lambda}\left[\sum_{p=0}^{M-2}e^{j(\phi+p\Delta)}n_p^* + \sum_{p=1}^{M-1}e^{-j(\phi+p\Delta)}n_p\right], \quad (A.6)$$

$$A = \frac{1}{(M-1)\lambda}\left[e^{j\phi}n_0^* + e^{-j(\phi+(M-1)\Delta)}n_{M-1} + \sum_{p=1}^{M-2}\left(e^{j(\phi+p\Delta)}n_p^* + e^{-j(\phi+p\Delta)}n_p\right)\right],$$

$$A = \frac{1}{(M-1)\lambda}\left\{\begin{array}{l}\underbrace{\left[\cos(\phi)n_{0,R} + \sin(\phi)n_{0,I} + \cos[\phi+(M-1)\Delta]n_{0,R} + \sin[\phi+(M-1)\Delta]n_{0,I}\right]}_{A1} \\[2em] \underbrace{+j\left[\sin(\phi)n_{0,R} - \cos(\phi)n_{0,I} + \cos[\phi+(M-1)\Delta]n_{0,I} - \sin[\phi+(M-1)\Delta]n_{0,R}\right]}_{A2} \\[2em] \underbrace{+2\sum_{p=1}^{M-2}\left(\cos(\phi+p\Delta)n_{p,R} + \sin(\phi+p\Delta)n_{p,I}\right).}_{A3}\end{array}\right. \quad (A.7)$$

Property 1. Let $\{X_k\}_{k=1\cdots n}$ be the set of n AWGN variables of $\mathbf{N}(0, \sigma_k^2)$ and $\{a_k\}_{k=1\cdots n}$ be the set of n constants, then we have [19]

$$\sum_{k=1}^{n} a_k X_k \longmapsto N\left(0, \sum_{k=1}^{n} a_k^2 \sigma_k^2\right). \tag{A.8}$$

According to Property 1, knowing that $n_{p,R}$ and $n_{p,I}$ are uncorrelated and of $\mathbf{N}(0, \sigma^2/2)$ for all $k = 1 \cdots n$, we deduce

$$A_1 \longmapsto N(0, \sigma^2),$$

$$A_2 \longmapsto N(0, \sigma^2), \tag{A.9}$$

$$A_3 \longmapsto N(0, 2(M-2)\sigma^2).$$

So we have

$$A \longmapsto N\left(0, \frac{(2M-3)\sigma^2}{(M-1)^2\lambda^2}\right) + jN\left(0, \frac{\sigma^2}{(M-1)^2\lambda^2}\right). \tag{A.10}$$

Similarly, the sum B of (A.6) can be expressed as

$$B = \frac{1}{(M-1)\lambda^2} \sum_{p=1}^{M-1} \left(n_p n_{p-1}^*\right)$$

$$= \frac{1}{(M-1)\lambda^2} \sum_{p=1}^{M-1} \left(n_{p,R} + jn_{p,I}\right)\left(n_{p-1,R} - jn_{p-1,I}\right),$$

$$B = \frac{1}{(M-1)\lambda^2} \sum_{p=1}^{M-1} \left(n_{p,R}n_{p-1,R} + n_{p,I}n_{p-1,I}\right)$$

$$+ j\left(n_{p,I}n_{p-1,R} - n_{p,R}n_{p-1,I}\right),$$

$$B = \frac{1}{(M-1)\lambda^2}$$

$$\times \left[\underbrace{\sum_{p=1}^{M-1} \left(n_{p,R}n_{p-1,R} + n_{p,I}n_{p-1,I}\right)}_{B1} \right.$$

$$\left. + j\underbrace{\sum_{p=1}^{M-1} \left(n_{p,I}n_{p-1,R} - n_{p,R}n_{p-1,I}\right)}_{B2} \right]. \tag{A.11}$$

Property 2. Let X_1 and X_2 be two independent AWGN variables of $\mathbf{N}(0, \sigma^2)$ and $X = X_1 X_2$, then we have

$$E[X] = E[X_1 X_2] = E[X_1]E[X_2] = 0,$$

$$E[X^2] = E\left[(X_1 X_2)^2\right] = E\left[(X_1)^2\right]E\left[(X_2)^2\right] = \sigma^4.$$

So variance of X is

$$V[X] = E\left[(X - E[X])^2\right] = E[X^2] = \sigma^4. \tag{A.12}$$

According to Property 2, the products $n_{p,R}n_{p-1,R}$, $n_{p,I}n_{p-1,I}$, $n_{p,R}n_{p-1,I}$, $n_{p,I}n_{p-1,R}$ follow the same law with zero mean and with standard deviation σ^2. According to the central limit theory, B_1 and B_2 are Gaussian with zero mean and a variance $2(M-1)\sigma^4$. So, we have

$$B \longmapsto N\left(0, \frac{2(M-1)\sigma^4}{(M-1)^2\lambda^4}\right) + jN\left(0, \frac{2(M-1)\sigma^4}{(M-1)^2\lambda^4}\right). \tag{A.13}$$

By substituting (A.10) and (A.13) in (A.5), equation (A.5) becomes

$$\hat{\Delta} - \Delta$$

$$= \text{angle}\left[1 + N\left(0, \frac{(2M-3)\sigma^2}{(M-1)^2\lambda^2}\right) + jN\left(0, \frac{\sigma^2}{(M-1)^2\lambda^2}\right)\right.$$

$$\left. + N\left(0, \frac{2(M-1)\sigma^4}{(M-1)^2\lambda^4}\right) + jN\left(0, \frac{2(M-1)\sigma^4}{(M-1)^2\lambda^4}\right)\right], \tag{A.14}$$

$$\hat{\Delta} - \Delta = \text{angle}\left[1 + \underbrace{N\left(0, \frac{(2M-3)\sigma^2}{(M-1)^2\lambda^2} + \frac{2(M-1)\sigma^4}{(M-1)^2\lambda^4}\right) + jN\left(0, \frac{\sigma^2}{(M-1)^2\lambda^2} + \frac{2(M-1)\sigma^4}{(M-1)^2\lambda^4}\right)}_{Z}\right]. \tag{A.15}$$

Assuming a large SNR, real part of Z can be approximated to 1 and its imaginary part can be approximated to 0, equation (A.15) can be approximated by using angle $(X) \approx \text{Im}(X)$:

$$\hat{\Delta} - \Delta \longmapsto N\left(0, \frac{\sigma^2}{(M-1)^2\lambda^2} + \frac{2(M-1)\sigma^4}{(M-1)^2\lambda^4}\right). \tag{A.16}$$

So, $\hat{\Delta} - \Delta$ can be expressed as a Gaussian noise of zero mean with variance $\sigma^2/(M-1)^2\lambda^2 + 2(M-1)\sigma^4/(M-1)^2\lambda^4$.

Assuming $\mu(\Delta)$ the elementary step of Δ, the error detection probability is given by

$$\Pr(\Delta) = \Pr\left(\left|\hat{\Delta} - \Delta\right| > \frac{\mu(\Delta)}{2}\right)$$

$$= 1 - \Pr\left(\left|\hat{\Delta} - \Delta\right| < \frac{\mu(\Delta)}{2}\right) \tag{A.17}$$

$$= 1 - \Pr\left(\hat{\Delta} - \Delta < \frac{\mu(\Delta)}{2}\right)$$

$$+ \Pr\left(\hat{\Delta} - \Delta < \frac{-\mu(\Delta)}{2}\right),$$

$$\Pr(\Delta) = 1 - \Pr\left(\hat{\Delta} - \Delta < \frac{\mu(\Delta)}{2}\right)$$

$$+ \left[1 - \Pr\left(\hat{\Delta} - \Delta < \frac{\mu(\Delta)}{2}\right)\right] \tag{A.18}$$

$$= 2\left[1 - \Pr\left(\hat{\Delta} - \Delta < \frac{\mu(\Delta)}{2}\right)\right].$$

Property 3. Let X be an AWGN variable of $\mathbf{N}(\mu, \sigma^2)$, then we have

$$\Pr(X < \alpha) = \frac{1}{2}\left[1 + \mathrm{erf}\left(\frac{\alpha - \mu}{\sigma\sqrt{2}}\right)\right]. \tag{A.19}$$

Finally, according to Property 3, we obtain

$$\Pr(\Delta) = 1 - \mathrm{erf}$$

$$\times \left(\frac{\mu(\Delta)/2}{\sqrt{2\left(\sigma^2/(M-1)^2\lambda^2 + 2(M-1)\sigma^4/(M-1)^2\lambda^4\right)}}\right). \tag{A.20}$$

B. Error Detection Probability of ϕ

To compute the error detection probability of ϕ, we assume that Δ is well estimated, then we have

$$\hat{\phi} = \mathrm{angle}\left[\sum_{p=0}^{M-1} \overline{C}_p^l e^{-jp\Delta}\right]$$

$$= \mathrm{angle}\left[\sum_{p=0}^{M-1} \left(\lambda e^{j(\phi+p\Delta)} + n_p\right)e^{-jp\Delta}\right],$$

$$\hat{\phi} = \mathrm{angle}\left[\sum_{p=0}^{M-1} \lambda e^{j\phi} + n_p e^{-jp\Delta}\right] \tag{B.1}$$

$$= \mathrm{angle}\left[M\lambda e^{j\phi} + \sum_{p=0}^{M-1} n_p e^{-jp\Delta}\right],$$

$$\hat{\phi} = \mathrm{angle}\left[M\lambda e^{j\phi}\left(1 + \frac{1}{M\lambda}\sum_{p=0}^{M-1} n_p e^{-jp\Delta}\right)\right].$$

We deduce

$$\hat{\phi} - \phi = \mathrm{angle}\left[1 + \frac{1}{M\lambda}\sum_{p=0}^{M-1} n_p e^{-jp\Delta}\right]$$

$$= \mathrm{angle}\left[1 + \frac{1}{M\lambda}\sum_{p=0}^{M-1} \left(n_{p,R} + n_{p,I}\right)\right. \tag{B.2}$$

$$\left. \times \left(\cos(p\Delta) - j\sin(p\Delta)\right)\right].$$

It can be approximated by using $\mathrm{angle}(X) \approx \mathrm{Im}(X)$

$$\hat{\phi} - \phi \approx \frac{1}{M\lambda}\sum_{p=0}^{M-1}\left[n_{p,I}\cos(p\Delta) - n_{p,R}\sin(p\Delta)\right]. \tag{B.3}$$

According to the central limit theory, we deduce,

$$\hat{\phi} - \phi \longmapsto N\left(0, \frac{\sigma^2}{2M\lambda^2}\right). \tag{B.4}$$

Assuming $\mu(\phi)$ the elementary step of ϕ, the error detection probability of ϕ is given by

$$\Pr(\phi) = \Pr\left(\left|\hat{\phi} - \phi\right| > \frac{\mu(\phi)}{2}\right)$$

$$= 1 - \Pr\left(\left|\hat{\phi} - \phi\right| < \frac{\mu(\phi)}{2}\right)$$

$$= 1 - \Pr\left(\hat{\phi} - \phi < \frac{\mu(\phi)}{2}\right)$$

$$+ \Pr\left(\hat{\phi} - \phi < \frac{-\mu(\phi)}{2}\right), \qquad (B.5)$$

$$\Pr(\phi) = 1 - \Pr\left(\hat{\phi} - \phi < \frac{\mu(\phi)}{2}\right)$$

$$+ \left[1 - \Pr\left(\hat{\phi} - \phi < \frac{\mu(\phi)}{2}\right)\right]$$

$$= 2\left[1 - \Pr\left(\hat{\phi} - \phi < \frac{\mu(\phi)}{2}\right)\right].$$

According to Property 3, we obtain

$$\Pr(\phi) = 1 - \text{erf}\left(\frac{\mu(\phi)/2}{\sqrt{\sigma^2/M\lambda^2}}\right). \qquad (B.6)$$

Acknowledgment

The authors would like to thank the CELTIC ENGINES project for its support of this work.

References

[1] DVB, "Frame structure channel coding and modulation for a second generation digital terrestrial television broadcasting system (DVB-T2)," ETSI EN 302755 V1.1.1 September 2009.

[2] U. Reimers, "Digital video broadcasting," *IEEE Communications Magazine*, vol. 36, no. 6, pp. 104–110, 1998.

[3] R. Van Nee and R. Prasad, *OFDM for Wireless Multimedia Communications*, Artech House, Boston, Mass, USA, 2000.

[4] M. J. F. G. García, O. Edfors, and J. M. Páez-Borrallo, "Peak power reduction for OFDM systems with orthogonal pilot sequences," *IEEE Transactions on Wireless Communications*, vol. 5, no. 1, pp. 47–51, 2006.

[5] S. H. Han and J. H. Lee, "An overview of peak-to-average power ratio reduction techniques for multicarrier transmission," *IEEE Wireless Communications*, vol. 12, no. 2, pp. 56–65, 2005.

[6] X. Li and L. J. Cimini, "Effects of clipping and filtering on the performance of OFDM," in *Proceedings of the 47th IEEE Vehicular Technology Conference (VTC '97)*, vol. 3, pp. 1634–1638, Phoenix, Ariz, USA, May 1997.

[7] A. E. Jones, T. A. Wilkinson, and S. K. Barton, "Block coding scheme for reduction of peak to mean envelope power ratio of multicarrier transmission schemes," *Electronics Letters*, vol. 30, no. 25, pp. 2098–2099, 1994.

[8] S. H. Müller and J. B. Huber, "OFDM with reduced peak-to-average power ratio by optimum combination of partial transmit sequences," *Electronics Letters*, vol. 33, no. 5, pp. 368–369, 1997.

[9] R. W. Bäuml, R. F. H. Fischer, and J. B. Huber, "Reducing the peak-to-average power ratio of multicarrier modulation by selected mapping," *Electronics Letters*, vol. 32, no. 22, pp. 2056–2057, 1996.

[10] A. D. S. Jayalath and C. Tellambura, "Reducing the peak-to-average power ratio of orthogonal frequency division multiplexing signal through bit or symbol interleaving," *Electronics Letters*, vol. 36, no. 13, pp. 1161–1163, 2000.

[11] B. S. Krongold and D. L. Jones, "PAR reduction in OFDM via active constellation extension," *IEEE Transactions on Broadcasting*, vol. 49, no. 3, pp. 258–268, 2003.

[12] J. Tellado-Mourelo, *Peak-to-average power ratio reduction for multicarrier Modulation*, Ph.D. thesis, Stanford University, September 1999.

[13] I. M. Mahafeno, Y. Louët, and J. F. Hélard, "Peak-to-average power ratio reduction using second order cone programming based tone reservation for terrestrial digital video broadcasting systems," *IET Communications*, vol. 3, no. 7, pp. 1250–1261, 2009.

[14] A. Aggarwal and T. H. Meng, "Minimizing the peak-to-average power ratio of OFDM signals using convex optimization," *IEEE Transactions on Signal Processing*, vol. 54, no. 8, pp. 3099–3110, 2006.

[15] S. Zabre, J. Palicot, Y. Louët, and C. Lereau, "SOCP approach for OFDM peak-to-average power ratio reduction in the signal adding context," in *Proceedings of the 6th IEEE International Symposium on Signal Processing and Information Technology (ISSPIT '07)*, pp. 834–839, Vancouver, Canada, August 2007.

[16] M. Sharif, M. Gharavi-Alkhansari, and B. H. Khalaj, "On the peak-to-average power of OFDM signals based on oversampling," *IEEE Transactions on Communications*, vol. 51, no. 1, pp. 72–78, 2003.

[17] R. van Nee and A. de Wild, "Reducing the peak-to-average power ratio of OFDM," in *Proceedings of the 48th IEEE Vehicular Technology Conference (VTC '98)*, vol. 3, pp. 2072–2076, Ottawa, Canada, May 1998.

[18] DVB, "Implementation guidelines for a second generation digital terrestrial television broadcasting system (DVB-T2)," ETSI TR 102 831 V0.9.17 November 2009.

[19] M. K. Simon, *Probability Distributions Involving Gaussian Random Variables*, Springer, New York, NY, USA, 2006.

9

Cyber Security for Smart Grid, Cryptography, and Privacy

Swapna Iyer

Department of Electrical and Computer Engineering, Illinois Institute of Technology, Chicago, IL 60616-3793, USA

Correspondence should be addressed to Swapna Iyer, siyer9@iit.edu

Academic Editor: Pierangela Samarati

The invention of "smart grid" promises to improve the efficiency and reliability of the power system. As smart grid is turning out to be one of the most promising technologies, its security concerns are becoming more crucial. The grid is susceptible to different types of attacks. This paper will focus on these threats and risks especially relating to cyber security. Cyber security is a vital topic, since the smart grid uses high level of computation like the IT. We will also see cryptography and key management techniques that are required to overcome these attacks. Privacy of consumers is another important security concern that this paper will deal with.

1. Introduction

One of the most important, complex, and intelligent network we have is the "power system". This system consists of circuits, wires, towers, transformers, sensors, and cables interlinked to provide us with uninterrupted power supply. This system is mainly a mechanical system and has very little electronics associated with it like sensors and communication. However, as technology has progressed rapidly and almost all the latest devices need electricity for their operation, it is necessary that we make our present power system more reliable and efficient [1].

We can say the demand for electricity is greater than its supply. The demand is not only high but also fluctuating. We could rely on renewable resources like solar energy and wind energy to meet the present need, but unfortunately, they turn out to be fluctuating too.

The smart grid enhances the functionality of the power delivery system. This is possible because smart grid uses sensors, communications, computation, and control in order to make the system smart and by applying intelligence to it in the form of control through feedback or in other words by using two way communication. In order to utilize the available resources, consumers need to change, and they need to act more "smart". They have to change from being passive consumers to being active consumers [1]. Smart grids aim to reduce the energy consumption, ensure reliability of power

supply, reduce carbon foot print, and minimize the costs associated with power consumption.

The smart grid system has many advantages, one of them being cost effectiveness. This is because the grid uses internet for communication purpose. However, using the internet means vulnerability to cyber attacks. As opposed to the original power system, the smart grid uses ethernet, TCP/IP and other operating systems, thus making the grid more susceptible to attacks. The smart grid should enhance the security of the power system, but protecting the grid is a more challenging task now. Once the system is attacked, the attacker may control several meters or disrupt the load balance of the system. Thus, we need to gain complete knowledge about cyber security, so we can eliminate it completely. We also need to focus on the cryptographic methods proposed by the National Institute of Standards and Technology (NIST) in order to avoid these cyber attacks.

In this paper, we will study smart grid security in more depth. The goal of this paper is to cover the security challenges related to cyber security, and we will also study how cryptography is used in order to eliminate cyber attacks. Finally, we will also discuss in brief privacy which is another smart grid security concern. The rest of the paper is organized as follows. We start by reviewing the challenges and goals of smart grid in Section 2. This is followed by the smart grid architecture in Section 3. We focus on cyber security in Section 4. Section 5 explains cryptography used for smart grid security in depth. Privacy in context with smart grid security is explained in Section 6. And finally, we conclude in Section 7.

2. The Smart Grid: Goals and Challenges

2.1. Goals. The present power grid has more than 9200 electric generating units, 1,000,000 plus megawatts of generating capacity connected by using 300,000 miles of transmission lines [2].

Electricity has one basic requirement; it needs to be utilized as soon as it is generated. The present grid does so successfully. However, now, the grid is overburdened. The reliability of the present grid is at stake, and this can be seen, since we have been witnessing more brownouts and blackouts recently.

Another thing that needs to be addressed when we consider the present grid is the efficiency. By making the grid more efficient, we can save millions of dollars. There is also a reverse case here; if there is an hour of power outage, the nation loses a tremendous amount of money. Electricity needs to be more affordable too. The rate of electricity is increasing gradually which makes it less affordable.

Majority of the electricity produced in the United States of America comes by burning coal. The carbon footprints that occur due to this contributes to global warming. If we introduce the use of renewable energy in our grid, we can reduce the carbon footprint.

We also need to compete globally with other countries that have better technology for energy distribution.

And finally, the grids security is of major concern. The current grid has a centralized architecture, and thus making it more vulnerable to attacks. A failure can hamper the country's banking, traffic, communication, and security system [2].

Thus, we introduce the smart grid system (Figure 1). We now have a smart power grid that creates a link between electricity, communications, and computer control. Many countries are actively participating in the development of smart grid; for example, the ETP created a joint vision for the European network of 2020 [3] and beyond, and the US established a federal smart grid task force under the Department of Energy (DoE).

The aim is first to control the electricity supply with utmost efficiency and also reduce the carbon emissions. A smart grid system basically needs to have the following properties (Figure 2) [4]:

(1) digitalization,

(2) intelligence,

(3) resilience,

(4) customization,

(5) flexibility.

Digitalization means to have a digital platform which makes the system fast and reliable. Flexibility would mean that the smart grid needs to be compatible, expandable, and adaptable. Intelligence would mean to inherit an intelligent

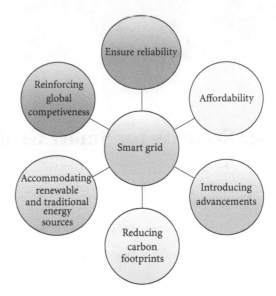

FIGURE 1: Smart grid goals.

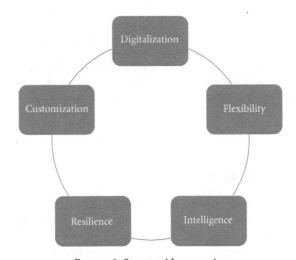

FIGURE 2: Smart grid properties.

technology. Resilience would mean that the system should not be affected by any attacks. And lastly, customization means the system needs to be client tailored.

The power grid today is already a very complex and intelligent system. It comprises thousands of miles of high voltage lines, an intelligent control system that controls it, and a communication system that distributes it. A smart grid would help us improve the efficiency and availability of the same power system by using better control strategies.

2.2. Challenges. Let us see what are the problems related to the current power grid system.

The current grid is "purpose built". This means that it is made in such a way that we cannot add any new control points and any security functions. The grid is bandwidth limited, and this restricts us from adding any extra information that would be required to ensure authentication. If there is no room for security, it implies the protocols runs relying on trust, and thus ignoring the possibility of any unknown entity.

In case of the new smart grid, the practice has changed; initially the devices used were purpose built, and these days, they are multipurpose. Instead of using dedicated lines for communication, we use the TCP/IP. Though the technology has drastically improved, the chances of being attacked have also increased rapidly.

Another issue is that smart meters would read the energy usage of a particular residence multiple times in an hour, which would lead to a loss of privacy for the consumer. That is because if one has a smart grid, then one can know whether a residence is occupied or not and also at what time what appliances are being used. This could lead to two different types of attack, either a simple theft or pricing the signals for monetary gains [5].

3. The Smart Grid Architecture

3.1. A General Model. The electricity delivery network basically consists of two subsystems, a transmission system and a distribution subsystem (Figure 3).

In the transmission network, electricity is moved in bulk from 345 kV to 800 kV over AC and DC lines. Power flows in one direction and is distributed to consumers at 132 kV. However, the smart grid will provide bidirectional metering unlike the present grid.

The grid includes a monitoring system and a smart meter which keeps track of the electricity consumed. It includes superconductivity transmission lines which help to reduce the resistive losses and also is compatible to other sources of energy like wind, solar, and so forth.

3.2. Functional Components. The three functional components of a smart grid are smart control centers, smart transmission networks, and smart substations. Let us take a look at them one by one as follows [4].

3.2.1. Smart Control Centers. The smart control centers will depend on the existing control centers. The main functions of a control center are as follows [4].

Monitoring/Visualization. The present control center performs monitoring based on the data collected via SCADA and RTUs (remote terminal units). In the future, information will be obtained from state measurement modules. It is better than the present module in terms of "running time" and "robustness". In the future, the outcomes will be combined with a wide area geographical information system (GIS), and a visual display will be provided. In this manner, more information will be covered. Also, in the future, the control centers will provide the root cause of a problem rather than just giving an alarming signal.

Analytical Capability. The future is expected to have online time domain-based analysis. These would include voltage stability and transient angular stability. The present grid

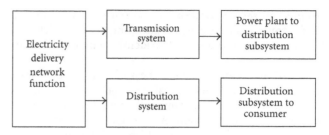

FIGURE 3: A general model.

does not provide the real-time dynamic characteristics of the system whereas in the future, we will have a dynamic model updates. Also, the future grid is expected to have a look ahead simulation capability.

Controllability. In the present grid, operations like separating, restoration, and so forth, depend on offline studies. In the future, these will be real time and dynamic. Fixed values are used for the protection and the control settings now, but in the future, proactive and adaptive approaches will be used. Also, there is no coordination when any decision is taken in the current technology. In future, there will be coordination in order to gain a better control.

Interaction with Electricity Market. The main aim of a smart grid system is to achieve high efficiency. For this, we need a control system that dynamically adjusts in accordance with the market. Sophisticated tools are used for this purpose. Also, the smart grid needs to accommodate renewable energy sources.

3.2.2. Smart Transmission Networks. There are new features that are included in the smart grid which involves signal processing, sensing, advanced materials, power electronics, communications and computing. These would improve the efficiency, utilization, quality, and security of the present system.

For long distance transmission, we use high-capacity AC and DC facilities. When the overhead lines are not possible, underground cables are used. High-temperature composite conductors and high-temperature superconducting cables are used for electrical transmission, since they have a higher current carrying capacity, low voltage drop, reduced line losses, light in weight, and better controllability. Six and twelve phase transmission lines are used which provide greater power transmission with reduced electromagnetic field and great phase cancellation.

Flexible and reliable transmission is made possible by using advanced flexible AC transmission system (FACTS) and high-voltage DC (HVDC) devices. FACTS are placed in the transmission network, and they improve the dynamic performance and stability. They will help grid to be free from transmission congestions. HVDC is used as a cost-effective alternative to AC lines.

Intelligent sensors are used with advanced signal processing to measure the line parameters and monitor the status around the sensor location. These sensors can detect the conductor temperature, detect galloping lines, predict initial failures of insulators and towers, identify fault locations, and so forth.

Based on these parameters, the operating conditions can be autonomously detected, analyzed, and responded in case of emergencies, thus maintaining the reliability and security of the transmission system. Also, smart grid systems have reduced catastrophic failures and less maintenance cost. Extreme event facility hardening systems are used to manage failure and restore the system rapidly [4].

3.2.3. Smart Substation. The equipments in the substation should be more reliable and efficient for functions like monitoring, controlling, operating, protecting, and maintaining. The main functions are the following [4]:

(1) smart sensing and measurement,

(2) communication,

(3) autonomous control and adaptive protection,

(4) data management and visualization,

(5) monitoring and alarming,

(6) diagnosis and prognosis,

(7) advanced interfaces with distributed resources,

(8) real-time modeling.

4. Cyber Security

4.1. Cyber Security Model. Like for any other network's security, the three main objectives that cyber security focuses on is availability, integrity, and confidentiality, that is, availability of power with integrity of information and confidentiality of customer's information.

Availability. The reason why we have smart grid is "availability". The basic goal of our network is to provide uninterrupted power supply to the users and to match user requirements.

Confidentiality. The grid network is responsible for the protection of a user's information. If the data is not protected, ample information about the user can be revealed to the attacker.

Integrity. The messages received from the user end should be authenticated. The network must ensure the information is not tampered. Also, the source of message should be authentic.

The smart grid's cyber infrastructure consists of electronic information and communication systems and services along with the information contained in these systems and services. This includes both the hardware and software too. Their basic functions are to process, store, and communicate information. This is done using a control system (SCADA) [6, 7]. The SCADA is a neutral system.

4.2. SCADA System. Supervisory control and data acquisition (SCADA) systems are basically centralized control systems that are used by our power distribution system. It is used for monitoring and controlling process [8].

The main blocks that a SCADA system includes are the following:

(i) HMI (human machine interface) presents processed data,

(ii) a supervisory computer that collects all the data and uses it for processing purpose,

(iii) remote terminal units (RTUs),

(iv) programmable logic controller (PLC),

(v) communication infrastructure.

By using the power system communication in the smart grid, the SCADA systems are connected to other systems like the internet or by certain dedicated lines. The vendors are using off the shelf products as part of the SCADA systems. These products are similar to the personal computers we use at home, and thus are susceptible to attacks and different threats [9].

A SCADA system is a necessary element in the grid infrastructure. It is used for two purposes, first the public transport system and second the public control system.

The cyber security basically can be attacked in three steps [10] as follows:

(1) the attacker has control over the SCADA system,

(2) the attacker identifies the system to launch an intelligent attack,

(3) attacker initiates the attack.

These SCADA systems are most vulnerable to attacks. In order to prevent the attackers from gaining control of SCADA system, automation will be required. The NIST has established smart grid cyber security coordination task group (CSCTG) which addresses and evaluates processes leading to comprehensive cyber security policies for smart grid [6].

The risks assessed by the CSCTG include [6, 11] the following:

(i) complexity of grid leading to weak point and openings to attackers,

(ii) cascading errors as a result of interconnected networks,

(iii) DoS (denial of service) attack,

(iv) attack on consumer privacy to excessive data gathering,

(v) attacks from annoyed employees and terrorists,

(vi) as number of nodes increases the number of entry points for an attacker also increases.

In order to obtain cyber security, we also need to have a robust hardware. We can discuss this further by dividing the hardware section in two parts: (a) new substations and (b) existing systems. In case of new substations, we can completely design the system to be immune against cyber security threats. For this, we can use managed switches. These are smart switches which perform multifunctions like access control, traffic prioritization, managing data flow, and so forth. However, since we already have an ethernet-based system laid, we must make changes to these systems such that they can withstand cyber attacks. For this, we can either update the present infrastructure or Install Security appliances. Security appliances are present between the ethernet connections and are used for examining and monitoring purposes. Another addition to existing systems would be the use of firewalls. They block unauthorized access to any network and work according to the user defined rules. We could also use a technology called VPN (virtual private network), where the connection between two stations is secured [12].

The Cyberspace Policy Review initiated by President Obama advised that "the Federal government should work with the private sector to define public-private partnership roles and responsibilities for the defense of privately owned critical infrastructure and key resources." Specifically, the review recommended that as "the United States deploys new Smart Grid technology, the Federal government must ensure that security standards are developed and adopted to avoid creating unexpected opportunities for adversaries to penetrate these systems or conduct large-scale attacks [11, 13]."

The Department of Energy should work with the federal energy regulatory commission to determine whether additional security mandates and procedures should be developed for energy-related industrial control systems. In addition, the United States deploys new smart grid technology, the federal government must ensure that security standards are developed and adopted to avoid creating unexpected opportunities for adversaries to penetrate these systems or conduct large-scale attacks [11].

Chairman Thompson issued the following statement regarding the legislation: "Any failure of our electric grid, whether intentional or unintentional would have a significant and potentially devastating impact on our nation. We must ensure that the proper protections, resources and regulatory authorities are in place to address any threat aimed at our power system. This legislation addresses these critical issues by providing a common sense approach to ensure continued security of the nation's electric infrastructure [14].".

The security concerns are increasing as the numbers of connections are increasing. There have been cases where cyber spies from China, Russia, and other countries are reported to have entered the United States electrical grid and tried to attack the system. The ability to resist attacks is one of the inevitable functions of the smart grid [15].

5. Cryptography and Key Management

In order to obtain cyber security, we must secure data using cryptography and different keys. In this section, we will study the various aspects related to cryptography and key management. We will first go through the different constraints related to cryptography followed by the cryptographic issues and solutions [16].

5.1. Constraints

5.1.1. Computational Constraints. Residential meters will have limitations when it comes to computational power and the ability to store cryptographic materials. The future devices are bound to have the basic cryptographic capabilities including the ability to support symmetric ciphers for authentication. The use of low-cost hardware with embedded cryptography is necessary but not enough to achieve high availability, integrity and confidentiality in the smart grid.

5.1.2. Channel Bandwidth. The communications that will take place in a smart grid system will take place over different channels that have different bandwidths. AES is a cipher that produces the same number of output bits as input bits. These bits cannot be compressed too, since they are encrypted and random in nature. In case we need to compress this data, we need to do so before encryption. Another factor to be taken into consideration is the cipher-based message authentication code (CMAC), which is added as a fixed overhead to a message and is typically 64 bits or 96 bits. These overheads turn out to be significant when we are dealing with short messages, since they would need large channel Bandwidth.

5.1.3. Connectivity. Standard public key infrastructure-based on peer-to-peer key establishment model where any peer may need to communicate with another is not desirable from a security standpoint for components. Many devices may not have connectivity to key servers, certificate authorities, online certificate status, and protocol Servers. Many connections between smart grid devices will have longer duration than typical internet connection.

5.2. General Cryptographic Issues

Entropy. Cryptographic key generation requires a good source of entropy that creates randomness which is unavailable for many devices.

Cipher Suite. A cipher suite that is open is needed in order to achieve interoperability. A decision about which block cipher, their modes, key sizes, and asymmetric ciphers forms the base of authentication operation.

Key Management Issues. Security protocols depend on security associations. There can be two types in which the security is authenticated: (1) use of Secret key and (2) use of certificate authority. In case we use secret keys, the keys have to be transported from a device to another. To transport these keys, we need a set of keys for each pair of communicating devices and all this needs to be well coordinated. There is also a hardware alternative for this, but that is a costlier option and involves a large amount of overhead. Digital certificates turn out to be cost effective solution as coordination is not required as it was in the case of public key system. Each device needs just one certificate for key management and one private key that is fixed from the time of installation. However, generating PKI and also having certificate authorities will also have a certain amount of overhead unnecessary for smaller systems.

Elliptic Curve Cryptography. A cryptographic Interoperability strategy (CIS) initiated by National Security Agency (NSA) for government systems selects approved cryptographic techniques. It consists of AES for encryption with 128 or 256 bits. Ephemeral unified model and Diffie-Hellman key agreement schemes, elliptic curve digital signature algorithm and secure hash algorithm (SHA) for hashing.

5.3. Cryptographic and Key Management Solutions

5.3.1. General Design Considerations

(i) Selection of cryptographic technique should be such that the design is robust and the algorithm is free of flaws.

(ii) Entropy issue can be solved by seeding a deterministic random bit generator (RBG) before distribution or use a key derivation function which comes with the device.

(iii) Use of cryptographic modules that is used to protect the cryptographic algorithm. We need to upgrade these modules timely, since smart grid equipments would be used for around twenty years and also replacing them would be a costlier affair.

(iv) Failure in encryption systems may occur due to implementation errors, compositional failures, insecure algorithms, or insecure protocols. These categories should be taken into consideration while designing.

(v) Since a random number generator is an integral part of the security system, its failures would result in a compromise of cryptographic algorithm or protocol.

(vi) There must be alternatives for authentication and authorization procedures in case we cannot connect to another system.

(vii) Availability must always be there since dropping or refusal to re-establish a connection may affect the critical communication.

(viii) The algorithms and key lengths should be such that the desired security strength is attained.

(ix) In order to maintain security of the keying materials and authentication data, we must protect it from unauthorized access or any device tampering. Physical security is required for this purpose.

5.3.2. Key Management System for Smart Grid. We use certificates that have validity, that is, certificates that have

not expired. If this certificate is issued to a device, that is, no longer reliable, either lost or stolen, then the certificate can be revoked. A certificate revocation list is used for this purpose. A device that uses the information in a certificate is called relying party (RP). RP has a checklist that must be considered when accepting a certificate.

The points that need to be checked are as follows

(i) if the certificate was issued by a trusted CA,

(ii) if certificate is still valid and not expired,

(iii) certificate should be in an authoritative CRL,

(iv) verification of the certificate subject and policy for which certificate is being used.

5.4. Approved Algorithms

Symmetric Key. Advanced encryption standards (AESs), triple data encryption algorithm (TDEA), or triple data encryption standard (TDES).

Asymmetric Key. Digital signature standard (DSS), digital signature algorithm (DSA), RSA digital signature algorithm (RSA), elliptic curve digital signature algorithm (ECDSA).

Secure Hash Standard. Secure hash standards (SHSs) and secure hash algorithm (SHA).

Message Authentication. CMAC, CCM, GCM/GMAC (Galois counter mode), and HMAC (hash message authentication code).

Key Management. SP800-108 KDF's.

Deterministic Random Number Generators. FIPS 186–2 APPENDIX 3.1 RNG, FIPS 186–2 APPENDIX 3.2 RNG, ANSI X9.31-1998 APPENDIX A2.4 RNG, ANSI X9.62-1998 ANNEX A.4 RNG, and ANSI X9.31 APPENDIX A.24 RNG using TDES and AES RNG, SP 800-90 RNG.

Nondeterministic Random Number Generators. Currently None.

Symmetric Key Establishment Techniques. FIPS 140–2 1G D.2.

Asymmetric Key Establishment Techniques. SP 800–56 A, SP 800–56 B, and FIPS 140–2 1G D.2.

These algorithms can be studied in detail from [17–34].

6. Privacy

Privacy cannot be defined. The basic definition of privacy would be "the right to be left alone". Privacy should not be confused with confidentiality. Confidentiality of information is information that can be accessed only by a few. In reference to the smart grid privacy means considering the rights, values and interests of customers (like their personal information, electric signatures, etc.). The data used by smart grid could be used to violate individuals [35].

A privacy impact assessment (PIA) is used for determining the privacy, confidentiality, and secure risks that arise due to the collection, use, and disclosure of personal information. PIA findings and recommendations are as follows [35].

(1) *Management and Accountability.* People should be appointed to ensure that the documented policies for information security and privacy are followed. Audit functions should be present in order to check the data access activity.

(2) *Notice and Purpose.* Before collecting data, using it, or sharing it, a notice must be prepared and exchanged.

(3) *Choice and Consent.* The consumer should be provided with the choices present in context to the energy usage data that could be revealed and their consent should be obtained.

(4) *Collection and Scope.* Only the information that is really necessary should be collected from the user by appropriate lawful means and with their consent.

(5) *Use of Retention.* The information that is collected should be used only for those purposes for what they were taken. Also, the information should be saved in such a way that no activity or information about the consumer can be found out from it. The data should be discarded once its purpose is over.

(6) *Individual Access.* Consumers should be able to see their individual data and can also request for correction if any of the data is inaccurate. They also have the right to know where their information is being shared.

(7) *Disclosure and Limiting Use.* The personal information cannot be shared by anyone not present in the initial notice and should only be used for the reason stated in the notice.

(8) *Security and Safeguards.* The personal information should be secure and must be protected from thefts, modification or unauthorized access.

(9) *Accuracy and Quality.* The personal information should be as accurate as possible and related to the purpose mentioned in the notice.

(10) *Openness, Monitoring, and Challenging Compliance.* A service recipient should be able to access the personal data and should be able to challenge the organizations compliance.

7. Conclusion

The various security concerns related to smart grid was proposed in this paper. Smart grid is an emerging project. Its implementation will result in numerous benefits for the society. However, it has to face a few challenges and concerns when it comes to security. We have studied these challenges in this paper. Cyber security is an integral part of the grids security concern. As the grid develops and expands in the future, the number of nodes that will be not susceptible to cyber attacks will increase. Domain architecture which is used to evaluate these challenges is explained in one of the sections. We then explain cryptography and key management techniques which are used to secure the system against cyber attacks. In this section, we covered the constraints for cryptography and also the proposed solutions. The last part of the paper deals with consumer privacy which is another important security parameter that cannot be neglected. In order to make the smart grid more popular, it should be free from any security drawbacks and hazards in order to have a better future.

Acknowledgment

I would like to thank Dr. Zuyi Li for his guidance and the help and inspiration he extended for this paper.

References

[1] C. W. Gellings, *The Smart Grid: Enabling Energy Efficiency and Demand Response*, The Fairmont Press, 2009.

[2] "The smart grid: an introduction," http://energy.gov/oe/downloads/smart-grid-introduction-0.

[3] "European smart grids technology platform," http://www.smartgrids.eu/documents/vision.pdf.

[4] F. Li, W. Qiao, H. Sun et al., "Smart transmission grid: vision and framework," *IEEE Transactions on Smart Grid*, vol. 1, no. 2, Article ID 5535240, pp. 168–177, 2010.

[5] S. Clements and H. Kirkham, "Cyber-security considerations for the smart grid," in *Proceedings of the Power and Energy Society General Meeting (2010 IEEE)*, pp. 1–5, July 2010.

[6] G. Iyer and P. Agrawal, "Smart power grids," in *Proceedings of the 2010 42nd Southeastern Symposium on System Theory (SSST 2010)*, pp. 152–155, March 2010.

[7] Z. Vale, H. Morais, P. Faria, H. Khodr, J. Ferreira, and P. Kadar, "Distributed energy resources management with cyber-physical SCADA in the context of future smart grids," in *Proceedings of the 15th IEEE Mediterranean Electrotechnical Conference (MELECON 2010)*, pp. 431–436, April 2010.

[8] "SCADA," http://en.wikipedia.org/wiki/SCADA.

[9] G. N. Ericsson, "Cyber security and power system communication—essential parts of a smart grid infrastructure," *IEEE Transactions on Power Delivery*, vol. 25, no. 3, Article ID 5452993, pp. 1501–1507, 2010.

[10] F. Boroomand, A. Fereidunian, M. A. Zamani et al., "Cyber security for smart grid: a human-automation interaction framework," in *Proceedings of the IEEE PES Innovative Smart Grid Technologies Conference Europe (ISGT Europe 2010)*, pp. 1–6, October 2010.

[11] "Cyberspace policy review," http://www.whitehouse.gov/assets/documents/Cyberspace_Policy_Review_final.pdf.

[12] A. Dreher and E. Byres, "Get smart about electrical grid cyber security," http://www.belden.com/pdfs/techpprs/PTD_Cyber_SecurityWP.pdf.

[13] "Introduction to NISTR 7628 guidelines for smart grid cyber security," 2010, http://csrc.nist.gov/publications/nistir/ir7628/introduction-to-nistir-7628.pdf.

[14] "Critical electric infrastructure protection act," http://ciip.wordpress.com/2009/04/30/critical-electric-infrastructure-protection-act/.

[15] "The security vulnerabilities of smart grid," 2009, http://www.ensec.org/index.php?option=com_content&view=article&id=198:the-security-vulnerabilities-of-smart-grid&catid=96:content&Itemid=345.

[16] "Guidelines for smart grid cyber security vol. 1, smart grid cyber security, architecture and high-level requirements," 2010, http://csrc.nist.gov/publications/nistir/ir7628/nistir-7628_vol1.pdf.

[17] "Advanced encryption standard (AES)," 2001, http://csrc.nist.gov/publications/fips/fips197/fips-197.pdf.

[18] M. Dworkin, "Recommendation for block cipher modes of operation-methods and techniques," 2001, http://csrc.nist.gov/publications/nistpubs/800-38a/sp800-38a.pdf.

[19] M. Dworkin, "Recommendation for block cipher modes of operation-the XYS-AES mode for confidentiality on storage device," 2010, http://csrc.nist.gov/publications/nistpubs/800-38E/nist-sp-800-38E.pdf.

[20] W. C. Barker, "Recommendation for the triple data encryption algorithm (TDEA) Block Cipher," 2008, http://csrc.nist.gov/publications/nistpubs/800-67/SP800-67.pdf.

[21] "Digital signature standards," 2009, http://csrc.nist.gov/publications/fips/fips186-3/fips_186-3.pdf.

[22] "FIPS PUB 186-2," 2000, http://csrc.nist.gov/publications/fips/archive/fips186-2/fips186-2-change1.pdf.

[23] "Secure hash standard," 2008, http://csrc.nist.gov/publications/fips/fips180-3/fips180-3_final.pdf.

[24] M. Dworkin, "Recommendation for block cipher modes of operation-the CMAC Mode for authentication," 2005, http://csrc.nist.gov/publications/nistpubs/800-38B/SP_800-38B.pdf.

[25] M. Dworkin, "Recommendation for block cipher modes of operation-the CCM mode for authentication and confidentiality," 2004, http://csrc.nist.gov/publications/nistpubs/800-38C/SP800-38C.pdf.

[26] M. Dworkin, "Recommendation for block cipher modes of operation-galois/counter mode (GCM) and GMAC," 2007, http://csrc.nist.gov/publications/nistpubs/800-38D/SP-800-38D.pdf.

[27] "The keyed hash message authentication code(HMAC)," 2002, http://csrc.nist.gov/publications/fips/fips198/fips-198a.pdf.

[28] L. Chen, "Recommendation for key derivation using pseudorandom functions," 2009, http://csrc.nist.gov/publications/nistpubs/800-108/sp800-108.pdf.

[29] "Recommendation guidance for FIPS PUB 140-1 and cryptographic module validation program," 2002, http://csrc.nist.gov/groups/STM/cmvp/documents/fips140-1/FIPS1401IG.pdf.

[30] S. S. Keller, "NIST-recommended random number generator based on ANSI X9.31 appendix A2.4 using the 3 key triple DES and AES algorithms," 2005, http://csrc.nist.gov/groups/STM/cavp/documents/rng/931rngext.pdf.

[31] E. Barker and J. Kelsey, "Recommendation for random number generation using deterministic random bit generator (revised)," 2007, http://csrc.nist.gov/publications/nistpubs/800-90/SP800-90revised_March2007.pdf.

[32] E. Barker, L. Chen, A. Regenscheid, and M. Smid, "Recommendation for Pair wise key establishment schemes using integer factorization cryptography," 2009, http://csrc.nist.gov/publications/nistpubs/800-56B/sp800-56B.pdf.

[33] E. Barker, D. Johnson, and M. Smid, "Recommendation for pair wise key establishment schemes using discrete logarithmic cryptography (revised)," 2007, http://csrc.nist.gov/publications/nistpubs/800-56A/SP800-56A_Revision1_Mar08-2007.pdf.

[34] "Implementation guidance for FIPS PUB 140-2 and the cryptographic module validation," 2010, http://csrc.nist.gov/groups/STM/cmvp/documents/fips140-2/FIPS1402IG.pdf.

[35] "Guidelines for smart grid cyber security vol. 2, privacy and smart grid," 2010, http://csrc.nist.gov/publications/nistir/ir7628/nistir-7628_vol2.pdf.

10

BVS: A Lightweight Forward and Backward Secure Scheme for PMU Communications in Smart Grid

Wei Ren,[1] Jun Song,[1] Min Lei,[2] and Yi Ren[3]

[1] *School of Computer Science, China University of Geosciences, Wuhan 430074, China*
[2] *School of Software Engineering, Key Laboratory of Network and Information Attack and Defense Technology of MoE, Beijing 100876, China*
[3] *Department of Information and Communication Technology, University of Agder (UiA), Grimstad, Norway*

Correspondence should be addressed to Wei Ren, weirencs@gmail.com

Academic Editor: Pierangela Samarati

In smart grid, phaser measurement units (PMUs) can upload readings to utility centers via supervisory control and data acquisition (SCADA) or energy management system (EMS) to enable intelligent controlling and scheduling. It is critical to maintain the secrecy of readings so as to protect customers' privacy, together with integrity and source authentication for the reliability and stability of power scheduling. In particular, appealing security scheme needs to perform well in PMUs that usually have computational resource constraints, thus designed security protocols have to remain lightweight in terms of computation and storage. In this paper, we propose a family of schemes to solve this problem. They are public key based scheme (PKS), password based scheme (PWS) and billed value-based scheme (BVS). BVS can achieve forward and backward security and only relies on hash functions. Security analysis justifies that the proposed schemes, especially BVS, can attain the security goals with low computation and storage cost.

1. Introduction

Smart grid is envisioned as a long-term strategy for national energy independence, controlling emission, and combating global warming [1]. Smart grid technologies utilize intelligent transmission to deliver electricity, together with distribution networks to enable two-way communications. These approaches aim to improve reliability and efficiency of the electric system via gathering consumption data, delivering dynamic optimization of operations, and arranging energy saving schedules.

The smart grid promises to transform traditional centralized, producer-controlled network to a decentralized, consumer-interactive network. For example, consumers react to pricing signals delivered by control unit from smart meters to achieve active load adjustment. Supervisory control And data acquisition (SCADA) or energy management system (EMS) may collect one data points every 1 to 2 seconds, whereas phaser measurement units (PMUs) may collect 30 to 60 data points per second [2].

The security of smart grid is a critical issue for its applicability, development and deployment [3–7]. On one hand, the security, and especially the availability of power supplying system, affects homeland security, as it is an indispensable infrastructure for pubic living system [8–10]. That is, any transient interruption will result in economic and social disaster. On the other hand, introduction of end devices such as PMUs requests for data and communication security to support secure and reliable uploading of measurements [11, 12].

As the PMUs are exposed far from the central control unit, they present as a security boundary line between defenses and attacks. Such frontier may be tampered by curious users who intend to make certain profits or, even worse, hacked by malicious attackers who target for damaging power scheduling performance [13, 14]. For example, in the former case, advanced customers may try to reduce the value of meter's readings by revising circuits or interfering signals outside; curious eavesdroppers may be interested in customers' power-consuming patterns to pry about the consumers' privacy such as daily behaviors or schedules. In the latter case, the attackers may invoke long-lasting peak values in meters to disturb the SCADA's scheduling strategies [15] or inject a worm to infect all meters to threaten the entire system resulting in a so-called billion-dollar bug [1]. To thwart the former security threaten, a straightforward way is to protect data confidentiality in PMU communications. Furthermore, to guarantee data integrity and data source authentication in PMU communications can mitigate the latter threat. Thus a prerequisite requirement arises—how to deliver and protect the encryption key and integrity key for such communications.

As the security issue for smart grid is an emerging new topic, currently available and customized solutions are a very few or undergoing development. Most existing work focuses on formulating the security problems [1–4, 7, 16] or build the security frameworks [5, 6, 8, 11, 17–19]. Especially, no existing work addresses key management issue for PMU communications in depth to the best of our knowledge. In this paper, we address data security and communication security between PMUs and control units in smart grid from the viewpoint of key management, including key generation, key deployment, and key evolution. After analyzing the data and communication security requirements, firstly, we propose several customized approaches and solutions.

Smart grid has some characteristics of itself own, for example, large number of deployment of end devices, real-time communications, resource constraints in tangible devices, to name a few. Thus, proper security solutions should beware of those specialities, for example, avoid disadvantages in applicable context to improve the applicability of proposed scheme. On the other hand, security design should be crafted for taking advantages of some properties of smart grid such as network architecture, domain context, and operational flow, as it may help to improve the overall performance. More specifically, we will dissect smart grid architecture to extract networking and system model and explore the inner mechanisms such as operational flow between SCADA and PMUs. We propose to solve the security problems by incorporating security scheme into the operational flow seamlessly to shrink the overall cost, and thus improve integrated performance. Such a design rationale makes use of inherent information in operational procedures as a security gradient and will be explained in the paper.

The major contributions of this paper are listed as follows.

(1) The security analysis, including network and system model, attack model and security requirements between PMU and SCADA communications in smart grid are extensively explored.

(2) We propose several lightweight schemes, including public key based scheme (PKS), password based Scheme (PWS), and billed value-based scheme (BVS) to tackle different application scenarios.

The rest of the paper is organized as follows. In Section 2, we discuss basic assumption and models used throughout the paper. Section 3 provides detailed description of our proposed schemes. We analyze security and performance aspects of the proposed scheme in Section 4. Finally, Section 5 concludes the paper.

2. Problem Formation

2.1. Network Model and System Model. The following related entities usually exist in smart grid applications.

(1) *PMUs.* Phaser measurement unit is an indispensable device for smart grid. As it may be exposed outside to potential adversaries, its security should be addressed firstly in the exploration of solutions. Each PMU has an automatic meter reading (AMR) to provide power values (or additionally a unit to delivery pricing information). The PMUs rely on the communication network to send measurements (or receive control instructions).

The characteristics of PMUs are as follows.

(i) Scalability. The number of PMUs is very large, could be in a scale of more than fifty thousands, depending on family quantity in a management domain, for example, in a county or a city scale.

(ii) Resource constraints. The computation and storage resources of PMUs are usually assumed to have constraints.

(iii) Compatibility. PMUs may have multiple variants for different categories of customers, and certain legacy systems or devices may try to be migrated or upgraded to a new version at first as more as possible.

(iv) Asymmetry. PMUs has a large volume of uploading traffics, but down-link traffics are comparatively much less than uploading traffics.

Therefore, incorporated security enhancement modules in PMUs should be affordable and have minimized revision for end customers. The design also needs to be suitable to multiple variants of PMUs, being compatible to general situations or legacy systems. We, thus, make the least assumption on the processing ability of PMUs. That is, their computation ability may be as low as a chip in sensor node, and storage space may be in megabyte magnitude. Thus, our solution can be applied in most architectures and perform better once higher processing platforms are available.

(2) *SGCC.* The control instructions are sent from smart grid control center, denoted as SGCC in this paper. It is a part of control unit of SCADA (or EMS). SGCC usually has enough computation and storage resources.

(3) *Customer.* The customers are always presented or related in smart grid applications; the PMU is not an isolated computing unit (this point is different with sensor node). Thus in security design, the human element could be considered and exploited if needed.

The communication network could be currently available home networks; we do not specify networking settings such as topology and parameters such as bandwidth to make our discussion be suitable in most general situations.

To summarize, we observe that in smart grid, two asymmetry or unbalance present: computation resources in PMUs and in SGCC; uploading and downloading communication volumes. They may affect some subtle tradeoff in design of security schemes. Moreover, human interaction may also be incorporated into the design.

2.2. Attack Model. Similar to the statement in related work [2], traditional communications involve devices that are in areas with physical access controls (such as fences and locked houses), but smart PMUs are deployed in the areas that could be accessible by both consumers and adversaries. Consequently, we have to assume that PMUs are located in a hostile environment and much stronger adversaries exist.

As attackers are assumed to be malicious and intended to tamper the system to gain some profits. For example, attackers may reduce the transmission data such as power consuming value for lower payment; they may also pulse the data in the transmission to corrupt the scheduling strategies; they may pry the communication patterns to speculate the privacy of consumers, such as daily behaviors; they may inject any forgeable data such as consuming value into the communication by manipulating PMUs, or even aim to crash partial or entire SCADA or EMS.

2.3. Security Requirement. The data are generated from PMUs and transmitted into communication networks. To protect such kind of data, security scheme should the fulfill security requirements as follows:

Data Confidentiality. Data confidentiality in transmission should be protected. Otherwise, utility consumption values will be known by attackers, which will leak much information on consumers' behaviors.

Data Integrity. Integrity of the data transferred in communication should be guaranteed so that any modification of the data can be detected.

Data Source Authentication. The source of the data should be verifiable by receivers to confirm the data authenticity and so as to exclude forged data.

Above requirements should be addressed in context of smart grid, or the solution should concern its applicability in smart grid environments. Such security requirements inevitably ask for a prerequisite demand—key management issue. The related keys such as the encryption key, integrity key, or authenticity key can be available and properly protected.

2.4. Design Goal. Based on above observations, we state the design goal as follows:

We search for a highly robust but lightweight scheme to protect data confidentiality, data integrity, and data source authentication in case of the presence of strong attackers and in the context of smart grid. To fulfill such objectives,

TABLE 1: Notation.

PKS	Public Key based Scheme
MK	Master Key
UID	Unique ID
PMU	Phaser Measurement Units
SGCC	Smart Grid Control Center
SEK	Session Encryption Key
PubK	Public Key
PriK	Private Key
PWS	Password based Scheme
PWD	Password
BVS	Billed Value based Scheme
V	Value of automatic meter readings
ETK	Evolutionary Transportation Key
$\{M\}_K$	Encryption of M using key K
$\parallel$	Concatenation

the prerequisite is how to generate, manage, and refresh underlying keys such as encryption key, integrity key, and authentication key. The encryption key is called session encryption key, denoted as SEK, which is only used for one uploading session of power values. The authentication key and integrity key are combined (or interchangeable) together and is called session integrity key, denoted as SIK, which is also used only for one session. The session period depends on the gathering interval of power values, scheduling policy, and security strength.

3. Proposed Schemes

In this section, we investigate a family of schemes for better understanding and explaining motivations. Each latter scheme may improve previous one by addressing some of its limitations in terms of performance or usability, or deal with several subtle tradeoff to achieve better overall performance and security.

We list all major notations used in the remainder of the paper in Table 1.

3.1. Public Key based Scheme—PKS. We firstly propose a basic public key based scheme, called PKS, to illustrate our motivations. To facilitate the encryption and message authentication code, the encryption key and integrity key are required. The naive scheme is using predistributed master key (*MK*) in the PMUs, but this solution has one weakness— if a PMU is compromised, the *MK* in this PMU will be leaked. Therefore, all derived keys from *MK* will be exposed if such derivation is only related to *MK*.

Each PMU has a *MK* that is preloaded into the PMU upon the deployment. PMU always has a unique id, called *UID*, which could be a designated sequence number of the PMU upon deployment and stored in on-chip read-only memory. Similar to *MK*, the UID is also stored by SGCC after the deployment of PMU. Customers are assumed to have a certificated public key generated by certificate authority (CA), usually a trusted third party for smart grid.

The Public Key based scheme (PKS) is described as following stages:

(1) Stage I—Preparation. Before session key establishment, SGCC checks whether the customer's PubK is revoked from Revocation List (RL). If not, go to next stage. Otherwise, stop or choose another scheme.

(2) Stage II—Session key seed establishment.

    (2.1) Establishment request (SKER). SGCC selects a random number $R = \{R_1 \| R_2\}$ and sends R that is encrypted by a customer's PubK to PMU. That is,

$$\text{SGCC} \longrightarrow \text{PMU} : \{Tm \| R_1 \| R_2\}_{\text{PubK}}, \qquad (1)$$

    where Tm is a time stamp denoting current time.

    (2.2) Establishment acknowledgement (SKEA). The customer relies her private key (PriK) to decrypt out R, checks whether Tm is in the proper range and sends back as follows:

$$\text{PMU} \longrightarrow \text{SGCC} : \{R_1 + 1 \| R_2 - 1\}_{\text{PriK}}. \qquad (2)$$

(3) Stage III—session key generation.

    (3.1) SEK generation. The customer uses following method to generate session encryption key: $\text{SEK} = \text{Hash}(R_1 \| \text{UID} \| \text{MK})$.

    (3.2) SIK generation. The customer uses following method to generate session integrity key: $\text{SIK} = \text{Hash}(R_2 \| \text{UID} \| \text{MK})$.

(4) Stage IV—data transmission. The PMU sends power value to SGCC:

$$\text{PMU} \longrightarrow \text{SGCC} : \{V\}_{\text{SEK}}, \{\text{Hash}(V)\}_{\text{SIK}}, \qquad (3)$$

where V is a value of meter reading in the last sample period.

Remarks.

(1) Two random values (R_1 and R_2) are used instead of one random value, can protect SEK and SIK independently. The exposure of one random number (i.e., R_1 in SEK or R_2 in SIK) will not result in the leakage of the other.

(2) Tm is used for defending replay attack. If Tm is not in the range, the SKER (session key establishment request) message will be ignored. The replay attack may result in DoS (denial of service) attack to PMUs. It can be mitigated by security policy that is out of the scope of the paper.

(3) SKEA (session key establishment acknowledgement) message confirms the authenticity of PMU and synchronizes the generation of session keys.

(4) SEK generation relies on $\{R_1 \| \text{UID} \| \text{MK}\}$. If MK is compromised by software flaws in program, UID may remain secure due to its hardware compromising hardness (namely, tamper-proofed read-only memory accessed only by PMU). R_1 guarantees the freshness and authenticity of SEK.

(5) The confidentiality and integrity of power data V are guaranteed by SEK and SIK.

Security Analysis. The security of SEK and SIK is guaranteed by the security of PriK. If the PriK is safely possessed, attackers cannot recognize SEK and SIK. UID is used for generating SEK and SIK, which increases the difficulties of hardware tampering by attackers. That is, even if MK is leaked by software compromising, the UID may still sustain secrecy, because it is a hardware extracted value and not easy to be revealed by only software compromising. Moreover, even though the attacker can further reveal UID by hardware scrutiny physically, they cannot be able to possess the PriK simultaneously, as it is securely and personally held by customers. The customers are assumed to safely possess their PriK and only use such keys in session establishment stage. Therefore, the security of SEK and SIK can be guaranteed.

Performance Analysis. We mainly consider performance at PMU side. The session key seed establishment stage induces the operations are 1 public key decryption and 1 public key encryption.

The session key generation stage incurs 2 hash function computation. Data transmission stage has 2 symmetric key encryption and 1 hash function computation. The communication includes two messages for key establishment and one message for data transmission. It shows that the operations in this stage almost remain to being minimized.

Usability and Cost Analysis. PKS involves customers' PriK, so customers usually have to possess some local device such as a USB disk to store such key (that is distributed by third trusted party). It may induce a USB port in PMU attached devices, which increases the cost of PMU devices. It also demands customers to safely possess a portable USB key, which may add customers' burden. The RL (revocation list) must be maintained or synchronized with CA (certificate authority) by SGCC. Or, SGCC will retrieve the RL if RL is only maintained by CA, it will introduce some response delay due to RL retrieval.

The customers are asked for participating the key establishment stage only when session keys are generated or updated. In proposed scheme, the session key establishment (or updating) stage are launched by SGCC, if customers and SGCC previously agree on one or multiple timeslots, for example, each Sunday 10:00 PM, which is only a management issue. If needed, the session key updating request can also be launched by customers, in this case customers may communicate with SGCC offline to negotiate a proper time-slot.

3.2. Password based Scheme: PWS. The public Key based Scheme (PKS) scheme is resilient to software compromise, but it assumes the existence of PKI (Public Key Infrastructure) system. To avoid such a restricted assumption, we propose a password based scheme, called PWS, to improve the flexibility and usability of the proposed solution.

In this scheme, password (denoted as PWD) is induced, which is a easily memorized (at least 8) digits in range [0, 9] so that PKI becomes unnecessary. The password are usually selected by customers for their favors so as to be easily memorized. The password usually is uploaded to SGCC off-line, for example, when create or start up the utility account or upon the deployment of PMUs.

The PWS scheme is described as follows:

(1) Stage I—session key seed establishment.

  (1.1) Establishment request (SKER). SGCC selects a random number $R = \{Tm\|R_1\|R_2\}$ and sends R encrypted by the customer's password PWD to PMU. That is

$$\text{SGCC} \longrightarrow \text{PMU} : \{Tm\|R_1\|R_2\}_{\text{PWD}}, \qquad (4)$$

  where Tm is current time stamp.

  (1.2) Establishment acknowledgement (SKEA). The customer decrypts out R via her PWD, checks whether Tm is in the range, and sends back as follows:

$$\text{PMU} \longrightarrow \text{SGCC} : \{R_1 + 1\|R_2 - 1\}_{\text{PWD}}. \qquad (5)$$

(2) Stage II—session key generation.

  (2.1) SEK generation. The customer uses following method to generate session encryption key:

$$\text{SEK} = \text{Hash}(R_1\|\text{UID}\|\text{MK}\|\text{PWD}). \qquad (6)$$

  (2.2) SIK generation. The customer uses following method to generate session integrity key:

$$\text{SIK} = \text{Hash}(R_2\|\text{UID}\|\text{MK}\|\text{PWD}). \qquad (7)$$

(3) Stage III—data transmission. The customer sends power value to SGCC as follows:

$$\text{PMU} \longrightarrow \text{SGCC} : \{V\}_{\text{SEK}}, \{\text{Hash}(V)\}_{\text{SIK}}. \qquad (8)$$

Enhancement. In PKS scheme, once PriK is exposed, all random number R are revealed. It is appealing that certain previous keys and together ciphertext encrypted by such keys are still safe even if current keys are exposed. This situation is so-called forward secrecy. To further enhance the security of scheme PWS, we propose to use key evolution method. Here, we call the key used for transporting random number R is a transportation key. We propose to use one-time hash value of PWD as the transportation key, and use hash chain as a key evolution strategy.

More specifically, at ith time in Stage I the encrypted key is not PWD but $\text{Hash}^{(i)}(\text{PWD}), (i \geqslant 1)$. That is, assuming at the ith time (or session) of transmission of random number R. The two steps in stage I are revised as follows:

(1.1) SGCC selects a random number $R = \{R_1\|R_2\}$ and sends R to PMU that is encrypted by hashed customer's password. That is,

$$\text{SGCC} \longrightarrow \text{PMU} : \{Tm\|R_1\|R_2\}_{\text{Hash}^{(i)}(\text{PWD})}. \qquad (9)$$

(1.2) The customer uses $\text{Hash}^{(i)}(\text{PWD})$ to decrypt out R, checks whether Tm is in the range, and sends back:

$$\text{PMU} \longrightarrow \text{SGCC} : \{R_1 + 1\|R_2 - 1\}_{\text{Hash}^{(i)}(\text{PWD})}. \qquad (10)$$

In this way, the encryption key for random number transportation will be evolved very time and be used for only once. Even attackers can reveal one encryption key, for example, $\text{Hash}^{(i)}(\text{PWD})$, they cannot conjecture previous encryption keys such as $\text{Hash}^{(j)}(\text{PWD})$ $(1 \leqslant j < i)$. The reason comes from the one-wayness of hash function. That is, given the image of the function, it is computationally infeasible to compute preimage. Therefore, this enhancement guarantees the forward secrecy of the transportation key.

In addition to the introduction of key evolution, a value SALT is further suggested to strengthen the limited length of PWD and defend off-line dictionary attack. As PWD needs to be easily memorized, the length of PWD usually is no longer than 8 digits. To extend the off-line brute force search space, SALT value can be used. The SALT will be safely stored in SGCC and PMU, respectively. The indeed PWD used for key evolution will be {PWD∥SALT} instead of PWD.

Security Analysis. The security of SEK and SIK is guaranteed by the security of PWD. SGCC is always assumed to securely possess the PWD, as it is in a trusted domain. If PWD is only memorized by consumers and its secrecy is maintained when it is typed on keyboard, attackers cannot recognize SEK and SIK due to the unknownness of PWD. Without PWD, attackers cannot reveal R that is the generating ingredient of session keys (namely, SEK and SIK).

Moreover, UID and MK are incorporated in the generation of SEK and SIK for the similar reason with public key based scheme. Especially, PWD is also proposed to embed into the generation of SEK and SIK, to further enhance the session key's secrecy.

The scheme can further provide forward secrecy of transportation key used for transferring random number R. That is, even a key $\text{Hash}^{(i)}(\text{PWD})$ for encryption of R are exposed, the keys such as $\text{Hash}^{(j)}(\text{PWD})$ $(1 \leqslant j < i)$ still remain secret.

Based on above analysis, the security of SEK and SIK can be guaranteed.

Performance Analysis. The operations induced at PMU side are 1 symmetric key decryption, 1 symmetric key encryption for key establishment, and 2 hash function computation for key generation.

Usability and Cost Analysis. PWS scheme may ask users to plug a small numeric keyboard into PMU attached device or PMU itself incorporates such a numeric keyboard panel, which slightly increases the cost of PMU. Nonetheless, the usability of scheme PWS is better than scheme PKS, as the USB key is not required and numeric keyboard is much cheaper than USB key. The PWD can be reinstated or updated by customers via off-line channel with SGCC.

3.3. Billed Value-Based Scheme: BVS.

PWS scheme can further be improved to avoid typing password by customers. We further propose a more lightweight scheme by using billed value. The billed value here means the last billed value for consumed utility. We assume that value is only known by SGCC and PMU, as we assume the utility consumption result is a private information of customers and should be kept secret (that is the underlying goal of proposed schemes). Suppose the billed value is BV, we use Hash(BV) to replace the functionality of PWD in PWS scheme. Note that the BV is always not equal to real-time consuming value V, as the billing period is always longer than data gathering period and billed value is a constant value in last billing period. For example, BV is altered once in one billing period, but the gathering value V is collected by SGCC much more frequently (depending on the control and scheduling strategies). The enhancement rationale for forward secrecy in PWS scheme can also be migrated to BVS scheme. Thus, the proposed BVS scheme is as follows.

(1) Stage I—session key seed establishment.

 (1.1) SGCC selects a random number $r = \{R_1 \| R_2\}$ and sends R encrypted by Hash(BV) to PMU. That is,

$$\text{SGCC} \longrightarrow \text{PMU} : \{R_1 \| R_2\}_{\text{Hash}^{(i)}(\text{Hash}(\text{BV}))}. \quad (11)$$

 (1.2) Customers use their $\text{Hash}^{(i)}(\text{Hash}(\text{BV}))$ to decrypt out R.

(2) Stage II—session key generation.

 (2.1) SEK generation. The customer uses following method to generate session encryption key:

$$\text{SEK} = \text{Hash}(R_1 \| \text{UID} \| \text{MK} \| \text{BV}). \quad (12)$$

 (2.1) SIK generation. The customer uses following method to generate session integrity key:

$$\text{SIK} = \text{Hash}(R_2 \| \text{UID} \| \text{MK} \| \text{BV}). \quad (13)$$

(3) Stage III—data transmission. The customer sends power value to SGCC as follows:

$$\text{PMU} \longrightarrow \text{SGCC} : \{V\}_{\text{SEK}}, \{\text{Hash}(V)\}_{\text{SIK}}. \quad (14)$$

Enhancement.

(1) The hash functions used in our scheme could be the same function or different functions, depending on the available storage space for implementation of hash function code. We suggest to use different hash functions as it will be more secure. That is, the transportation key is $\text{Hash}_1^{(i)}(\text{Hash}_2(\text{BV}))$.

(2) The synchronization of SGCC and PMU on BV is straightforward if the clock of PMU and SGCC can be strictly synchronized. Normally, the transaction is cutoff at the end of billing period, for example, at the 1:00 AM of the first day of each month. At that moment, the PMU will save this value (also the last uploading value) before 1:00 AM as a billing value. That value is the utility consumption of last payment period. Hence, it performs as a common shared secret between PMU (customer) and SGCC in a natural way, and it is automatically and periodically updated to maintain freshness.

(3) If the clock of PMU is not strictly synchronized, we propose the following policy—multiple transmission of BV. That is, in the first day of each month before 1:00 AM, PMU stores any current V as BV and attaches it to multiple messages. That is,

$$\text{PMU} \longrightarrow \text{SGCC} : \{V \| \text{BV} \| \text{BV}_{\text{TAG}}\}_{\text{SEK}},$$
$$\{\text{Hash}(V \| \text{BV} \| \text{BV}_{\text{TAG}})\}_{\text{SIK}}, \quad (15)$$

where BV_{TAG} presents a tag for notifying SGCC that the BV is attached.

(4) As the success of update of BV is critical for key synchronization, we propose another policy by using confirmed reply if two-way communication is available (in fact, two-way communication is usually available in smart grid). That is, the two-way messages include confirmation from SGCC on the receipt of BV, as follows:

$$\text{PMU} \longrightarrow \text{SGCC} : \{V \| \text{BV} \| \text{BV}_{\text{TAG}}\}_{\text{SEK}},$$
$$\{\text{Hash}(V \| \text{BV} \| \text{BV}_{\text{TAG}})\}_{\text{SIK}},$$
$$\text{SGCC} \longrightarrow \text{PMU} : \{\text{BV} \| \text{BV}_{\text{TAGACK}}\}_{\text{SEK}},$$
$$\{\text{Hash}(\text{BV} \| \text{BV}_{\text{TAGACK}})\}_{\text{SIK}}. \quad (16)$$

(5) In PWS scheme, only forward secrecy of the transportation key are ensured. That is, from $\text{Hash}_2^{(i)}(\text{BV})$ attackers can compute $\text{Hash}_2^{(i+1)}(\text{BV})$, but not $\text{Hash}_2^{(i-1)}(\text{BV})$. To further enhance the secrecy of transportation key, we propose an enhancement method for both forward secrecy and backward secrecy. Here, backward secrecy means that even if the current key is exposed, the future keys cannot be correctly conjectured. Concretely, we propose the

following key evolution strategy, assuming the ith transportation of random number R:

$$\text{SEED} \longleftarrow \text{Hash}_2(BV),$$

$$\{L \| R\} \longleftarrow \text{SEED},$$

$$\text{ETK}_L \longleftarrow \text{Hash}^{(n+1-i)}(L),$$

$$\text{ETK}_R \longleftarrow \text{Hash}^{(i)}(R), \tag{17}$$

$$\text{ETK} \longleftarrow \{\text{ETK}_L \| \text{ETK}_R\},$$

$$\text{SGCC} \longrightarrow \text{PMU} : \{R_1 \| R_2\}_{\text{ETK}},$$

where ETK means evolutionary transportation key, used for the transportation of random number R.

In this way, the encryption key for random number will be changed very time and be used for only once. Even attackers can reveal one encryption key, for example, $\text{Hash}^{(n+1-i)}(L)$, they cannot conjecture future encryption keys such as $\text{Hash}^{(n+1-j)}(L)(i < j < n)$. The reason is the one-wayness of hash function. Therefore, the backward secrecy of transportation key ETK is guaranteed. Besides, the value of n is stored in the table of database in SGCC and preloaded into PMU.

(6) As the key is updated in bidirections to provide forward and backward secrecy, the backward secrecy needs the predetermination of maximal evolution times $n + 1$. If the maximal number is reached, or if sampling times i is increased to $n + 1$ within one billing period, we propose to update BV by using $BV \longleftarrow \text{Hash}_2(BV)$ and reset i to 1. The updating period of transporting key result in the alternation of random number R, and further SEK and SIK. The updating period depends on the security policy and data gathering frequency.

(7) In one billing period, all SEKs and SIKs are generated by different random number R that are transported using the derived keys from same BV. As key evolution is involved, the loss of synchronization of i at PMU and SGCC in one billing period will result in the decryption failure of random number R at the PMU side. The minor adjustment can solve this problem. At SGCC side, the random number could have some relation between R_1 and R_2, for example, $R = \{R_1 \| R_2 = \text{Hash}_1(R_1)\}$. At PMU side upon receipt of $\{R_1 \| R_2\}_{\text{ETK}}$, PMU will decrypt it with supposed ETK. If decrypted value presents the designated relation, the synchronization is maintained.

(8) As the security of BV is critical for BVS scheme, we also propose some strategies to protect BV's secrecy. The secret BV can be a function of public BV. We leave some flexibility of BV value's customized tuning. For example, customers can select a policy on how to generate secrete BV from public BV value, when paying for the utility, and upload the selection into SCADA. Such policy could be an option in policy list. The synchronization of BV between PMU and SCADA can be confirmed by customers upon paying for the utility bill and checking PMU. We assume PMU has a screen to display assumed BV when customers type designated on-board button, and customer can also upload PMU her selected policy by pressing the same button. The public BV will not lead to the exposure of secrete BV, unless corresponding policy is exposed.

Security Analysis. The basic analysis is similar to PWS scheme. The security of SEK and SIK is guaranteed by the security of BV, which is assumed to be the private information of customers. The one-time usage of BV derived encryption key improve the confidentiality of random number, which is an ingredient of SEK and SIK. Together with UID, MK and BV, the security of SEK and SIK can be guaranteed.

Especially, the bidirection hash-chain based derivation guarantees both forward and backward secrecy of the transportation key ETK, so both forward and backward secrecy of R are maintained. As R is the seed of session key SEK and SIK, the both forward and backward secrecy of session keys are guaranteed.

Performance Analysis. The scheme induces the operations are 1 symmetric key encryption, symmetric key decryption, 2 hash function computation. The SEK and SIK generation requires a one-way message from SGCC to PMU. Besides, the enhancement induces more computation, but all are hash function calculation that have low overhead.

Usability and Cost Analysis. Last available BV value can be stored in SGCC and PMU, so customers do not need to remember a password. The security of BV is critical, so it may save in some separated devices such as on-chip rewritable memory to protect its secrecy.

4. Analysis

4.1. Security Analysis. We state the analysis formally by presenting following propositions.

Proposition 1. *If PriK is secretly possessed, PKS will be secure.*

Proof. If PriK is secretly possessed, R will remain secure. If R is secret, computation of SEK and SIK is equivalent to random guess due to the one-wayness of hash function. Thus, if SEK is a secret, the data secrecy of V will be ensured. If SIK is a secret, the message integrity and message source authentication will be ensured. The reason is the one wayness of hash function and the secrecy of SIK.

Proposition 2. *If PWD is maintained secret, the scheme PWS will achieve security goals.*

Proof. Straightforward.

Definition 3. Forward secrecy. Given a key K, it is computationally infeasible to conjecture K_f, where K_f is the key before last key evolution. That is, $|\Pr\{K_f \mid K, K \leftarrow f(K_f)\} - \Pr\{K_f\}| < \epsilon(n)$, where $\epsilon(n)$ is a negligible polynomial related to a security parameter n. n usually is the security strength in length. $f(\cdot)$ is the key evolution function. $\Pr\{K_f\}$ denotes the probability of revealing K_f.

Definition 4. Backward secrecy. Given a key K, it is computationally infeasible to conjecture K_b, where K_b is the key after key evolution. That is, $|\Pr\{K_b \mid K, K_b \leftarrow f(K)\} - \Pr\{K_b\}| < \epsilon(n)$, where $\epsilon(n)$ is a negligible polynomial related to security parameter n. n usually is the security strength in length. $f(\cdot)$ is the key evolution function. $\Pr\{K_b\}$ denotes the probability of revealing K_b.

Lemma 5. *One-way function is sufficient for forward secrecy, and necessary for forward secrecy if only one evolutionary key is stored and shared by communication peers.*

Proof. The proof for sufficient condition is straightforward. Next, we proof it is a necessary condition. As only one evolutionary key is stored and shared at communication peers, denoted as K, the next generated key is the function of K. That is, $K_f = f(K)$, where $f(\cdot)$ is a function taking as input K. If $|\Pr\{K_f \mid K\} - \Pr\{K_f\}| = 0$, we have $\Pr\{f(K) \mid K\} = \Pr\{f(K)\}$. $f(\cdot)$ is thus a real random number generation, for example, randomly sample function from a key space. In other words, $f(K) = K_f, (K_f \leftarrow_r \{0,1\}^{|K|})$, where $\leftarrow_r$ means random selection. As communication peers use key evolution for secure communication, they have to maintain holding a shared secret after key evolution. Thus, if $f(\cdot)$ is a real random number generation (RNG), the key evolution is unserviceable because the shared pairwise secret is lost. To maintain holding shared secret after key evolution, it needs to satisfy $|\Pr\{K_f \mid K\} - \Pr\{K_f\}| < \epsilon(n)$, where $\epsilon(n)$ is a negligible polynomial related to security parameter $n = |K|$. Therefore, $f(\cdot)$ has to take as input K and must has one-wayness, as desired.

Proposition 6. *BVS has optimal forward and backward secrecy.*

Proof. For forward and backward security, one-way function is required. BVS guarantees forward and backward security by using only single one-way function. The first half key is generated by forward secure key evolution method; the other half key is generated by backward secure key evolution method. Due to the one-wayness of one-way function, the reveal of key after key evolution can only be done by random guess. Suppose $\text{ETK}_L = L_1, \text{ETK}_R = L_2$. That is, $\Pr\{K_b \mid K, K_b \leftarrow f(K)\} = 1/2^{L_1}$, and $\Pr\{K_f \mid K, K \leftarrow f(K_f)\} = 1/2^{L_2}$. Besides, $L_1 + L_2 = |K| = n$. Thus, $\Pr\{K_f, K_b \mid K, K \leftarrow f(K_f), K_b \leftarrow f(K)\} = 1/2^{L_1} \times 1/2^{L_2} = 1/2^{L_1+L_2} = 1/2^n$. Thus BVS has forward and backward secrecy.

Next, we proof it is optimal. If we define overall security strength is the minimum of backward secrecy strength and forward secrecy strength, the key revealing probability will be $\text{MAX}\{1/2^{L_1}, 1/2^{L_2}\}$. Thus, when $L_1 = L_2 = |K|/2$, the overall secrecy strength achieves an optimal strength $1/2^{n/2}$.

TABLE 2: Scheme comparison.

Scheme	Security	Performance (PMU side)	Usability
PKS	PriK	PKD + Hash	PKI + USB Key
PWS	PWD + forward security	SKD + Hash	Keyboard
BVS	BV + forward + backward security	SKD + Hash	/

Above proof is valid even for any attack model for communication link (of course, we only consider any attack models that have finite computational ability, namely, polynomial attackers).

Proposition 7. *Scheme PKS is not forward secure, but scheme PWS is forward secure.*

Proof. Straightforward.

Proposition 8. *Scheme PWS is not backward secure, but scheme BVS is forward and backward secure.*

Proof. In BVS scheme, $\text{ETK}_L \leftarrow \text{Hash}^{(n+1-i)}(L)$. On one hand, if ETK_L is exposed, attacker cannot conjecture future encryption keys $\text{Hash}^{(n+1-j)}(L)(i < j < n)$. Thus, the backward secrecy are guaranteed. On the other hand, if $\text{ETK}_R \leftarrow \text{Hash}^i(R)$ is exposed, attacker cannot conjecture future encryption keys $\text{Hash}^{(j)}(R)(j < i)$. Thus, the forward secrecy is ensured. Hence, either ETK_L or ETK_R cannot be conjectured. ETK, thus, has forward secrecy and backward secrecy, as desired.

4.2. Performance Analysis. The additional computation of BVS only involves hash functions, so the computational cost is manageable. The hash function codes can be reused. For example, one hash function is SHA256; the other is SHA512. The incurred storage for codes is also lightweight. As hash function is typical lightweight cryptographic primitives, it is also extensively applied in computing platforms with much lower computational ability than PMU such as RFID tag [20]. Moreover, the hardware implementation of hash functions has competitive performances [21–23], which further guarantee the applicability of hash functions in PMUs.

Regarding the usability, BVS has the best performances. It has no requirement for PKI comparing with PKS scheme and has no requirement for password inputting device comparing with PWS scheme. We list the comparisons between three schemes in Table 2. (Acronym: PKD—public key decryption and SKD—symmetric key decryption.)

5. Conclusion

In this paper, we proposed a family of lightweight security schemes for session key seed establishment and session key generation to guarantee data secrecy, data integrity, and data source authentication in communications from PMUs to SGCC (SCADA or EMS control center). We proposed public key based scheme (PKS) and password based scheme (PWS) for different application scenarios. Billed value-based scheme (BVS) was proposed and emphasized, as it can achieve forward and backward security by only relying on hash functions and has appealing usability or flexibility. Security and performance analysis justified that the proposed scheme BVS can achieve forward and backward secrecy with lightweight hash function computation.

Acknowledgments

This work was supported by Special Fund for Basic Scientific Research of Central Colleges, China University of Geosciences (Wuhan) under Grant no. 090109, Major State Basic Research Development Program of China (973 Program) (no. 2007CB311203), National Natural Science Foundation of China (no. 60821001), and Ph.D. Programs Foundation of Ministry of Education of China (no. 20070013007).

References

[1] P. McDaniel and S. McLaughlin, "Security and privacy challenges in the smart grid," *IEEE Security and Privacy*, vol. 7, no. 3, pp. 75–77, 2009.

[2] H. Khurana, M. Hadley, N. Lu et al., "Smart-grid security issues," *IEEE Security and Privacy*, vol. 8, no. 1, pp. 81–85, 2010.

[3] F. Boroomand, A. Fereidunian, M. A. Zamani et al., "Cyber security for smart grid: a human-automation interaction framework," in *Proceedings of the IEEE PES Innovative Smart Grid Technologies Conference Europe (ISGT Europe '10)*, pp. 1–6, November 2010.

[4] S. Clements and H. Kirkham, "Cyber-security considerations for the smart grid," in *Proceedings of the 2010 IEEE Power and Energy Society General Meeting (PES '10)*, pp. 1–5, September 2010.

[5] A. R. Metke and R. L. Ekl, "Security technology for smart grid networks," *IEEE Transactions on Smart Grid*, vol. 1, no. 1, pp. 99–107, 2010.

[6] D. Wei, Y. Lu, M. Jafari et al., "An integrated security system of protecting smart grid against cyber attacks," in *Proceedings of the Innovative Smart Grid Technologies (ISGT '10)*, pp. 1–7, 2010.

[7] M. Amin, "Challenges in reliability, security, efficiency, and resilience of energy infrastructure: toward smart self-healing electric power grid," in *Proceedings of the IEEE Power and Energy Society General Meeting (PES '08)*, pp. 1–5, Pittsburgh, Pa, USA, July 2008.

[8] G. N. Ericsson, "Cyber security and power system communication—essential parts of a smart grid infrastructure," *IEEE Transactions on Power Delivery*, vol. 25, no. 3, pp. 1501–1507, 2010.

[9] J. T. Seo and C. Lee, "The green defenders," *IEEE Power and Energy Magazine*, vol. 9, no. 1, pp. 82–90, 2011.

[10] J. Kim and J. Lee, "A model of stability," *IEEE Power and Energy Magazine*, vol. 9, no. 1, pp. 75–81, 2011.

[11] K. M. Rogers, R. Klump, H. Khurana, A. A. Aquino-Lugo, and T. J. Overbye, "An authenticated control framework for distributed voltage support on the smart grid," *IEEE Transactions on Smart Grid*, vol. 1, no. 1, pp. 40–47, 2010.

[12] Y. Wang, I. R. Pordanjani, and W. Xu, "An event-driven demand response scheme for power system security enhancement," *IEEE Transactions on Smart Grid*, vol. 2, no. 1, pp. 23–29, 2011.

[13] K. Moslehi and R. Kumar, "A reliability perspective of the smart grid," *IEEE Transactions on Smart Grid*, vol. 1, no. 1, pp. 57–64, 2010.

[14] Y. Wang, W. Li, and J. Lu, "Reliability analysis of wide-area measurement system," *IEEE Transactions on Power Delivery*, vol. 25, no. 3, pp. 1483–1491, 2010.

[15] J. Ma, P. Zhang, H. j. Fu et al., "Application of phasor measurement unit on locating disturbance source for low-frequency oscillation," *IEEE Transactions on Smart Grid*, vol. 1, no. 3, pp. 340–346, 2010.

[16] K. Budka, J. Deshpande, J. Hobby et al., "Geri—bell labs smart grid research focus: economic modeling, networking, and security amp; privacy," in *Proceedings of the 1st IEEE International Conference on Smart Grid Communications (SmartGridComm '10)*, pp. 208–213, November 2010.

[17] A. Vaccaro, M. Popov, D. Villacci, and V. Terzija, "An integrated framework for smart microgrids modeling, monitoring, control, communication, and verification," *Proceedings of the IEEE*, vol. 99, no. 1, pp. 119–132, 2011.

[18] T. Zhang, W. Lin, Y. Wang et al., "The design of information security protection framework to support smart grid," in *Proceedings of the 2010 International Conference on Power System Technology (POWERCON '10)*, pp. 1–5, 2010.

[19] T. M. Overman and R.W. Sackman, "High assurance smart grid: smart grid control systems communications architecture," in *Proceedings of the 1st IEEE International Conference on Smart Grid Communications (SmartGridComm '10)*, pp. 19–24, November 2010.

[20] T. L. Lim and Y. Li, "A security and performance evaluation of hash-based rfid protocols," in *Proceedings of the 5th China International Conferences on Information Security and Cryptology (Inscrypt '09)*, vol. 5487 of *Lecture Notes in Computer Science*, pp. 406–424, 2009.

[21] A. L. Selvakumar and C. S. Ganadhas, "The evaluation report of sha-256 crypt analysis hash function," in *Proceedings of the International Conference on Communication Software and Networks (ICCSN '09)*, pp. 588–592, June 2009.

[22] B. Baldwin, A. Byrne, M. Hamilton et al., "FPGA implementations of SHA-3 candidates: cubehash, grostl, lane, shabal and spectral hash," in *Proceedings of the 12th Euromicro Conference on Digital System Design: Architectures, Methods and Tools, (DSD '09)*, pp. 783–790, Patras, Greece, August 2009.

[23] N. Sklavos and P. Kitsos, "Blake hash function family on fpga: from the fastest to the smallest," in *Proceedings of the 2010 IEEE Computer Society Annual Symposium on VLSI (ISVLSI '10)*, pp. 139–142, September 2010.

11

Gaussian Pulse-Based Two-Threshold Parallel Scaling Tone Reservation for PAPR Reduction of OFDM Signals

Lei Guan and Anding Zhu

School of Electrical, Electronic & Communications Engineering, University College Dublin, Dublin 4, Ireland

Correspondence should be addressed to Lei Guan, lei.guan@ucd.ie

Academic Editor: Stefania Colonnese

Tone Reservation (TR) is a technique proposed to combat the high Peak-to-Average Power Ratio (PAPR) problem of Orthogonal Frequency Division Multiplexing (OFDM) signals. However conventional TR suffers from high computational cost due to the difficulties in finding an effective cancellation signal in the time domain by using only a few tones in the frequency domain. It also suffers from a high cost of hardware implementation and long handling time delay issues due to the need to conduct multiple iterations to cancel multiple high signal peaks. In this paper, we propose an efficient approach, called *two-threshold parallel scaling*, for implementing a previously proposed Gaussian pulse-based Tone Reservation algorithm. Compared to conventional approaches, this technique significantly reduces the hardware implementation complexity and cost, while also reducing signal processing time delay by using just two iterations. Experimental results show that the proposed technique can effectively reduce the PAPR of OFDM signals with only a very small number of reserved tones and with limited usage of hardware resources. This technique is suitable for any OFDM-based communication systems, especially for Digital Video Broadcasting (DVB) systems employing large IFFT/FFT transforms.

1. Introduction

Orthogonal Frequency Division Multiplexing (OFDM) is one of the most popular modulation schemes employed in modern wireless communication systems, such as DVB (Digital Video Broadcasting), WiMAX (Worldwide Interoperability for Microwave Access), and LTE (Long Term Evolution). OFDM offers many advantages, including high spectral efficiency, supporting high data rates, and tolerance to multipath fading [1]. Unfortunately, OFDM signals often have a high Peak-to-Average Power Ratio (PAPR) due to the summation of many independent subcarrier-modulated signals with random phases. High peaks occur very rarely, but the power amplifier (PA) in the transmitter may be overdriven deep into saturation on these rare occurrences, which can result in very high instantaneous spectral regrowth that causes interferences to other users. To prevent such phenomena, the PA must be "backed-off" into its linear region from the saturation point by approximately the PAPR level of the input signal, which consequently leads to very low power efficiency of the transmitter.

PAPR reduction techniques are proposed to reduce the high peaks of the transmit signal to a satisfactory level before transmission, allowing the PA to be operated at a higher power level to achieve high power efficiency without introducing severe distortion. In past years, many PAPR reduction techniques for OFDM signals have been proposed, such as precoding [2], clipping and filtering [3], nonlinear companding [4, 5], Selective Mapping (SLM) [6, 7], and Partial Transmit Sequences (PTS) [8, 9]. As discussed in [10], an effective PAPR reduction technique should have a high capability of PAPR reduction while causing minimal distortion to the signal. Especially, significant out-of-band distortion should be avoided; otherwise extra compensation efforts must be made elsewhere to avoid violating spectrum mask specifications defined by standardization bodies. In the mean time, processing time of the algorithm must be short enough to avoid delaying the data transmission, and it must be simple and easy to implement in the system with low cost.

Tone Reservation (TR) is a technique whereby a small number of subcarriers (tones) are reserved in the frequency domain to create a signal in the time domain which can cancel the high peaks in the information-carrying signals at the OFDM transmitters. TR is one of the most efficient methods for reducing the PAPR without introducing any additional distortion to the original information data. It has been adopted in the new DVB standard [11]. This technique has been further developed since it was first proposed by Tellado in [12]. An active-set approach was proposed in [13] to find the optimum reserved cancellation signal. In [14], two efficient schemes were proposed for selecting an optimal reserved set to handle the secondary peaks problem, while in [15], a multistage TR was proposed to maximize the PAPR reduction performance without increasing the number of reserved tones. However, TR still suffers from a high computational cost due to the difficulties of generating effective cancellation signal in the time domain from only a small number of reserved tones in the frequency domain. Another critical problem is that, as discussed in [16], generally, current TR-based PAPR reduction techniques require more than 20 iterations before getting a satisfactory performance. Large number of iterations will introduce long handling delays, which should be avoided in the real time communication system.

Previously, we proposed an efficient technique in [17] by creating a Gaussian pulse-like cancellation signal that facilitates a simple procedure for reducing high peaks while minimizing the occurrence of secondary peaks. But only the basic concept of the approach was presented. The algorithm was just implemented in a software environment, for example, MATLAB, and important issues related to practical hardware implementation were not discussed. In this paper, we further develop this idea and propose an efficient technique, called two-threshold parallel scaling (TTPS), which can be employed to implement the Gaussian pulse-based Tone Reservation algorithm on digital hardware chips with very low cost. This algorithm is realized on a field programmable gate array (FPGA) board using the Xilinx Virtex-4 chip. Experimental results show that this approach can effectively reduce the PAPR of OFDM signals with significantly lower complexity and shorter handling delay compared to conventional approaches.

This paper is organized as follows. In Section 2, we briefly reintroduce the Tone Reservation technique based on Gaussian pulses proposed previously. The two-threshold parallel scaling based Tone Reservation algorithm for PAPR reduction of OFDM signals is presented in Section 3, and the FPGA hardware implementation of the algorithm is given in Section 4. The results and performance validations are shown in Section 5, with a conclusion in Section 6.

2. Gaussian Pulse-Based Tone Reservation

For an OFDM modulation with N subcarriers, a block of N symbols X_k ($k = 0, 1, 2, \ldots, N-1$) is transmitted in parallel, and the baseband signal in the discrete time domain can be written as

$$x_n = \frac{1}{\sqrt{N}} \sum_{k=0}^{N-1} X_k e^{(2\pi j/N)kn}, \quad n = 0, \ldots, N-1. \quad (1)$$

The transmitted sequence x_n can be generated by the Inverse Fast Fourier Transform (IFFT) at the transmitter and restored by Fast Fourier Transform (FFT) at the receiver as follows:

$$x_n = \text{IFFT}(X_k), \qquad X_k = \text{FFT}(x_n). \quad (2)$$

The Peak-to-Average Power Ratio of the transmitted signal can be expressed as

$$\text{PAPR}(x) = 10 \log_{10} \left(\frac{\max |x_n|^2}{E\left[|x_n|^2\right]} \right), \quad (3)$$

where $|x_n|$ returns the magnitude of x_n, and $E[\bullet]$ represents the expectation operation.

The basic idea of Tone Reservation is that a small number of subcarriers are reserved in the frequency domain for generating a signal in the time domain that cancels the high peaks of information-carrying signals. In such a system, the data-bearing vector $\mathbf{X}$ and the reserved tones vector $\mathbf{C}$ in the frequency domain lie in disjoint frequency subspaces, namely, they cannot both have nonzero values at a given tone, which can be expressed as

$$X_k + C_k = \begin{cases} C_k, & k \in L, \\ X_k, & k \in L^c, \end{cases} \quad (4)$$

where L denotes the subset of reserved tones, and $L \ll N$, N represents the set of all tones in the data frame, that is, the size of the IFFT/FFT. L^c is the complement set of L in N and represents the set of information tones. C_k is the cancellation signal in the frequency domain, and its counterpart signal c_n in the time domain can be obtained through an IFFT. If the transmit sample x_n exceeds the desired clipping threshold, a c_n will be added to the information signal, which produces a new composite signal

$$\overline{x}_n = x_n + c_n = \text{IFFT}(X_k + C_k). \quad (5)$$

Consequently, the new PAPR becomes

$$\text{PAPR}(x) = 10 \log_{10} \left(\frac{\max |x_n + c_n|^2}{E\left[|x_n|^2\right]} \right), \quad (6)$$

where the PAPR can be reduced by optimizing c_n so that $\max |x_n + c_n|^2$ can be smaller than $\max|x_n|^2$.

Since the subcarriers are orthogonal to each other and symbol demodulation is performed in the frequency domain on a tone-by-tone basis, the reserved subcarriers can be discarded at the receiver, and only the data-bearing subchannels are used to determine the transmitted bit stream. This approach can effectively reduce the PAPR of OFDM signals without introducing any additional distortion to the information data. However, TR suffers a high computational cost due to the difficulties of finding an effective cancellation signal. This is because the cancellation signal must be generated in the frequency domain using the minimum number of tones to maximize data throughout.

At the same time, it is preferable also to have a narrow pulse in the time domain to prevent the generation of secondary peaks. Unfortunately, these two requirements conflict with each other. In conventional TR approaches, the cancellation signal is mainly generated from either trial-and-error processes [12] or its generation involves complex optimization procedures [13].

In order to simplify the procedures of generating the cancellation signal, in our previous work [16], a truncated Gaussian pulse-based approach was proposed. Because the Gaussian pulse has the unique property that it is the signal which is its own Fourier transform, it can be simultaneously optimized in both the time domain and the frequency domain. In the time domain, a Gaussian pulse is often defined as

$$g_\sigma(t) = e^{-t^2/2\sigma^2}, \qquad (7)$$

where σ represents the pulse width. The Fourier transform of (7) is

$$G_\sigma(\omega) = \sqrt{2\pi}\sigma e^{-\sigma^2\omega^2/2}. \qquad (8)$$

In the discrete time domain, the pair of the Gaussian pulse and its FFT can be expressed as

$$e^{j\cdot(2\pi/N)\cdot(1/2)n^2} \longleftrightarrow e^{-j\cdot(2\pi/N)\cdot(1/2)k^2}, \qquad (9)$$

where $n \in [0, N-1]$ is the time index, and $k \in [0, K-1]$ is the frequency index for the FFT length. As is clear from (9), the FFT of this particular sampled Gaussian pulse in the time domain is exactly a sampled Gaussian pulse in the frequency domain.

In Tone Reservation, in order to avoid affecting data carriers, we use a truncated Gaussian pulse in the frequency domain, in which only the reserved tones have nonzero values. This is achieved by approximating a Gaussian pulse using a discrete window function, whose coefficients can be calculated as follows:

$$G_{[m+1]} = e^{-(1/2)(\alpha(m-(L/2))/(L/2))^2}, \quad \text{where } 0 < m < L-1, \qquad (10)$$

where α represents the reciprocal of the standard deviation, and the width of the window is inversely related to α. This equation describes the amplitude of the Gaussian pulse, and the phase is set to zero. The value L represents the number of tones reserved, typically, $L = 16$ or 32. Zeros are then padded to the coefficients to form a data frame with the same size of IFFT/FFT as that used in the system. According to the properties of the FFT, a narrow pulse with low side lobes can be generated in the time domain with the IFFT operation, as shown in Figure 1. Compared to other types of cancellation signals, the advantage of this Gaussian pulse-based cancellation signal is that it appears as a narrow pulse in both the time domain and the frequency domain. Consequently, only a very small number of tones are required to be reserved in the TR techniques employing this cancellation signal, which increases the spectrum usage of TRs.

3. Two-Threshold Parallel Scaling Tone Reservation

In an OFDM system, signal samples are processed by IFFT/FFT on a frame-by-frame basis, and thus PAPR reduction is also conducted frame by frame. A predefined Gaussian pulse-based cancellation signal with a fixed FFT size can be generated in advance. For instance, if a size of 1024 is used in the FFT and 16 tones are reserved, this cancellation signal will only have nonzero values in the 16 reserved tone locations in the frequency domain and the rest of the tones are zero. After IFFT, this signal has one sharp peak with small ripples spreading over the frame in the time domain. If there are peaks exceeding the required threshold in the information-carrying signal, the magnitude of the peaks and their corresponding location are detected. The peak of the predefined cancellation signal can be circularly shifted to the peak location and scaled by the value of the difference between the peak and the threshold and then subtracted from the original information signal, so that the power of the peak tones can be reduced to the desired target level. As shown in Figure 2, this process can be conducted in several iterations, starting from the highest peak and canceling one peak per iteration. This iterative single-peak cancellation approach causes significant time delay if multiple peaks need to be canceled, which may not be feasible in real time communications.

This Gaussian pulse-based Tone Reservation process can be conducted fully in the time domain, with only circular shift and amplitude scaling operations involved. The circular shift operation in the time domain does not affect the data tones in the frequency domain. For instance, we assume the predefined Gaussian pulse is p_n, and it is scaled by μ_i and circular shifted by $(n - n_i)$ to form the cancellation signal c^i at the ith iteration as

$$c_n^i = -\mu_i p_{[(n-n_i)_N]}. \qquad (11)$$

Its frequency domain representation can be obtained from

$$C_k^i = \text{FFT}(c_n^i) = \text{FFT}(-\mu_i p_{[(n-n_i)_N]}). \qquad (12)$$

Applying the linear circular shift property of the FFT operation, we obtain

$$C_k^i = -\mu_i \cdot \text{FFT}(p_{[(n-n_i)_N]}) = (-\mu_i) \cdot C_k \cdot e^{-(2\pi j/N)kn_i}, \qquad (13)$$

where

$$C_k = \text{FFT}(p_n). \qquad (14)$$

We can see that C_k^i also only has nonzero values in the same reserved tones as those of C_k. This means that the peak cancellation operations at each iteration are independent from each other, and thus multiple cancellation signals can be generated in parallel in the time domain and summed together to compose the final cancellation signal. The total cancellation signal can be expressed as

$$c_{\text{total}} = \sum_{i=1}^{M} c_n^i. \qquad (15)$$

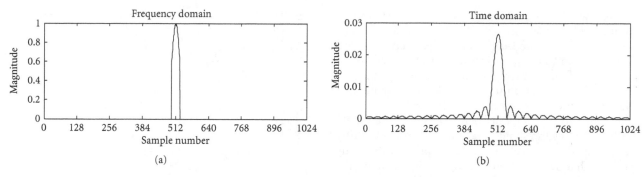

FIGURE 1: A truncated Gaussian pulse in the frequency domain and its corresponding waveform in the time domain.

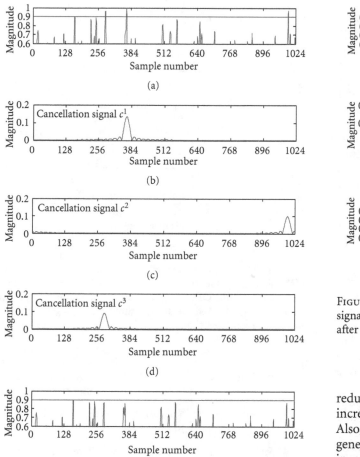

FIGURE 2: Multiple iterations cancellation process: (a) the original OFDM signal with threshold shown in solid line; (b) the cancellation signal generated during the 1st iteration; (c) the cancellation signal generated during the 2nd iteration; (d) the cancellation signal generated during the 3rd iteration; (e) the OFDM signal after PAPR reduction with 3 iterations.

For example, the three peak cancellation signals in Figure 2 can be added together to make one cancellation signal in Figure 3.

By applying this parallel process, multiple peaks can be simultaneously cancelled, and thus time delay can be

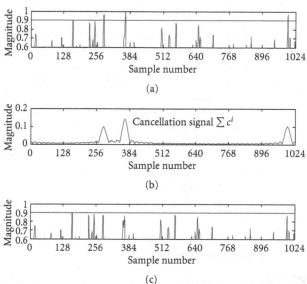

FIGURE 3: Parallel cancellation process: (a) the original OFDM signal; (b) the composite cancellation signal; (c) the OFDM signal after PAPR reduction.

reduced. However, the system complexity and cost are increased since multiple cancellation branches are required. Also, in a real system, since the transmit data is randomly generated, the numbers of peaks exceeding the threshold in each data frame vary, so that some frames will have more peaks than others if only one fixed threshold is used for peak detection. In order to reduce cost, only a limited number of parallel branches can be employed in a real system. For the data frames where the number of peaks exceeds the number of available branches, peak sorting algorithms must be applied to pick out the top B peaks for cancellation, where B indicates the maximum number of available branches. Implementation of the sorting algorithm can be costly because comparisons have to be made among peaks and each comparison result between two peaks should be recorded until the top B peaks have been successfully sifted out. Furthermore, only cancelling a limited small number of peaks in each data frame cannot guarantee a reduction in PAPR sufficient to satisfy system requirements.

To cope with these problems, in this work, we propose a *two-threshold parallel scaling* (TTPS) approach with two iterations, which is a good compromise between serial and parallel operations. Firstly, we introduce two thresholds for peak detection: one with higher magnitude, A_H and the other one with lower magnitude, A_L. We then conduct the parallel cancellation in two iterations. In the first iteration, we detect the rare and high peaks using the high threshold A_H but use the low threshold A_L as the reference for setting the scaling factor to cancel the peaks. In other words, only the peaks with a magnitude above A_H are detected, but the magnitudes of these peaks are reduced to the level of A_L after peak cancellation. In the second iteration, the low threshold A_L is used for both peak detection and peak cancellation. An example of the time domain process is shown in Figure 4, where the high threshold A_H is illustrated by a broken line while the low threshold A_L is shown in a solid line. Clearly, more peaks are detected above A_L than those above A_H. However, because we scale the cancellation signal to cancel the high peaks above A_H to the level of A_L during the first iteration, these high peaks are no longer valid in the second iteration. This avoids repeating cancellation of high peaks and reduces the burden of the second iteration. After two iterations, almost all of the peaks above the low threshold can be cancelled. The block diagram of this approach is given in Figure 5. Compared to the single threshold approach, this two-threshold parallel scaling approach can effectively cancel almost twice the number of peaks with two iterations using the same hardware resource.

4. FPGA Implementation

The field programmable gate array (FPGA) has many advantages in digital signal processing, including high density integration, parallel operation mechanisms, high speed processing, and flexible implementation. It has become one of the main choices for implementing PAPR reduction algorithms in real systems [18, 19]. In this section, we illustrate how to implement the proposed TTPS-based Tone Reservation algorithm on FPGA chips.

The high-level hardware implementation architecture is shown in Figure 6. The original OFDM signal is represented in complex form with real and imaginary parts, each of which is converted to the digital domain with 16-bit wide input registers. The most significant bit of those 16 bits is the sign bit while the others are used to quantitatively represent the value of the real and imaginary parts. The details of each block are given as follows:

(1) *Input Magnitude and Phase Calculation*. The coordinate rotation digital computer (CORDIC) algorithm [20] is used to calculate the magnitude x_{mag} and the phase c_{pshift} of the complex input I/Q OFDM signal. The phase information is represented in the form of $\sin(\theta)$ and $\cos(\theta)$ equations.

(2) *Threshold Registers*. Two thresholds are preset in this unit. Since the OFDM signal is represented in complex form with signed 16-bit registers and its

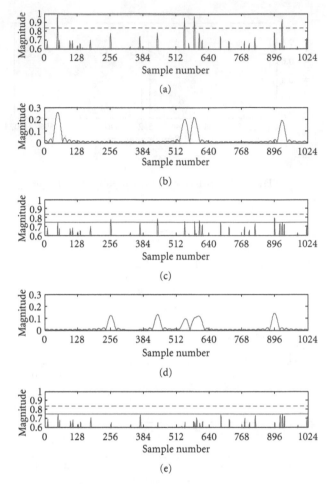

FIGURE 4: The proposed cancellation process: (a) the original OFDM signal; (b) the 1st cancellation signal based on the high threshold A_H; (c) the OFDM signal after first iteration; (d) the 2nd cancellation signal based on the low threshold A_L; (e) the OFDM signal after second iterations.

magnitude cannot exceed $2^{16} = 65536$, one unsigned 16-bit register is adequate to represent the threshold.

(3) *Signal Clipping*. This unit is used to clip the input signal if its magnitude exceeds the threshold.

(4) *Peak Detection*. The detection and recording of the magnitudes of the valid peaks are implemented in this unit. In addition, the location information of the peaks is generated, appearing as the sample index of each data frame. The output signals of this unit are defined as follows: p_{valid} is a 1-bit register which will be set to 1 for one cycle only when a valid high peak is detected; p_{locat} is a N-bit register to represent the location information; p_{mag} represents the delta magnitude of a peak above the threshold. The peak detection process is shown in Figure 7.

(5) *RAM-Based Peak Information Storage*. This unit is used to record the information of the first B peaks of each current data frame. Three parameters, magnitude, phase, and location, are stored in two 32-bit

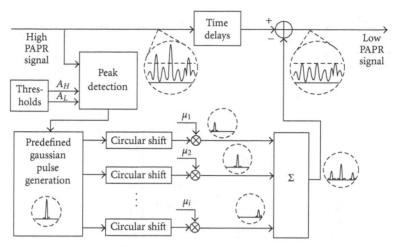

FIGURE 5: Block diagram of the proposed TTPSTR algorithm.

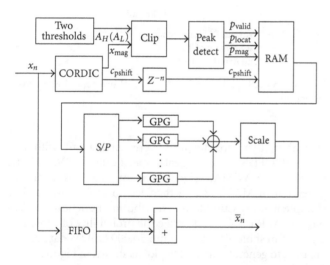

FIGURE 6: High-level FPGA implementation of the proposed approach.

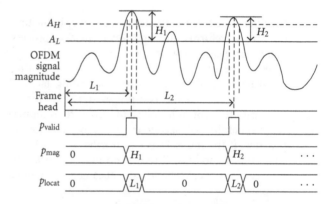

FIGURE 7: Peak detection process: L_k, $k = 1, 2, \ldots, B$ represents the location information of the ith peak, while H_k, $k = 1, 2, \ldots, B$ gives the delta magnitude of the peak referring to the threshold.

RAMs for each peak. The magnitudes and locations are stored in the most significant 16 bits and the least significant 16 bits of the first RAM, respectively. Similarly the phase information $\sin(\theta)$ and $\cos(\theta)$ are stored in the most and the least significant 16 bits of the second part of RAM, respectively.

(6) *Serial-to-Parallel Operation (S/P).* This unit provides the possibility to cancel multiple peaks per iteration. Three serial sequences, with the magnitude, location, and phase information of the valid peaks, are converted to B parallel-structure-based sequences. For each parallel sequence, one cancelation signal will be assigned by the *Gaussian Pulse Generation* unit below. The serial-to-parallel conversion and parallel cancellation signals generation process are shown in Figure 8.

(7) *Gaussian Pulse Generation (GPG).* The original Gaussian pulse signal is pregenerated in MATLAB and prestored in one 32-bit wide ROM on board, the

most and the least significant 16 bits of which are assigned to represent the real part and imaginary part, respectively. The kth cancelation signal $c^{i,k}$ at ith iteration is defined as follow:

$$c_n^{i,k} = p_{\mathrm{mag}} \cdot c_{\mathrm{pshift}} \cdot p_{[(n-n_{i,k})_N]}, \tag{16}$$

where $p_{\mathrm{mag}} = x_{\mathrm{mag}} - A_L$ is the magnitude amount exceeding the threshold A_L, and $c_{\mathrm{pshift}} = \cos(\theta) + j \cdot \sin(\theta)$ represents the phase information. The scaling factor is $-\mu_{i,k} = p_{\mathrm{mag}} \cdot c_{\mathrm{pshift}}$, and $p_{[\cdot]}$ is the circular shift term of the original cancellation pulse p_n. In order to make the implementation more efficient, the circular shift operation was carried out as an initial-address-variable-RAM read operation. Based on the peak location information L_i, the initial value of the address for circular shift operation can be easily generated.

(8) *Scaling and Summation of Cancellation Signals.* Once all of the B parallel cancellation signals have been assigned, the final cancellation signal can be straightforwardly obtained by summing them all

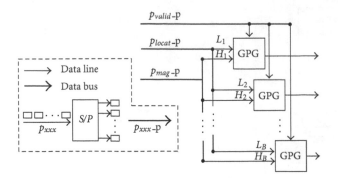

FIGURE 8: Serial-to-Parallel conversion (within the dashed line block) and parallel cancellation signals generation process. The symbol p_{xxx} represents the signal p_{valid}, p_{locat}, and p_{mag}, while p_{xxx}-p presents the corresponding parallel signals; L_i is the initial value of an address generator for circular shift operation, while H_i is used to scale the normalized cancellation unit.

together. Due to the existence of side lobes in the time domain waveforms, during the summation process, secondary peaks may be generated when two target peaks to be cancelled are very close to each other. In order to avoid this occuring, a scaling factor λ can be applied to the composite signal to reduce the amplitude of side lobes in order to minimize the probability of secondary peak occurrence. In practice, if the highest peak is normalized to 1, $\lambda = 0.7$ shows a good PAPR reduction performance. The final composite cancellation signal can be represented as follows:

$$\tilde{c}_n^i = \lambda \sum_{k=1}^{B} c_n^{i,k}, \qquad (17)$$

where λ represents the scaling factor, and B is the limit of the maximum number of peaks that can be cancelled in each iteration. Selection of the value of B involves a compromise: larger B values produce higher performance but introduce a higher implementation cost.

(9) *FIFO-Based Delay Unit.* Proper time alignment should be employed before subtracting the peaks from the original signal. Since there is no sorting algorithm or a large number of iterations, the handling time of the peak cancellation process is fixed.

(10) *Peak Cancellation (Subtracter):* In this unit, the peak cancellation signal is subtracted from the time-aligned complex input I/Q signal to form an output OFDM signal with a low PAPR.

The implementation cost and performance will be evaluated in the following section.

5. Results and Performance Evaluation

5.1. PAPR Reduction Performance Evaluation. In order to evaluate the performance of TTPS-based Tone Reservation

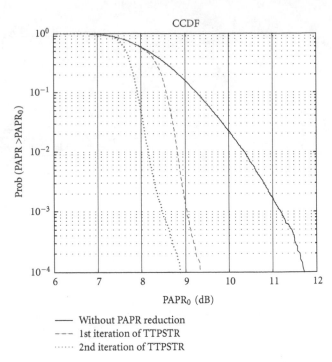

— Without PAPR reduction
--- 1st iteration of TTPSTR
····· 2nd iteration of TTPSTR

FIGURE 9: CCDF plots of a WiMAX signal before and after PAPR reduction.

algorithm, two separate tests were carried out with two different OFDM-based signals, specifically a DVB-T2 4K signal and a WiMAX signal. The original test data was generated in MATLAB and then fed to the hardware. The Complementary Cumulative Distribution Function (CCDF) plot of PAPR is used to describe the probability of exceeding a given threshold $PAPR_0$. Around 50,000 OFDM data blocks are used to generate the CCDF plot as shown in Figures 9 and 10.

For the WiMAX signal with 64-QAM, the IFFT/FFT size was 1024, where 16 tones were reserved to generate the Gaussian pulse-based cancellation signal. The CCDF plots before and after PAPR reduction by using the proposed TTPS-TR algorithm are shown in Figure 9. The original PAPR is around 11.8 dB at 0.01%(1e-4) probability. After the first iteration, the PAPR is reduced to 9.3 dB and further reduced to 8.9 dB after the second iteration. The total PAPR reduction is around 3 dB after two iterations using the proposed TTPS-TR approach. In the second test, a DVB-T2 4k signal with 16-QAM was generated, and this signal contained 4096 tones, 32 of them were reserved for PAPR reduction. The CCDF plots of this signal are shown in Figure 10. Again, more than 2 dB improvement can be achieved at the 0.01% probability level with only two iterations.

By employing Gaussian pulses, only a very small proportion of the tones needs to be reserved in the frequency domain to generate a sharp peak cancellation signal in the time domain, which significantly reduces the spectrum resource usage caused by Tone Reservation. For example, in the WiMAX test above, only 16 of 1024 tones, 1.56%, are reserved, while for the DVB-T2 signal, 32 of 4096 tones,

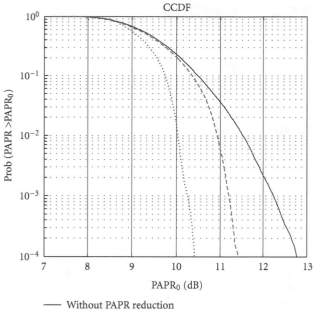

FIGURE 10: CCDF plots of a DVB-T2 signal before and after PAPR reduction.

TABLE 1: The key parameter settings in TTPS-TR.

	Settings (WiMAX)	Settings (DVB-T2)	Comments
A_H	0.72	0.74	High threshold
A_L	0.66	0	Low threshold
B	6	6	Number of cancellation branches
λ	0.7	0.6	Scaling factor

Note: the peak amplitude of the signal is normalized to 1.

TABLE 2: FPGA resource utilization.

	Usage[1]	Total	Percentage[2]
DSP48s	36	192	18%
Slice flip flops	2601	30720	8%
Slices	1950	15360	12%
4-input LUTs	3208	30720	10%
RAMB16s	20	192	10%

[1] Based on Table 1 settings for TTPS-TR.
[2] Based on Xilinx Virtex-4 XC4VSX35 chip.

0.78%, were occupied by TR. Furthermore, by employing Gaussian pulses, the number of reserved tones does not proportionally increase with the FFT size since the time domain cancellation signal can be optimized with a predecided small number of tones in the frequency domain. This means that the proposed technique will produce more benefits in a system employing a larger size of IFFT/FFT, such as the DVB-T2 system, where 4K, 8K, 16K, and 32K IFFT/FFT transforms are used [11].

One fact should be pointed out that the performance of our proposed TTPS TR largely depends on the number of parallel branches within each iteration process. This must be a compromise between the implementation cost and the PAPR reduction performance. Generally, the larger the number of parallel branches used, the better the PAPR performance achieved but a greater implementation cost will be required.

5.2. Implementation Cost Assessment. As an example, the proposed approach was implemented on a Xilinx Virtex-4 XC4VSX35 FPGA chip with the Xtreme DSP development Kit. The top module of the implementation is shown in Figure 11, while the parameter settings and the hardware resource utilization are given in Tables 1 and 2, respectively.

As indicated in Table 1, in our test, six cancellation branches were employed. Since one complex multiplier can be realized with four real multipliers, the number of hardware multipliers used is $4 \times 6 = 24$, and considering the scalar scaling operation, another 2 real multipliers are required for each branch. The total number of the multipliers used is $24 + 2 \times 6 = 36$. This number is compared to the number of DSP48s needed in the FPGA in Table 2. Because the multiplier is one of the most complex and expensive components in FPGA hardware, the number of multiplier resources used is the main hardware cost of the implementation. Overall, the proposed algorithm only occupies a small percentage of the Virtex-4 chip, shown in Table 2.

In this work, we only illustrate how to implement the proposed Gaussian pulse-based Tone Reservation algorithm using two-threshold parallel scaling on FPGA chips, but the proposed technique is not solely limited to FPGAs. The same structure can also be readily implemented in other types of digital circuits, for example, general digital signal processing (DSP) chips or application-specific integrated circuits (ASICs).

6. Conclusions

In this paper, we propose an efficient two-threshold parallel scaling approach for implementing the Gaussian pulse-based Tone Reservation algorithm on digital hardware for reducing the peak-to-average power ratio of OFDM signals. The proposed technique was implemented on a Xilinx Virtex-4 series FPGA chip and tested with WiMAX and DVB signals. Experimental results demonstrated that the PAPR of OFDM signals can be effectively reduced with only a small number of tones reserved and with just two iterations. By employing the proposed technique, this Gaussian pulse-based cancellation signal can be generated in advance and stored in memory. The full PAPR reduction process can be conducted in the time domain using simple circular shift and magnitude scaling, which significantly reduces the implementation complexity of the Tone Reservation technique.

The proposed technique can be easily integrated into any OFDM-based wireless transmitters and is especially

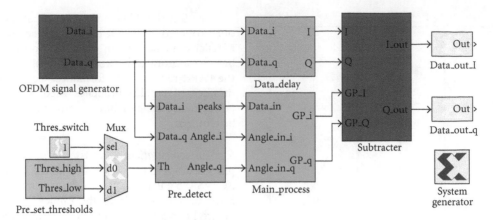

FIGURE 11: The top module of FPGA implementation.

useful for Digital Video Broadcasting systems where Tone Reservation is written in the standards and large IFFT/FFT transforms are employed. By using the proposed PAPR reduction technique, the number of high peaks in OFDM signals can be dramatically decreased, and thus Bit-Error Rate (BER) and the level of out-of-band spectral leakage caused by nonlinearity of RF power amplifiers can be significantly reduced.

Acknowledgment

This work was supported by the Science Foundation Ireland under the Principal Investigator Award at the University College Dublin, Dublin, Ireland.

References

[1] R. Prasad, *OFDM for Wireless Communications Systems*, Artech House, Boston, Mass, USA, 2004.

[2] M. J. Hao and C. H. Lai, "Precoding for PAPR reduction of OFDM signals with minimum error probability," *IEEE Transactions on Broadcasting*, vol. 56, no. 1, pp. 120–128, 2010.

[3] X. Li and L. J. Cimini Jr., "Effects of clipping and filtering on the performance of OFDM," *IEEE Communications Letters*, vol. 2, no. 5, pp. 131–133, 1998.

[4] T. Jiang and G. Zhu, "Nonlinear companding transform for reducing peak-to-average power ratio of OFDM signals," *IEEE Transactions on Broadcasting*, vol. 50, no. 3, pp. 342–346, 2004.

[5] J. Hou, J. Ge, D. Zhai, and J. Li, "Peak-to-average power ratio reduction of OFDM signals with nonlinear companding scheme," *IEEE Transactions on Broadcasting*, vol. 56, no. 2, pp. 258–262, 2010.

[6] R. W. Bäuml, R. F. H. Fischer, and J. B. Huber, "Reducing the peak-to-average power ratio of multicarrier modulation by selected mapping," *Electronics Letters*, vol. 32, no. 22, pp. 2056–2057, 1996.

[7] H. B. Jeon, K. H. Kim, J. S. No, and D. J. Shin, "Bit-based SLM schemes for PAPR reduction in QAM modulated OFDM signals," *IEEE Transactions on Broadcasting*, vol. 55, no. 3, pp. 679–685, 2009.

[8] S. H. Müller and J. B. Huber, "OFDM with reduced peak-to-average power ratio by optimum combination of partial transmit sequences," *Electronics Letters*, vol. 33, no. 5, pp. 368–369, 1997.

[9] J. C. Chen, "Application of quantum-inspired evolutionary algorithm to reduce PAPR of an OFDM signal using partial transmit sequences technique," *IEEE Transactions on Broadcasting*, vol. 56, no. 1, pp. 110–113, 2010.

[10] T. Jiang and Y. Wu, "An overview: peak-to-average power ratio reduction techniques for OFDM signals," *IEEE Transactions on Broadcasting*, vol. 54, no. 2, pp. 257–268, 2008.

[11] European Standard, ETSI EN 302 755 V1.1.1, "Frame structure channel coding and modulation for a second generation digital terrestrial television broadcasting system (DVB-T2)," September 2009.

[12] J. Tellado, *Peak-to-average power reduction for multi-carrier modulation*, Ph.D. thesis, Stanford University, September 1999.

[13] B. S. Krongold and D. L. Jones, "An active-set approach for OFDM PAR reduction via tone reservation," *IEEE Transactions on Signal Processing*, vol. 52, no. 2, pp. 495–509, 2004.

[14] D. W. Lim, H. S. Noh, J. S. No, and D. J. Shin, "Near optimal PRT set selection algorithm for tone reservation in OFDM systems," *IEEE Transactions on Broadcasting*, vol. 54, no. 3, pp. 454–460, 2008.

[15] D. W. Lim, H. S. Noh, H. B. Jeon, J. S. No, and D. J. Shin, "Multi-Stage TR Scheme for PAPR Reduction in OFDM Signals," *IEEE Transactions on Broadcasting*, vol. 55, no. 2, pp. 300–304, 2009.

[16] M. Mroué, A. Nafkha, J. Palicot, B. Gavalda, and N. Dagorne, "Performance and implementation evaluation of TR PAPR reduction methods for DVB-T2," *International Journal of Digital Multimedia Broadcasting*, vol. 2010, Article ID 797393, 10 pages, 2010.

[17] C. A. Devlin, Z. Anding, and T. J. Brazil, "Gaussian pulse based tone reservation for reducing PAPR of OFDM signals," in *Proceedings of the 65th IEEE Vehicular Technology Conference (VTC '07)*, pp. 3096–3100, Dublin, Ireland, April 2007.

[18] C. Dick and H. Tarn, "FPGA realization of peak-to-average power ratio reduction techniques for OFDM wireless systems," in *Proceedings of the 41st Asilomar Conference on Signals, Systems and Computers (ACSSC '07)*, pp. 1969–1975, Pacific Grove, Calif, USA, 2007.

[19] "Crest Factor Reduction for OFDMA Systems," Application Note 475, Altera Corporation Inc., San Jose, Calif, USA, November 2007.

[20] YU. H. Hu, "CORDIC-based VLSI architectures for digital signal processing," *IEEE Signal Processing Magazine*, vol. 9, no. 3, pp. 16–35, 1992.

12

Cognitive Radio for Smart Grid: Theory, Algorithms, and Security

Raghuram Ranganathan,[1,2] Robert Qiu,[1,2] Zhen Hu,[1,2] Shujie Hou,[1,2]
Marbin Pazos-Revilla,[1,2] Gang Zheng,[1,2] Zhe Chen,[1,2] and Nan Guo[1,2]

[1] Department of Electrical and Computer Engineering, Center for Manufacturing Research,
Tennessee Technological University, Cookeville, TN 38505, USA
[2] Cognitive Radio Institute, Tennessee Technological University, Cookeville, TN 38505, USA

Correspondence should be addressed to Raghuram Ranganathan, raghu_ucf@yahoo.com

Academic Editor: Chi Zhou

Recently, cognitive radio and smart grid are two areas which have received considerable research impetus. Cognitive radios are intelligent software defined radios (SDRs) that efficiently utilize the unused regions of the spectrum, to achieve higher data rates. The smart grid is an automated electric power system that monitors and controls grid activities. In this paper, the novel concept of incorporating a cognitive radio network as the communications infrastructure for the smart grid is presented. A brief overview of the cognitive radio, IEEE 802.22 standard and smart grid, is provided. Experimental results obtained by using dimensionality reduction techniques such as principal component analysis (PCA), kernel PCA, and landmark maximum variance unfolding (LMVU) on Wi-Fi signal measurements are presented in a spectrum sensing context. Furthermore, compressed sensing algorithms such as Bayesian compressed sensing and the compressed sensing Kalman filter is employed for recovering the sparse smart meter transmissions. From the power system point of view, a supervised learning method called support vector machine (SVM) is used for the automated classification of power system disturbances. The impending problem of securing the smart grid is also addressed, in addition to the possibility of applying FPGA-based fuzzy logic intrusion detection for the smart grid.

1. Introduction

1.1. Cognitive Radio.
Cognitive radio (CR) is an intelligent software defined radio (SDR) technology that facilitates efficient, reliable, and dynamic use of the underused radio spectrum by reconfiguring its operating parameters and functionalities in real time depending on the radio environment. Cognitive radio networks promise to resolve the bandwidth scarcity problem by allowing unlicensed devices to transmit in unused "spectrum holes" in licensed bands without causing harmful interference to authorized users [1–4]. In concept, the cognitive technology configures the radio for different combinations of protocol, operating frequency, and waveform. Current research on cognitive radio covers a wide range of areas; including spectrum sensing, channel estimation, spectrum sharing, and medium access control (MAC).

Due to its versatility, CR networks are expected to be increasingly deployed in both the commercial and military sectors for dynamic spectrum management. In order to develop a standard for CRs, the IEEE 802.22 working group was formed in November 2004 [5]. The corresponding IEEE 802.22 standard defines the physical (PHY) and medium access control (MAC) layers for a wireless regional area network (WRAN) that uses white spaces within the television bands between 54 and 862 MHz, especially within rural areas where usage may be lower. Details of the IEEE 802.22 standard including system topology, system capacity, and the projected coverage for the system are given in the next section.

1.2. The 802.22 System.
The IEEE 802.22 is the first standardized air interface for CR networks based on opportunistic utilization of the TV broadcast spectrum [6, 7]. The main objective of the IEEE 802.22 standard is to provide broadband connectivity to remote areas with comparable performance to broadband technologies such as cable and

DSL, in urban areas. In this regard, the FCC selected the predominantly unoccupied TV station channels operating in the VHF and UHF region of the radio spectrum.

1.2.1. System Topology. The 802.22 system is a point-to-multipoint wireless air interface consisting of a base station (BS) that manages a cell comprised of number of users or customer premises equipments (CPEs) [8]. The BS controls the medium access and "cognitive functions" in its cell and transmits data to the CPEs in the downlink, while receiving data in the uplink direction from the CPEs. The various CPEs perform distributed sensing of the signal power in the various channels of the TV band. In this manner, the BS collects the different measurements from the CPEs and exploits the spatial diversity of the CPEs to make a decision if any portion of the spectrum is available.

1.2.2. Service Coverage. Compared to other IEEE 802 standards such as 802.11, the 802.22 BS coverage range can reach up to 100 KM, if not limited by power constraints. The coverage of different wireless standards is shown in Figure 1. The WRAN has the highest coverage due to higher transmit power and long-range propagation characteristics of TV bands.

1.2.3. System Capacity. The WRAN systems can achieve comparable performance to that of DSL, with downlink speeds of 1.5 Mbps and uplink speed of 384 Kbps. The system would thus be able to support 12 simultaneous CPEs, resulting in an overall system download capacity of 18 Mbps.

The specification parameters of the IEEE 802.22 standard is summarized in Table 1.

1.3. Smart Grid. Smart grid explores and exploits two-way communication technology, advanced sensing, metering and measurement technology, modern control theory, network grid technology, and machine learning in the power system to make the power network stable, secure, efficient, flexible, economical, and environmentally friendly.

Novel control technology, information technology, and management technology should be effectively integrated to realize the smart information exchange within the power system from power generation, power transmission, power transformation, power distribution, power scheduling to power utilization. The goal of smart grid is to systematically optimize the cycle of power generation and utilization.

Based on open-system architecture and shared information mode, power flow, information flow, and transaction flow can be synchronized. In this way, the operation performance of power enterprises can be increased. From power customer's perspective, demand response should be implemented. Customers would like to participate in more activities in the power system and power market to reduce their electric bills.

Distributed energy resources, for example, solar energy, wind energy, and so on, should also play an important role in the smart grid. Versatile distributed energy resources can perform the peak power shaving and increase the

TABLE 1: IEEE 802.22 characteristics.

Parameter	Specification
Typical cell radius (km)	30–100 km
Methodology	Spectrum sensing to identify free channels
Channel bandwidth (MHz)	6, (7, 8)
Modulation	OFDM
Channel capacity	18 Mbps
User capacity	Downlink: 1.5 Mbps Uplink: 384 kbps

stability of the power system. However, distributed energy generation imposes new challenges on the power system. Power system planning, power quality issue, and so on should be reconsidered.

To support the smart grid, a dedicated two-way communications infrastructure should be set up for the power system. In this way, secure, reliable, and efficient communication and information exchange can be guaranteed. In addition, the various devices, equipments, and power generation facilities of the current power system should be updated and renovated. Novel technologies for power electronics should be used to build advanced power devices, for example, transformer, relay, switch, storage, and so on.

To incorporate the smart features into the power system, computationally intelligent techniques, that is, machine learning and dimensionality reduction, should be widely applied. Machine learning is a scientific discipline that is concerned with the design of algorithms for computers to imitate the behavior of human beings, which includes learning to recognize complex patterns and make decisions based on experience, automatically and intelligently. Dimensionality reduction is the process of reducing the number of random variables under consideration to control the degrees of freedom. Several areas for applying computationally intelligent techniques to the smart grid have been identified in [9]. These areas are smart sensing and metering, autonomous control, adaptive protection, advanced data management and visualization, intelligent interfaces with distributed resources and market, decision support systems for system operation, and planning. The concept of compressing electrical power grids using the singular value decomposition (SVD) analysis is proposed in [10] to reduce the network traffic. The main idea is to determine what parts of the system are more strongly coupled from the grid admittance matrix [10].

In the smart grid, there will be more than one element, agent, controller, or decision maker. The control algorithm for the system with a single agent cannot be well suited for the distributed control or noncooperative control. From the multiagent control issue perspective, Game theory gives a general control methodology to deal with interaction, competition, and cooperation among decision makers in the complex system. Game theory is widely used in social sciences, economics, engineering, and so on. For the smart grid, the energy consumption scheduling issue has been

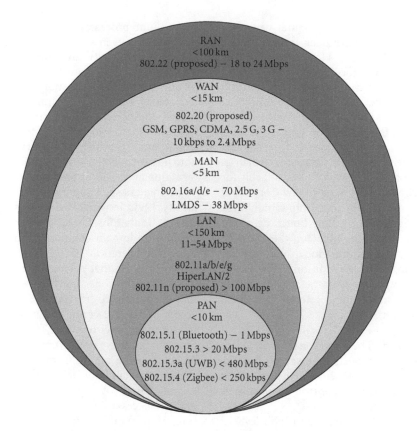

FIGURE 1: Comparison of 802.22 with other wireless standards.

formulated as a game theory problem [11]. The aim of scheduling is to reduce the total energy cost as well as PAR in the load demand [11]. Based on the assumption that the charge for each subscriber is proportional to his/her total daily load, the energy consumption game can be solved distributively with minimum exchanging information [11]. Meanwhile, the unique Nash equilibrium of the energy consumption game is the optimal solution to the central scheduling problem [11]. The work in [11] has been extended by [12]. Different control strategies based on the degree of information sharing in the network have been studied [12]. Partial knowledge setting and blind setting are considered. The proposed distributed stochastic energy consumption scheduling algorithms can still successfully exploit the limited information to improve the overall load profile [12]. In the context of the electrical power system, auction theory is a popular approach to deal with the power control issue from an economic point of view. Auction theory is a kind of game theory that deals with the behavior of agents in auction markets. Operation of a multiagent system for microgrid control has been presented in [13]. Auction theory has been exploited as the foundation of the proposed algorithm, the main idea being that every distributed energy resource or controllable load decides what is best for it, taking into account the overall benefit [13].

From the discussion of the control algorithm in smart grid, it is safe to say that pricing-based algorithms, pricing-based utility functions, and pricing models should be

considered to optimize the system. A quasidynamic pricing model [14] has been proposed to minimize the electricity bill of cooperative users. The price comprises of a base price and a penalty term. Two methods are described. Deadline-driven continuous variable method is suitable for an energy cost optimization with less interruptible tasks, while the time slot-based method is appropriate for more interruptible tasks [14]. One optimal real-time pricing algorithm has been mentioned in [15]. Energy pricing is an essential tool to develop efficient demand-side management strategies [15]. The proposed algorithm can be implemented in a distributed manner to maximize the aggregate utility of all users and minimize the cost imposed to the energy provider [15].

1.4. Power System Disturbance Classification.

It is critical for power system operators to discern power system disturbances characteristics in order to take control measures to ensure power system security and reliability. This issue has become even more challenging due to the expansion of power system interconnections and integration of distributed generators and renewable energy resources [16, 17]. Wide area measurement system (WAMS) implements the disturbance detection by collecting measurements from local sensors (wire, cable, or wireless) and managing it on a central server [18–22].

Power system disturbance classification has been conducted using pattern recognition in [23–25] based on power system measurements like voltage quality, power flow, or frequency. Artificial intelligence, such as neural networks, and particle swarm optimization have been introduced for complex signal classification [26, 27]. However, the implementation of these algorithms is too complicated and not practical. To circumvent this, a machine-learning method called support vector machine (SVM) can be employed to quickly and accurately classify various common power system disturbances using the frequency data at various points in the power system. The objective is to eventually enable automated classification of disturbances, which is currently easy for a person to accomplish, yet difficult for a computer. SVM, which was first proposed by Cortes and Vapnik [28], transforms unknown data from a nonlinear space to a linear space. Subsequently, any linear algorithm can be applied to form the knowledge for the machine operation. SVM can achieve a unique global optimum for a convex optimization problem. In addition, SVM is not affected by the uncertainty in the parameters. Due to its various advantages, SVM is increasingly preferred in the field of pattern recognition and classification [26, 27].

1.5. Securing the Smart Grid. The smart grid is aimed at transforming the already aging electric power grid in the United States into a digitally advanced and decentralized infrastructure with heavy reliance on control, energy distribution, communication, and security.

In order to develop this infrastructure, a high level of interconnectivity and reliability among its nodes is required. Sensors, advanced metering devices, electrical appliances, and monitoring devices, just to mention a few, will be highly interconnected allowing for the seamless flow of data. Reliability and security in this flow of data between nodes, as shown in Figure 2, is crucial due to the low latency and cyber attacks resilience requirements of the smart grid.

A distributed interconnection among these nodes will be ubiquitous, just as finding a similar level of connectivity among cellular phones or computing nodes in a large organization. The smart grid environment, however, poses a new set of communications and security paradigms. Due to their complexity and importance to the realization of the smart grid infrastructure, it is extremely important to study the interactions among the nodes, more specifically, in terms of their communications and security.

Taking into account that reliability and security will impose constraints on the majority of the devices connected to the Smart Grid, if not all, it would be wise to consider communication standards, protocols, and devices that are designed from the ground up to be secured, logically and physically. Since a great portion of the traffic generated within the grid will be traveling on an unsecured medium such as the Internet, it is imperative to minimize the amount of potential security loopholes. Additionally, the human variable should also be taken into account in the security model, as part of the security infrastructure.

When it comes to security, communication is key, and information should be properly disseminated to all the parties involved, ensuring that everyone has a clear and common understanding of security needs facilitating their implementation and operation. Training and informing users about processes, study of human behavior, and the perception of events related to the processes is as important to the entire security equation, as it is to engineer a secured infrastructure. As a matter of fact, the greatest security threat to any infrastructure is human error, as opposed to the technology securing it. Communications in the smart grid is a key component of the entire infrastructure, and logically we divide it into two sections, the backbone communications (interdomain), which will carry communications among domains such as those shown in Figure 2, and the communications at the local area network (intradomain) limited by perimeters such as a customer's house, or a distribution facility [29]. It would be important to note that due to current limitations, the focus of research on our testbed will be on intradomain communications, without disregard for future considerations of the interdomain aspect.

We can say that current and emerging technologies in telecommunications, most of which are expected to fall in the wireless realm (Wimax, Zigbee, 802.11, etc.), can accommodate the communications needs of both inter and intradomain environments, however, not without flaws. From a security standpoint, these technologies are not designed to be secure from the ground up. For example, Zigbee is a standard for short-range communications, and manufacturers of Zigbee compliant chips produce them without necessarily considering the security issue. In addition, chip manufacturers print the chip model on top of the chip itself as a standard practice. The chip specifications can therefore be easily downloaded, and potential flaws of the chip can be easily exploited by attackers. Additionally, by default, many of these chips do not carry any internal security features and, therefore, rely on external chips, or on higher level software applications for this purpose. An easy access to the external chip by any malicious attacker could potentially disable any installed security features. This and other similar scenarios lead us to think that the smart grid should be driven by technologies and standards that consider security as their primary concern.

The smart grid has been conceived as being distributed in nature and heavily dependent on wireless communications. Today's SOHO (small office/home office) and enterprise-graded wireless devices include security features to mitigate attacks, the vast majority still relying on conventional rule-based detection. It has been shown that conventional rule-based detection systems, although helpful, do not have the capability of detecting unknown attacks. Furthermore, as presented in [30], these conventional IDSs would not be able to detect such an attack if it is carefully crafted, since the majority of these rules are solely based on strict thresholds.

2. Review

2.1. Cognitive Radio Network Testbed. A Cognitive Radio (CR) network testbed is being built at Tennessee Technological University [31, 32]. The idea of applying a cognitive radio network testbed to the smart grid was developed at Tennessee Technological University in the middle of 2009 in a funded research proposal [33]. Subsequently, this idea has been strengthened in [31, 34–37]. The objective of this

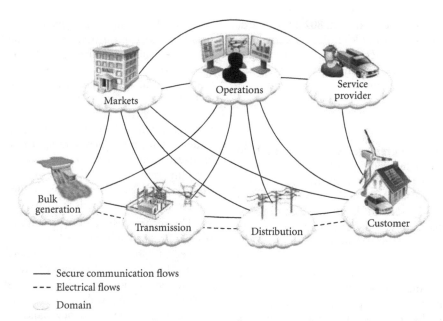

— Secure communication flows
--- Electrical flows
⬭ Domain

FIGURE 2: Interaction among actors in smart grid domains through secure communication flows and flows of electricity.

testbed is to achieve the convergence of cognitive radio, cognitive radar, and smart grid [38].

The cognitive radio network testbed being built is unique and real-time oriented. It is designed to provide much more stand-alone computing power and reduce the response time delay. The cognitive radio network testbed is comprised of tens of nodes, with each node based on a self-designed motherboard, and commercial radio frequency (RF) boards. On the self-designed motherboard, there are two advanced and powerful field programmable gate arrays (FPGAs) that can be flexibly configured to implement any function. Therefore, this network testbed can also be applied to the smart grid.

To our understanding, the benefits of applying cognitive radio to the smart grid are summarized in Table 2. Firstly, cognitive radio can operate over a wide range of frequency bands. It has frequency agility. This feature is especially useful for smart grid because the frequency spectrum today is so crowded, and cognitive radio provides the capability of reusing unused frequency bands for the smart grid. Secondly, cognitive radio enables high-speed data transmission for the smart grid. This is due to the wide-band nature of cognitive radio. The data rate can be as high as tens of Mbps, in contrast to the ZigBee that can only provide a data rate of tens to hundreds of kbps. Thirdly, cognitive radio has the potential to transmit data over a long-distance. Recently, the federal communications commission (FCC) has decided to allow using unused TV bands for wireless communications. The TV bands are ideal for long distance mass data transmission. Cognitive radio in a wireless regional area network (WRAN) scenario is designed to utilize the unused TV bands. Employing cognitive radio, the smart grid can communicate over a long distance over the air. Fourthly, cognitive radio boasts of cognitive learning and adaptation capability. It has the ability to learn the environment, reason

TABLE 2: Advantages of applying cognitive radio to smart grid.

Salient features	Description
Frequency diversity	CR can operate over unused frequency bands
Transmission speed	Data rates of up to tens of Mbps can be achieved
Range	CR can transmit over long distances in a WRAN scenario
Adaptability	CR has inherent intelligence to adapt to changes in the environment
Programmability	Built on an SDR platform, the CR can be selectively programmed

from it, and adapt accordingly. Cognitive radio makes the smart grid "smarter" and more robust. Fifthly, cognitive radio is based on the software defined radio (SDR) platform, which is a programmable radio. Hence, cognitive radio is capable of performing different applications and tasks. In addition, security, robustness, reliability, scalability, and sustainability of the smart grid can be effectively supported by cognitive radio due to its flexibility and reprogrammability.

2.2. Smart Grid Communications. Smart grid technology has attracted significant research focus in recent years from the power and communications standpoint [39, 40]. CRs provide a promising solution to the growing spectrum scarcity problem by intelligently accessing unused regions of spectrum originally licensed to primary users (PUs). One of the key requirements for the smart grid is a robust and efficient communications infrastructure that can address both the current and future energy management needs [41, 42]. With the advent of modern communications technologies, and the recently defined IEEE 802.22 standard, CR networks are believed to be a viable choice for smart grid applications. The opportunistic access of the TV broadcast spectrum as outlined in the 802.22 standard can be realized as one of the cognitive network functions.

3. Examples

In this section, examples are presented employing machine learning and signal processing techniques for dimensionality reduction, recovery of smart meter transmissions, power system disturbances classification, and fuzzy logic-based intrusion detection. This section is divided as follows. In Section 3.1, dimensionality reduction techniques such as PCA, KPCA, and LVMU, in combination with SVM, are used as a preprocessing tool in a spectrum sensing application for Wi-Fi signals. The SVM technique is used for power system disturbances classification in Section 3.2. In Section 3.3, the sparsity of the smart meter transmissions is exploited to recover the BPSK-modulated smart meter data, by employing the recently proposed bayesian compressed sensing, and compressed sensing kalman filter methods. Finally, the critical issue of smart grid security is addressed in Section 3.4, and a possible approach to realize this is provided using FPGA-based fuzzy logic.

3.1. Dimensionality Reduction Applied to Cognitive Radio with Experimental Validation. In radar and sensing signal processing, the control of degrees of freedom (DOF)—or intrinsic dimensionality—is the first step, called preprocessing. The network dimensionality, on the other hand, has received attention in information theory literature. The techniques of the dimensionality reduction can be explored to extract the intrinsic dimensionality of the high-dimensional data.

Dimensionality reduction methods are innovative and important tools in machine learning [43]. The original dimensionality data collected from our living world may contain a lot of features however, usually these features are highly correlated and redundant with noise. Hence, the intrinsic dimensionality of the collected data is much fewer than the original features. Dimensionality reduction attempts to select or extract a lower dimensionality expression but retain most of the useful information. In the first example, both linear methods such as principal component analysis (PCA) [44], nonlinear methods such as kernel principal component analysis (KPCA) [45], and landmark maximum variance unfolding (LMVU) [46, 47] are studied, by combining them with the support vector machine (SVM) [48–53]—the latest breakthrough in machine learning, in the context of spectrum sensing for cognitive radio.

Measured Wi-Fi signals with high signal-to-noise ratio (SNR) are employed in the first example. The DOF of the Wi-Fi signals is extracted by three dimensionality reduction techniques in this example. The advantages of applying dimensionality reduction techniques are verified by comparing with the results obtained without dimensionality reduction.

3.1.1. Wi-Fi Signal Measurements. Wi-Fi time-domain signals have been measured and recorded using an advanced digital phosphor oscilloscope (DPO) whose model is Tektronix DPO72004 [54]. The DPO supports a maximum bandwidth of 20 GHz and a maximum sampling rate of 50 GS/s. It is capable of recording up to 250 M samples per channel. In the measurements, a laptop accesses the Internet through a wireless Wi-Fi router, as shown in Figure 3. An antenna with a frequency range of 800 MHz to 2500 MHz is placed near the laptop and connected to the DPO. The sampling rate of the DPO is set to 6.25 GS/s. Recorded time-domain Wi-Fi signals are shown in Figure 4. The duration of the recorded Wi-Fi signals is 40 ms.

The recorded 40 ms Wi-Fi signals are divided into 8000 slots, with each slot lasting 5 μs. These slots can be viewed as spectrum sensing slots. The time-domain Wi-Fi signals within the first 1 μs of every slot are then transformed into the frequency domain using the Fast Fourier Transform (FFT), which is equivalent to FFT-based spectrum sensing. In this paper, the frequency band of 2.411–2.433 GHz is considered. The resolution in the frequency domain is 1 MHz. Therefore, for each slot, 23 points in the frequency domain can be obtained, of which 13 points will be selected in the following experiment.

3.1.2. Experimental Validation. SVM will be exploited to classify the states (busy $l_i = 1$ or idle $l_i = 0$) of the measured Wi-Fi data with or without dimensionality reduction, given the true states. SVM will classify the states of the spectrum data at different time slots.

The DOF of the Wi-Fi frequency domain signals is extracted using the original 13 dimensions. The flow chart of the SVM processing combined with dimensionality reduction methods, including data processing, is shown in Figure 5.

The false alarm rate obtained by combining SVM with dimensionality reduction and employing only SVM is shown in Figure 6. The results are averaged over 50 experiments. In each experiment, the number of training sets is 200, and the number of testing sets is 1800.

The original dimension of the frequency domain data is varied from 1 to 13 for the SVM method. In addition, the SVM method is combined with the extracted dimensions from 1 to 13, obtained with dimensionality reduction.

In the whole experiment, a Gaussian RBF kernel with $2\sigma^2 = 5.5^2$ is used for KPCA. The parameter $k = 3$, in which k is the number of nearest neighbors of y_i (x_i) (including both training and testing sets) for LMVU. The optimization toolbox SeDuMi 1.1R3 [55] is applied to solve the optimization step in LMVU. The SVM toolbox SVM-KM [56] is used to train and test the SVM processes. The kernels selected for SVM are heavy-tailed RBF kernels with parameters $\gamma = 1$, $a = 1$, and $b = 1$. These parameters are kept constant for the whole experiment.

Experimental results show that with dimensionality reduction, the spectrum sensing performance is much better with fewer features than that without dimensionality reduction.

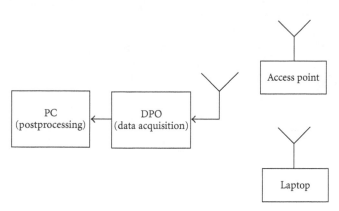

FIGURE 3: Setup of the measurement of Wi-Fi signals.

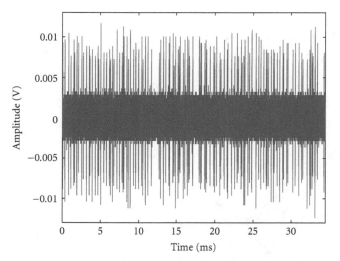

FIGURE 4: Recorded Wi-Fi signals in time domain.

3.2. Classifying Power System Disturbances Using SVM. Due to the large variability exhibited by the few power system disturbance data sets available, data sets are generated mathematically in this section for training purposes. In this way, a large number of data sets can be generated and used in training to ensure accurate SVM models.

Based on frequency and time domain analysis, and derived from typical disturbances, mathematical models for each disturbance can be formulated by the following signal equations:

(i) generation trip,

$$u(t) = \sin(\omega_0 t) + \alpha_1 e^{-c_1(t_{11}-t_{12})} \sin\left(\beta_1 \omega_0 (t_{11} - t_{12})\right) + \cdots$$

$$\alpha_2 e^{-c_2(t_{21}-t_{22})} \sin\left(\beta_2 \omega_0 (t_{11} - t_{12})\right) + \cdots, \tag{1}$$

(ii) line trip,

$$u(t) = (1 - \alpha(u(t_2) - u(t_1))) \sin(\omega_0 t), \tag{2}$$

(iii) frequency oscillation,

$$u(t) = \sin(\omega_0 t) + \alpha e^{-c(t-t_1)} \sin\left(\beta \omega_0 (t - t_1)\right) \prod (t_2 - t_1), \tag{3}$$

where various terms are defined as follows: time window $\prod(t_2 - t_1) = u(t_2) - u(t_1)$, ω_0 is a random frequency of basic frequency fluctuation, α is an additional signal factor, β is an additional frequency factor, c is the time constant, and t is the time period.

After carefully selecting the obtained parameters, such as amplitude, angles, frequency, and time period of each subfrequency component, enough examples can be generated by manipulating these parameters by random deviation within a tolerance range. Figures 7, 8, and 9 are the mesh patterns of 200 mathematical examples for the generation trip, line trip, and frequency oscillations, respectively.

SVM is a linear classifier in the parameter space, but it becomes a nonlinear classifier as a result of the nonlinear mapping of the space of the input patterns into the high-dimensional feature space [27]. Training an SVM model is a quadratic-optimization problem [57, 58]. The hyperplane represented by $\langle \omega, x \rangle + b = 0$ is constructed, so that the margin between the hyperplane and nearest point is maximized, where ω is the vector of hyperplane coefficients, b is a bias term, and $\langle \cdot \rangle$ denotes the inner product of two vectors.

Therefore, the classification function is $f(x; \omega, b) = \langle \omega, x \rangle + b$. An n-class classifier is constructed using the maximum value of the function $f_{ij}(x; \omega, b) = \langle \omega_{ij}, x \rangle + b_{ij}$, $k = 1, \ldots, n$. For SVM, the problem can be solved by training data x_i^k, where $i = 1, \ldots, m$ data points.

Thus, the mathematical function between class i and class j is represented by the following equations:

$$f_{ij}(x; \omega, b) = \langle \omega_{ij}, x \rangle + b_{ij}$$

$$\text{Minimize: } \frac{1}{2} \langle \omega_{ij}, \omega_{ij}^T \rangle + \frac{C}{n} \sum_{n=1}^{N} \xi_n^{ij}$$

$$\text{Constraints: } y_n^{ij} \left(\langle \omega_{ij}, \omega_{ij}^T \rangle + b_{ij} \right) \geq 1 - \xi_n^{ij}, \tag{4}$$

$$\text{where } \xi_n^{ij} \geq 0,$$

$$y_n^{ij} = \begin{cases} +1 & \text{if } y_n = i\text{th class,} \\ -1 & \text{if } y_n = j\text{th class.} \end{cases}$$

The machine-learning package Weka is used to classify the data using an SVM multiclass algorithm. After being transformed to the Weka format, the input data includes three categories: generation trip, oscillation, and line trip. The data contains 200 examples of each category which is then divided into 2 equal sized groups. The first set is used for training, and the second set is used for verification. The verification results are as follows: generation trip can be classified with a success rate of 0.985, compared to 0.853 for the line trip, and 0.626 for the frequency oscillation.

3.3. Compressed Sensing-Based Smart Meter Reading. Compressed sensing, also known as compressive sensing, compressive sampling, or sparse sampling, is a technique for finding sparse solutions to underdetermined linear systems [59–63]. The concept of applying compressed sensing to smart meter reading was first proposed in [64]. A smart

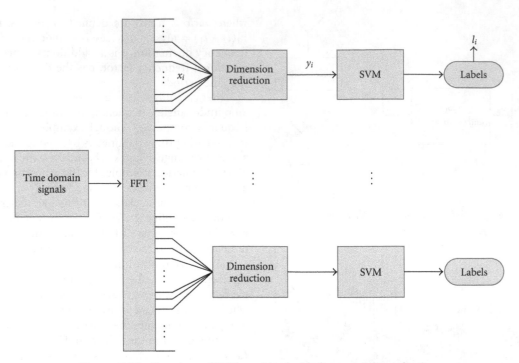

FIGURE 5: The flow chart of SVM combined with dimensionality reduction.

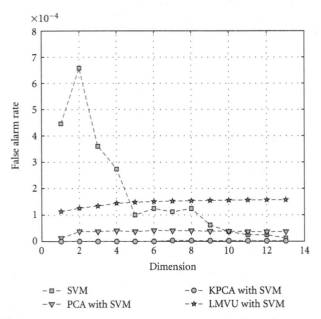

FIGURE 6: False alarm rate.

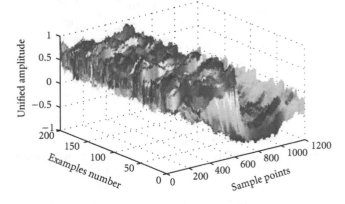

FIGURE 7: Mesh patterns of 200 examples for generation trip.

meter is an intelligent electrical meter that conveys information to the central power station regarding significant changes in the power load either through two-way wireless or power line communications. Since the power consumption in a particular home does not dynamically vary, the number of smart meters simultaneously transmitting is very small compared to the total number of meters in a particular cognitive smart grid network. As a result, the sparsity of the smart meter data transmission to the central processing node

or access point (AP) was exploited in [64] for applying the principle of compressed sensing. However, in [64], it was assumed that the noise is bounded. In this paper, the newly proposed techniques of Bayesian compressive sensing [65], and compressed sensing kalman filter [66] are applied for smart meter reading when the noise is Gaussian distributed.

3.3.1. Bayesian Compressed Sensing. Consider an N-dimensional signal y that is compressible in some basis function A, that is, y can be accurately reconstructed with a small number K of basis-function coefficients, where $K \ll N$. In other words, the basis coefficient vector s is a sparse vector with a majority of components close to 0. Compressive sensing states that it is possible to recover these basis-function coefficients with fewer measurements $M < N$ of y. This is accomplished by a linear transformation of y

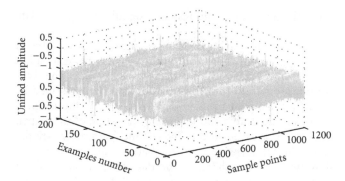

FIGURE 8: Mesh patterns of 200 examples for line trip.

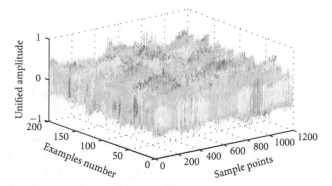

FIGURE 9: Mesh patterns of 200 examples for frequency oscillation.

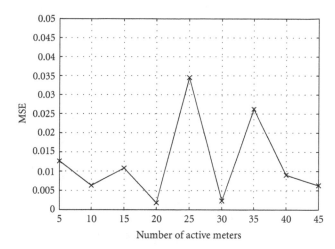

FIGURE 10: MSE achieved by BCS for different number of active meters.

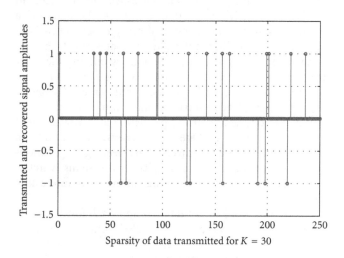

FIGURE 11: Sparsity of data transmitted for $K = 30$.

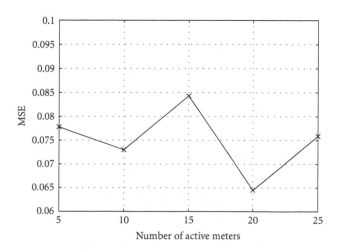

FIGURE 12: MSE achieved by CSKF for different number of active meters.

onto an $M \times N$ matrix H to generate an M-dimensional measurement vector z. Mathematically, z can be represented as

$$z = y^T A H. \tag{5}$$

Since we have $y = As$, (5) becomes

$$z = Hs. \tag{6}$$

The expression in (6) is an underdetermined system; hence, the estimate of s is ill conditioned. However, since s is sparse with respect to A, (6) can be solved as a l_1 norm minimization problem as follows:

$$\hat{s} = \arg \min_s \left[\|z - Hs\|_2^2 + \lambda \|s\|_1 \right]. \tag{7}$$

The scalar λ decides the weightage given to the Euclidean error and the sparseness constraints in the first and second terms of (7), respectively.

The above optimization problem can be solved using many linear programming techniques such as basis pursuit (BP) [67], matching pursuit (MP) [68], and orthogonal matching pursuit (OMP) [69]. In [65], a Bayesian approach is employed to estimate s from the compressed measurements z. Hence, by imposing a Laplace sparseness prior on s, and assuming a Gaussian likelihood model for z, the solution for (7) becomes a maximum a posterior (MAP) estimate for s.

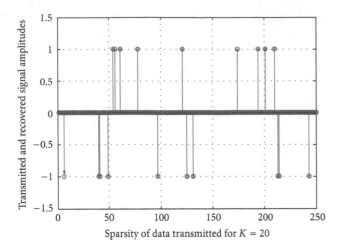

FIGURE 13: Sparsity of data transmitted for $K = 20$.

3.3.2. Kalman Filter-Based Compressed Sensing. The kalman filter is a recursive filter that estimates the state of a process or system from a series of noisy observations [70–72]. The kalman filter optimally estimates the true state of the system by making a prediction, estimating the error in the prediction, and computing a weighted average of the predicted value and the measured value. Therefore, the mathematical equations for the kalman filter can be separated into time updates or prediction and measurement updates or correction. Due to its versatility, the kalman filter has been used in diverse engineering applications such as digital signal processing, control systems, wireless communications, image processing, and weather forecasting [73–78].

Recently, a new kalman filtering approach for the recovery of sparse signals was proposed, called compressed sensing embedded kalman filter (CSKF-1) [66, 79]. The CSKF-1 adopts the pseudomeasurement (PM) technique [80] to incorporate a fictitious measurement in the kalman filtering process to satisfy the sparseness constraint. The PM can be expressed as

$$0 = \hat{H}s - \delta,$$
$$\hat{H} = [\text{sign}(s(1), s(2), \dots, s(N))],$$
(8)

where $\text{sign}(s(k)) = 1$ if $s(k) \geq 0$, and -1 otherwise.

δ is the tuning parameter which controls the sparsity of the solution state vector.

3.3.3. System Description and Signal Model. As mentioned in the previous section, the smart meter data transmission to the AP is sparse in nature, that is, only a small percentage of meters would be actively transmitting data at any time. Therefore, the principles of compressed sensing can be readily applied to the recovery of the data reports. The main advantage of employing compressed sensing is that it allows the smart meters to transmit simultaneously, as opposed to the popular carrier sense multiple access (CSMA) protocol, which uses a random backoff to avoid collisions in

transmissions. This could result in significant delay in data recovery.

The system consists of N smart meters managed by an AP. In each frame, synchronization and channel estimation is performed, followed by data transmission. The synchronization and channel estimation can be performed by transmitting a pilot signal to the meters during the assigned periods in the frame and is beyond the scope of this paper. However, it is assumed that the channel parameters are flat fading in nature, with a large coherence time indicating a slow time-varying channel. The data transmission section in the frame is divided into several time slots during which the active smart meters can simultaneously transmit their readings. In mathematical form, the data transmission received by the AP at time t can be expressed as

$$z(t) = \sum_{i=1}^{N} p_i(t)c_is_i + w(t)$$
(9)

c_i is the flat-fading channel parameter between meter i and the AP, $p_i(t)$ is the pseudorandom spreading code at time t for meter i, s_i is the data transmitted by meter i, $w(t)$ is the Gaussian distributed noise term. The spreading code is known only to the AP and meters, preventing unauthorized people from accessing and tampering with the data. Suppose that the data transmission period has T time slots, then the above signal model can be rewritten in matrix-vector form as follows:

$$Z = HS + W,$$
(10)

where

$$H = PC,$$
(11)
$$C = \text{diag}(c_1, c_2, \dots, c_N),$$
(12)
$$P_{t,i} = [p_i(1), p_i(2), \dots, p_i(T)]^T,$$
(13)
$$Z = [z(1), z(2), \dots, z(T)]^T,$$
(14)
$$S = [s_1, s_2, \dots, s_N]^T,$$
(15)
$$W = [w(1), w(2), \dots, w(T)]^T.$$
(16)

Since the number K of meters simultaneously transmitting is small, $K \ll N$. As a result, the vector S in (15) is sparse. It can therefore be easily inferred that (10) is identical to the CS equation (6), with the exception of additive Gaussian noise. Hence, the recovery of the smart meter reading would correspond to the optimization problem in (7). In the simulations, the total number of smart meters, N, in the cognitive smart grid network is considered to be 250, and the length of the observation vector/time slots T is 100. Binary phase shift keying (BPSK) modulation is considered. The mean square error (MSE) between the actual data vector and the estimated data vector is used as the measure of performance. The MSE is plotted for different number of active meters K or sparsity of the data transmission.

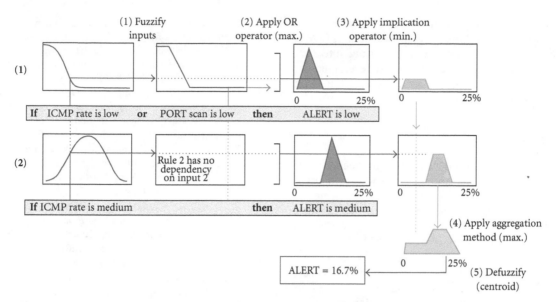

FIGURE 14: Fuzzy Logic example applied to IDS.

3.3.4. Bayesian Compressive Sensing for Smart Meter Reading. In this section, the smart grid data recovery problem in (6) is treated as a linear regression problem and is considered from a Bayesian perspective, as proposed in [65]. A hierarchical sparseness prior is imposed on S, and sparse Bayesian learning using the relevance vector machine (RVM) [81] is performed. The MSE achieved by the BCS algorithm for different values of K is illustrated in Figure 10. For the case of $K = 30$, the sparsity of the data transmitted along with the recovered data is illustrated in Figure 11.

3.3.5. Compressed Sensing Kalman Filter Approach. In this section, the recently proposed CSKF algorithm is employed for the recovery of data at the AP. The total number of smart meters in the network is assumed to be 250, and T is 150. The MSE yielded for various number of active meters K is shown in Figure 12, respectively. A comparison between the amplitudes of the transmitted and recovered signal versus the sparsity of meter transmission is shown in Figure 13.

3.4. FPGA-Based Fuzzy Logic Intrusion Detection for Smart Grid. Artificial intelligence techniques such as fuzzy logic, bayesian inference, neural networks, and other methods can be employed to enhance the security gaps in conventional IDSs. As shown in Figure 14, a fuzzy logic approach was used in [82], in which different variables that influence the inference of an attack can be analyzed and later combined for the decision-making process of a security device. Additionally, if each security device serving as an IDS is aware not only of itself, but also of a limited number (depending on local resources and traffic) of surrounding trusted IDS devices, the alerts that these other devices generate can be used to adjust local variables or parameters to better cope with distributed attacks and more accurately detect their presence.

The research and development of robust and secure communication protocols, dynamic spectrum sensing, and distributed and collaborative security should be considered as an inherent part of smart grid architecture. An advanced decentralized and secure infrastructure needs to be developed with two-way capabilities for communicating information and controlling equipment, among other tasks, as indicated in the recently published "Guidelines for Smart Grid Cyber Security Vol.1" by the National Institute of Standards and Technologies. The complexity of such an endeavor, coupled with the amalgam of technologies and standards that will coexist in the development of the smart grid, makes it extremely necessary to have a common platform of development, with flexibility and reliable performance.

Field programmable gate arrays (FPGAs) development platforms share these advantages, not to mention the fact that a single silicon FPGA chip can be used to study several smart grid technologies and their implementations. FPGA chips offer significant potential for application in the smart grid for performing encryption and decryption, intrusion detection, low-latency routing, data acquisition and signal processing, parallelism, configurability of hardware devices, and high-performance and high-bandwidth tamper-resistant applications. Dr. William Sanders, a member of the Smart Grid Advisory Committee of the National Institute of Standards and Technology (NIST), has been in the recent years among the most influential persons in the research of smart grid security. His research team and several collaborating universities proposed the use of a Trustworthy Cyber Infrastructure for the Power Grid (TCIPG) that focuses on the security of low-level devices and communications, as well as trustworthy operation of the power grid under a variety of conditions including cyber attacks and emergencies [83]. TCIPG proposes a coordinated response and detection at multiple layers of the cyber-infrastructure hierarchy including but not limited to sensor/actuator and substation levels. At these levels of the hierarchy, software defined radio and wireless communications technologies could be used and studied to prevent attacks such as wireless jamming.

Dr. Sanders also proposes the use of specifications-based IDS in protecting advanced metering infrastructures (AMIs) [84]. A distributed FPGA-based network with adaptive and cooperative capabilities can be used to study several security and communication aspects of this infrastructure both from the attackers and defensive point of view.

4. Conclusions

In this paper, the integration of two emerging technologies, namely, the cognitive radio and smart grid is addressed. The concept of dimensionality reduction is presented as a possible preprocessing method to extract the intrinsic dimensionality of high-dimensional data. Using Wi-Fi signal measurements, the effectiveness of the PCA, KPCA, and LVMU dimensionality reduction techniques in conjunction with the SVM method is provided in a spectrum sensing application. In addition, the SVM technique is used for suitably classifying the power system disturbances. For the recovery of sparse smart meter transmissions, experimental results obtained by employing the Bayesian compressed sensing and compressed sensing kalman filter approaches are given for BPSK data. Finally, the critical issue of smart grid security is addressed, and a possible approach for achieving this is presented using FPGA-based fuzzy logic intrusion detection.

Acknowledgments

This work is funded by the National Science Foundation through Grants (ECCS-0901420), (ECCS-0821658), and (ECCS-0622125) and the Office of Naval Research through two Contracts (N00014-07-1-0529 and N00014-11-1-0006).

References

[1] J. Mitola III and G. Q. Maguire Jr., "Cognitive radio: making software radios more personal," *IEEE Personal Communications*, vol. 6, no. 4, pp. 13–18, 1999.

[2] S. Haykin, "Cognitive radio: brain-empowered wireless communications," *IEEE Journal on Selected Areas in Communications*, vol. 23, no. 2, pp. 201–220, 2005.

[3] G. Ganesan, Y. Li, B. Bing, and S. Li, "Spatiotemporal sensing in cognitive radio networks," *IEEE Journal on Selected Areas in Communications*, vol. 26, no. 1, pp. 5–12, 2008.

[4] J. Bazerque and G. Giannakis, "Distributed spectrum sensing for cognitive radio networks by exploiting sparsity," *IEEE Transactions on Signal Processing*, vol. 58, no. 3, pp. 1847–1862, 2010.

[5] C. Cordeiro, K. Challapali, D. Birru et al., "IEEE 802.22: an introduction to the first wireless standard based on cognitive radios," *Journal of Communications*, vol. 1, no. 1, pp. 38–47, 2006.

[6] C. Cordeiro, K. Challapali, D. Birru, and N. Sai Shankar, "IEEE 802.22: the first worldwide wireless standard based on cognitive radios," in *Proceedings of the 1st IEEE International Symposium on New Frontiers in Dynamic Spectrum Access Networks (DySPAN '05)*, pp. 328–337, Baltimore, Md, USA, November 2005.

[7] C. Cordeiro, K. Challapali, and M. Ghosh, "Cognitive PHY and MAC layers for dynamic spectrum access and sharing of TV bands," in *Proceedings of the 1st International Workshop on Technology and Policy for Accessing Spectrum*, vol. 222, p. 3, ACM, New York, NY, USA, 2006.

[8] C. Stevenson, G. Chouinard, Z. Lei, W. Hu, S. Shellhammer, and W. Caldwell, "IEEE 802.22: the first cognitive radio wireless regional area network standard," *IEEE Communications Magazine*, vol. 47, no. 1, pp. 130–138, 2009.

[9] Z. Jiang, "Computational intelligence techniques for a smart electric grid of the future," in *Proceedings of the 6th International Symposium on Neural Networks on Advances in Neural Networks (ISNN '09)*, pp. 1191–1201, 2009.

[10] Z. Wang, A. Scaglione, and R. J. Thomas, "Compressing electrical power grids," in *Proceedings of the 1st IEEE International Conference on Smart Grid Communications (SmartGridComm '10)*, pp. 13–18, 2010.

[11] A. Mohsenian-Rad, V. Wong, J. Jatskevich, and R. Schober, "Optimal and autonomous incentive-based energy consumption scheduling algorithm for smart grid," in *Proceedings of the Innovative Smart Grid Technologies (ISGT '10)*, pp. 1–6, Citeseer, Gaithersburg, Md, USA, January 2010.

[12] S. Caron and G. Kesidis, "Incentive-based energy consumption scheduling algorithms for the smart grid," in *Proceedings of the 1st IEEE International Conference on Smart Grid Communications*, pp. 391–396, Gaithersburg, Md, USA, October 2010.

[13] A. L. Dimeas and N. D. Hatziargyriou, "Operation of a multiagent system for microgrid control," *IEEE Transactions on Power Systems*, vol. 20, no. 3, pp. 1447–1455, 2005.

[14] S. Hatami and M. Pedram, "Minimizing the electricity bill of cooperative users under a Quasi-Dynamic Pricing Model," in *Proceedings of the 1st IEEE International Conference on Smart Grid Communications (SmartGridComm '10)*, pp. 421–426, IEEE, 2010.

[15] P. Samadi, A. Mohsenian-Rad, R. Schober, V. Wong, and J. Jatskevich, "Optimal real-time pricing algorithm based on utility maximization for smart grid," in *Proceedings of the IEEE International Conference on Smart Grid (SmartGridComm '10)*, Gaithersburg, Mass, USA, October 2010.

[16] J. F. Hauer, N. B. Bhatt, K. Shah, and S. Kolluri, "Performance of "WAMS East" in providing dynamic information for the North East blackout of August 14, 2003," in *Proceedings of the IEEE Power Engineering Society General Meeting*, pp. 1685–1690, IEEE, Denver, Colo, USA, June 2004.

[17] D. Divan, G. A. Luckjiff, W. E. Brumsickle, J. Freeborg, and A. Bhadkamkar, "A grid information resource for nationwide real-time power monitoring," *IEEE Transactions on Industry Applications*, vol. 40, no. 2, pp. 699–705, 2004.

[18] B. Qiu, L. Chen, V. Centeno, X. Dong, and Y. Liu, "Internet based frequency monitoring network (FNET)," in *Proceedings of the IEEE Power Engineering Society Winter Meeting*, vol. 3, pp. 1166–1171, IEEE, 2002.

[19] A. G. Phadke, "Synchronized phasor measurements in power systems," *IEEE Computer Applications in Power*, vol. 6, no. 2, pp. 10–15, 1993.

[20] Z. Zhong, C. Xu, B. J. Billian et al., "Power system frequency monitoring network (FNET) implementation," *IEEE Transactions on Power Systems*, vol. 20, no. 4, pp. 1914–1921, 2005.

[21] S. Tsai, Z. Zhong, J. Zuo, and Y. Liu, "Analysis of wide-area frequency measurement of bulk power systems," in *Proceedings of the IEEE Power Engineering Society General Meeting*, Montreal, Canada, June 2006.

[22] C. Chang, A. Liu, and C. Huang, "Oscillatory stability analysis using real-time measured data," *IEEE Transactions on Power Systems*, vol. 8, no. 3, pp. 823–829, 2002.

[23] C. Chunling, X. Tongyu, P. Zailin, and Y. Ye, "Power quality disturbances classification based on multi-class classification SVM," in *Proceedings of the 2nd International Conference on Power Electronics and Intelligent Transportation System (PEITS '09)*, vol. 1, pp. 290–294, IEEE, 2009.

[24] P. Gao and W. Wu, "Power quality disturbances classification using wavelet and support vector machines," in *Proceedings of the 6st International Conference on Intelligent Systems Design and Applications, (ISDA '06)*, pp. 201–206, October 2006.

[25] A. M. Gaouda, S. H. Kanoun, M. M. A. Salama, and A. Y. Chikhani, "Pattern recognition applications for power system disturbance classification," *IEEE Transactions on Power Delivery*, vol. 17, no. 3, pp. 677–683, 2002.

[26] F. Melgani and Y. Bazi, "Classification of electrocardiogram signals with support vector machines and particle swarm optimization," *IEEE Transactions on Information Technology in Biomedicine*, vol. 12, no. 5, pp. 667–677, 2008.

[27] I. Guler and E. D. Ubeyli, "Multiclass support vector machines for EEG-signals classification," *IEEE Transactions on Information Technology in Biomedicine*, vol. 11, no. 2, pp. 117–126, 2007.

[28] C. Cortes and V. Vapnik, "Support-vector networks," *Machine Learning*, vol. 20, no. 3, pp. 273–297, 1995.

[29] N. I. of Standards and Technologies, "Guidelines for grid security, vol 1," Tech. Rep., 2010, http://csrc.nist.gov/publications/PubsNISTIRs.html.

[30] M. Pazos-Revilla and A. Siraj, "An experimental model of an fpga-based intrusion detection systems," in *Proceedings of the 26th International Conference on Computers and Their Applications*, 2011.

[31] R. C. Qiu, Z. Chen, N. Guo et al., "Towards a real-time cognitive radio network testbed: architecture, hardware platform, and application to smart grid," in *Proceedings of the 5th IEEE Workshop on Networking Technologies for Software-Defined Radio and White Space*, June 2010.

[32] Z. Chen, N. Guo, and R. C. Qiu, "Building A cognitive radio network testbed," in *Proceedings of the IEEE Southeastcon*, Nashville, Tenn, USA, March 2011.

[33] R. C. Qiu, "Cognitive radio network testbed," Funded Research Proposal for Defense University Research Instrumentation Program (DURIP), August 2009, http://www.defense.gov/news/Fiscal 2010 DURIP Winners List.pdf.

[34] R. C. Qiu, "Cognitive radio and smart grid," Invited Presentation at IEEE Chapter, February 2010, http://iweb.tntech.edu/rqiu.

[35] R. C. Qiu, "Cogntiive radio institute," Funded research proposal for 2010 Defense Earmark, 2010, http://www.opensecrets.org/politicians/earmarks.php?cid=N00003126.

[36] R. C. Qiu, "Smart grid research at TTU," Presented at Argonne National Laboratory, February 2010, http://iweb.tntech.edu/rqiu/publications.htm.

[37] R. Qiu, Z. Hu, G. Zheng, Z. Chen, and N. Guo, "Cognitive radio network for the Smart Grid: experimental system architecture, control algorithms, security, and microgrid testbed," *IEEE Transactions on Smart Grid*. In press.

[38] R. C. Qiu, M. C. Wicks, Z. Hu, L. Li, and S. J. Hou, "Wireless tomography(part1): a novel approach to remote sensing," in *Proceedings of the 5th International Waveform Diversity and Design Conference*, Niagara Falls, Canada, August 2010.

[39] M. Amin and B. Wollenberg, "Toward a smart grid: power delivery for the 21st century," *IEEE Power and Energy Magazine*, vol. 3, no. 5, pp. 34–41, 2005.

[40] J. Cupp and M. Beehler, "Implementing smart grid communications," 2008.

[41] A. Ghassemi, S. Bavarian, and L. Lampe, "Cognitive radio for smart grid communications," in *Proceedings of the 1st IEEE International Conference on Smart Grid Communications (SmartGridComm '10)*, pp. 297–302, IEEE, Gaithersburg, Md, USA, 2010.

[42] N. Ghasemi and S. M. Hosseini, "Comparison of smart grid with cognitive radio: solutions to spectrum scarcity," in *Proceedings of the 12th International Conference on Advanced Communication Technology (ICACT '10)*, vol. 1, pp. 898–903, February 2010.

[43] J. Lee and M. Verleysen, *Nonlinear Dimensionality Reduction*, Springer, London, UK, 2007.

[44] I. T. Jolliffe, *Principal Component Analysis*, Springer, London, UK, 2002.

[45] B. Schölkopf, A. Smola, and K. R. Müller, "Nonlinear component analysis as a kernel eigenvalue problem," *Neural Computation*, vol. 10, no. 5, pp. 1299–1319, 1998.

[46] K. Q. Weinberger and L. K. Saul, "Unsupervised learning of image manifolds by semidefinite programming," *International Journal of Computer Vision*, vol. 70, no. 1, pp. 77–90, 2006.

[47] K. Weinberger, B. Packer, and L. Saul, "Nonlinear dimensionality reduction by semidefinite programming and kernel matrix factorization," in *Proceedings of the 10th International Workshop on Artificial Intelligence and Statistics*, pp. 381–388, 2005.

[48] V. Vapnik, *The Nature of Statistical Learning Theory*, Springer, London, UK, 2000.

[49] V. Vapnik, *Statistical Learning Theory*, Wiley, New York, NY, USA, 1998.

[50] V. Vapnik, S. Golowich, and A. Smola, "Support vector method for function approximation, regression estimation, and signal processing," in *Advances in Neural Information Processing Systems*, M. Mozer, M. Jordan, and T. Petsche, Eds., pp. 281–287, MIT Press, Cambridge, Mass, USA, 1997.

[51] C. J. C. Burges, "A tutorial on support vector machines for pattern recognition," *Data Mining and Knowledge Discovery*, vol. 2, no. 2, pp. 121–167, 1998.

[52] A. J. Smola and B. Schölkopf, "A tutorial on support vector regression," *Statistics and Computing*, vol. 14, no. 3, pp. 199–222, 2004.

[53] N. Cristianini and J. Shawe-Taylor, *An Introduction to Support Vector Machines: and Other Kernel-Based Learning Methods*, Cambridge University Press, Cambridge, UK, 2000.

[54] Z. Chen and R. C. Qiu, "Prediction of channel state for cognitive radio using higher-order hidden Markov model," in *Proceedings of the IEEE Southeast Conference*, pp. 276–282, March 2010.

[55] J. Sturm, "The advanced optimization laboratory at McMaster university, Canada. SeDuMi version 1.1 R3," 2006.

[56] S. Canu, Y. Grandvalet, V. Guigue, and A. Rakotomamonjy, *Svm and Kernel Methods Matlab Toolbox*, Perception Systmes et Information, INSA de Rouen, Rouen, France, 2005.

[57] D. Fradkin and I. Muchnik, "Support vector machines for classification," *Discrete Methods in Epidemiology*, vol. 70, pp. 13–20, 2006.

[58] K. Bennett and C. Campbell, "Support vector machines: hype or hallelujah?" *ACM SIGKDD Explorations Newsletter*, vol. 2, no. 2, pp. 1–13, 2000.

[59] D. L. Donoho, "Compressed sensing," *IEEE Transactions on Information Theory*, vol. 52, no. 4, pp. 1289–1306, 2006.

[60] Y. Tsaig and D. L. Donoho, "Extensions of compressed sensing," *Signal Processing*, vol. 86, no. 3, pp. 549–571, 2006.

[61] E. Candès, "The restricted isometry property and its implications for compressed sensing," *Comptes Rendus Mathematique*, vol. 346, no. 9-10, pp. 589–592, 2008.

[62] E. Candès, J. Romberg, and T. Tao, "Robust uncertainty principles: exact signal reconstruction from highly incomplete frequency information," *IEEE Transactions on Information Theory*, vol. 52, no. 2, pp. 489–509, 2006.

[63] Z. Tian and G. B. Giannakis, "Compressed sensing for wideband cognitive radios," in *Proceedings of IEEE International Conference on Acoustics, Speech and Signal Processing (ICASSP '07)*, vol. 4, pp. 1357–1360, 2007.

[64] L. Husheng, M. Rukun, L. Lifeng, and R. Qiu, "Compressed meter reading for delay-sensitive and secure load report in smart grid," in *Proceedings of the 1st IEEE International Conference on Smart Grid Communications (SmartGridComm '10)*, 2010.

[65] S. Ji, Y. Xue, and L. Carin, "Bayesian compressive sensing," *IEEE Transactions on Signal Processing*, vol. 56, no. 6, pp. 2346–2356, 2008.

[66] A. Carmi, P. Gurfil, and D. Kanevsky, "Methods for sparse signal recovery using Kalman filtering with embedded pseudo-measurement norms and quasi-norms," *IEEE Transactions on Signal Processing*, vol. 58, no. 4, pp. 2405–2409, 2010.

[67] S. S. Chen, D. L. Donoho, and M. A. Saunders, "Atomic decomposition by basis pursuit," *SIAM Review*, vol. 43, no. 1, pp. 129–159, 2001.

[68] S. G. Mallat and Z. Zhang, "Matching pursuits with time-frequency dictionaries," *IEEE Transactions on Signal Processing*, vol. 41, no. 12, pp. 3397–3415, 1993.

[69] J. A. Tropp and A. C. Gilbert, "Signal recovery from random measurements via orthogonal matching pursuit," *IEEE Transactions on Information Theory*, vol. 53, no. 12, pp. 4655–4666, 2007.

[70] R. Meinhold and N. Singpurwalla, "Understanding the Kalman filter," *American Statistician*, vol. 37, no. 2, pp. 123–127, 1983.

[71] R. Kalman et al., "A new approach to linear filtering and prediction problems," *Journal of Basic Engineering*, vol. 82, no. 1, pp. 35–45, 1960.

[72] S. Haykin, *Adaptive Filter Theory*, Pearson Education, Dorling Kindersley, India, 2008.

[73] E. Wan and R. van der Merwe, "The unscented Kalman filter for nonlinear estimation," in *Proceedings of the Adaptive Systems for Signal Processing, Communications, and Control Symposium (AS-SPCC '00)*, pp. 153–158, IEEE, 2000.

[74] G. Evensen, "The ensemble Kalman filter: theoretical formulation and practical implementation," *Ocean Dynamics*, vol. 53, no. 4, pp. 343–367, 2003.

[75] L. Ma, K. Wu, and L. Zhu, "Fire smoke detection in video images using Kalman filter and Gaussian mixture color model," in *Proceedings of the International Conference on Artificial Intelligence and Computational Intelligence (AICI '10)*, vol. 1, pp. 484–487, IEEE, Sanya, China, 2010.

[76] L. Ljung, "Asymptotic behavior of the extended Kalman filter as a parameter estimator for linear systems," *IEEE Transactions on Automatic Control*, vol. 24, no. 1, pp. 36–50, 2002.

[77] R. van der Merwe and E. Wan, "The square-root unscented Kalman filter for state and parameter-estimation," in *Proceedings of the IEEE International Conference on Acoustics, Speech,* *and Signal Processing (ICASSP '01)*, vol. 6, pp. 3461–3464, IEEE, Salt Lake City, Utah, USA, 2001.

[78] A. Lakhzouri, E. Lohan, R. Hamila, and M. Renfors, "Extended Kalman filter channel estimation for line-of-sight detection in WCDMA mobile positioning," *EURASIP Journal on Applied Signal Processing*, vol. 2003, pp. 1268–1278, 2003.

[79] D. Kanevsky, A. Carmi, L. Horesh, P. Gurfil, B. Ramabhadran, and T. Sainath, "Kalman filtering for compressed sensing," in *Proceedings of the 13th Conference on Information Fusion (FUSION '10)*, pp. 1–8, Edinburgh, UK, July 2010.

[80] S. J. Julier and J. J. LaViola, "On Kalman filtering with nonlinear equality constraints," *IEEE Transactions on Signal Processing*, vol. 55, no. 6, pp. 2774–2784, 2007.

[81] M. E. Tipping, "Sparse bayesian learning and the relevance vector machine," *Journal of Machine Learning Research*, vol. 1, no. 3, pp. 211–244, 2001.

[82] M. Pazos-Revilla, *Fpga based fuzzy intrusion detection system for network security*, M.S. thesis, Tennessee Technological University, Cookeville, Tenn, USA, 2010.

[83] W. Sanders, "Tcip: trustworthy cyber infrastructure for the power grid," Tech. Rep., Information Trust Institute, University of Illinois at Urbana-Champaign, 2011.

[84] R. Berthier, W. Sanders, and H. Khurana, "Intrusion detection for advanced metering infrastructures: requirements and architectural directions," in *Proceedings of the 1st IEEE International Conference on Smart Grid Communications (SmartGridComm '10)*, pp. 350–355, IEEE, Gaithersburg, Md, USA, October 2010.

13

Distributed Storage Manager System for Synchronized and Scalable AV Services across Networks

Frank X. Sun,[1] John Cosmas,[2] Muhammad Ali Farmer,[1] and Abdul Waheed[1]

[1] *British Institute of Technology & E-Commerce, 258-262 Romford Road, London E7 9HZ, UK*
[2] *Department of Electronic & Computer Engineering, School of Engineering and Design, Brunel University, Middlesex UB8 3PH, UK*

Correspondence should be addressed to Frank X. Sun, frank@bite.ac.uk

Academic Editor: Stefania Colonnese

This paper provides an innovative solution, namely, the distributed storage manager that opens a new path for highly interactive and personalized services. The distributed storage manager provides an enhancement to the MHP storage management functionality acting as a value added middleware distributed across the network. The distributed storage manager system provides multiple protocol support for initializing and downloading both streamed and file-based content and provides optimum control mechanisms to organize the storing and retrieval of content that are remained accessible to other multiple heterogeneous devices.

1. Introduction

In the Savant project (http://dea.brunel.ac.uk/project/Savant/), as part of the overall system architecture providing the end-to-end application for producing, delivering, and using of enriched interactive TV content, the content access system (CAS) presents the scalable (where scalability means content personalization, device independence and network independence) and synchronized service to the user by means of multiple heterogeneous devices [1]. It is designed as a home media server which adapts the service so that it can be consumed in a personalized way using three different device classes with different properties: a conventional TV set for traditional viewing, a TabletPC as a portable powerful, highly interactive personal device, and a PDA as a portable lightweight personal device. While the TV set is connected directly to the home media server, the portable devices will communicate with the server using IP via a WLAN connection. Additional content to be synchronized with the main content, such as a signer or multiple camera views, can be delivered over broadband or broadcast networks. The CAS supports the presentation synchronization transparently.

Multimedia home platform (DVB-MHP) is an open middleware system standard designed by the DVB project for interactive digital television. The MHP enables the reception and execution of interactive, Java-based applications on a TV set. Interactive TV applications can be delivered over the broadcast channel, together with audio and video streams. These applications can be, for example, information services, games, interactive voting, e-mail, SMS, or shopping. Although there is a certain amount of storage management incorporated with multimedia home platform (MHP 1.2) specification, this is not sufficient for the storage requirements of the home media server system [2]. At present, the storage management functionality specified by MHP is restricted and based on the Java File I/O. These operations permit file access to persistently stored content and access to content downloaded using a specific broadcast channel. Nonetheless, additional control mechanisms are necessary to sort out multiple content formats that are consumed by the terminal in a variety of ways. In addition, there is no support for managing the downloading and extraction of content by means of multiple protocols used within the broadcast network. Therefore, an additional storage management system needs to be defined and implemented.

This paper provides an innovative solution, namely, the distributed storage manager that opens a new path for highly interactive and personalized services. The presented

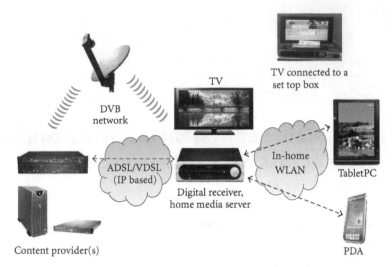

FIGURE 1: Scalable rich media TV service.

functionality of distributed storage manager provides an enhancement to the MHP 1.2 storage management functionality acting as a value-added middleware distributed across the network. The distributed storage manager system provides multiple protocol support for initializing and downloading both streamed and file-based content and provides optimum control mechanisms to organize the storing and retrieval of content that are remained accessible to other multiple heterogeneous devices such as Set Top Box, TabletPC, and PDA. A novelty distribution module based on the CORBA distributed computing environment which was embedded in the distributed storage manager was designed. The distributed storage manager provides location transparency of service and the functionality to transport multimedia content from server to client or vice versa.

This paper first describes the key parts of the content access system and then describes the architecture of the distributed storage manager system, introduces each of the components, and describes their functions within the system. Finally, conclusions are drawn.

2. Content Access System (CAS) Architecture

For the purpose of supporting service scalability, a content access system has been developed [3]. The content access system (CAS) was considered as an engine for controlling and managing services. It presents the scalable service to the user by means of multiple heterogeneous devices (Figure 1). The setup of the CAS consists of a home media server (HMS), a Fujitsu-Siemens Activity 300, and three clients, a TabletPC (Fujitsu-Siemens Stylistic (ST Series)), a PDA (Fujitsu-Siemens PocketLoox), and a TV which is connected to a set top box (another Fujitsu-Siemens Activity 300).

The HMS receives all information from the service delivery system (SDS), stores essence and metadata, and makes it accessible for the clients via the client service system. With the exception of the client devices, all components built

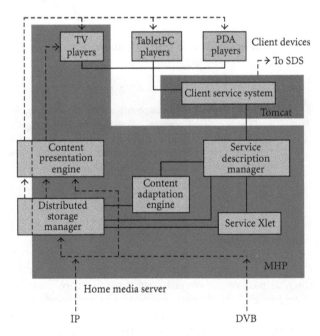

FIGURE 2: System architecture of content access system.

upon MHP (multimedia home platform) middleware shown in Figure 2 reside on the HMS.

The CAS presents the scalable service to the user by means of multiple heterogeneous devices. The core element of the CAS is a home server at the premises of the customer that provides fine-granular scalability and personalization of the service. It will adapt the service such that it can be consumed using three different device classes with different properties: a conventional TV set for linear viewing, a TabletPC as a portable powerful, highly interactive personal device, and a PDA as a portable lightweight personal device. To realize this, content transcoding may be necessary on the home server. While the TV set will be connected directly to the home server, the portable devices will communicate with the server using IP via a WLAN connection. Using the service on the three different device classes is termed service scalability. If service components have been transmitted using multiple networks, it is the responsibility of the CAS to reassemble these components to form a composite service and to present them synchronously.

The content presentation engine presents and synchronizes content to the user in the form specified by the user interface, so it has two purposes: content delivery and content synchronization. The service description manager is responsible for receiving, updating, maintaining, and interpreting the service description and triggers processes depending on the information found there. It resides inside the MHP world and is composed of two logical subparts, called passive and active parts, respectively. The content adaptation engine is responsible to adapt multimedia content such that it can be displayed on a variety of terminals with different resources and can be transferred over networks of varying properties. The service Xlet fulfils two purposes within the CAS. First it signals a DVB service, for example, a TV programme, which carries a specific service. After tuning into the channel, the service Xlet is started through the MHP application manager. The service Xlet then controls the application in the CAS. The second function of the service Xlet is to transfer the metadata to the CAS modules.

3. Distributed Storage Manager System Architecture

3.1. Functional Overview of Distributed Storage Manager System. Although there is a certain amount of storage management facilities incorporated with MHP, this is rather rudimentary and not sufficient for the storage requirements of terminal system since it is restricted and based on the Java.File.IO package. Also an MHP-enabled terminal requires additional content management and control specifically if content/data is being delivered over multiple transport protocols, channels, and networks. There are not control mechanisms to organize multiple content formats that are consumed by the terminal in various ways. Additional storage and retrieval management is required for multimedia content that is associated with the main AV multimedia content. The current storage management mechanisms provided by MHP do not distinguish between the various uses of content, and it does not implement any particular searching mechanism, so it makes the process of content retrieval inefficient. So a storage manager system for MHP was required as part of the terminal middleware to accomplish a rather complex task involving the access and extraction of content via different DVB data delivery channels, such as DVB object carousel, DVB PES, DVB private sections, DVB IP sections (multicast IP/UDP packages via MPE), and various IP transport channels. In addition, the location of content extracted over such channels must be recorded in a consistent manner. This permits the search and retrieval of the absolute file location of content in an efficient and timely manner.

The storage manager system has access to an interface to download content on to multiple heterogeneous devices.

There are three different user devices as the heterogeneous devices:

(i) Set top box (Fujitsu-Siemens Activy 300) is connected with TV and remote control. It provides large storage, and its components include a wavelancard, IP connection (also accessible via UMTS), and a DVB card.

(ii) TabletPC (Fujitsu-Siemens Stylistic (ST Series)) is operated via touch screen and keyboard and used as a portable device at home. Its components are a DVB-T card and a wavelancard for the local network.

(iii) PDA (Fujitsu-Siemens PocketLoox) is used as the mobile device for "on-the-move" usage. It is equipped with storage media and can automatically connect to the STB. Its components are wavelancard and UMTS connection.

So as one of the fundamental objectives of the storage manager system was to allow multiple heterogeneous devices and multiple server processes in a distributed environment. There is no mechanism for distributing content to different types of terminal devices within MHP, so the storage management system has to be implemented on a distributed platform. Therefore, an additional storage management system needs to be defined and implemented to provide solutions to these issues.

Meanwhile, the storage manager system is responsible for storing, retrieving, and organising input content from the object carousel, private sections (broadcast channel), and IP content (DSL, GPRS) via the broadband channel as well as transcoded content from the content adaptation engine. The storage manager provides the access control with functions to trigger and extract content from the delivery channels, that is, DVB broadcast channel and IP broadband channel [4–7]. These functions include the following:

(i) DSMCC object carousel, DVB PES, and DVB private sections downloading from the DVB transport stream,

(ii) IP extraction within multiprotocol encapsulation (private sections)

(iii) IP extraction from the broadband channel.

The storage manager, is also responsible for the storing, retrieval, managing and maintaining of persistently stored content decided by the user and also manages the removal of no longer used content. The SM runs on the home media server; it provides a mechanism for organizing and managing the persistent storage on the home media server. When any content is persistently saved to disk, any metadata describing the content is also persistently saved with the content. The storage manager also stores metadata that describes the user profile/preferences during the system initialization process.

A structured database is generated by the storage manager from metadata, which contains the location of content on the hard disk. The storage manager also is responsible for providing absolute file locations of content that is stored on disk to external other CAS system components, for example, service description manager or content adaptation engine. The storage manager allows external access to it and executes storage manager functionality. This therefore allows these external other CAS components to drive the content presentation engine and present content to the user. The storage manager provides a reference or pointer (URL or absolute file path) of the content and forwards it to the calling component. The storage manager reports the current location of content to the service description manager, thus keeping the service description up to date.

3.2. Storage Manager System Functional Components. The storage manager system enables applications to store and retrieve content to/from the home media server persistent file systems. For the storage manager (SM) to communicate to external software components (i.e., service description manager, content adaptation engine), java events/listeners are used and an external interface is provided for external software entities to submit requests to the storage manager.

The SM triggers the carousel download when a service has been selected. The SM sets the carousel root based on MHP properties and the selected service locator (DVB locator). It also controls access to the content contained within the carousel. The request coming from the service description manager for carousel content consists of the relative file path of the desired carousel content. The relative file path is combined with the carousel root, and then the absolute file path of the content is provided. After the SM has confirmed that the content is available on the carousel, then the absolute file location is returned.

A section filter (ring filter) is used to extract data carried within the private sections of the transport stream (DVB over IP). This software component assumes that the payload of the private section is IP packets, that is, MPE. The payload of the IP packets and the use of the IP packets are design specific. The Java.net package is used to create sockets thus supporting the sending and receiving of IP (UDP) packets via the return channel. The SM loads a user profile once a login has been successful. The contents of the user profile are design specific although the profile should at least provide the SM with the user's persistent root directory.

The current implementation supports transmission of media items over the DSMCC object carousel and private sections. After receiving a DVB locator, the module decides by way of the DVB SI if the media item is transferred in an object carousel or in private sections. The term "media item" is used for a set of files, for example, HTML pages usually refer to pictures, style sheets, and other files. Media items in the object carousel are stored immediately after they were requested. This means that the file has to be in the carousel when the request comes in. The actual extraction of files from the object carousel is part of the MHP implementation. The module therefore uses the MHP DSMCC API to make use of it.

After a media item has been stored, the storage manager informs its listeners by events that there is a new content available. There are two kinds of events: one indicates that the storing succeeded (Storage Event), and the other one indicates that the storing failed (Request Failed Event). Failure of storing media items can occur for instance if some sections of a media item get lost. The components of storage manager and their relationships are listed below and shown in Figure 3.

(i) Properties manager: the properties manager is used to store and load system properties, terminal characteristics, user preferences, and user profiles.

(ii) Persistent storage: the persistent storage facility is provided by the storage manager.

(iii) Storage manager implementer: the storage manager implementer provides the root class of the storage manager subsystem and provides overall control of the software components created by it.

(iv) Media item manager: the media item manager is defined for the storage manager so that the storage manager knows which media item it has downloaded, where to find the media item it should remove (i.e., delete from the persistent storage), and how to do a clean-up operation.

(v) Download clients: the download clients defines an interface for all the clients to trigger a file download and proposes a common abstract interface for all download clients.

(vi) Carousel manager: the carousel manager is central instance to manager locating and attaching of DSM-CC object carousel.

(vii) Content location table: the content location table is used to construct a table, based on the supplied metadata, containing information about content.

(viii) Content container object: it represents a storage container for content description data fields including a content item's relative filename, absolute file name, a collection of associate content relative filenames, segment start time, and segment duration.

3.3. Storage Event Dispatching Algorithm. When a request media item event is issued by the service description manager, the storage manager uses the following algorithm to determine if and how the media item should be downloaded and which storage event is thrown:

(i) with checking in the persistent storage file, if the media item is already locally available and has already been cached, then the event will be ignored;

(ii) if the media item has an RTSP (real-time streaming protocol) media locator point to the service delivery system (SDS), save the information that it is available in the media item management and dispatch event that the media item is now available with this media locator;

(iii) if the media item has a DVB locator, initiate download of media item and when successfully downloaded, save the information that it is locally available in the media item management and dispatch event that the media item is now available (overwriting its current availability status) with a new local media locator.

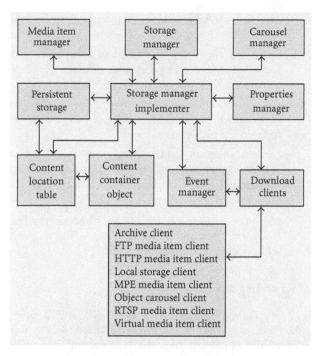

Figure 3: The distributed storage manager system components.

If media item has a DVB locator (not RTSP, ftp, or http), then the media item is normally downloaded with the appropriate download client. As usual, the media item management is notified that the media item has been downloaded. The media item might already be available because it has a second RTSP media locator. So if the media item has two media locators (RTSP and DVB), then the storage manager dispatches two storage events: one for the RTSP that is dispatched directly after the media item has been requested that indicates the content is available on the service delivery system (SDS). In parallel, the storage manager is downloading the content signaled in the DVB locator and when this download is finished, dispatches a second storage event for the same media item, saying that the media item is now available in the persistent storage, thus sparing the SDS from further requests.

3.4. Principle of Storage Manager System Operations. The storage manager (SM) is initialised at terminal boot up during the MHP environment initialisation. This is done during the system runtime. Therefore, the SM is integrated into the implemented MHP stack extending its current rudimentary persistent storage system. Since the storage manager implementer is the root software entity, it is responsible for the initialisation of all other SM software components and processes.

Upon initialisation the storage manager is loaded by the java runtime class loader. The storage manager implementer sets the service locator when the user selects a new service. An empty content location table (CLT) is initialised by the storage manager implementer; the CLT attempts to locate the persistent storage configuration file. This configuration

file contains CLT entries of content that were persistently stored during the previous terminal operation. The file is then parsed recreating new content container objects (CCOs) of the previous persistent storage entries. The newly created CCOs are then added by the CLT.

The requests from the service description manager are handled by storage manager to make media items content available. The SM finds out where to get the requested media item from by analyzing the media locator and uses the appropriate module to access the content. By analyzing the request media item event, the SM gets the type of download and then passes the request to appropriate download client to download. Download client defines the interfaces for the internal storage manager modules. Each download client handles one media item transport mechanism; it also provides a common method to dispatch events and to call a suitable download client for a specific media item request.

Upon receiving a request from an external software subsystem, the request is passed to the storage manager implementer where the request is processed. If the request is for the absolute location of content, the relative filename is extracted from the request. The storage manager implementer then queries the CLT that performs a binary search of CCO. The CCO performs a matching function and validates the existence of the file using the stored absolute file location. If this search is successful, the corresponding CCO is extracted by the CLT and passed to the storage manager implementer. The storage manager implementer extracts the absolute file location and associate content file names and returns them to the external software sub-system that initiates the request. If no match is found or the validation test fails, an NULL is returned.

Since some form of content requires associated content (e.g., an HTML page may embed an image, therefore the location of this image is also required), the storage manager stores the mapping between content file names and associate content file names. If the request is to store a content item, the storage manager implementer extracts the relative filename and associate content file names from the request. The storage manager implementer then searches the absolute file location and relative filename. A new CCO is created by the storage manager implementer, which then instructs the CLT to store the CCO. If the request is to delete a content item, the storage manager implementer instructs the CLT to search and retrieve the target CCO. If found and the CCO validates the existence of the content file, the storage manager implementer instructs to remove the content with the corresponding absolute file location from the hard disk.

When a terminating signal is received by the MHP system, that is, the session had ended, the mechanism is provided by the storage manager implementer to allow the MHP system to inform the storage manager implementer of the termination. When this notification is received, the storage manager implementer instructs the CLT to create a backup of all persistently stored entries to the persistent storage configuration file.

3.5. Components and System Testing. To test all the internal components and input and output of the storage manager, three testing environments were created to allow it to be tested in an integrated way. All the testing processes in the testing environments were as predicted and were successful. The three testing environments are presented as follows.

(i) Simulate MHP: a class known as "simulate MHP" was created to load all the storage manager components into a regular Java runtime environment. The aim of this environment is to enable all components to be tested. It is clear that since crucial parts of the distributed storage manager rely on MHP, not all components can be tested with this or will fully work even if they run.

(ii) Offair package (Stand-alone CAS without DVB input): an environment was created that relies on MHP but not on DVB input (off-air package). The aim of this environment is to set up the full workflow in the CAS. This especially allows testing communication between the components. Therefore, all components should implement the off-air functionality. The off-air storage manager class simulates downloading files by having all files available as local files and throwing storage events after some predefined schedules. It sends storage events that contain new locators for requested media items after some configurable time. So it is basically a translator of media locators. The information when which media item should arrive can be found in an XML configuration file located in the carousal directory. This file is parsed by the off-air storage manager config file parser that creates pairs of media items and time "stamps" to simulate that the media item is downloaded after a certain time. To schedule the requested media items (if they have been found in the configuration file), the media item arrival scheduler is used. This environment focuses on home media server functionalities rather than TV client functionalities. The prerequisite here is to have the MHP-RI available, and this means that this environment is set up on the terminal. This environment would allow testing of all (server) components in their "natural" environment and testing of storage manager functionalities that do not need DVB input (FTP, etc.). Such an environment would be independent of DVB streams, so that it does not have to rely on the creation of a DVB stream for the off-air testing.

(iii) Stand-alone version with DVB input: play prepared DVB transport stream from hard drive. The storage manager gets its DVB input not from the DVB channel but from a DVB stream stored on disk. This also includes video playback of main video on TV.

By using the three integrated testing environments, the following points were accomplished, and all the components testing results have passed:

(i) storage manager Impl: testing of the initialization of all software components and interfaces within storage manager;

(ii) carousel manager: testing the interfaces to the MHP API by downloading DSM-CC object carousel;

(iii) download client: the download of content onto the hard disk from various download clients and the addition of CCO within the CLT;

(iv) media item management: testing of media item downloaded to the CAS. Add/remove a media item to/from the persistent storage;

(v) content location table: testing of the insertion, retrieval, and deletion of CCO. Testing of access methods and "synchronized" blocks and testing of binary search performance.

(vi) content container object: testing of access methods for storing and retrieving file names, file locations, and associated content file names.

3.6. Networking and Services

3.6.1. Distribution and the Use of CORBA. One of the fundamental objectives of the storage manager was to allow multiple clients and multiple server processes in a distributed environment. For this purpose, CORBA was used as its object request broker (Figure 4). CORBA is a mechanism in software for normalizing the method-call semantics between application objects residing either in the same address space (application) or remote address space (same host, or remote host, on a network). All CORBA code is encapsulated in storage manager servant, storage manager server and storage manager client classes that work at the interface level of the calling classes. This allows the CORBA transport layer to be replaced by different CORBA implementations.

To translate overloaded class methods into separate CORBA methods, this work goes into an IDL (interface definition language) file, which autogenerates the CORBA code during its compile process. The JDK1.3+ comes with the idlj compiler, which is used in this case to map IDL definitions into Java declarations and statements. The storage manager servant, storage manager server, and storage manager client class codes must deal with the translation step between the overloaded methods and the differently named CORBA equivalents.

3.6.2. Naming Service. Each object is registered with the naming service (Figure 5) at instantiation. It operates in a manner analogous to a file directory structure, adding the names of objects to each node of a branch, where the first level branch is the "context" and the second level the component. When CORBA methods need to find an object, a request is sent to the naming service to get the object's location. The naming service is in charge and searches by name. Components must be uniquely named, otherwise the original component will be overwritten by subsequent ones.

3.6.3. Event Service. The event service usually, but not necessarily, runs on the same machine as the naming service, listens for event notifications from the server(s), and is responsible for getting these events across the network. The

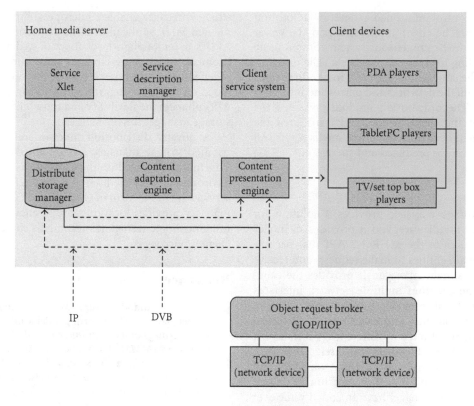

FIGURE 4: Structure of distributed platform for storage manager.

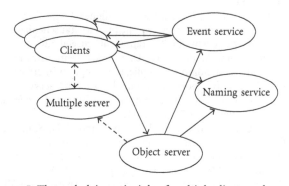

FIGURE 5: The underlying principle of multiple clients and servers.

event service uses the "push" model, that is, events are pushed out from the service to all registered clients. A concrete class on the object server sends a notify message over the event service to its companion on the client.

3.6.4. Object Server.
This process is at the centre of the distributed storage manager architecture. The object server class contains the main entry point for the object server process.

Once the object server has an ORB, it can register the CORBA service. It starts by getting a reference to the root of the naming service. This returns a generic CORBA object and then transferred into a naming context object to register a CORBA service with the naming service.

For the client deployment, once a reference to the naming service has been obtained, it can be used to access the naming service and find the service such that the media item transfer service is found, and then the download media item method is invoked.

With the use of the distribution module (Figure 4), the request and response messages between the client and the server are exchanged through the 10 Mbps Ethernet LAN for the TV sets (set top box), for the portable device (PDA, Tablet PC) via a WLAN connection. A web server was constructed with the home media server, and the basis for communication (requests and responses) is HTTP. The storage manager instantiates and controls all components that run within the Tomcat environment. The object request brokers (ORBs) in both sides use the GIOP/IIOP (generic inter-orb protocol/internet inter-ORB protocol) protocol to exchange the messages. The client applications call the functions supported by storage manager to get the multimedia contents transparently from the object server, which is dispersed on the communication network.

3.6.5. Distribution Module Testing.
To test the functionality of the distribution module, an application was developed on the basis of the distributed storage manager API. This application provides the interactive video retrieval service for video on demand (VOD). The distributed storage manager provides the client devices with various operations

to transport and control multimedia data in a location transparent manner. The client application and the server objects running on the heterogeneous system communicate interactively according to the VOD scenarios. The distribution module uses the storage manager API to obtain various multimedia data from the networks and parses and interprets the data encoded. The distribution module presented the interpreted data to the client devices and transferred the inputs from the client devices to the home media server. All the testing processes are as predicted and successful.

4. Conclusions

The distributed storage manager provides a solution for extending the MHP middleware, and it provides an implementation of interfaces to the MHP 1.2 API that permits other external software entities to make requests and receive responses from the storage manager. It provides the capability to retrieve content from multiple network interfaces utilizing various protocols provided by the MHP platform; this permits the downloading and extraction of file-based and streaming content delivered by different DVB transport protocols, namely, DSM-CC object carousel, DVB PES, MPEG-2 private sections, multicast UDP/IP via MPE, and various IP transport protocols. The presented functionalities of the distributed storage manager have an added value over the already provided functionalities by the most recent MHP version 1.2, also it supports for currently popular DVB-IPDC data carousels such as FLUTE to deliver files over the Internet or unidirectional systems from one or more senders to one or more receivers.

The distributed storage manager also provides multiple protocol support for initializing and downloading both streamed and file-based content. In addition, complex but optimum control mechanisms are provided to organize the storing and retrieval of content that are remained accessible to other multiple heterogeneous devices.

The distributed storage manager also organizes the downloaded content upon the hard disk to permit efficient retrieval of content file locations and provides access mechanisms to the downloaded content. It performs the task of organizing content that involves providing a structured database to store the mapping of absolute file locations, relative file names, and relative associate file names on the hard disk. This permits the distributed storage manager to service applications/external software components (i.e., content presentation engine) or decoders/players with the physical location of requested content. It also permits other external software entities to make requests and receive responses from the storage manager.

Compared to the storage management incorporated with multimedia home platform, the distributed storage manager permits a metadata search and retrieval of stored content based on a set of generated keywords; in addition, submission of multiple keywords is permitted. The resulting list will contain various content tiles with their matching score and allows a faster content presentation to the end user.

The distributed storage manager works with DVB-J (service Xlet) application that is executed via MHP. The storage manager enables, interoperability of various implemented MHP applications. The distributed storage manager API is a set of high-level functions, data structures, and protocols which represent a standard interface for platform-independent application software. It is object oriented and is based on the Java programming language. Furthermore, the API enhances the flexibility and reusability of the distributed storage manager functionalities.

A novelty distribution module embedded in the distributed storage manager was designed and implemented. This module is based on the CORBA distributed computing environment, and the interfaces that define the distribution services are in the form of OMG IDL. The distributed storage manager provides location transparency of service and the functionality to transport multimedia content from server to client or vice versa.

References

[1] P. Wolf, G. Durand, G. Kazai, M. Lalmas, and U. Rauschenbach, "A metadata model supporting scalable interactive TV services," in *Proceedings of the 11th International Multi-Media Modelling Conference (MMM '05)*, Melbourne, Australia, January 2005.

[2] J. Cosmas, A.n Lucas, K. Krishnapillai, and M. Akhtar, "Storage manger system for DVB terminals," in *Proceedings of the Telecommunications, Networks and Broadcasting(PG Net '01)*, EPSRC, Liverpool UK, June 2001.

[3] U. Rauschenbach, W. Putz, P. Wolf, R. Mies, and G. Stoll, "A scalable interactive service supporting synchronized delivery over broadcast and broadband networks," http://dea.brunel.ac.uk/project/savant/pub/IBC04-SAVANT-rauschenbach_et_al-updated.pdf.

[4] U. Rauschenbach, J. Heuer, and K. Illgner, "Next-Generation interactive broadcast services," http://www.rauschenbach.net/Publications/docs/wsdb2004_rauschenbach_etal.pdf

[5] B. Heidkamp, A. Pohl, and U. Schiek, "Demonstrating the feasibility of standardized application program interfaces that will allow mobile/portable terminals to receive services combining UMTS and DVB-T," *International Journal of Services and Standards*, vol. 1, no. 2, pp. 228–42, 2004.

[6] A. Centonza, T. J. Owens, J. Cosmas, and Y. H. Song, "Differentiated service delivery in cooperative IP-based broadcast and mobile telecommunications networks," *IMA Journal of Management Mathematics*, vol. 18, pp. 245–267, 2007.

[7] Y. Zhang, C. H. Zhang, J. Cosmas et al., "Analysis of DVB-H network coverage with the application of transmit diversity," *IEEE Transactions on Broadcasting*, vol. 54, no. 3, pp. 568–577, 2008.

14

Utility-Based Joint Routing, Network Coding, and Power Control for Wireless Ad Hoc Networks

Kaiqian Ou, Yinlong Xu, Xiumin Wang, and Wang Liu

School of Computer Science and Technology, Key Laboratory on High Performance Computing,
University of Science and Technology of China, Anhui Province 230026, China

Correspondence should be addressed to Yinlong Xu, ylxu@ustc.edu.cn

Academic Editor: Zongpeng Li

Energy saving and high delivery reliability are two essential metrics in wireless ad hoc networks. In this paper, we propose a joint power control and network coding (PCNC) scheme which regulates the transmission power to reduce the overall energy usage and uses network coding to improve reliability by reducing the number of packet retransmissions. To argue for PCNC scheme, we investigate both unicast and multicast routing scenarios. To evaluate routing optimality, we adopt expected utility as a metric, which integrates energy cost, reliability, and benefit value. Based on the expected utility, we explore the optimality in both unicast and multicast routing. For unicast routing, we propose an optimal algorithm. We show the NP-hardness of multicast routing problem, and also design a heuristic solution. Results from simulations demonstrate that PCNC improves the performance in terms of expected utility compared with existing techniques.

1. Introduction

Wireless ad hoc networks drew lots of attention in recent years because of its potential applications in various areas. However, ad hoc networks suffer the energy shortage due to the limited power supply devices [1, 2] and unreliable communication caused by the unstable wireless medium [3, 4]. Therefore, *saving energy* and *improving message delivery reliability* are two important issues in the design of wireless ad hoc protocols.

Wireless communications (e.g., sending a message) are usually the most energy-consuming events in wireless networks. Thus, one of the most straight approaches to reduce energy consumption is decreasing the transmission power at the senders. However, decreasing the transmission power will reduce the reliability of the link, which may incur packet loss during data propagation [5]. Packet loss leads to packet retransmissions, which consumes more energy. To balance energy cost and reliability, several approaches have been proposed, especially, transmission power control (TPC) and network coding (NC).

TPC, which has been studied in [5, 6], focuses on adjusting transmission power level on each sender to reduce the

energy consumption. In [5], TPC is applied to study the tradeoff between end-to-end reliability and energy consumption based on the probability link model. Different from [5], Li et al. [6] integrated TPC with retransmission to address the problem of energy-efficient reliable routing for wireless ad hoc networks. With TPC, the transmission power can be decreased at each node for the packet retransmissions. Their experimental results also demonstrate the benefits of adopting TPC and retransmission.

Recently, NC has received extensive research attentions in networking area. Instead of just forwarding the input packets, a relay node with NC encodes input packets into some encoded ones and sends them out. After receiving the required number of encoded packets, a receiver can decode out the original packets. Recent work [7] shows that NC can improve reliability by reducing the number of packet retransmissions in wireless lossy networks.

Motivated by the advantages of TPC (reducing transmission power) and reliability benefit of NC (reducing retransmission times), this paper studies the tradeoff between energy cost and reliability using a joint power control and network coding (PCNC) scheme. We will study the benefits of PCNC on unicast and multicast in wireless ad hoc network and adopt a widely used metric, *expected utility* [8–11], which integrates link cost, link stability, and system benefit to evaluate the performance of the system. We define the system utility as

$$U = AR - C, \qquad (1)$$

where the cost C of a system is the total expected energy consumption, and the benefit A of a system is the gain of successful message delivery, and R is the reliability of the routing. Delivery reliability and energy cost depend on not only routing path, but also how to conduct TPC and NC at senders. Therefore, the challenge is that a routing algorithm based on PCNC needs to determine not only the optimal routing path (or tree), but also the optimal combination of transmission power assignment and coding strategy at each sender.

The main contributions of our work are summarized as follows.

(1) We systematically integrate routing, TPC, and NC in wireless ad hoc networks based on utility metric.

(2) For unicast, we propose an optimal routing algorithm to determine the maximum utility path with the optimal combination of transmission power assignment and coding strategy at each sender along the path.

(3) For multicast, we show that finding an optimal multicast tree to maximize the expected utility is NP-hard and propose a heuristic approach named MIEUDF.

(4) Simulation results show that our proposed routing schemes outperform existing schemes in terms of expected utility in both unicast and multicast scenarios.

The rest of the paper is organized as follows. We first introduce related work in Section 2. Section 3 gives the preliminaries, which show the network coding scheme and the link model. The utility metric is described in Section 4. In Section 5, we propose the optimal routing algorithm for unicast session. The heuristic solution of multicast routing is proposed in Section 6. The simulation results are presented in Section 7. Finally, we conclude the paper in Section 8.

2. Related Work

Transmission power control (TPC), which allows a sender to adjust its transmission power level, is used to improve the performance of the network. Correia et al. [12] adopted TPC to decrease energy consumption while maintaining the reliability of the channel in wireless sensor networks. Pierpaolo et al. [13] proposed a distributed TPC method to improve the energy efficiency of routing algorithms in ad hoc networks. By integrating TPC with retransmission, Li et al. [6] proposed energy-efficient reliable routing schemes in wireless ad hoc networks.

Network coding (NC) is an approach pioneered by Ahlswede et al. [14], with which a relay node encodes the input packets and outputs the encoded ones. It has been shown that NC offers exciting benefits in terms of throughput, reliability, cost, and delay in wireless networks [15–18]. Specifically,

TABLE 1: Summary of key notations.

Notation	Meaning
x	The number of equal-size packets in a message
A	Benefit value of given message
V	Set containing all nodes in a network
$d_{u,v}$	The distance between node u and v
p_u	Transmission power level of node u
n_u	Predetermined number of transmitted packets on node u
$r_{u,v}$	Packet link reliability over link (u, v)
$R_{u,v}$	Message link reliability over link (u, v)
$R_{u \sim v}$	Message path reliability along path from node u to v
C_u	Pre-determined energy consumption on sender u
U^Q	Expected utility along path Q
REU_u	Remaining expected utility of node u to a given destination
U^T	Expected utility through tree T
IEU_u	Incremental expected utility of added destination u in MIEUDF

the reliability gain of NC was studied recently in [7, 19, 20]. The work in [19] confirmed that NC could increase the reliability by reducing the number of transmissions in unicast communication. In multicast, the work in [7, 20] showed that NC improves network reliability.

A new metric called *expected utility* was developed and shown achieving a better performance than other metric (cost and reliability)[10]. Later, expected utility was widely used to evaluate system performance [8, 9, 11]. Based on expected utility metric, M. M. Lu and J. Wu [8] applied network coding to routing problems in unreliable wireless environments and demonstrated that network coding improves the system performance. J. Wu, M. Lu, and F. Li [9] explored the optimality of opportunistic routing (OR) for a utility-based routing, and studied [11] the data-gathering problem in wireless sensor networks by adopting the utility-based metric.

3. Preliminaries

We summarize the main notations used in this paper in Table 1. Suppose that a given message consisting of x equal-size packets is assigned with a benefit value A, that is, the system will obtain benefit value A for each destination successfully receiving the message.

3.1. Network Coding Scheme and Assumptions. Network coding scheme allows intermediate node(s) between the source and destination(s) to encode the incoming packets, and then forward the encoded ones. In this paper, we assume that the given original message is divided by source node into x fixed-sized packets, $B_1, B_2, \ldots, B_x$. In this paper, we assume that random linear network coding over a finite field $GF(q)$ is adopted in the wireless network, that is, a transmitted packet is a linear combination of $B_1, B_2, \ldots, B_x$ with coefficients are

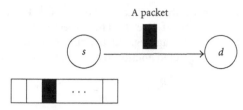

FIGURE 1: Link model: node s sends a packet of message to node d over link (s, d).

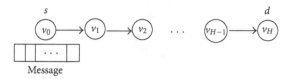

FIGURE 2: Unicast path example: node s sends a message to node d over path $Q = \langle s = v_0, v_1, v_2, \ldots, v_{H-1}, v_H = d \rangle$.

randomly selected from $GF(q)$ [21]. Some more assumptions on coding scheme are as follows.

(1) There is a limitation on the number of encoded packets of a message transmitted (also called *pre-determined number*) at each sender i, denoted as n_i, which is adjustable as in [8]. If no limitation on the number of transmitted packets, the power cost may be extremely high for energy-limited devices.

(2) An intermediate node will transmit its pre-determined number of encoded packets only when it has received x independent encoded packets. Without this assumption, more energy consumption is wasted on sending useless packets that cannot be used to reconstruct the original message.

Based on the above coding scheme, a message is transmitted hop-by-hop from source to destination in form of encoded packets. However, a message is not guaranteed to be successfully delivered to a destination, due to pre-determined number rather than unlimited number of transmitted encoded packets. The pre-determined number should reflect the importance of the corresponding message, because an important message requires high reliability and more encoded packets being transmitted. The increment of the number of transmitted packets can directly increase the transmission reliability (see Section 4.3). Under this coding scheme, the tradeoff between expected energy consumption and message delivery reliability is explored in the rest of this paper.

3.2. Link Model. In this paper, we use the similar link model in [5], which is also widely used in other works [22–24]. Assume that the transmitted packets are fixed-size of B bits, and all nodes transmit at the same rate.

Consider the link shown in Figure 1, where a packet of a message is transmitted from node s to d through the zero mean additive white Gaussian noise (AWGN) channel. Following [5], the probability of packet successful reception is given by (this formula is achieved using AWGN channel with Rayleigh fading assuming the sender does not have information about the fading state, See [5] for more details)

$$r_{s,d}(d_{s,d}, p_s) = \exp\left(-\frac{d_{s,d}^k(2^B - 1)}{\beta p_s}\right), \quad (2)$$

where B is the packet size, $d_{s,d}$ is the distance between node s and d, p_s is the chosen transmission power level at node s, and k is the propagation power loss exponent, usually assumed to be between 2 to 4. As in [5], the noise power and fading parameter are assumed to be constant across the network, denoted as β. Since B, k, and β are all assumed to be constant, a sender can adjust its transmission power to control the probability of packet successful reception over a link.

In this section, we introduced two adjustable parameters at each sender i, transmission power level p_i and pre-determined number n_i of transmitted packets. In the next section, we will analyze how these adjustable parameters at senders affect energy consumption and message delivery reliability, and hence the expected utility.

4. Utility Metric Model

In this section, we first introduce utility metric for both unicast path and multicast tree as functions of energy consumption and transmission reliability. Then, we study how to calculate energy consumption and message link/path reliability based on TPC and NC.

4.1. Utility for Unicast. We first consider a simple case, where a source node s sends a message to a destination node d using a link (s, d), as illustrated in Figure 1. Denote *pre-determined energy consumption* at node s as C_s which is defined as the transmission power times the pre-determined number of transmitted packets and *message link reliability* as $R_{s,d}$ which is defined as the probability of x independent encoded packets being successfully received by d. The system has the probability of $R_{s,d}$ to obtain benefit value A at the cost of C_s, and may consume energy C_s obtaining zero benefit with the probability of $1 - R_{s,d}$ with less than x independent encoded packets being successfully received by d. The expected utility over this link is

$$R_{s,d}(A - C_s) + (1 - R_{s,d})(-C_s) = R_{s,d} \times A - C_s. \quad (3)$$

We then consider a general case with single destination where source node s sends the message to destination d over path $Q = \langle s = v_0, v_1, v_2, \ldots, v_{H-1}, v_H = d \rangle$, as shown in Figure 2. For a multihop path scenario, the probability of destination d successfully receiving the message is *message path reliability*, that is, the probability that a message is successfully transmitted over all links along Q rather than message link reliability in Formula (3). Let $R_{v_t \sim v_h}$ denote the message path reliability from node v_t to v_h along

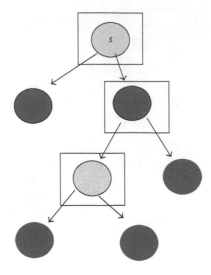

D: nodes in red

SS: nodes in rectangle

FIGURE 3: Multicast tree example: node s sends a message to multiple destinations in D through the tree.

the path. According to network coding scheme described in Section 3.1, each intermediate node will relay the message to its downstream node only after it successfully receives the message from the source. So, $R_{v_t \sim v_h} = \prod_{i=t}^{h-1} R_{v_i,v_{i+1}}$. Since the probability of destination d successfully receiving the message is $R_{v_0 \sim v_H}$, the system gets expected benefit $R_{v_0 \sim v_H} \times A$. For an intermediate node v_i, the probability of consuming pre-determined energy is equal to the probability that the message is successfully transmitted from source to v_i, that is, $R_{v_0 \sim v_i}$. Therefore, expected energy consumption at node v_i is equal to $C_{v_i} \times R_{v_0 \sim v_i}$. The total expected energy cost along the path is the sum of the expected energy consumption at each sender, that is, $\sum_{i=0}^{H-1} C_{v_i} \times R_{v_0 \sim v_i}$. Then, the expected utility of path Q, denoted as U^Q, is expected benefit contributed by the single destination minus the total expected energy cost at all senders along the path

$$U^Q = R_{v_0 \sim v_H} \times A - \sum_{i=0}^{H-1} C_{v_i} \times R_{v_0 \sim v_i}, \quad (4)$$

where $R_{v_0 \sim v_i} = \prod_{j=0}^{i-1} R_{v_j,v_{j+1}}$.

4.2. Utility for Multicast. We consider the scenario consisting of multiple destinations where a source node s sends the message to multiple destinations through a multicast tree as shown in Figure 3. Let T be the multicast tree, and D be the *set of destinations*, including all leaves and some intermediate nodes of T. A node $i \in D$ may contribute benefit value A to the system with a probability of $R_{s \sim i}$ because the probability of node i successfully receiving the message is $R_{s \sim i}$. Let SS be the *set of senders* on the tree, including the source and all intermediate nodes. A node $j \in SS$ may have pre-determined energy consumption with a probability of $R_{s \sim j}$ because node j consumes energy only after it successfully receives

the message from the source s. We use U^T to represent the expected utility of tree T. The expected utility of the multicast tree is the aggregated benefit of all destinations minus the total expected energy cost at all senders on the tree:

$$U^T = \sum_{i \in D} R_{s \sim i} \times A - \sum_{j \in SS} R_{s \sim j} \times C_j, \quad (5)$$

where $R_{s \sim t} = \prod_{\forall (u,v) \in s \sim t} R_{u,v}$.

4.3. Energy Consumption and Message Reliability. In this subsection, we study how to calculate energy consumption and message link reliability based on the two parameters at each sender, transmission power and pre-determined number of transmitted packets.

Let (u, v) be a link, where node u is the sender and node v is u's downstream node. Assume that the transmission power and the pre-determined number of transmitted packets at u are p_u and n_u, respectively. According to the definition of predetermined energy consumption,

$$C_u = p_u \times n_u. \quad (6)$$

In the following, we are to calculate $R_{u,v}$ based on p_u and n_u. From (2), the *packet delivery reliability over link $r_{u,v}$*, that is, the probability of a packet being successfully transmitted over a link can be obtained as

$$r_{u,v}(p_u, d_{u,v}) = \exp\left(-\frac{d_{u,v}^k (2^B - 1)}{\beta p_u}\right). \quad (7)$$

Since the message link reliability $R_{u,v}$ is the probability that x independent encoded packets being successfully transmitted over link (u, v), we can calculate $R_{u,v}$ by summing up the probability that exactly $j (j \geq x)$ packets successfully transmitted over the link. Without loss of generality, we assume that different packet transmissions are independent. Therefore, the packet transmissions can be regarded as a Bernoulli experiment. So, the probability of successfully receiving exact j packets follows binomial distribution, $\binom{n_u}{j} \cdot r_{u,v}^j (1 - r_{u,v})^{n_u - j}$.

By summing up the total $n_u - x + 1$ probabilities that exact j ($n_u \geq j \geq x$) out of n_u packets are successfully received by node v, we obtain the expression of the message link reliability over link (u, v) as

$$R_{u,v} = \sum_{j=x}^{n_u} \binom{n_u}{j} r_{u,v}^j (1 - r_{u,v})^{n_u - j}, \quad (8)$$

where $r_{u,v} = \exp(d_{u,v}^k (2^B - 1)/\beta p_u)$.

From (6) and (8), the predetermined energy consumption at u, C_u, and the massage link reliability over link (u, v), $R_{u,v}$, both depend on the adjustable transmission power and pre-determined number of transmitted packets at sender u. In the following, we use $C_u(p_u, n_u)$ to denote the predetermined energy consumption at node u, and $R_{u,v}(p_u, n_u)$ to denote the message link reliability over link (u, v).

By applying (6) and (8) to (4) or (5), we can calculate the expected utility for a given path or tree based on the transmission power level and the pre-determined number of transmitted packets at each sender.

5. Unicast Routing

In this section, we will model unicast routing and propose an optimal unicast routing algorithm.

5.1. Problem Statement. In a wireless ad hoc network, a source node s initiates a unicast session to send a message to a destination d. The problem is to find a unicast path to deliver the message from s to d such that the expected utility is maximized. Let Q be a unicast path from s to d, $R_{s\sim i}^Q$ be the message path reliability from source s to node i along the path Q, where i is a node on Q. Let C_j^Q be the pre-determined energy consumption at sender j. According to (4), the expected utility along path Q is

$$R_{s\sim d}^Q \times A - \sum_{j \in SS^Q} R_{s\sim j}^T \times C_j^Q, \qquad (9)$$

where SS^Q is the set of senders on path Q. Then, the maximum utility unicast problem can be formulated as

$$\text{Maximize} \quad U^Q = R_{s\sim d}^Q \times A - \sum_{j \in SS^Q} R_{s\sim j}^Q \times C_j^Q, \qquad (10)$$

$$\text{Subject to} \quad p_j \in LS, \quad j \in SS^Q, \quad n_j \in NS,$$

where Q is a feasible path from s to d, $LS = \{p_{\max}/L, 2p_{\max}/L, \dots, p_{\max}\}$ is the set of transmission power levels available at each sender, $p_{\max}$ is the maximum possible power level, $NS = \{x, x+1, x+2, x+3, \dots\}$ is the set of the feasible pre-determined number of transmitted packets (*note: at least x packets must be received by a node; otherwise, the destination cannot reconstruct the original message*). In Formula (10), $R_{s\sim i}^Q$ and C_j^Q can be calculated according to Formula (6) and (8), respectively.

The difficulty of optimal unicast routing is that the routing algorithm needs to determine not only the optimal routing path, but also the optimal selections of both transmission power and pre-determined number of transmitted packets at each sender along the path.

5.2. Optimal Solution. In this subsection, we propose an optimal unicast routing algorithm. An important observation is that the calculation of path utility can be conducted in a recursive way. Consider a path $Q = \langle s = v_0, v_1, v_2, \dots, v_{H-1}, v_H = d \rangle$, as shown in Figure 2. Define the expected utility of subpath from v_i to v_H as the *remaining expected utility* (REU) of node v_i, denoted as REU_{v_i}. Specially, $\text{REU}_{v_0} = \text{REU}_s = U^Q$ and $\text{REU}_d = \text{REU}_{v_H} = A$ because the initial benefit value of the message is A. From (4), the recursive expression of REU is

$$\text{REU}_{v_i} = \begin{cases} A & \text{if } i = H, \\ R_{v_i, v_{i+1}} \text{REU}_{v_{i+1}} - C_{v_i} & \text{if } 0 \le i \le H-1. \end{cases} \qquad (11)$$

Therefore, we can recursively apply Formula (11) starting from destination d to calculate the expected utility of any sub-path. Since $R_{v_i, v_{i+1}} \le 1$ and $C_{v_i} > 0$, each iterative

step of the calculation will reduce REU from the original value of A. To find the maximum utility path to destination d is equal to finding the minimum REU reduction path starting from the destination. So, the utility-based routing problem is similar to shortest path problem. But there are some differences: (1) our problem measures the distance in terms of expected utility rather than cost; (2) the solution of our problem requires to determine not only the next hop but also the values of both the transmission power and the pre-determined number of transmitted packets at each sender.

Based on the Dijkstra's algorithm for shortest path problem, we design a routing Algorithm 1 to maximize the expected utility from a source node to a destination node.

In Algorithm 1, V is the set of all nodes in a network. p_u and n_u are the transmission power and pre-determined number of transmitted packets at u, respectively. p_u^* and n_u^* are the corresponding optimal values of p_u and n_u to maximize the expected utility over the link (u, v). The existence of p_u^* and n_u^* is guaranteed by the following theorem.

Theorem 1. *For any link (u, v), the optimal values of both transmission power level p_u^* and pre-determined number of transmitted packets n_u^* exist such that the expected utility $R_{u,v}(p_u, n_u) \times \text{REU}_v - C_u(p_u, n_u)$ over the link is maximized.*

Proof. See The appendix.

The algorithm starts from the destination with the initial message benefit value A and REUs of other nodes are initially set to $-\infty$. At the beginning, V consists of all nodes in the network. In each iteration, this algorithm not only selects the node that reduces the REU to the least, that is, the node with largest REU will be removed from V, but also determines the corresponding optimal values of the transmission power and pre-determined number of transmitted packets at the selected node. The REU will be reduced at each intermediate node going backwards from the destination to the source node. When source s is selected and removed from V, the algorithm stops and outputs optimal path from s to d. Since Algorithm 1 is similar to Dijkstra algorithm, the time complexity of Algorithm 1 is $O(|V|^2)$.

When a routing path for a given source-destination pair is determined, the source divides the message into x packets, generates n_s^* encoded packets, and transmits them using transmission power p_s^* to its downstream node along the optimal path. Only after receiving x linearly independent packets from the upstream node, an intermediate node i begins to send n_i^* encoded packets with optimal transmission power p_i^* to the next hop.

6. Multicast Routing

In this section, we first formulate the maximum utility multicast routing problems, which is shown to be NP-hard. Then, a heuristic solution for multicast routing problem is proposed.

6.1. Problem Statement. Given a wireless network with a set of nodes V, a source node $s \in V$ initiates a multicast session

```
(1) for all v ∈ V do
(2)      REUv ← −∞.
(3)      assign benefit value to destination d : REU_d ← A.
(4) end for
(5) while s ∉ V do
(6)      Find node v ∈ V with the largest REU.
(7)      Remove node v from V.
(8)      For each node u ∈ V RELAX(v, u).
(9) end while
(10) procedure Relax(v, u)
(11)     Find the optimal p*_u and n*_u to maximize R_{u,v}(p_u, n_u)×
(12)     REU_v − C_u(p_u, n_u).
(13)     if REU_u < R_{u,v}(p*_u, n*_u) × REU_v − C_u(p*_u, n*_u). then
(14)         Update REU_u with p*_u and n*_u.
(15)     end if
(16) end procedure
```

ALGORITHM 1: Unicast(V, s, d, A).

and sends a message to a set of destinations $D \subseteq V$. It is to find a multicast tree to deliver the message from the source to all destinations such that the expected utility is maximized. The problem is called maximum-utility multicast routing problem (MUMRP).

Let $R_{s \sim i}^T$ be the message path reliability from source s to a node i along a muticast tree T. Denote the set of senders on T as SS^T. Let C_j^T be the pre-determined energy consumption at sender $j \in SS^T$. According to Formula (5), the expected utility of tree T is

$$\sum_{i \in D} R_{s \sim i}^T \times A - \sum_{j \in SS^T} R_{s \sim j}^T \times C_j^T. \tag{12}$$

Then, the MUMR problem can be formulated as

$$\text{Maximize} \quad U^T = \sum_{i \in D} R_{s \sim i}^T \times A - \sum_{j \in SS^T} R_{s \sim j}^T \times C_j^T,$$

$$\text{Subject to} \quad p_j \in LS, \quad n_j \in NS, \quad j \in SS^T, \tag{13}$$

where T is a feasible multicast tree connecting the source to all destinations in D. $LS = \{p_{max}/L, 2p_{max}/L, \ldots, p_{max}\}$ and $NS = \{x, x + 1, x + 2, x + 3, \ldots\}$ are the same as in Section 5. In (13), $R_{s \sim i}^T$ and C_j^T can be calculated according to Formulae (6) and (8), respectively.

The difficulty to find a multicast tree with maximum-utility lies in that it not only determines the optimal tree but also optimal values of transmission power and pre-determined number of transmitted packets at each sender of the tree.

The maximum-utility broadcast routing problem (MUBRP) is a special case of MUMRP. If the reliability of eligible links is 1 and pre-determined number of packets is fixed across the network, MUBRP can be reduced to the geometric minimum broadcast cover problem (GMBC) [25], which is shown to be NP-hard. Hence, MUBRP and further MUMRP are both NP-hard. In the following, we design heuristic solutions for MUMRP.

6.2. Heuristic Solution for MUMRP. In this subsection, we propose a heuristic solution for MUMRP. For MUMRP, each destination node in D will contribute benefit value A with successful message reception in a multicast session. Based on Prim's algorithm, we propose a greedy-based heuristic, *maximum incremental expected utility destination first* algorithm (MIEUDF), which greedily inserts a path that connects a destination to the current tree such that the incremental expected utility (IEU) of the added destination is maximized. The IEU of the new added destination is defined as its expected benefit minus corresponding expected energy cost. The MIEUDF algorithm iteratively adds the destination with the maximum IEU from the set of remaining destinations to an existing tree. The algorithm in pseudocode is presented in Algorithm 2. In Algorithm 2, IEU_i denotes the IEU of destination i. The aggregated expected utility of the multicast tree is denoted as U_{all}. The multicast tree generated is recorded in T.

The algorithm starts with a tree consisting of only the source node s and U_{all} being zero. At the beginning, the IEU of each destination is assigned with the expected utility along the optimal path from source to itself generated by Algorithm 1. The optimal path from source s to any destination u is recorded as $s \sim *u$, and all generated optimal paths build up a tree rooted at s.

At each step of *Repeat* loop in the algorithm, the destination with largest IEU, say u, is removed from D and connected to the existing tree T through its optimal path, and contributes IEU_u to U_{all}. For any relay node t along the new inserted branch of tree T, its transmission power and pre-determined number of transmitted packets, p_t^* and n_t^*, will be determined. Then, IEU of any other destination v will be increased by the expected energy cost along the inserted branch if $s \sim *v$ share some sub-path with the branch, because the expected energy consumption for the sharing sub-path has been included in the newly inserted branch. During each iterative step, not only a destination is connected to the existing T, but also the corresponding optimal values of the transmission power and pre-determined

(1) **for all** $v \in D$ **do**
(2)   IEU$_v$ and $s \sim *v$ assigned by UNICAST(V, s, v, A).
(3) **end for**
(4) T with only root s
(5) $U_{\text{all}} \longleftarrow 0$.
(6) **while** $D \neq \varnothing$ **do**
(7)   remove the maximum IEU destination u from D.
(8) $U_{\text{all}} \leftarrow U_{\text{all}} + \text{IEU}_u$.
(9)   insert the branch connecting u to T.
(10)   determine p_t^* and n_t^* for each sender t along the inserted
(11)   branch of T.
(12) **for** each node $v \in D$ **do**
(13)   **if** $s \sim *v$ shares sub-path with the inserted branch **then**
(14)   increase IEU$_v$ by expected power cost along the
(15)   sharing sub-path.
(16)   **end if**
(17)   **end for**
(18) **end while**

ALGORITHM 2: MIEUDF(V, D, s, A, T).

number of transmitted packets of the newly added senders are determined. When D is empty, the algorithm stops and outputs a multicast tree T connecting the source to all destinations in D. Since Algorithm 2 calls Algorithm 1 $|D|$ times, its time complexity is $O(|D| \times |V|^2)$.

After multicast routing tree is determined, s divides the message into x packets, generates n_s^* encoded packets, and broadcasts the encoded packets to its downstreaming nodes along the tree using transmission power p_s^*. Only after receiving x linearly independent packets from its parent node, an intermediate node i in the tree begins to send n_i^* encoded packets to its children with transmission power level p_i^*.

7. Simulation

In this section, we give an evaluation of our proposed PCNC-based utility routing algorithms. To evaluate the performance of PCNC-based utility routing scheme (PCNC), we compare PCNC with two existing methods: power control with retransmission-based routing scheme (PCRE) and NC-based routing scheme (NC).

Compared with PCNC, PCRE only allows original packets to be transmitted in a network. With PCRE, the transmission power of sender will be adjusted to the optimum power that maximizes the expected utility. For comparison purposes, the redundancy ratio in PCNC is calculated, and then this ratio will be used as the average times of retransmission for each packet at each forward node in PCRE.

Compared with PCNC, each sender in NC scheme will simply adjust its transmission power to be proportional to the distance between itself and its intended receiver and will select the optimum number of encoded packets transmitted to maximize expected utility. In the following simulations, the transmission power of each sender will be adjusted to

d^2, where d is the corresponding distance between the sender and its intended receiver, as in [8, 9].

7.1. Simulation Settings. We set up the simulations in a 20×20 square field, where nodes are randomly deployed. All nodes are homogeneous with the same available transmission power set $LS = \{p_{\max}/L, 2p_{\max}/L, \ldots, p_{\max}\}$. We set $p_{\max} = 60$, $L = 10$. The path-loss exponent k and constant $\beta/(2^B - 1)$ are set to 2 and 5, respectively.

For unicast routing, we fix the position of the source s and the destination d at locations $(2, 2)$ and $(18, 18)$, respectively. Other nodes are randomly deployed. For multicast routing, we randomly deploy nodes including source s. We conduct the experiments with different numbers of nodes and different numbers of packets in a message. The experiments are conducted 50 times for each setting, and the average is used to compare the performances of the three comparable algorithms.

7.2. Simulations for Unicast Routing. For unicast routing, we conduct experiments with two benefit values, 3000 and 6000.

We first evaluate the impact of message size x on utility-based unicast routing schemes. In the experiments, the message size x varies from 4 to 12, with a fixed total number of nodes 30. The experimental results are shown in Figure 4. We observe that PCNC outperforms PCRE and NC with various x value under two benefit values, and both PCNC and NC achieve much more expected utility than PCRE, whose utilities are almost negative. The significant performance gap between PCNC/NC and PCRE is because that NC makes any encoded packet transmitted identically useful for recovering a message, and gives redundancy for a whole message rather than a single packet using retransmission scheme. With the same pre-determined number of transmitted packets, NC increases the message delivery reliability significantly compared with retransmission, especially with larger x. Hence, with PCRE, the initial benefit value A will be reduced rapidly to negative, going backwards from the destination to the source. Compared with NC, PCNC increases the expected utility about 17%~125% with benefit value 3000, and 8%~ 28% with benefit value 6000, respectively. The reason that PCNC has better performance over NC is that with TPC, each intermediate node has more alternative choices on transmission power rather than fixed to d^2, and thus optimal choice can reduce power consumption and hence increase the expected utility.

We then evaluate the performance of the three algorithms with different numbers of nodes from 10 to 50. x is set to 6 in these groups of simulations. The experimental results are shown in Figure 5. The expected utilities of three algorithms slightly increase as the number of nodes grows. This is because a larger number of nodes results in more routing path choices from the source to a destination, and more routing path choices may lead to better performance in terms of expected utility. We also observe that PCNC achieves the largest expected utility among the three algorithms, and PCRE attains the smallest expected utility. Compared with PCRE, PCNC and NC increase expected utility significantly under two benefit values. Compared with NC, PCNC increases the expected utility about 25%~36% with benefit value 3000, and 8%~14% with benefit value 6000, respectively.

7.3. Simulation for Multicast.
In this subsection, we evaluate the performance of our proposed heuristic MIEUDF for MUMRP. To evaluate the performance of MIEUDF, we also compare it with two other comparative methods, PCRE and NC. We use two benefit values 1000 and 2000 in the following experiments.

We first compare the performance of PCNC with two comparable algorithms, PCRE and NC, under different message sizes. The message size x varies from 4 to 12. In this group of experiments, we limit the total nodes number to 20, including 10 destination node. These nodes are randomly dispersed in the target field. The experimental results is shown in Figure 6. From Figure 6, we observe that with various message sizes, the performance of PCNC is better than that of PCRE and NC under two benefit values 1000 and 2000. Note that PCRE in multicast scenarios achieves much higher expected utility than in unicasting scenarios, where almost all utilities are negative. It is because that a number of destinations contribute benefits to system in multicast instead of a single destination in unicast, and that the source may be deployed near to destination(s) rather than far away in unicast. Compared with PCRE, PCNC increases the expected utility by 76%~413% with benefit value 1000 and by 52%~523% with benefit value 2000. And compared with NC, PCNC increases the expected utility by 16%~70% with benefit value 1000 and by 5%~14% with benefit value 2000.

We also evaluate the performance of MIEUDF with different number of destinations in the target field. We set the total number of nodes to 40, and vary the number of destinations from 10 to 30. The message size x is set to 8.

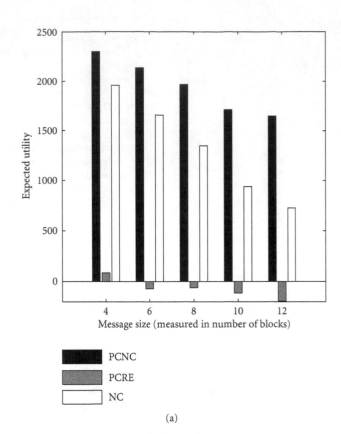

(a)

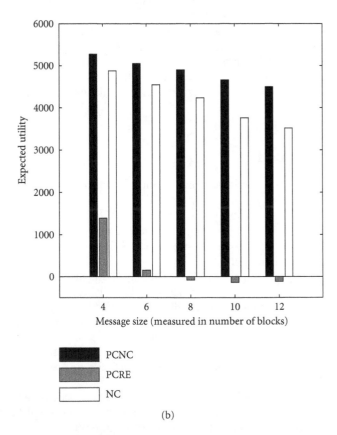

(b)

FIGURE 4: The comparison between three schemes (PCNC, PCRE, and NC) with different message sizes for unicast routing, when (a) $A = 3000$ and (b) $A = 6000$.

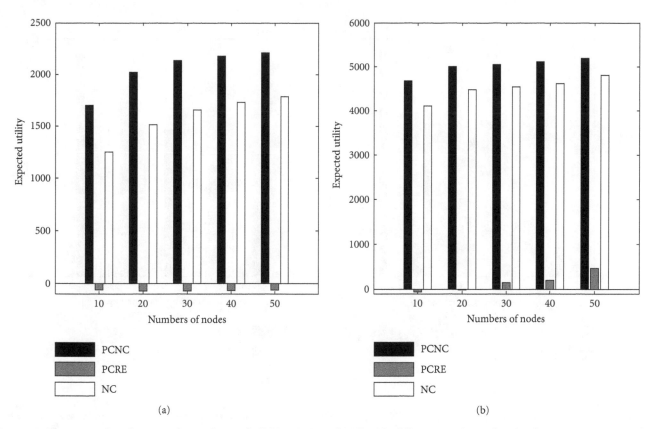

FIGURE 5: The comparison between three schemes (PCNC, PCRE, and NC) with different numbers of nodes for unicast routing, when (a) $A = 3000$ and (b) $A = 6000$.

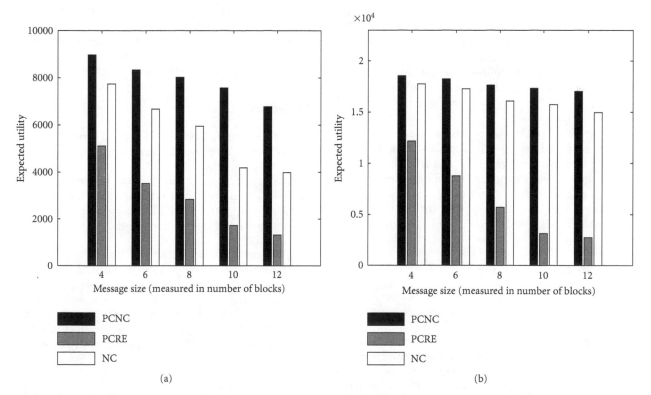

FIGURE 6: The comparison among three schemes (PCNC, PCRE, and NC) with different message sizes for multicast routing, when (a) $A = 1000$ and (b) $A = 2000$.

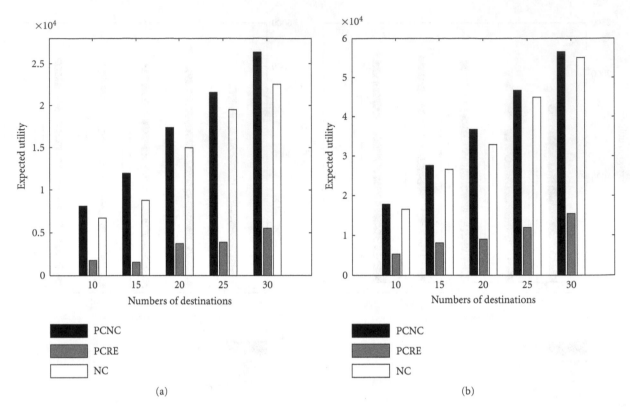

FIGURE 7: The comparison among three schemes (PCNC, PCRE, NC) with different numbers of destinations for mulitcast routing, when (a) $A = 1000$ (b) $A = 2000$.

Figure 7 illustrates the expected utilities of three schemes PCNC, PCRE, and NC under two benefit values 1000 and 2000. From Figure 7, we observe that PCNC achieves the expected utilities of multicast tree 3~6 times and 2~3 times greater than that of PCRE with benefit values 1000 and 2000, respectively. Additionally, compared with NC, PCNC increases the expected utilities of multicast tree by 10%~36% and by 4%~13% with benefit values 1000 and 2000, respectively.

From the above results, we conclude that the performance of our proposed heuristic MIEUDF based on PCNC is better than other two schemes, PCRE and NC. The reason is that PCNC-based heuristic not only applies NC to enhance the message delivery reliability but also selects the optimal transmission power to reduce power consumption, and hence increases the expected utility of multicast session.

8. Conclusion

In this paper, we combine power control technique with network coding scheme to attain a tradeoff between energy consumption and message delivery reliability. We adopt a probability link model to reflect the relationship between transmission power and link reliability, and introduce a single metric expected utility to integrate energy consumption and reliability. Based on the expected utility metric, we propose an optimal algorithm to achieve the maximum expected utility for unicast routing, and design a heuristic for multicast

routing problems, respectively. Simulation results demonstrate that our proposed scheme PCNC outperforms other two alternative schemes, PCRE and NC. In the future, we would like to extend the utility metric to analyze throughput, delay, and other performance metrics when power control technique is integrated with network coding schemes.

Appendix

Proof of Theorem 1. We first introduce a lemma. Then based on this lemma, we prove the correctness of Theorem 1.

Lemma 1. *For any link (u, v), if the transmission power of sender u is fixed, then there exists an optimal pre-determined number of transmitted packets on node u such that the expected utility over this link can be maximized.*

Proof. Assume that a message consists of x packets. Since the transmission power level of node u, p_u, is fixed, the packet link reliability over this link, denoted as $r_{u,v}$, can be determined according to (2). Since both p_u and $r_{u,v}$ are fixed, we drop the subscript of $r_{u,v}$ and p_u as r and p, respectively. We use n_u to represent pre-determined number of sender u.

Based on (3) and (8), the expected utility over this link can be derived:

$$\sum_{j=x}^{n_u} \binom{n_u}{j} \cdot r^j (1-r)^{n_u-j} \cdot A - n_u \cdot p. \qquad (A.1)$$

From the above equation, we can easily observe that the utility is a function of n_u (only depending on the variable n_u). Thus, we use $U(n_u)$ to denote the link expected utility. Then, we can derive the expression of $\Delta U(n_u)$:

$$\Delta U(n_u) = U(n_u + 1) - U(n_u)$$
$$= \binom{n_u}{x - 1} \cdot r^x (1 - r)^{n_u + 1 - x} \cdot A - p. \qquad (A.2)$$

Proving the existence of optimal pre-determined number n_u^* to maximize $U(n_u)$ is equal to proving that there exists an n_u^* such that $\Delta U(n_u^* - 1) > 0$ and $\Delta U(n_u^*) \le 0$;

$$\Delta U(n_u) = \binom{n_u}{x - 1} r^x (1 - r)^{n_u + 1 - x} A - p$$

$$= \frac{n_u(n_u - 1) \cdots (n_u - x + 2)}{(x - 1)!} r^x (1 - r)^{n_u + 1 - x} A - p$$

$$< \frac{n_u^{x-1}}{(x - 1)!} r^x (1 - r)^{n_u + 1 - x} A - p$$

$$= n_u^{x-1} (1 - r)^{n_u} \frac{r^x A (1 - r)^{1-x}}{(x - 1)!} - p. \qquad (A.3)$$

Since $r^x A(1 - r)^{1-x}/(x - 1)!$ and p are both constant, the decreasing rate of $(1 - r)^{n_u}$ is larger than the increasing rate of n_u^{x-1}, as n_u increases. Therefore, for a sufficiently large n_u, $n_u^{x-1}(1 - r)^{n_u}$ will be less than or equal to $(p \cdot (x - 1)!)/r^x A(1 - r)^{1-x}$, which results in $\Delta U(n_u) \le 0$. Thus, Lemma 1 is proved.

Proof of Theorem 1. Suppose that there are L discrete power levels available to node u, that is, $\{p_{\max}/L, 2p_{\max}/L, \ldots, p_{\max}\}$. The problem to prove there exist optimal values of both transmission power and pre-determined number of transmitted packets at node u to maximize utility can be decomposed into L subproblems with fixed transmission power according to L discrete power levels.

Based on Lemma 1, an optimal pre-determined number of transmitted packets to maximize expected utility exists for each of these L sub-problems. We use $N_1^*, N_2^*, \ldots, N_L^*$ to represent the optimal pre-determined number of transmitted packets with corresponding transmission power level $p_{\max}/L, 2p_{\max}/L, \ldots, (L-1)p_{\max}/L, p_{\max}$, respectively. We use $U(N_j^*, j \cdot p_{\max})/L)$ to denote these L utilities, where $1 \le j \le L$. The maximum utility among these L utilities is the global optimum.

Acknowledgments

This paper was supported by the National Natural Science Foundation of China (NSFC) under Grant no. 61073038, and the National High Technology Research and Development Program of China under Grant no. 2009AA01A348.

References

[1] J. H. Chang and L. Tassiulas, "Energy conserving routing in wireless ad-hoc networks," in *Proceedings of the 19th Annual Joint Conference of the IEEE Computer and Communications Societies (IEEE INFOCOM '00)*, pp. 22–31, Tel Aviv, Israel, March 2000.

[2] Q. Li, J. Aslam, and D. Rus, "Online power-aware routing in wireless adhoc networks," in *Proceedings of the Annual ACM International Conference on Mobile Computing and Networking (ACM MOBICOM '01)*, pp. 97–107, Rome, Italy, July 2001.

[3] A. Cerpa, M. Potkonjak, J. L. Wong, and D. Estrin, "Temporal properties of low power wireless links: modeling and implications on multi-hop routing," in *Proceedings of the 6th ACM International Symposium on Mobile Ad Hoc Networking and Computing (MOBIHOC '05)*, pp. 414–425, May 2005.

[4] D. Couto, D. Aguayo, B. Chambers, and R. Morris, "Performance of multihop wireless networks : shortest path is not enough," *SIGCOMM Computer Communication Review*, vol. 33, no. 1, pp. 83–88, 2003.

[5] A. Khandani, E. Modiano, J. Abounadi, and L. Zheng, "Reliability and route diversity in wireless networks," in *Proceedings of the Conference on Information Sciences and Systems (CISS '05)*, Baltimore, Md, USA, March 2005.

[6] X.-Y. Li, Y. Wang, H. Chen, X. Chu, Y. Wu, and Y. Qi, "Reliable and energy-efficient routing for static wireless Ad Hoc networks with unreliable links," *IEEE Transactions on Parallel and Distributed Systems*, vol. 20, no. 10, pp. 1408–1421, October 2009.

[7] M. Ghaderi, D. Towsley, and J. Kurose, "Reliability gain of network coding in lossy wireless networks," in *Proceedings of the The 27th Conference on Computer Communications (IEEE INFOCOM '08)*, pp. 2171–2179, April 2008.

[8] M. M Lu and J. Wu, "Erasure-coding based utility routing in multihop wireless network," in *Proceedings of the 6th IEEE International Conference on Mobile Ad-Hoc and Sensor Systems (IEEE MASS '09)*, pp. 168–177, Macau, China, October 2009.

[9] J. Wu, M. Lu, and F. Li, "Utility-based opportunistic routing in multi-hop wireless networks," in *Proceedings of the 28th International Conference on Distributed Computing Systems (ICDCS '08)*, pp. 470–477, June 2008.

[10] M. Lu and J. Wu, "Social welfare based routing in Ad Hoc networks," in *Proceedings of the 2006 International Conference on Parallel Processing (ICPP '06)*, pp. 211–218, August 2006.

[11] M. Lu and J. Wu, "Utility-based data-gathering in wireless sensor networks with unstable links," *Lecture Notes in Computer Science*, vol. 49, no. 4, pp. 13–24, 2008.

[12] L. H. A. Correia, D. F. Macedo, A. L. dos Santos, A. A. F. Loureiro, and S. M. S. Nogueira, "Transmission power control techniques for wireless sensor networks," *Elsevier Computer Networks*, vol. 51, no. 17, pp. 4765–4779, 2007.

[13] P. Bergamo, A. Giovanardi, A. Travasoni, D. Maniezzo, G. Mazzini, and M. Zorzi, "Distributed power control for energy efficient routing in AD Hoc networks," *Wireless Networks*, vol. 10, no. 1, pp. 29–42, 2004.

[14] R. Ahlswede, N. Cai, S. Y. R. Li, and R. W. Yeung, "Network information flow," *IEEE Transactions on Information Theory*, vol. 46, no. 4, pp. 1204–1216, 2000.

[15] J. Jin, T. Ho, and H. Viswanathan, "Comparison of network coding and non-network coding schemes for multi-hop wireless networks," in *Proceedings of the IEEE International Symposium on Information Theory*, pp. 197–201, July 2006.

[16] M. Ghaderi, D. Towsley, and J. Kurose, "Reliability benefit of network coding," Tech. Rep., Computer Science Department,

University of Massachusetts Amherst, Amherst, Mass, USA, 2007.

[17] M. Kurth, A. Zubow, and J. P. Redlich, "Cooperative opportunistic routing using transmit diversity in wireless mesh networks," in *Proceedings of the 27th IEEE Communications Society Conference on Computer Communications (INFOCOM '08)*, pp. 1310–1318, Phoenix, Ariz, USA, April 2008.

[18] K. Zeng, W. Lou, and H. Zhai, "On end-to-end throughput of opportunistic routing in multirate and multihop wireless networks," in *Proceedings of the 27th IEEE Communications Society Conference on Computer Communications (IEEE INFOCOM '08)*, pp. 816–824, April 2008.

[19] D. S. Lun, M. Médard, and R. Koetter, "Network coding for efficient wireless unicast," in *Proceedings of the IEEE International Zurich Seminar on Digital Communications*, pp. 74–77, February 2006.

[20] C. Zhan, Y. Xu, J. Wang, and V. Lee, "Reliable multicast in wireless networks using network coding," in *Proceedings of the 6th IEEE International Conference on Mobile Adhoc and Sensor Systems (MASS '09)*, pp. 506–515, Macau, China, October 2009.

[21] T. Ho, M. Médard, R. Koetter et al., "A random linear network coding approach to multicast," *IEEE Transactions on Information Theory*, vol. 52, no. 10, pp. 4413–4430, 2006.

[22] A. E. Khandani, J. Abounadi, E. Modiano, and L. Zheng, "Reliability and route diversity in wireless networks," *IEEE Transactions on Wireless Communications*, vol. 7, no. 12, Article ID 4712690, pp. 4772–4776, 2008.

[23] L. A. Petingi, "Reliability study of mesh networks modeled as random graphs," in *Proceedings of the International Conference on Mathematical Models for Engineering Science (MMES '10)*, pp. 85–93, November 2010.

[24] J.-Q. Jin, T. Ho, and H. Viswanathan, "Comparison of network coding and non-network coding schemes for multihop wireless networks," in *Proceedings of the IEEE International Symposium on Information Theory*, pp. 197–201, July 2006.

[25] M. Cagalj, J.-P. Hubaux, and C. Enz, "Minimumenergy broadcast in all-wireless networks: NP-completeness and distribution issues," in *Proceedings of the Annual ACM International Conference on Mobile Computing and Networking (ACM MOBICOM '02)*, pp. 172–182, Atlanta, Ga, USA, 2002.

15

Location Discovery Based on Fuzzy Geometry in Passive Sensor Networks

Rui Wang,[1] Wenming Cao,[2] and Wanggen Wan[1]

[1] School of Communication and Information Engineering, Shanghai University, Shanghai 200072, China
[2] School of Information Engineering, Shenzhen University, Shenzhen 518060, China

Correspondence should be addressed to Rui Wang, rwang@shu.edu.cn

Academic Editor: Chi Zhou

Location discovery with uncertainty using passive sensor networks in the nation's power grid is known to be challenging, due to the massive scale and inherent complexity. For bearings-only target localization in passive sensor networks, the approach of fuzzy geometry is introduced to investigate the fuzzy measurability for a moving target in R^2 space. The fuzzy analytical bias expressions and the geometrical constraints are derived for bearings-only target localization. The interplay between fuzzy geometry of target localization and the fuzzy estimation bias for the case of fuzzy linear observer trajectory is analyzed in detail in sensor networks, which can realize the 3-dimensional localization including fuzzy estimate position and velocity of the target by measuring the fuzzy azimuth angles at intervals of fixed time. Simulation results show that the resulting estimate position outperforms the traditional least squares approach for localization with uncertainty.

1. Introduction

Wireless sensor network localization in smart grid is an important area that attracted significant research interest. As a national smart grid constructed, it is important for developers to consider target localization problems to ensure both the smart grid operation efficiently. The objective of location discovery in sensor networks for smart grid is to estimate the location of a target from measurements collected by a single moving sensor or several fixed sensors at distinct and known locations.

For passive bearings-only localization, the sensor node detects the signals transmitted by a target to generate directional information in the form of bearing measurements. These measurements are triangulated to estimate the target location. While triangulation yields a unique intersection point for bearing lines in the absence of measurement errors, the noise present in bearing and observer measurements requires an optimal solution to be formulated based on noisy measurements; hence, statistical techniques for bearings-only target localization is introduced.

The pioneering work of Stansfield [1] provided a closed-form small error approximation of the maximum likelihood estimator in 1947. It is shown in [2] that the Stansfield estimator is asymptotically biased, where the traditional maximum likelihood (TML) formulation is examined in detail including a bias and variance analysis. A linearized least squares approach to bearings-based localization is given in [3]. The linearized and iterative algorithms typically require an initial estimate of the target location [2–5]. Liu et al. [6] proposed a vertical localization method using Euclidean geometry theory.

The practical passive target localization in sensor networks is characterized by a certain degree of uncertainty, which may result from approximate definition of the measurand, limited knowledge of the real environment, variability of influence quantities, inexact values of reference standards or parameters used in the model, background noise of the electronic devices, and so on. Especially, there exists uncertainty (fuzziness) with sensor locations and measurements, which can be studied based on fuzzy geometry. Rosenfeld [7] first discussed some concepts and properties of fuzzy plane geometry. Buckley and Eslami [8, 9] proposed another theory of fuzzy plane geometry, where the distances between fuzzy points, fuzzy area, and fuzzy circumference is considered as fuzzy numbers. Inspired by the authors in [7–9], the approach of fuzzy geometry is introduced to investigate the passive bearings-only target localization for the case of fuzzy linear observer trajectory in passive sensor networks.

The paper is organized as follows. The concept of fuzzy geometry is provided in Section 2. A novel analysis approach of passive bearings-only target localization based on fuzzy geometry theory for the case of fuzzy linear observer trajectory is proposed in Section 3. Simulation examples are presented in Section 4 to validate the theoretical findings of the paper. Section 5 concludes the paper.

2. Fuzzy Geometry

In this section, fuzzy points and fuzzy lines in fuzzy geometry are introduced. Place a "bar" over a capital letter to denote a fuzzy subset of R^n ($n = 1, 2, 3$) such as, $\overline{X}, \overline{Y}, \overline{A}$, and $\overline{B}$. Any fuzzy set is defined by its membership function. If $\overline{A}$ is a fuzzy subset of R^n ($n = 1, 2, 3$), we write its membership function with $\mu((x_1, \ldots, x_n) \mid \overline{A})$ in $[0, 1]$ for all x. The α-cut of any fuzzy set $\overline{X}$ of R^n, $\overline{X}(\alpha)$, is defined as $\{x : \mu((x_1, \ldots, x_n) \mid \overline{A}) \geq \alpha\}$, $0 < \alpha \leq 1$, and $\overline{X}(0)$ is the closure of the union of $\overline{X}(\alpha)$, $0 < \alpha \leq 1$. $\overline{X}$ is denoted as a fuzzy vector, and $\vec{x}$ is denoted as a traditional vector.

2.1. Fuzzy Points

Definition 1. A fuzzy point at $p = (a_1, a_2, \ldots, a_n)$ in R^n ($n = 1, 2, 3$), written $\overline{P}(a_1, \ldots, a_n)$, is defined by its membership function:

(1) $\mu((x_1, \ldots, x_n) \mid \overline{P}(a_1, \ldots, a_n))$ is upper semicontinuous;

(2) $\mu((x_1, \ldots, x_n) \mid \overline{P}(a_1, \ldots, a_n)) = 1$, if and only if $(x_1, \ldots, x_n) = (a_1, \ldots, a_n)$;

(3) $\overline{P}(\alpha)$ is a compact, convex, subset of R^n for all α, $0 < \alpha \leq 1$.

Next; we define the fuzzy distance between fuzzy points. Let $d(u, v)$ be the usual Euclidean distance metric between points u and v in R^n; we define the fuzzy distance $\overline{D}$ between two fuzzy points $\overline{P_1} = \overline{P}(a_{11}, \ldots, a_{n1})$, $\overline{P_2} = \overline{P}(a_{12}, \ldots, a_{n2})$.

Definition 2. Consider $\Omega(\alpha) = \{d(u, v) : u \text{ is in } \overline{P}(a_1, b_1)(\alpha)$ and v is in $\overline{P}(a_2, b_2)(\alpha)\}$, $0 \leq \alpha \leq 1$, then, $\mu(d \mid \overline{D}) = \sup\{\alpha : d \in \Omega(\alpha)\}$.

Theorem 1. One has $\overline{D}(\alpha) = \Omega(\alpha), 0 \leq \alpha \leq 1$, and $\overline{D}$ is a real fuzzy number.

Definition 3. A fuzzy metric $\overline{M}$ is a mapping from pairs of fuzzy points $(\overline{P_1}, \overline{P_2})$ into fuzzy numbers so that

(1) $\overline{M}(\overline{P_1}, \overline{P_2}) = \overline{M}(\overline{P_2}, \overline{P_1})$,

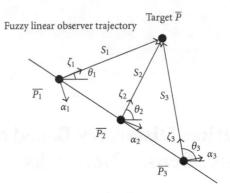

FIGURE 1: Fuzzy geometry for bearings-only target localization (3 sensors along fuzzy linear observer trajectory) in R^2 space.

(2) $\overline{M}(\overline{P_1}, \overline{P_2}) = \overline{0}$, if and only if $\overline{P_1}, \overline{P_2}$ are both fuzzy points at $(a_1, a_2, \ldots, a_n)$,

(3) $\overline{M}(\overline{P_1}, \overline{P_2}) \leq \overline{M}(\overline{P_1}, \overline{P_3}) + \overline{M}(\overline{P_3}, \overline{P_2})$ for any fuzzy points $\overline{P_1}, \overline{P_2}$, and $\overline{P_3}$.

2.2. Fuzzy Lines

Definition 4 (Two-point form). Let $\overline{P_1}, \overline{P_2}$ be two fuzzy points in R^n space ($n = 2, 3$). Define

$$
\begin{aligned}
&\Omega(\alpha) \\
&= \left\{
\begin{aligned}
&(x_1, x_2, \ldots, x_n) : \frac{x_1 - b_1}{a_1 - b_1} = \frac{x_2 - b_2}{a_2 - b_2} = \cdots = \frac{x_n - b_n}{a_n - b_n}, \\
&(a_1, a_2, \ldots, a_n) \in \overline{P_1}(\alpha), (b_1, b_2, \ldots, b_n) \in \overline{P_2}(\alpha)
\end{aligned}
\right\},
\end{aligned}
$$

$$0 \leq \alpha \leq 1. \tag{1}$$

Then the fuzzy line $\overline{L}$ is

$$\mu\left((x_1, \ldots, x_n) \mid \overline{L}\right) = \sup\{\alpha : (x_1, \ldots, x_n) \in \Omega(\alpha)\}. \tag{2}$$

3. Fuzzy Geometry Analysis for Bearings-Only Target Localization in R^2 Space

Based on fuzzy geometry, a detailed analysis of the interplay between the target localization geometry and the fuzzy estimation bias for the case of fuzzy linear observer trajectory in R^2 space is provided, which can realize the 3-dimensional localization including fuzzy estimate coordinate and target velocity by measuring the fuzzy azimuth angles at intervals of fixed time.

3.1. Fuzzy Geometry for Bearings-Only Target Localization in R^2 Space. Fuzzy geometry for bearings-only target localization in R^2 space is discussed. The fuzzy geometric relationship between one-sensor locations $\overline{P_i}$, and the target is shown in Figure 1. Assume a fuzzy linear observer trajectory

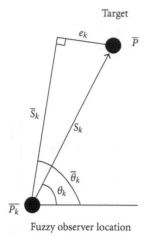

FIGURE 2: Fuzzy geometric relationship between a sensor and a target.

with three bearing measurements θ_1, θ_2, and θ_3 collected by three sensors at fuzzy observer locations $\overline{P_1}, \overline{P_2}$, and $\overline{P_3}$, respectively. The target localization is denoted as $\overline{P} = [x, y]$. In practical sensor networks, angle measurements are corrupted with some fuzzy factors.

Then define unit function α_k and ζ_k in Figure 1,

$$\alpha_k = \begin{bmatrix} \sin \theta_k \\ -\cos \theta_k \end{bmatrix},$$

$$\zeta_k = \begin{bmatrix} \cos \theta_k \\ \sin \theta_k \end{bmatrix}. \tag{3}$$

Using fuzzy points $\overline{P_i}$ in the plane, define

$$\text{Angle}_k(\alpha) = \left\{ \theta_k \mid \theta_k \in \overline{P_i}(\alpha) \right\}, \quad 0 \leq \alpha \leq 1. \tag{4}$$

Then, the membership function of fuzzy angle $\overline{\Theta_k}$ is

$$\mu\left(\theta_k \mid \overline{\Theta_k} \right) = \sup\left\{ \alpha : \theta_k \in \text{Angle}_k(\alpha) \right\}. \tag{5}$$

The target localization is related to the fuzzy observer locations through the fuzzy line equation. For fuzzy points $\overline{P_i}$ in the plane, by Definition 3, define

$$\Omega_{3i}(\alpha) = \left\{ (x, y) : \frac{y - v_i}{x - u_i} = \frac{p_y - v_i}{p_x - u_i}, (u_i, v_i) \in \overline{P_i}(\alpha) \right\}, \tag{6}$$

$$0 \leq \alpha \leq 1.$$

Then, the membership function of fuzzy line $\overline{P_i P}$ is

$$\mu\left((x, y) \mid \overline{P_i P} \right) = \sup\left\{ \alpha : (x, y) \in \Omega_{3i}(\alpha) \right\}. \tag{7}$$

Define

$$\Omega_{3\overline{P_1 P_2 P_3}}(\alpha)$$

$$= \left\{ \begin{array}{l} (x, y) : \dfrac{y - v_1}{x - u_1} = \dfrac{v_2 - v_1}{u_2 - u_1} = \dfrac{v_3 - v_1}{u_3 - u_1}, (u_1, v_1) \in \overline{P_1}(\alpha), \\ \qquad\qquad (u_2, v_2) \in \overline{P_2}(\alpha), (u_3, v_3) \in \overline{P_3}(\alpha) \end{array} \right\}$$

$$0 \leq \alpha \leq 1. \tag{8}$$

Then, the membership function of fuzzy line $\overline{P_1 P_2 P_3}$ is

$$\mu\left((x, y) \mid \overline{P_1 P_2 P_3} \right) = \sup\left\{ \alpha : (x, y) \in \Omega_{3\overline{P_1 P_2 P_3}}(\alpha) \right\}. \tag{9}$$

$\overline{P_k}$ fuzzy observer location of the sensor in the plane is illustrated in Figure 2.

It is shown from Figure 2 that the fuzzy error e_k is obtained by

$$e_k = s_k \sin\left(\overline{\theta}_k - \theta_k \right), \tag{10}$$

where s_k is fuzzy distance between $\overline{P_k}$ and $\overline{P}$ which satisfies Definition 2.

Define

$$\Omega(\alpha) = \left\{ \begin{array}{l} x = \overline{x_1} + d\left(\overline{P_1}, \overline{P_2} \right) \bullet \dfrac{\sin\left(\overline{\theta}_2 + \psi \right)}{\sin\left(\left| \overline{\theta}_2 - \overline{\theta}_1 \right| \right)} \bullet \cos\left(\overline{\theta}_1 \right) \\[2ex] y = \overline{y_1} + d\left(\overline{P_1}, \overline{P_2} \right) \bullet \dfrac{\sin\left(\overline{\theta}_2 + \psi \right)}{\sin\left(\left| \overline{\theta}_2 - \overline{\theta}_1 \right| \right)} \bullet \sin\left(\overline{\theta}_1 \right) \\[2ex] \psi = \text{arctg}\left(\dfrac{\overline{y_2} - \overline{y_1}}{\overline{x_2} - \overline{x_1}} \right) \end{array} \middle| \begin{array}{l} (\overline{x_1}, \overline{y_1}) \in \overline{P_1}(\alpha), \\ (\overline{x_2}, \overline{y_2}) \in \overline{P_2}(\alpha) \\[1ex] \overline{\theta}_1 \in \left\{ \theta_1 \mid \theta_1 \in \overline{P_1}(\alpha) \right\} \\[1ex] \overline{\theta}_2 \in \left\{ \theta_2 \mid \theta_2 \in \overline{P_2}(\alpha) \right\} \\[1ex] 0 \leq \alpha \leq 1 \end{array} \right\}. \tag{11}$$

Then, the membership function of fuzzy location (x, y) of the target is

$$\mu\left((x, y) \mid \overline{P} \right) = \sup\{ \alpha : (x, y) \in \Omega(\alpha) \}, \tag{12}$$

where $d(\overline{P_1}, \overline{P_2})$ is fuzzy distance with fuzzy points $\overline{P_1}$ and $\overline{P_2}$ which satisfies Definition 2. By the formulas (3)–(12), for the case of N sensors deployed along using the fuzzy object programming, we have the fuzzy location of the target as follows:

$$\text{Min} \quad e = \sum_k w_k e_k,$$

$$\text{S.T.} \quad e_k = s_k \sin\left(\overline{\theta}_k - \theta_k\right), \quad k = 1, 2, \dots, N,$$

$$\Omega_i(\alpha) = \left\{ \begin{array}{l} x = \overline{x}_i + d\left(\overline{P}_i, \overline{P}_j\right) \bullet \dfrac{\sin\left(\overline{\theta}_j + \psi\right)}{\sin\left(\left|\overline{\theta}_j - \overline{\theta}_i\right|\right)} \bullet \cos\left(\overline{\theta}_i\right) \\[4mm] y = \overline{y}_i + d\left(\overline{P}_i, \overline{P}_j\right) \bullet \dfrac{\sin\left(\overline{\theta}_j + \psi\right)}{\sin\left(\left|\overline{\theta}_j - \overline{\theta}_i\right|\right)} \bullet \sin\left(\overline{\theta}_i\right) \\[4mm] \psi = \text{arctg}\left(\dfrac{\overline{y}_j - \overline{y}_i}{\overline{x}_j - \overline{x}_i}\right) \end{array} \middle| \begin{array}{l} \left(\overline{x}_i, \overline{y}_i\right) \in \overline{P}_i(\alpha), \\[3mm] \left(\overline{x}_j, \overline{y}_j\right) \in \overline{P}_j(\alpha) \\[3mm] \overline{\theta}_i \in \left\{\theta_i \mid \theta_i \in \overline{P}_i(\alpha)\right\} \\[3mm] \overline{\theta}_j \in \left\{\theta_j \mid \theta_j \in \overline{P}_j(\alpha)\right\} \\[2mm] 0 \le \alpha \le 1 \end{array} \right\}, \tag{13}$$

$$i = 1, 2, \dots, N-1, \quad j = i+1, \, i+2, \dots, N.$$

Then, the membership function of fuzzy location (x, y) of the target is

$$\mu\left((x, y) \mid \overline{P}_i\right) = \sup\{\alpha : (x, y) \in \Omega_i(\alpha)\}, \tag{14}$$

where, $d(\overline{P}_i, \overline{P}_j)$ is fuzzy distance with fuzzy points $\overline{P}_i$ and $\overline{P}_j$ which satisfies on Definition 2. Define

$$\Omega_{3\overline{P_i P_{i+1} P_{i+2}}}(\alpha) = \left\{ \begin{array}{l} (x, y) : \dfrac{y - v_i}{x - u_i} = \dfrac{v_{i+1} - v_i}{u_{i+1} - u_i} = \dfrac{v_{i+2} - v_i}{u_{i+2} - u_i}, \\[3mm] (u_i, v_i) \in \overline{P}_i(\alpha), \, i = 1, \dots, N-2 \end{array} \right\},$$

$$0 \le \alpha \le 1 \tag{15}$$

the membership function of fuzzy line $\overline{P_i P_{i+1} P_{i+2}}$ is

$$\mu\left((x, y) \mid \overline{P_i P_{i+1} P_{i+2}}\right) = \sup\left\{\alpha : (x, y) \in \Omega_{3\overline{P_i P_{i+1} P_{i+2}}}(\alpha)\right\}. \tag{16}$$

Next, the target velocity needs to be determined, which is based on the time-neighboring estimate locations and time intervals. Similarly, there also exists some fuzziness among target locations and time intervals. Let $\overline{P}_i(\alpha)$, $\overline{P}_{i+1}(\alpha)$ be the estimate location at time t_i, t_{i+1}, respectively. The time interval $t_{i+1} - t_i$ is denoted as the fuzzy number $\overline{T}_{i+1} = (a/b/c)$; define

$$\Omega_{v_{i+1}}(\alpha) = \left\{ v_{i+1} = \dfrac{d(p_i, p_{i+1})}{\varepsilon_{i+1}} \middle| \right.$$

$$\left. p_i \in \overline{P}_i(\alpha), p_{i+1} \in \overline{P}_{i+1}(\alpha), \varepsilon_{i+1} \in \overline{T}_{i+1} \right\}. \tag{17}$$

Then, the fuzzy target velocity $\overline{V_{i+1}}$ at time t_{i+1} is

$$\mu\left(v_{i+1} \mid \overline{V_{i+1}}\right) = \sup\{\alpha : v_{i+1} \in \Omega_{v_{i+1}}(\alpha)\}. \tag{18}$$

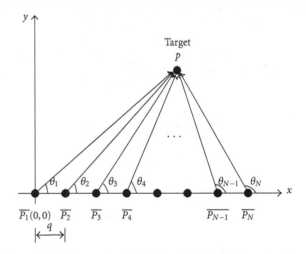

FIGURE 3: Fuzzy geometry of target localization for the case of fuzzy linear observer trajectory.

Based on the above formulas (13), (14), (17), (18), define

$$\Omega_{i+1}(\alpha) = \left\{ v_{i+1} = \dfrac{d\left((x_i, y_i), (x_{i+1}, y_{i+1})\right)}{\varepsilon_{i+1}} \middle| \begin{array}{l} (x_{i+1}, y_{i+1}) \\[3mm] (x_i, y_i) \in \overline{P}_i(\alpha), \\[1mm] (x_{i+1}, y_{i+1}) \in \overline{P}_{i+1}(\alpha), \\[1mm] \varepsilon_{i+1} \in \overline{T}_{i+1} \end{array} \right\}. \tag{19}$$

Then, in R^2 space, the 3-dimensional fuzzy estimate $\overline{\wp_{i+1}}$ including the fuzzy target locations and fuzzy velocity at time t_i is

$$\mu\left((x_{i+1}, y_{i+1}, v_{i+1}) \mid \overline{\wp_{i+1}}\right)$$

$$= \sup\{\alpha : (x_{i+1}, y_{i+1}, v_{i+1}) \in \Omega_{i+1}(\alpha)\}. \tag{20}$$

3.2. Fuzzy Geometry Theory for the Case of Fuzzy Linear Observer Trajectory in R^2 Space. Figure 3 shows the fuzzy

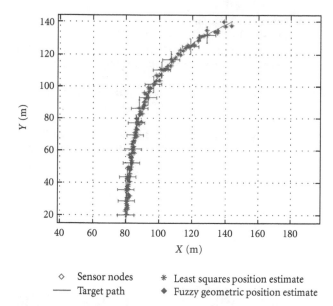

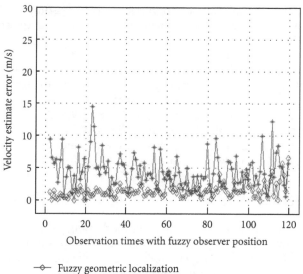

◇ Sensor nodes   ✳ Least squares position estimate
—— Target path   ◆ Fuzzy geometric position estimate

FIGURE 4: illustration of the moving target trajectory, defuzzified position estimate and some interval values, and least squares position estimate.

—◇— Fuzzy geometric localization
—✳— Least squares localization

FIGURE 6: Velocity estimate error comparison with fuzzy observer positions.

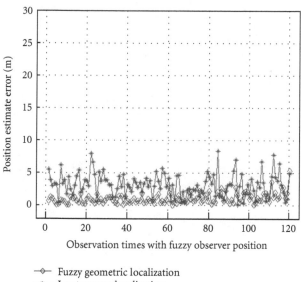

—◇— Fuzzy geometric localization
—✳— Least squares localization

FIGURE 5: Position estimate error comparison with fuzzy observer positions.

geometry of target localization for the case of fuzzy linear observer trajectory. Let observer location $\overline{P_1}$ be the origin of the fuzzy plane, denoted as $\overline{P_1}(0,0)$.

Theorem 2. *Suppose that the neighboring observers are separated by the fuzzy distance q, then*

(1) *any fuzzy geometry of target localization for the case of fuzzy linear observer trajectory can be equivalently represented by Figure 3, which can be realized with the rotation and translation of absolute coordinates of the target location and observer locations,*

(2) *for the fuzzy linear observer trajectory shown in Figure 3, the fuzzy centroid of the observer locations is*

$$c = \left[\frac{1}{2}(N-1)q \quad 0\right]. \tag{21}$$

Proof. Obvious by fuzzy geometry theory.

4. Experiments Analysis

Three sensor nodes are deployed in R^2 space to implement the 3-dimensional fuzzy estimation including the target position and velocity. Due to the uncertainty in practical sensor networks, sensor observation positions are estimated by $\overline{S_1}(0,0)$, $\overline{S_2}(100,0)$, and $\overline{S_3}(200,0)$ based on fuzzy theory, where the coordinates of sensor $(\overline{X}, \overline{Y})$ are a triangle fuzzy number, denoted as $(x - 5/x/x + 5, \ y - 5/y/y + 5)$, which determine a fuzzy linear observer trajectory. For the same bearing measurements, let the standard deviation of measurement error be 0.01 rad, time interval $\overline{T}(1) = 1\,\text{s}$. The bearings-only localizations based on fuzzy geometry and least squares methods [10] are analyzed and compared in Figure 4.

The sensor positions are estimated as the arbitrary points which belong to the fuzzy points $\overline{S_1}(0,0)$, $\overline{S_2}(100,0)$, and $\overline{S_3}(200,0)$, respectively. Figure 4 illustrates the moving target trajectory, the defuzzified position estimate of the target using weighted average operator and some interval values, and the position estimate based on least squares method. Figures 5 and 6 compare the position estimate error and velocity estimate error between the two methods. It shows that the precision of fuzzy geometric localization is better than that of least squares localization in uncertain sensor networks. The resulting position estimate outperforms the traditional least squares approach for bearings-only localization with uncertainty. When the target arrived at the coordinate (112, 120), set $\alpha = 0.6$, then the fuzzy position estimate interval is $([110.8, 114.8], [117.3, 121.3])(0.6)$. The defuzzified position estimate is (112.8, 119.3), and the defuzzified estimate error is 1.05 m, and the defuzzified estimate velocity is 3.01 m/s. Therefore, the defuzzified 3-dimensional fuzzy estimation is (112.8, 119.3, 3.01). Simulation results validate the rationality and the effectiveness that fuzzy geometry is applied in the bearings-only target localization for two-dimensional sensor networks.

5. Conclusion

A fuzzy geometric localization approach using passive sensor networks in smart grid is proposed based on fuzzy geometry. The fuzzy analytical bias expressions and the constraints are derived considering fuzzy measurements and fuzzy observer positions. The interplay between the target localization geometry and the fuzzy estimation bias is analyzed in detail for the case of fuzzy linear observer trajectory. The experiment results validate that the resulting fuzzy estimate outperforms the traditional least squares approach in a number of respects for localization with uncertainty. Future work will focus on the various kinds of fuzzy observer trajectories and higher-dimensional localization problem in practical sensor networks.

Acknowledgments

This research work is supported by the National Natural Science Foundation of China (60873130, 60872115), the Shanghai's Leading Academic Discipline Project of Shanghai Municipal Education Committee (J50104), and the project of Shanghai Science Committee (10511501303, 10511501300).

References

[1] R. G. Stansfield, "Statistical theory of D. F. fixing," *Journal Institution Electrical Engineering*, vol. 94, no. 15, pp. 186–207, 1947.

[2] M. Gavish and A. J. Weiss, "Performance analysis of bearing-only target location algorithms," *IEEE Transactions on Aerospace and Electronic Systems*, vol. 28, no. 3, pp. 817–828, 1992.

[3] D. J. Torrieri, "Statistical theory of passive localization systems," *IEEE Transactions on Aerospace and Electronic Systems*, vol. 20, no. 2, pp. 183–198, 1984.

[4] W. H. Foy, "Position-location solutions by Taylor-series estimation," *IEEE Transactions on Aerospace and Electronic Systems*, vol. 12, no. 2, pp. 187–194, 1976.

[5] S. Nardone, A. G. Lindgren, and K. F. Gong, "Fundamental properties and performance of conventional bearings-only target motion analysis," *IEEE Transactions on Automatic Control*, vol. 29, no. 9, pp. 775–787, 1984.

[6] Z. X. Liu, W. X. Xie, and X. Yang, "Target location method based on intersection of lines of sight in the netted passive sensor system," *Journal of Electronics and Information Technology*, vol. 27, no. 1, pp. 17–20, 2005.

[7] A. Rosenfeld, "The diameter of a fuzzy set," *Fuzzy Sets and Systems*, vol. 13, no. 3, pp. 241–246, 1984.

[8] J. J. Buckley and E. Eslami, "Fuzzy plane geometry I: points and lines," *Fuzzy Sets and Systems*, vol. 86, no. 2, pp. 179–187, 1997.

[9] J. J. Buckley and E. Eslami, "Fuzzy plane geometry II: circles and polygons," *Fuzzy Sets and Systems*, vol. 87, no. 1, pp. 79–85, 1997.

[10] D. Kutluyil, "Bearings-only target localization using total least squares," *Signal Processing*, vol. 85, no. 9, pp. 1695–1710, 2005.

16

A Survey of Linear Network Coding and Network Error Correction Code Constructions and Algorithms

Michele Sanna and Ebroul Izquierdo

School of Electronic Engineering and Computer Science, Queen Mary, University of London, London E1 4NS, UK

Correspondence should be addressed to Michele Sanna, michele.sanna@eecs.qmul.ac.uk

Academic Editor: Ning Chen

Network coding was introduced by Ahlswede et al. in a pioneering work in 2000. This paradigm encompasses coding and retransmission of messages at the intermediate nodes of the network. In contrast with traditional store-and-forward networking, network coding increases the throughput and the robustness of the transmission. Linear network coding is a practical implementation of this new paradigm covered by several research works that include rate characterization, error-protection coding, and construction of codes. Especially determining the coding characteristics has its importance in providing the premise for an efficient transmission. In this paper, we review the recent breakthroughs in linear network coding for acyclic networks with a survey of code constructions literature. Deterministic construction algorithms and randomized procedures are presented for traditional network coding and for network-control network coding.

1. Introduction

The theoretical foundations of network coding were first provided by Ahlswede et al. [1]. The idea originated in the sphere of satellite communications, in the scenario in Figure 1. A satellite acts as relay node for the bidirectional communication between two ground stations in nonline-of-sight. The relay receives the data from the ground stations, and it broadcasts a function of the two messages (Figure 1(b)). Each station can decode the respective message from the transmitted and the received information, with a remarkable saving of bandwidth.

Ahlswede et al. applied the idea of coding at intermediate nodes to general multinode networks, referring to it as the *network information flow* problem. Network coding allows network nodes to perform decoding and reencoding of the received information, resulting in the retransmission of messages that are a function of the incoming messages, as opposed to traditional routing (which can be regarded as a special case of network coding). The network equivalent of the satellite example is the butterfly network (Figure 2). The benefit of coding at the bottleneck edge is the increased rate with respect to the case of traditional networking, in which the intermediate node can only forward one packet at a time. The major achievement of network coding is, thus, the possibility of reaching the full theoretical capacity of the network with the transmission rate in multiple-source multicast scenarios [1].

Network coding has generated a number of fertile theoretical and applicative studies, and it is foreseen to be successfully implemented in future applications. In wireless and cognitive radio networks, the physical superposition of the signals can be seen as a benefit instead of an interference and exploited for coding at physical level [2, 3]. The communication can be protected against attacks from malicious nodes [4], eavesdropping entities [5, 6], and impairments such as noise and information losses [7, 8] thanks to the property of the network of acting as a coding operator. In peer-to-peer networks, the distribution of a number of encoded versions of the source data avoids the well-known problem of the missing block at the end of the download [9, 10].

The perspective of application of network coding in several fields follows the theoretical studies that laid the foundations of this new transmission paradigm. The basics of network coding are reviewed in this paper, ranging from transmission models to the vast topic of code construction

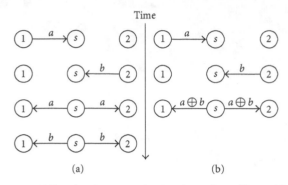

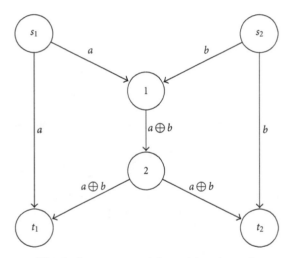

FIGURE 1: Bidirectional communication through satellite. With the traditional method (a) the satellite (s) can receive and retransmit one message at a time. With network coding (b) *a xor b* is broadcasted to both ground nodes, which are able to decode the respective messages.

FIGURE 2: The single-source two-sinks multicast butterfly network.

based on information vectors. Determining the coding operations for specific networks allows transmission with desired properties, especially in the case of coding for error control. The approaches based on vector transmission have been extensively studied, and a large variety of code construction methods have been proposed.

Linear codes on acyclic networks is the main topic of this paper due to the large landscape of recent and ongoing research activities. Simple transmission models can be formulated thanks to the mathematical tools available to treat linear algebraic problems. These models are used to help dealing with the transmission from the point of view of a coding operator. Coherent and noncoherent transmission models are distinguished whether knowledge of the network transfer characteristic is available at the transmitter and receiver sides or not. Packet-based and symbol-based transmission is feasible in case of coherent network coding, whereas noncoherent models need a packet-based transmission to cope with an oblivious model of the network.

The construction of the network code is a problem of prior setup of the network before transmission. Two main

distinctions of construction approaches are made. Deterministic algorithms are considered when full knowledge of the network is available and infrequent topology changes are expected. Randomized approaches are considered to construct the network code in a distributed way.

Coding against noise, packet losses and attacks from malicious entities extend classic theory to channel operators by considering a physical spatial dimension for coding. Models for transmission with error control coding and constructions of the network code are discussed for coherent and noncoherent models of transmission.

The paper is organized as follows. In Section 2, we review linear network coding and the recent developments in terms of the mathematical tools to comprehend linear network codes. Section 3 presents deterministic and randomized methods for network code construction. Network error correction theory and construction algorithms for coherent and noncoherent transmission are presented in Section 4. Section 5 concludes the paper.

2. Linearly Solvable Networks

The formulation of network coding has been studied as the problem of determining the existence of the coding functions (solvability of the code). As presented in [1], no assumption was made about the nature of the coding functions. However, linear coding allows to use a plethora of well-known mathematical tools that makes it appealing from the "engineeristic" point of view.

Consider a communication network as a directed graph $\mathcal{G} = (V, E)$, composed of a vertex set V and a directed edge set E. For coding purposes, all edges in the graph have integer capacity. One or more edges with unit capacity are considered between the nodes connected by higher rate links.

Linear network coding was introduced by Li et al. [11]. In linear network coding, the transmitted messages are linear combinations of the messages at the input edges of each node (Figure 3). A linear code multicast (LCM) is a set of linear encoding functions corresponding to each edge of E, which can correctly carry an information flow from a set of sources $S = [s_1, s_2, \ldots, s_{|S|}]$ to a set of sink nodes $T = [t_1, t_2, \ldots, t_{|T|}]$.

Given a nonsource node i with input edges $d \in \text{In}(i)$ and output nodes $e \in \text{Out}(i)$, we refer to i as $\text{tail}(e)$ and $\text{head}(d)$. Let $U_d, d \in \text{In}(i)$ be the messages in the incoming edges to i, then the message U_e transmitted on edge e is

$$U_e = \sum_{d \in \text{In}(e)} \beta_{d,e} U_d. \tag{1}$$

The coding coefficients $\beta_{d,e}$ constitute the *local encoding kernel* of an edge e, for all $e \in E$, whereas the *global encoding kernel* of an edge is the result of local coding at all nodes in upstream-to-downstream order, until edge e:

$$k_e = \sum_{d \in \text{In}(e)} \beta_{d,e} k_d. \tag{2}$$

Typically in delay-free networks, messages of m bits are considered as symbols in a finite field $\mathbb{F}_q$ of size q, for example, a Galois field of size $q = 2^m$ or a ring of polynomials

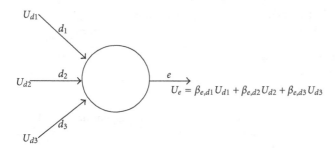

FIGURE 3: Linear coding of messages at intermediate nodes.

of maximum degree $\log_2(q) - 1$. In networks with delays, we consider similar algebra, based on a ring of polynomials whose coefficients are rational functions in a delay variable [12].

2.1. Algebraic Approach to Acyclic Networks.

Let's consider a network without cycles and with instantaneous transmission. The basic theory can be then extended to networks with delayed transmission and cycles. The algebraic approach to the transfer characteristic was proposed by Koetter and Médard [12].

Linear coding across the network induces a linear transformation on the source vector message. An adjacency matrix F is defined as an $|E| \times |E|$ matrix

$$[F]_{e,d} = \begin{cases} \beta_{d,e}, & \text{if tail}(e) = \text{head}(d), \\ 0, & \text{otherwise.} \end{cases} \quad (3)$$

The network transform characteristic can be then modeled by a system matrix M induced by the linear code [12]

$$M = A(1 - F[\beta])^{-1}B, \quad (4)$$

where A is a source-symbol routing matrix, and B is the routing matrix at the receivers. Consider a network with a max-flow h to each destination. A source codebook is a vector space $\mathcal{C} \subseteq \mathbb{F}_q^h$ spanned by the LCM. The source bitstream is arranged in a vector codeword $\mathbf{x} = [x_1, x_2, \ldots, x_h] \in \mathcal{C}$, with symbols $x_i \in \mathbb{F}_q$. The codeword received by a sink node is a vector of messages $\mathbf{y} = [y_1, y_2, \ldots, y_h]$, obtained by means of the network transformation as [12]

$$\mathbf{y} = \mathbf{x}M. \quad (5)$$

The network operates a transformation, that projects the source codebook into the receiver codebook by the system matrix M. The receiver decodes the source messages by inverting such transformation.

Successful transmission is achieved if the encoding vectors span the coding space. In order to transmit a correct code and span, the coding space at the sinks, the paths must retain linear independence. In other words, each path has to be a base for the coding space.

The coefficients of the source-to-network routing matrix A, transfer matrix F, and network-to-sink routing matrix B have to be determined. In order for the code to be correct and

span, the coding space at the sinks, the system matrix M has to have rank equal to h.

In multisource multicast scenarios, the system matrix takes the form of a composite matrix in which each submatrix is a system matrix relative to the unicast transmission from each source to each sink. The rank of this matrix has to be equal to the respective source-to-sink flow. Determining the coefficients is regarded as the problem of linear code construction. Randomized algorithms as well as deterministic and iterative construction algorithms have been proposed and are discussed in Section 3.

If the code projected at the receivers has length bigger than the rate and it is a minimum distance separable (MDS) code, the codewords at the receivers have minimum distance $d_{\min,t} = \text{mincut}(t) - h + 1$. Network error correction (NEC) was proposed to use the network transfer characteristic for error control purposes [7, 8]. Additional property are required for M in case of NEC, as discussed in Section 4.

2.2. Properties of a Linear Network Code.

The existence of an LCM on a given network depends on the network topology, the number of edge-disjoint paths from each source to each receiver, and the base field size q. Linear network coding was demonstrated to be sufficient to reach the max-flow rate in single-source multicast networks. In other words, an h-dimensional LCM always exists if the base field is large enough [11, 13]. The lower bound for the alphabet size in single-source scenarios was stated to be $\mathcal{O}(\sqrt{|T|})$, where $|T|$ is the number of destination nodes [14]. Deterministic search of the coefficients might need a bigger field size because of the particular method used for the construction; for example, the preservative approach in [15] needs a field with size $\mathcal{O}(|T|h)$. The condition is not tight for the existence of the code, but it is necessary for the algorithm to terminate successfully. Langberg et al. have suggested that the minimum number of coding-capable nodes that can sustain a flow h to $|T|$ destinations is $\mathcal{O}(h^2|T|)$ and has demonstrated that finding this number as well as the minimum required field size is both NP-complete problems [16].

The first deterministic algorithm for code search was presented by Li et al. [11]. Koetter and Médard proposed an algebraic solution in polynomial form [12]. Fragouli et al. proposed a solution of network coding translating it to a graph coloring problem, where a number of known tools from discrete mathematics can be used for the code construction [17]. A class of deterministic algorithm code construction for single-source networks has then originated inspired by the *flow path* approach by Li et al. as well as randomized criteria which are both discussed in Section 3.

2.2.1. Multiple Sources.

Most of the results about linear network coding are referred to a single-source scenario, due to the sufficiency of linear codes to reach the network capacity in single-source multicast. This result subsumes the sufficiency of linear codes for multiple flows generated at the same source node [18].

A. R. Lehman and E. Lehman provided a taxonomy of network information flows distinguishing between problems

TABLE 1: Construction possibility depending on network model and the implementation.

	Coherent	Noncoherent
Symbol based	Centralized (deterministic or semirandomized)	—
Packet based	Centralized (deterministic or semirandomized)	Distributed (randomized)

that do not benefit from network coding and problems where network coding increases the throughput [14]. Among the latter class, it was identified that a series of network where linear codes that solve the flow problem do not exist. Further studies on network coding with tools such as matroids and guessing games claim similar results about linear solvability of networks. Non-Shannon-type information inequalities were introduced by Zhang and Yeung in 1998 and were used to calculate the capacity of a network, demonstrating that such capacity cannot be expressed with Shannon-type inequalities [19]. With this premise, Dougherty et al. studied network coding using matroids theory and demonstrated the limits of linear codes, claiming a gap in the maximum linear coding capacity [20–22].

A similar result was demonstrated in the context of graph entropy. The solvability of specific cases was demonstrated by Riis by solving the network coding problem with a guessing game approach [23, 24]. It follows from these works that linear coding fails in solving multiple-source network coding problems. The capacity region of generic networks was studied by Song et al. who gave inner and outer bounds [25]. Successively, the admissible coding region was fully characterized by refining the capacity bounds [26].

Network coding for correlated information sources can be seen as a form of distributed source coding [27]. The channel compresses the sources by means of network coding with a generalization of multilevel diversity coding [28]. The network can be seen as a Slepian-Wolf coder and achieves higher throughput in the general case than separate source and network coding [29].

Few deterministic algorithms cope with the multiple-source multicast code construction. Still, efficient construction can be achieved with algorithms for generic codes [11, 13] or with randomized routines [30]. Linear correlation is indeed exploited by random linear codes, as discussed in [31]. A randomized approach based on matroids theory that encompasses multiple sources was presented in [32].

2.2.2. Networks with Cycles. Although most of the network coding literature is dedicated to acyclic networks, practical applications need to cope with possible cycles in the network. The instantaneous model can be reformulated from single-symbol network coding to symbols pipelines as in convolutional coding. The algebra behind the model is based on polynomial rings [12]. Rational power series are used on finite fields as generalized linear coding kernels. Global encoding kernels can be written by resemblance with (2)

$$k_e(z) = \sum_{d \in \text{In}(e)} \beta_{d,e}(z) k_d(z),$$ (6)

where the local kernel $\beta(z) \in z^{t(d,e)} GF\langle z \rangle$, $t(d, e)$ is the delay from d to e. A matrix structure for the transfer characteristic can be described in agreement with the algebraic formulation of acyclic networks.

Convolutional codes and some construction algorithms were also studied by Erez and Feder [33], by Huang et al. [34] and by Barbero and Ytrehus [35]

A general theoretic model was provided by Li and Sun [36]. They proposed a general coding framework in terms of discrete valuation rings (DVR). Their case subsumes convolutional code as a particular case. Convolutional codes for error correction were recently presented by Prasad and Rajan [37, 38]

LCM in acyclic networks being well known, in the next Section, we discuss construction algorithms for the acyclic case only.

3. Construction of Linear Network Codes

Code construction techniques for LCM in acyclic networks can be classified by means of different aspects (see Table 1). One fundamental distinction on the transmission model is whether the sender or receiver have knowledge of the network coding functions. The model of network coding can be then considered *coherent* or *noncoherent*. Coherent network coding assumes that coding and decoding happen with full knowledge of the network transfer characteristic. This can happen if the code is constructed in a centralized manner, where a supernode or a central authority imposes the encoding kernels to the rest of the network. Deterministic and semirandomized approaches are feasible with centralized construction, given that in both cases the central authority ensures that the code is correct for the network. Packet-based and symbol-based communication is feasible with deterministic approaches.

In case of noncoherent modeling, the network topology and the channel transfer characteristic are not known neither by the receiver or the transmitter. Randomized approaches are implemented in a distributed way, where each node randomly combines the incoming messages before retransmission. Randomized approaches need packet-based communication, since the receiver builds a decoding matrix based on the information delivered implicitly in the packets.

Linear codes and matroids have been an active topic of research. Based on a theory of linear solvability equivalence, any linearly solvable network can naturally induce a representable network matroid. For code construction through matroids, the use of linear algebra and projective planes has been proposed [41] as well as the approach of matrix completion [40].

We present now some algorithms for network code construction, divided by deterministic and randomized approaches.

TABLE 2: Comparison of deterministic algorithms for network code construction. $|E|$ is the total number of edges in the network, $|V|$ the number of nodes, and $|T|$ the number of sinks. $\mathcal{M}(h)$ is the time required to perform an $h \times h$ matrix multiplication. Langberg suggest that the correct running times of the algorithms of Jaggi et al. are different when the number of edges is small [16].

	Field size (q)	Time complexity
Yeung et al. [39], Algorithm 2.19	$\binom{|E|+h-1}{h-1}$	$\mathcal{O}(|E|)$
Jaggi et al. [15] LIF	$2|T|$	$\mathcal{O}(|E||T|h^2)$
Jaggi et al. [15] DLIF	$|T|$	$\mathcal{O}(|E||T|h(h+|T|))$
Jaggi et al. [15] fast	$2|E||T|$	$\mathcal{O}(|E||T|h + |T|\mathcal{M}(h))$
Langberg et al. [16]	$|T|$	$\mathcal{O}(|E||T|^2h + h^4|T|^3(|T|+h))$
Harvey et al. [40]	$|T|$	$\mathcal{O}(|T|h^3 \log h)$

3.1. Deterministic Construction. Two main approaches to coherent construction have been discussed in literature [42]. A first approach called *flow path* was firstly proposed for generic codes by Li et al. and later improved for multicast by Jaggi et al. in their preservative design [15]. Another approach based on matroids theory and *matrix completion* was proposed by Harvey et al. [40].

The approach of Li et al. achieves generic network codes, for example, yields to linear independence of the coding vectors among the largest possible set of edges. The algorithm of Li et al. is greedy and not computationally efficient [11].

Jaggi et al.'s algorithm [15] constructs a single-source LCM which achieves linear independence of the coding vectors for a specific set of nodes T with a smaller field size than previous implementations (see Table 2). This preservative approach is so far the most followed by deterministic construction algorithms. The algorithm achieves linear independence of the global encoding vectors of edges on the h paths from the source to each sink, so that they always form a base for the coding space. It considers the edges one at a time in topological order for the calculation of the local encoding vectors and ensures the preservation of linear independence at all steps. To choose the local encoding kernels, a semirandomized procedure chooses randomly the vectors and test the linear independence—linear information flow (LIF). A completely deterministic choice of local encoding kernels is also proposed (Deterministic LIF, DLIF).

In the same work, a fast routine is also presented, in which, breaking the flow path criterion, the coefficients of all edges are chosen randomly [15]. As opposed to distributed randomized approaches, the rank of the transfer matrix is checked by the central entity before transmission. In case of code failure, the routine is performed again. Success probabilities of such routines are discussed in the next section and in Table 3. The total execution time for the three algorithms is compared in Table 2.

Jaggi et al. also present a variant of the preservative algorithm, which considers path failures [15]. The idea is to consider artificial edges feeding the nodes with random symbols, to simulate path errors. All failure patterns are checked during the design, at the cost of an exponential increase of complexity as the network grows in size. More efficient robust designs are considered in Section 4.

Langberg et al. presented an algorithm that reduces the network to an equivalent minimal set of encoding nodes and applies the preservative design on the equivalent graph [16].

The result is a less time-consuming algorithm with the same validity of an LCM calculated in a complete network.

An algorithm for code construction based on matroids theory is presented by Harvey et al. A problem of independent matching of matroids that applied to transfer matrices of the network is proposed, followed by a maximum-rank completion that gives then rank equal to h to M [40]. In this way, the algorithm can be also applied to multiple-source multicast problems as opposed to the aforementioned algorithms which work for single-source networks. The procedure is terminated in less time than Jaggi et al.'s algorithms and requires a smaller base field [40]. The complexity of the algorithm in the single-source multicast version is compared with the other algorithms in Table 2.

3.2. Randomized Construction. When the network topology is unknown or variable, randomized approaches turn out to be the best solution. Packet-based transmission is necessary for the receiver to deduce the network code. The choice of the coding coefficients is performed autonomously by each node for the respective outgoing edges. The receivers are eventually able to decode the message by deducing the characteristic from the incoming packets. Decoding is done by means of two possible techniques. With subspace coding at the source, the receivers can examine the space spanned by the symbols across the packets and deduce the source space. The source may instead attach a series of 1s in turn to each packet header and 0s to the others. Namely, the input message can be expressed as $[I_\omega, X]$, where X is a $\omega \times K$ matrix whose rows are packets of K symbols. The receiver can then extrapolate the the global encoding kernels $A(1-F)^{-1}B_t$ from the packet headers [45].

Necessary condition for the construction of the decoding matrix is that the network code spans the coding space. Ho et al. stated that a sufficiently large base field is enough to ensure the existence of the code and the possibility of successfully decoding the transmission [31]. The probabilities of successful randomized construction and the required field size for the existence of such code are resumed in Table 3. Table 3 also shows the probability of generating a correct network code in presence of network degradation.

A correct network code in presence of link failures or errors only exists if the source codebook has a degree of redundancy $\delta_t = \text{mincut}(t) - \omega$, for all $t \in T$, where $\omega = \dim(\mathcal{C}) \leq h$ [43]. Error correction via network coding is presented in the next section, where we also analyze some

TABLE 3: Lower bounds for success probability of randomized coding and the required field size. Upper table shows the success probability, that is, the probability of having successful transmission with coding redundancy ($\delta_t = \text{mincut}(t) - \dim(\mathcal{C})$, for all $t \in T$) with and without degradation in the network up to d [43]. The lower table shows the success probability of generating a minimum distance separable (MDS) code with distance $D_{\min,t} = \text{mincut}(t) - \dim(\mathcal{C}) + 1$, with and without codebook redundancy [44]. J is the set of internal nodes.

	Without degradation ($d = 0$)	With degradation ($d > 0$)	
$\Pr(D_{\min,t} \le \delta_t + 1 - d, \forall t \in T)$	$1 - \sum_{t \in T} \binom{\delta_t + |J| + 1}{|J|}/(q-1)^{\delta_t + 1}$	$1 - \sum_{t \in T} \binom{|E|}{\delta_t - d}\binom{d + |J| + 1}{|J|}/(q-1)^{d+1}$	[43]
Field size q	$\sum_{t \in T} \binom{|E|}{\delta_t}$	$1 - (\sum_{t \in T} \binom{|E|}{\delta_t - d}\binom{d + |J| + 1}{|J|})^{1/d+1}$	
	Without redundancy ($\delta_t = 0$)	With redundancy ($\delta_t > 0$)	
MDS, $\Pr(D_{\min,t} \le \delta_t + 1, \forall t \in T)$	$(1 - |T|/(q-1))^{|J|+1}$	$(1 - \sum_{t \in T} \binom{|E|}{\delta_t}/(q-1))^{|J|+1}$	[44]
Field size q	$|T||E|$	$\sum_{t \in T} \binom{|E|}{\delta_t}$	

evolutions of the aforementioned algorithms that construct codes for error protection.

4. Network Error Correction

The transmission in the network can be jeopardized by the injection of errors or erasure of symbols. Errors are caused by channel noise or by the insertion of extraneous messages by malicious nodes. Loss of packets can happen because of traffic jams in the network.

Traditional error correcting codes add redundancy to the transmission in the time domain. The network itself offers another mechanism for error correction by adding redundancy in the spatial domain. Network error correction (NEC) was proposed by Cai and Yeung, to drive network coding mechanisms to recover erroneous symbols as well as lost packets with network error-correcting codes [7, 8]. NEC extends all the knowledge of classic coding theory, such as coding distance, weight measures, and coding bounds including the network as a coding operator. Normal network coding can be regarded as a special case of NEC without error control properties. The formulation of the problems of existence and construction of the network code can be extended to the NEC case.

Ho et al. presented a theoretical framework of network failure management [46]. A distinction between link failure and node failure is made, the difference residing in losing all the links from a faulty node, and consequently all the paths through that node. NEC in general includes both possibilities by considering the potential loss of a number of links. They present then two recovery schemes: A receiver-based recovery scheme, in which, under loss of information flow, each receiver can react and recover the lost information, and a network-wide recovery scheme, in which all nodes contribute to the recovery procedure [46]. Network coding against errors usually achieves a receiver-centric error correction.

The algebraic model of transmission can be extended by considering errors as random alterations of the symbols on the edges and erasures as symbol cancellations. This alteration is considered as an additive $1 \times |E|$ error vector $\mathbf{z}$ as

$$\mathbf{y} = (\mathbf{x}A + \mathbf{z})(1 - F)^T B. \tag{7}$$

The error pattern of $\mathbf{z}$ is a $1 \times |E|$ vector $\rho_\mathbf{z}$ with unitary components in the corresponding nonzero components of

$\mathbf{z}$. In the following, we present bounds, weights, and coding distance definitions as well as some construction algorithms for NEC codes.

We consider a network with a max flow equal to $\text{mincut}(t)$ to each destination $t \in T$. The source codebook $\mathcal{C}$ at the source can be redundant, that is, it is an ω-dimensional subspace of the vector space $\mathbb{F}_q^h$ spanned by an LCM. The coding space projected at the receiver retains the ω dimensions in presence of network degradations under certain conditions and thus support the transmission at a controllable error rate, thanks to the NEC code. A code is defined as l-error correcting if each destination can successfully recover the source message in presence of at most l total errors. Additionally the existence of linear MDS codes allows superior control over error injections. The code characteristics are discussed in the next section.

As for normal network coding, for NEC transmission, a coherent or a noncoherent model of the network may be considered, generating different approaches to the assignment of the network code. With the coherent model, a deterministic construction of MDS codes is possible under some prerequisites (e.g., field size), as explained in Section 4.1. Noncoherent models need a statistical study of the transmission and can be formalized as a transmission over a random linear operator channel (LOC) or a random matrix channel. Randomized network coding for error correction has been studied from the point of view of the existence of the code with certain error correction characteristic. Coding and decoding for random coding are tackled by different approaches. Assuming a packet-based transmission model, statistical decoding can be performed at the receiver as proposed in [47], whereas subspace coding has been proposed in [48] and further explored in [49]. Randomized coding and stochastic matrix channels are discussed in Section 4.2.

Network Bounds and Weights. The coding bounds for network codes have been defined in [7, 8]. Hamming bound, Singleton bound, Sphere-packing bound, and Gilbert-Varshamov bound define the relation between codebook size (subspace dimensions), field size, network capacity, and coding distance. A refined formulation for destinations with unequal rates to the sinks has been presented by Yang et al. [50].

Following these definitions, we can regard the NEC with the same characteristics of classic linear channel codes in terms of the correction and detection of error and the correction of erasures. A codebook redundancy at the receiver can be defined as

$$\delta_t = \text{mincut}(t) - \text{dim}((C)). \tag{8}$$

The minimum coding distance has been defined in terms of coding redundancy at each sink as [47]

$$d_{\text{min},t} = \delta_t + 1 \tag{9}$$

and can be applied in the scope of symbol-based transmission, that is, the codewords at the receiver t are vectors of symbols in $\mathbb{F}_q$ as in (5). From the definition of coding distance follows that the number of correctable errors at the receiver t is $l = \lfloor (d_{\text{min},t} - 1)/2 \rfloor$, and the number of detectable errors is $d_{\text{min},t} - 1$. In MDS codes, the definition of minimum distance follows classic coding theory as the minimum among the network Hamming distances between the message vectors. The existence of MDS codes has been discussed by Zhang [47] (see Table 4 for the required conditions).

Silva et al. give a reinterpretation of coding metrics [49]. They make use of matrix codes formed by the packetized structure of the transmission. Minimum rank distance (MRD) codes are defined as matrix codes with a minimum distance between the elements X and Y as

$$d_R(X, Y) = \text{rank}(Y - X). \tag{10}$$

These codes attain the Singleton bound with respect to the rank metric.

Yang et al. introduced two classes of coding weights of the vectors involved in symbol-based transmission referred to the received vector $\mathbf{y}$, error vector $\mathbf{z}$, and message vector $\mathbf{x}$ [51]. Given the classic definition of Hamming weight $w_H(\mathbf{z})$ as the number of components in the vector $\mathbf{z}$ that differ from the corresponding zero vector, a first class of descriptors can be defined as follows [51].

Network Hamming weight of the received vector $\mathbf{y}$:

$$W_t^{\text{rec}}(\mathbf{y}) = \min w_H(\mathbf{z}), \tag{11}$$

where the minimum is searched among all the error vectors $\mathbf{z}$ that result in receiving the word $\mathbf{y} = \mathbf{z}F_t$ at the receiver. Network Hamming weight of the error vector $\mathbf{z}$:

$$W_t^{\text{err}}(\mathbf{z}) = W_t^{\text{rec}}(\mathbf{z}F_t). \tag{12}$$

Network Hamming weight of the message vector $\mathbf{x}$:

$$W_t^{\text{msg}}(\mathbf{x}) = W_t^{\text{rec}}(\mathbf{x}M). \tag{13}$$

Another form of network Hamming weights can be defined for the error vector $\mathbf{z}$ in terms of the mincut of the network and on the rank of the transmission matrix resulting from the error pattern [51], that is: Mincut of an error vector $\mathbf{z}$:

$$w_c(\mathbf{z}) = \text{mincut}(\rho_{\mathbf{z}}), \tag{14}$$

where mincut indicates the mincut of edges included in the error pattern $\rho_{\mathbf{z}}$.
Rank of an error vector:

$$w_r(\mathbf{z}) = \text{rank}(\rho_{\mathbf{z}}), \tag{15}$$

where the rank of the error pattern indicates the rank of the matrix formed by the rows in $(1 - F)^T B$ corresponding to the edges in $\rho_{\mathbf{z}}$.
The network Hamming weight can be expressed as

$$w_n(\mathbf{z}) = \min w_H(\mathbf{z}'), \tag{16}$$

where the minimum is searched among all the error vectors $\mathbf{z}'$ that result in receiving the same word as for $\mathbf{z}$ when the transmitted word is $\mathbf{x} = \mathbf{0}$, which is substantially equivalent to the definition given before for the first class of network weights.

Like for generic network codes, a coherent or a noncoherent model of the network can be assumed. The coherent model assumes that the receiver decodes the transmission with a priori knowledge of the topology and the network code. Coding coefficients in case of centralized and deterministic construction are feasible with both symbol-based and packet-based approaches. Randomized routines need packet-based transmission to record the encoding kernels in the packet header.

The noncoherent model assumes that the network code is not known at the moment of the decoding. The effort of exploiting the network characteristic moves from the network to the transmitter and the receiver, respectively. The idea of linear channel operator (LOC) has been studied by various authors [48, 52, 53] and has demonstrated to be useful to model a random channel with error control coding properties.

In the following subsection, we present some of the algorithms for NEC code construction in single-source multicast networks.

4.1. Deterministic Construction. Deterministic algorithms for code construction assume that the topology of the network is known, and the possible events of error injection can be systematically analyzed. Because of the coherent model of transmission, it is possible to have MDS symbol-based codes. Nevertheless, packet-based transmission is always possible and might encourage superior error correction capacity, by exploiting at the receiver the fact that all packets share the same network code [54].

Error resiliency of generic LCM were presented before the formalization of NEC. A first deterministic algorithm was presented by Jaggi et al. together with their preservative approach to LCM [15]. The idea is to consider artificial edges feeding the nodes with random symbols, to simulate path errors. All failure patterns are checked during the design, presenting an exponential increase of computational complexity.

Yang et al. proposed two completely deterministic and centralized algorithms achieving the refined Singleton bound, including unequal flows to the sinks [50]. Network code and codebook are reciprocally matched to achieve at

TABLE 4: Comparison of centralized algorithms for single-source multicast network error correction code construction. $|E|$ is the total number of edges in the network, $|T|$ the number of sinks, d is the minimum distance at all sinks, h is the multicast rate, n_s the number of outgoing channels from the source. In Bahramgiri and Lahouti's algorithms: $R^{(d)}$ is the set of failure patterns with at most $d-1$ failures of edges in common with other paths, Ω includes all possible sets of paths [55].

	Field size (q)	Time complexity
Yang et al. [50], Algorithm 1	$|T|\binom{|E|}{d-1}$	$\mathcal{O}(n_s|T|\omega\binom{|E|}{d-1}(n_s^2+|T|\binom{|E|}{d-1}))$
Yang et al. [50], Algorithm 2	$|T|\binom{h+|E|-2}{d-1}$	$\mathcal{O}(h|T|^2|E|\binom{h+|E|-2}{d-1}(h^2|T|^2+|T|\binom{h+|E|-2}{d-1}))+h^3d|E||T|\binom{|E|}{d-1})$
Matsumoto [56]	$|T|\binom{|E|}{d-1}$	$\mathcal{O}(h|E||T|\binom{|E|}{d-1}(|T|\binom{|E|}{d-1}+h+d))$
Bahramgiri and Lahouti [55], RNC1	$|T|\binom{h-1}{h-d}$	$\mathcal{O}(|E||T|(n-d+1)^3\binom{h-1}{h-d}(1-\binom{h-1}{h-d}|T|/q)^{-1})$
Bahramgiri and Lahouti [55], RNC2	$|T||R^{(d)}|\binom{h-1}{h-d}$	$\mathcal{O}(|E||T||R^{(d)}|(n-d+1)^3\binom{h-1}{h-d}(1-\binom{h-1}{h-d}|T||R^{(d)}|/q)^{-1})$
Bahramgiri and Lahouti [55], RNC3	$|T|\prod_T|\Omega|$	$\mathcal{O}(|E||T|(n-d+1)^3\prod_T|\Omega|(1-|T|\prod_T|\Omega|/q)^{-1})$
Guang et al. [57], lin. ind. test	$|T|\binom{|E|}{d-1}$	$\mathcal{O}(|E|(\omega+d-1)|T|\binom{|E|}{d-1}(1+\omega+(|E|+1)/2))$
Guang et al. [57], deterministic	$|T|\binom{|E|}{d-1}$	$\mathcal{O}(|E||T|\binom{|E|}{d-1}(|T|\binom{|E|}{d-1}(\omega+(|E|+1)/2)+\omega+d-1))$

each receiver the maximum distance $d_{\min,t} = \text{mincut}(t) - \omega + 1$. The first algorithm determines the network coding kernels first and then constructs a proper codebook. The encoding kernels spanning the coding space are chosen, then the codebook is chosen using the basis for the network code that keep the minimum coding distance [50]. The second algorithm determines a codebook by means of traditional block-code generation and then constructs the network code. It is iterative, that is, it constructs the code edge by edge in upstream to downstream order. The choice of local coding kernel that retain the coding distance is done by eliminating the kernels that do not support the source rate under all failure patterns (that do not reduce the mincut under the rate). This technique is a generalization of the linear independence of the preservative design. The processing load and the required field size of these two algorithms are compared in Table 4.

Matsumoto proposed another centralized and deterministic algorithm, improving the algorithm of Jaggi et al. for error protection [56]. The base idea is to build an extended network with imaginary nodes feeding the regular edges and expanding the number of edge disjoint paths to the sinks. To let the new paths be independent from the regular ones, the preservative algorithm is run on the extended network. This algorithm possesses similar requirements to Yang's algorithms, as showed in Table 4.

Bahramgiri and Lahouti also proposed some variants of construction algorithms in line with Jaggi et al.'s design [55]. Three versions are considered: A first scheme called robust network coding 1 (RNC1) chooses the local kernels with a criterion of partial linear independence. All ω-subsets of the paths from source to sink have to be independent. A random subroutine is considered in this case, and the linear independence is verified. When $\text{mincut}(t) - \omega$ paths fail, the receiver can always recover ω information symbols but cannot cope with the alteration of paths intended to other sinks; thus, the scheme is successful only in case of erasures in a unicast scenario. A second scheme (RNC2) considers a subset of paths which have any edge in common to any other path to other sinks. The scheme increases the complexity

by a factor equal to the number of paths with joint edges, but copes with all path failures in case of erasures. A third scheme (RNC3) considers the use of backup paths. In all construction algorithms, $\text{mincut}(t)$ edge-disjoint paths are considered from source to sink, not considering edges in other possible paths. Backup paths superpose with the edge-disjoint and use inactive edges as a backup in case any the other paths fail. In the algorithm, at each step, the partial independence is verified among ω-subsets of all possible paths. This scheme increases the complexity by a factor equal to the number of possible ω-subsets of paths. The three algorithms are compared in Table 4 and discussed in detail in [55].

Another greedy algorithm was proposed by Guang et al. embracing the principles of the preservative design [57]. Linear independence of local encoding kernels is guaranteed for all error patterns with linear independence testing or with a deterministic implementation similar to Jaggi et al.'s LIF and DLIF criteria, with a global complexity given in Table 4. Consider that the formulae in Table 4 have been adapted to fit a simplified notation with equal parameters for all receivers. For example, the formula for Guang et al.'s algorithm [57] considers the complexity of constructing the code for up to a number of failures, whereas we reformulate for a maximum of $d_{\min} - 1 = h - \omega$ errors.

4.2. Randomized Construction. Randomized construction is performed when there is no knowledge of the network topology. Network coding kernels are chosen randomly, then the transfer characteristic is exploited at the receiver side. The transmission is supposed to be packet based because the receiver has to deduce the network transfer characteristic from a set of transmitted data. Algebraically, the transmission has the formulation [47]:

$$\begin{bmatrix} X & Y \end{bmatrix}\begin{bmatrix} A \\ I \end{bmatrix}(1-F)^{-1}B_t = Y_t, \tag{17}$$

where X is a $\omega \times K$ matrix whose rows are packets of K symbols transmitted on each of the ω paths, and Z is an $|E| \times$

K matrix of error symbols affecting the edges. Y_t is a $h \times K$ matrix of symbols received by sink $t \in T$. A randomized choice of the local encoding kernel produces a random matrix channel. The coding space projected at the receiver is correct under random link failures with increasing probability as the base field size increases. Koetter and Médard stated, in the sphere of regular codes, that, depending on the field size, a randomly generated code can be correct with up to a certain number of errors if the failure patterns that do not reduce the capacity under a threshold h with probability $q \leq (|\mathcal{F}||T|h) + 1$ [12]. The probability of failure of a randomized choice of the code in presence of link failures was also demonstrated by Ho et al. [31].

These probabilities were studied by Balli et al. who refined the formulation of success probability for randomized codes with codebook redundancy at the source ($\delta_t =$ mincut(t) $- \omega$) and variable degradation. This formulation assumes that the codebook redundancy is used to contrast network degradation up to a number of errors d. It also gives the probability mass function of the minimum distance [43]. These probabilities and the minimum field size required for existence are compared in Table 3.

Guang et al. calculated the probability of the randomly generated code to be minimum distance separable (MDS) codes, besides begin space spanning under d errors [44]. The given formulae express the success probability of having an MDS code with minimum distance equal or bigger than the code redundancy. These probabilities are also shown in Table 3.

There are mainly two techniques for transmitting with randomized network coding. If the global encoding kernels are implicitly communicated to the receiver (for instance in the header of the packets, as in Chou's practical framework [45]) the decoding matrix can be constructed at the receiver by parsing the packed headers. On the contrary, subspace coding is a new coding technique which does not consider the transfer characteristic of the network for decoding. These two transmission techniques have in common the distributed and randomized choice of the encoding kernels and are compared in the following.

4.2.1. Statistical Decoding.
Zhang proposed decoding criteria in packet-based network coding, with the algebraic formulation as in (17). Similarly to Chou's practical framework, in packet-based statistical decoding, the sender appends to each packet a unitary base to the coding space. Namely, it inserts unitary vectors in the packet header at the source as $[I_\omega, X]$, so that the receiver can read the global encoding kernels from the received packets and build a decoding matrix [45]. Such approach is coherent in the sense that the receivers need to know the network topology, but it is decentralized in the choice of the encoding kernels.

The decoding equation deduced from the packet headers is to be solved for error patterns of Z with increasing rank. The message parts of all solutions is unique for error patterns up to $1/2(d_{min} - 1)$ [47]. A brute force decoding algorithm based on the minimum possible rank of error patterns is proposed, and a fast decoder with Gaussian elimination is also presented, which exploits the fact that all symbols in a packet are subject to the same coding [47]. The latter formulation was also proposed as a technique which corrects errors up to $d_{min} - 2$ with reasonably favorable probability, thus, beyond the capacity of a normal error-correcting code [54].

Zhang et al. also proposed a method based on hybrid FEC/NEC to increase error correction capability of the network code [54, 58]. In traditional *detection/deletion* methods, an error detection code is used within a packet. The hybrid system uses a local FEC code to detect errors at intermediate nodes and record the error pattern in the packets. Then network error decoding at the receiver is performed with knowledge of the error pattern, thus, achieving correction performance close to the bound of erasure correction [54].

The reliability of the decoding matrix built from the packet header can be a problem. Errors in the packet header (which affects the reception of global kernel errors and attacks from malicious nodes) are treated with similar techniques in literature. The difference is that random alterations in the packet header can be corrected, whereas adversaries may have the capability of altering the header to make it pointless at the receiver [47]. To some extent, coding against attacks from Byzantine adversaries has been related to subspace coding because of the moot reliability of the information in the packet header.

Jaggi et al. proposed in various works a simple distributed algorithms for robust encoding at the source against Byzantine adversaries [4]. The model for error injection assumes an intelligent entity with knowledge of sender and receiver intentions. Three situations are discussed: The malicious entity has knowledge of a part of the transmission paths (shared secret) of all the transmissions occurring in the network (omniscient adversary) or can jeopardize only part of the transmitted packets (limited adversary) resembling a noise injection up to a certain error rate. The proposed coding strategy is asymptotically rate optimal, that is, it achieves the Singleton bound. A generic network code is used for the internal nodes, whereas the source generates random combinations, and the receiver performs statistical decoding.

4.2.2. Subspace Coding.
The subspace coding approach was first proposed by Köetter and Kschischang [48]. The transition matrix of the network becomes a channel with unknown coding properties. A linear operator channel (LOC) model can be used to model this kind of channels as studied by Yang et al. [52]. Capacity of LOCs was studied in the coherent and noncoherent case. Although channel training techniques make possible to perform statistical decoding, subspace coding assumes a *channel oblivious* model, in which neither the transmitter nor the receiver has knowledge of the network topology or encoding kernels.

The transformation operated by the network as LOC can be expressed similarly to (17). Considering the transmission of packets spanning an input space V, the sinks receive packets spanning another space U related to the input space by an operator

$$U = H_k(V) \oplus Z, \tag{18}$$

where H_k is an erasure operator which returns a k subspace of V (corresponding to a packet erasures in the network) and Z is an error space which adds a dimension (injection of erroneous symbols). These spaces are in general subspaces of an ambient space W with dimension h. A distance between subspaces of W can be formulated, giving a valid metric for $P(W)$, that is, the subspace set of all subspaces of W (the Grassmanian of W) [48]. Such a metric is

$$d(A, B) = \dim(A + B) - \dim(A \cap B) \qquad (19)$$

and opens up the possibility of building codes for operator channels (subspace codes). A subspace code $\mathcal{C}$ is a subset of $P(W)$, that is, a nonempty set of subspaces of W. Any subspace V in C can be transmitted by injecting a basis and can be reconstructed at the receiver from the receiver space U if the minimum distance of $\mathcal{C}$ is bigger than $2(t + \rho)$ (where the distance is defined as in (19) and t and ρ being the dimension of Z and the number of erasures, resp.) [48]. Sphere packing, sphere covering, and Singleton bounds were given for the subspace metric [48]. A Reed-Solomon construction based on linearized polynomials was also studied [48].

Silva et al. studied other metrics for subspace coding, such as the rank metric. They propose a generalized decoding problem for a family of maximum rank distance codes exploiting partial knowledge of network degradation in terms of erasures (knowledge of error location but not the value) and deviations (knowledge of error value but not the location) [49]. Their approach with rank metric is based on Gabidulin codes which is analogous to the subspace metric approach with Reed-Solomon codes.

On the other hand, Bossert and Gabidulin derived a generalization of Koetter and Kschischang construction. A class of codes with the subspace metric was defined as the intersection of rank-metric codes with lifting construction [59]. Code constructions with prescribed distance and Gilbert-type bounds were given in [60]. Gadouleau and Yun further studied packing and covering properties with subspace and rank metrics [61].

Silva and Kschischang also proposed a metric which better models the effect of adversarial error injections, which is the *injection* metric [62]. This metric allows better design of nonconstant-dimension codes than the subspace metric. The construction of codes for the injection metric, as well as much more other topics in subspace coding, are still open issues. This branch of network coding is not well known yet, so it is expected to provide a wide landscape of topics for future research.

The potential advantages of using subspace coding over coherent network coding have been pointed out by Zhang [63]. Coherent network correction keeps its advantages over subspace coding against random channel errors. On the other hand, the performance for erasure correction is the same for both approaches, whereas against attacks for malicious nodes the approach of rank-metric codes can achieve higher performance, because it does not need to record the encoding kernels in the header. On the other hand, centralized and deterministic approaches to code construction are seemingly impractical because such complete knowledge of the network may not be available at any instant.

5. Conclusions

In this paper, we have reviewed the recent breakthrough achievements in network coding theory. Most of the well-established knowledge of network coding is due to the work in the theory and construction algorithms for linear coding, network error correction theory, and construction algorithms. Further indepth study of network coding can be found in the books by Yeung [28], Ho and Lun [64], Fragouli and Soljanin [65, 66] and in the upcoming book edited by Médard and Sprintson [67].

Acknowledgment

This research was partially supported by the European Commission under contract FP7-247688 3DLife and FP7-248474 SARACEN.

References

[1] R. Ahlswede, N. Cai, S. Y. R. Li, and R. W. Yeung, "Network information flow," *IEEE Transactions on Information Theory*, vol. 46, no. 4, pp. 1204–1216, 2000.

[2] P. A. Chou and Y. Wu, "Network coding for the internet and wireless networks," Tech. Rep., Microsoft Research, June 2007.

[3] S. Katti, H. Rahul, W. Hu, D. Katabi, M. Medard, and J. Crowcroft, "XORs in the air: practical wireless network coding," *IEEE/ACM Transactions on Networking*, vol. 16, no. 3, pp. 497–510, 2008.

[4] S. Jaggi, M. Langberg, S. Katti et al., "Resilient network coding in the presence of byzantine adversaries," *IEEE Transactions on Information Theory*, vol. 54, no. 6, pp. 2596–2603, 2008.

[5] N. Cai and T. Chan, "Theory of secure network coding," *Proceedings of the IEEE*, vol. 99, no. 3, pp. 421–437, 2011.

[6] D. Silva and F. R. Kschischang, "Universal secure network coding via rank-metric codes," *IEEE Transactions on Information Theory*, vol. 57, no. 2, pp. 1124–1135, 2011.

[7] R. W. Yeung and N. Cai, "Network error correction. I. Basic concepts and upper bounds," *Communications in Information & Systems*, vol. 6, no. 1, pp. 19–35, 2006.

[8] N. Cai and R. W. Yeung, "Network error correction. II. Lower bounds," *Communications in Information & Systems*, vol. 6, no. 1, pp. 37–54, 2006.

[9] K. Jain, L. Lovász, and P. A. Chou, "Building scalable and robust peer-to-peer overlay networks for broadcasting using network coding," *Distributed Computing*, vol. 19, no. 4, pp. 301–311, 2007.

[10] C. Gkantsidis and P. R. Rodriguez, "Network coding for large scale content distribution," in *Proceedings of the 24th Annual Joint Conference of the IEEE Computer and Communications Societies (INFOCOM '05)*, vol. 4, pp. 2235–2245, March 2005.

[11] S. Y. R. Li, R. W. Yeung, and N. Cai, "Linear network coding," *IEEE Transactions on Information Theory*, vol. 49, no. 2, pp. 371–381, 2003.

[12] R. Koetter and M. Médard, "An algebraic approach to network coding," *IEEE/ACM Transactions on Networking*, vol. 11, no. 5, pp. 782–795, 2003.

[13] R. W. Yeung and S.-Y. R. Li, "Polynomial time construction of generic linear network codes," in *Proceedings of the 43rd Allerton Conference on Communication, Control and Computing,* September 2005.

[14] A. R. Lehman and E. Lehman, "Complexity classification of network information flow problems," in *Proceedings of the 41st Annual Allerton Conference on Communication, Control and Computing,* 2003.

[15] S. Jaggi, P. Sanders, P. A. Chou et al., "Polynomial time algorithms for multicast network code construction," *IEEE Transactions on Information Theory,* vol. 51, no. 6, pp. 1973–1982, 2005.

[16] M. Langberg, A. Sprintson, and J. Bruck, "Network coding: a computational perspective," *IEEE Transactions on Information Theory,* vol. 55, no. 1, pp. 147–157, 2009.

[17] C. Fragouli, E. Soljanin, and A. Shokrollahi, "Network coding as a coloring problem," in *Proceedings of the Conference on Information Science and Systems (CISS '04),* Princeton, NJ, USA, 2004.

[18] T. H. Chan, "On the optimality of group network codes," in *Proceedings of the IEEE International Symposium on Information Theory (ISIT '05),* pp. 1992–1996, September 2005.

[19] Z. Zhang and R. W. Yeung, "On characterization of entropy function via information inequalities," *IEEE Transactions on Information Theory,* vol. 44, no. 4, pp. 1440–1452, 1998.

[20] R. Dougherty, C. Freiling, and K. Zeger, "Networks, matroids, and non-Shannon information inequalities," *IEEE Transactions on Information Theory,* vol. 53, no. 6, pp. 1949–1969, 2007.

[21] R. Dougherty, C. Freiling, and K. Zeger, "Insufficiency of linear coding in network information flow," *IEEE Transactions on Information Theory,* vol. 51, no. 8, pp. 2745–2759, 2005.

[22] R. Dougherty, C. Freiling, and K. Zeger, "Linearity and solvability in multicast networks," *IEEE Transactions on Information Theory,* vol. 50, no. 10, pp. 2243–2256, 2004.

[23] S. Riis, "Graph entropy, network coding and guessing games," Tech. Rep. CoRR abs/0711.4175, 2007, http://www.eecs.qmul.ac.uk/~smriis/RiisTRGraphEntro.pdf.

[24] S. Riis, "Reversible and irreversible information networks," *IEEE Transactions on Information Theory,* vol. 53, no. 11, pp. 4339–4349, 2007.

[25] L. Song, R. W. Yeung, and N. Cai, "Zero-error network coding for acyclic networks," *IEEE Transactions on Information Theory,* vol. 49, no. 12, pp. 3129–3355, 2003.

[26] X. Yan, R. W. Yeung, and Z. Zhang, "The capacity region for multi-source multi-sink network coding," in *Proceedings of the IEEE International Symposium on Information Theory (ISIT '07),* pp. 116–120, June 2007.

[27] J. Barros and S. D. Servetto, "Network information flow with correlated sources," *IEEE Transactions on Information Theory,* vol. 52, no. 1, pp. 155–170, 2006.

[28] R. W. Yeung, *Information Theory and Network Coding,* Springer, New York, NY, USA, 1st edition, 2008.

[29] A. Ramamoorthy, K. Jain, P. A. Chou, and M. Effros, "Separating distributed source coding from network coding," *IEEE Transactions on Information Theory,* vol. 52, no. 6, pp. 2785–2795, 2006.

[30] Y. Wu, V. Stankovic, Z. Xiong, and S. Y. Kung, "On practical design for joint distributed source and network coding," *IEEE Transactions on Information Theory,* vol. 55, no. 4, pp. 1709–1720, 2009.

[31] T. Ho, M. Médard, R. Koetter et al., "A random linear network coding approach to multicast," *IEEE Transactions on Information Theory,* vol. 52, no. 10, pp. 4413–4430, 2006.

[32] M. Gadouleau and A. Goupil, "A matroid framework for noncoherent random network communications," *IEEE Transactions on Information Theory,* vol. 57, no. 2, pp. 1031–1045, 2011.

[33] E. Erez and M. Feder, "Efficient network code design for cyclic networks," *IEEE Transactions on Information Theory,* vol. 56, no. 8, pp. 3862–3878, 2010.

[34] J. Huang, L. Wang, T. Zhang, and H. Li, "Unified construction algorithm of network coding in cyclic networks," in *Proceedings of the 15th Asia-Pacific Conference on Communications (APCC '09),* pp. 749–753, October 2009.

[35] A. I. Barbero and Ø. Ytrehus, "Cycle-logical treatment for "Cyclopathic" networks," *IEEE Transactions on Information Theory,* vol. 52, no. 6, pp. 2795–2804, 2006.

[36] S. Y. R. Li and Q. T. Sun, "Network coding theory via commutative algebra," *IEEE Transactions on Information Theory,* vol. 57, no. 1, pp. 403–415, 2011.

[37] K. Prasad and B. S. Rajan, "Network error correction for unit-delay, memory-free networks using convolutional codes," in *Proceedings of the IEEE International Conference on Communications (ICC '10),* May 2010.

[38] K. Prasad and B. S. Rajan, "On network-error correcting convolutional codes under the BSC edge error model," in *Proceedings of the IEEE International Symposium on Information Theory (ISIT '10),* pp. 2418–2422, June 2010.

[39] R. W. Yeung, S. Y. R. Li, N. Cai, and Z. Zhang, "Network coding theory part I: single source," *Foundations and Trends in Communications and Information Theory,* vol. 2, no. 4, pp. 241–329, 2006.

[40] N. J. A. Harvey, D. R. Karger, and K. Murota, "Deterministic network coding by matrix completion," in *Proceedings of the 16th Annual ACM-SIAM Symposium on Discrete Algorithms (SODA '05),* pp. 489–498, SIAM, Vancouver, Canada, 2005.

[41] R. Dougherty, C. Freiling, and K. Zeger, "Linear network codes and systems of polynomial equations," *IEEE Transactions on Information Theory,* vol. 54, no. 5, pp. 2303–2316, 2008.

[42] S.-Y.R. Li, Q. T. Sun, and Z. Shao, "Linear network coding: theory and algorithms," *Proceedings of the IEEE,* vol. 99, no. 3, pp. 372–387, 2011.

[43] H. Balli, X. Yan, and Z. Zhang, "On randomized linear network codes and their error correction capabilities," *IEEE Transactions on Information Theory,* vol. 55, no. 7, pp. 3148–3160, 2009.

[44] X. Guang and F.-W. Fu, "The failure probability at sink node of random linear network coding," in *Proceedings of the IEEE International Conference on Information Theory and Information Security (ICITIS '10),* pp. 876–879, Beijing, China, December 2010.

[45] P. C. Yunnan, P. A. Chou, Y. Wu, and K. Jain, "Practical network coding," in *Allerton Conference in Communication, Control and Computing,* Monticello, Ill, USA, October 2003.

[46] T. Ho, M. Médard, and R. Koetter, "An information-theoretic view of network management," *IEEE Transactions on Information Theory,* vol. 51, no. 4, pp. 1295–1312, 2005.

[47] Z. Zhang, "Linear network error correction codes in packet networks," *IEEE Transactions on Information Theory,* vol. 54, no. 1, pp. 209–218, 2008.

[48] R. Köetter and F. R. Kschischang, "Coding for errors and erasures in random network coding," *IEEE Transactions on Information Theory,* vol. 54, no. 8, pp. 3579–3591, 2008.

[49] D. Silva, F. R. Kschischang, and R. Köetter, "A rank-metric approach to error control in random network coding," *IEEE Transactions on Information Theory,* vol. 54, no. 9, pp. 3951–3967, 2008.

[50] S. Yang, R. W. Yeung, and C. K. Ngai, "Refined coding bounds and code constructions for coherent network error correction," *IEEE Transactions on Information Theory*, vol. 57, no. 3, pp. 1409–1424, 2011.

[51] S. Yang, R. W. Yeung, and Z. Zhang, "Weight properties of network codes," *European Transactions on Telecommunications*, vol. 19, no. 4, pp. 371–383, 2008.

[52] S. Yang, S.-W. Ho, J. Meng, and E.-H. Yang, "Optimality of subspace coding for linear operator channels over finite fields," in *IEEE Information Theory Workshop (ITW '10)*, pp. 1–5, Cairo, Egypt, January 2010.

[53] D. Silva, F. R. Kschischang, and R. Kotter, "Communication over finite-field matrix channels," *IEEE Transactions on Information Theory*, vol. 56, no. 3, pp. 1296–1305, 2010.

[54] Z. Zhang, "Some recent progresses in network error correction coding theory," in *Proceedings of the 4th Workshop on Network Coding, Theory, and Applications (NetCod '08)*, pp. 1–5, January 2008.

[55] H. Bahramgiri and F. Lahouti, "Robust network coding against path failures," *IET Communications*, vol. 4, no. 3, pp. 272–284, 2010.

[56] R. Matsumoto, "Construction algorithm for network error-correcting codes attaining the Singleton bound," *IEICE Transactions on Fundamentals of Electronics, Communications and Computer Sciences*, vol. E90-A, no. 9, pp. 1729–1735, 2007.

[57] X. Guang, F.-W. Fu, and Z. Zhang, "Construction of network error correction codes in packet networks," in *Proceedings of the IEEE International Symposium on Network Coding (NetCod '11)*, Beijing, China, July 2011.

[58] Z. Zhang, X. Yan, and H. Balli, "Some key problems in network error correction coding theory," in *Proceedings of the IEEE Information Theory Workshop on Information Theory for Wireless Networks (ITW '07)*, pp. 131–135, July 2007.

[59] M. Bossert and E. M. Gabidulin, "One family of algebraic codes for network coding," in *Proceedings of IEEE International Symposium on Information Theory (ISIT '09)*, vol. 4, pp. 2863–2866, IEEE Press, Seoul, Korea, 2009.

[60] E. M. Gabidulin and M. Bossert, "Algebraic codes for network coding," *Problems of Information Transmission*, vol. 45, no. 4, pp. 343–356, 2009.

[61] M. Gadouleau and Z. Yan, "Packing and covering properties of subspace codes for error control in random linear network coding," *IEEE Transactions on Information Theory*, vol. 56, no. 5, article no. 6, pp. 2097–2108, 2010.

[62] D. Silva and F. R. Kschischang, "On metrics for error correction in network coding," *IEEE Transactions on Information Theory*, vol. 55, no. 12, pp. 5479–5490, 2009.

[63] Z. Zhang, "Theory and applications of network error correction coding," *Proceedings of the IEEE*, vol. 99, no. 3, pp. 406–420, 2011.

[64] T. Ho and D. S. Lun, *Network Coding: An Introduction*, Cambridge University Press, Cambridge, UK, 2008.

[65] C. Fragouli and E. Soljanin, "Network coding fundamentals," *Foundations and Trends in Networking*, vol. 2, no. 1, pp. 1–133, 2007.

[66] C. Fragouli and E. Soljanin, "Network coding applications," *Foundations and Trends in Networking*, vol. 2, no. 2, pp. 135–269, 2007.

[67] M. Médard and A. Sprintson, Eds., *Network Coding: Fundamentals and Applications*, Cambridge University Press, Cambridge, UK, 2011.

17

Building Automation Networks for Smart Grids

Peizhong Yi, Abiodun Iwayemi, and Chi Zhou

Electrical and Computer Engineering Department, Illinois Institute of Technology, Chicago, IL 60616-3793, USA

Correspondence should be addressed to Chi Zhou, zhou@iit.edu

Academic Editor: Robert C. Qiu

Smart grid, as an intelligent power generation, distribution, and control system, needs various communication systems to meet its requirements. The ability to communicate seamlessly across multiple networks and domains is an open issue which is yet to be adequately addressed in smart grid architectures. In this paper, we present a framework for end-to-end interoperability in home and building area networks within smart grids. 6LoWPAN and the compact application protocol are utilized to facilitate the use of IPv6 and Zigbee application profiles such as Zigbee smart energy for network and application layer interoperability, respectively. A differential service medium access control scheme enables end-to-end connectivity between 802.15.4 and IP networks while providing quality of service guarantees for Zigbee traffic over Wi-Fi. We also address several issues including interference mitigation, load scheduling, and security and propose solutions to them.

1. Introduction

The smart grid is an intelligent power generation, distribution, and control system. It enhances today's power grid with intelligence, bidirectional communication capabilities and energy flows [1]. These enhancements address the efficiency, stability, and flexibility issues that plague the grid at present. In order to achieve its promised potential, the smart grid must facilitate services including the wide-scale integration of renewable energy sources, provision of real-time pricing information to consumers, demand response programs involving residential and commercial customers, and rapid outage detection. All these tasks demand the collection and analysis of real-time data. This data is then used to control electrical loads and perform demand response.

In order to obtain the full benefit of smart grids, their communication infrastructure must support device control and data exchanges between various domains which comprise the smart grid. The smart grid must be allied with smart consumption in order to achieve optimum power system efficiency. This necessitates the integration of smart buildings, appliances, and consumers in order to reduce energy consumption while satisfying occupant comfort. Building automation systems (BASs) already provide this intelligence, enabling computerized measurement, control and management of heating, ventilation, air-conditioning (HVAC), lighting, and security systems to enhance energy efficiency, reduce costs, and improve user comfort. Buildings consume 29% of all electricity generated in the United States [2]; therefore, the ability of BASs to communicate and coordinate with the power grid will have a tremendous effect on grid performance. Home area networks (HANs) provide similar capabilities for residential buildings. They facilitate the interconnection of smart appliances with smart meters to automatically regulate residential electricity usage and respond to pricing signals from the utility [3].

Zigbee is a low cost, low power, low data rate and short-range communication technology based on the IEEE 802.15.4 standard. United States National Institute for Standards and Technology (NIST) has defined Zigbee and the Zigbee smart energy profile (SEP) as the one of the communication standards for use in the customer premise network domain of the smart grid [4]. However, due to Zigbee's limited transmission range, it must be a combined with longer-range communication technologies such as IEEE802.11 in order to provide end-to-end connectivity across the smart grid.

In this paper, we discuss the different issues relevant to communication infrastructures for building automation system in smart grid. We begin with an introduction of whole system architecture of a smart grid system based on a perfect power system [5] including premises networks, field area networks, and a power system controller. We designed and implemented a Zigbee-based building energy management testbed system. Our system integrates a Zigbee-enhanced building automation system with the smart grid to harness energy management schemes such as demand response, real-time power pricing, peak load management, and distributed generation. We also propose a quality of service (QoS) aware 802.15.4/802.11 interoperability framework for home area network and building area network (BAN) which prioritizes wireless sensor network (WSN) traffic over Wi-Fi networks. In our scheme, WSN packets are classified according to their QoS requirements. They are then aggregated and tunneled over the Wi-Fi to the BASs server. We also proposed a frequency agility-based interference mitigation scheme to avoid interference from neighboring Wi-Fi networks. Distributed load scheduling based on optimal stopping rules [6] was proposed in the paper which can reduce the peak load and adjust utility operation time based on electricity pricing and waiting time. We also discuss open issues including security and data compression.

The rest of paper is organized as follows. Section 2 describes a smart grid system architecture. In Section 3, the Zigbee-based building energy management system was introduced. Our proposed QoS-aware 802.15.4/802.11 interoperability framework is presented in Section 4. Frequency-agility-based interference mitigation algorithm is proposed in Section 5. Section 6 presents our proposed optimal stopping rule-based distributed load scheduling scheme. Several open issues including smart grid security and data compression discussed in Section 7. Finally, the paper is concluded in Section 8.

2. System Architecture

The smart grid is the convergence of information technology, communications, and power system engineering to provide a more robust and efficient electrical power system [7]. Smart grids consist of sensing, communication, control, and actuation systems which enable pervasive monitoring and control of the power grid [8]. These features enable utilities to accurately predict, monitor and control the electricity flows throughout the grid. They also transform the power grid into a bidirectional power system in which customers can supply as well as receive power from the grid, converting the grid into a distributed power generation system [9].

The smart grid utilizes the hierarchical structure detailed in [8] and displayed in Figure 1. The foundation of this structure is the power system infrastructure consisting of power conversion, transportation, consumption, and actuation devices. They include power plants, transmission lines, transformers, smart meters, capacitor banks, reclosers, and various devices. Smart meters enable bidirectional power flows between utilities and consumers, enabling consumers to produce and supply energy to the grid, thereby becoming "prosumers". This development promises significant improvements in power system reliability, as alternative power sources can supply the grid during utility power outages. It also increases system efficiency, as line losses

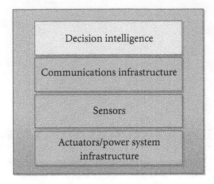

FIGURE 1: Smart grid structure.

due to long-distance transmission are eliminated. These smart grid capabilities will foster greater incorporation of renewable energy sources such as wind and solar power into the grid, thereby reducing the dependence on fossil-fuel power generation and reducing greenhouse gas emissions.

The second layer of the smart grid architecture is the sensors. Power system reliability is significantly improved via embedded sensors distributed throughout nodes within the power system. These sensors enable real-time fault detection and isolation via bidirectional digital communication links. They also provide granular system health data that can be used for rapid system analysis, fault preemption, and trending. Smart meters also provide users and utilities with real-time power consumption data and enable the remote monitoring and control of building loads and home appliances. Consumers can also receive real-time pricing information to facilitate informed decision making.

The communications infrastructure is the glue that binds all these various layers together and consists of wide, local building and home area networks. They consist of broadband technologies such as 802.16 WiMAX, 802.11 Wi-Fi, optical fiber, 802.15.4/Zigbee, and power line carrier schemes. Zigbee has found great application in smart metering, home, and building automation control due to its low-cost, flexibility, wide-spread support, and intervendor interoperability.

At the top of the system is the decision intelligence block which encompasses substation automation, fault-management, load distribution, and other control strategies deployed to guarantee power system stability and balance power demand and supply.

The smart grid concept has been extended to smaller smart grid networks known as smart microgrids. A smart microgrid is a localized smart grid covering specific geographical regions, such as suburban neighborhoods or university campuses, and incorporating local or onsite power generation.

Building automation systems provide centralized and automated management of major or critical loads within building. Building automation aims to reduce energy costs, improve energy efficiency and facilitate off-site building management [10–12]. The primary requirements for building automation applications are low cost, ease of installation, and flexibility/reconfigurability.

TABLE 1: Zigbee radio frequency characteristics.

Frequency	Region	Modulation scheme	Bit rate (kbps)	Channels	Channel spacing
868 MHz	Europe	BPSK	20	1	N/A
915 MHz	America and Asia	BPSK	40	10	2 MHz
2.4 GHz	Global	O-QPSK	250	16	5 MHz

3. Zigbee-Based Home Automation

3.1. Zigbee/IEEE 802.15.4. Zigbee is a low-rate, low-power, wireless personal area networking scheme [10] based on the IEEE 802.15.4 standard. It is designed for short-distance communication and supports a maximum data rate of 250 kbps without encryption.

Zigbee devices are ideal for smart grid and building automation applications, because they are wireless, low cost, and robust. Wireless nodes also provide flexibility, easy redeployment, and reconfiguration. The integration of Zigbee radios with light switches, occupancy sensors, temperature sensors, and smoke detectors enables measurement and control of all the building loads. The low power consumption of Zigbee is achieved by very low system duty cycles, with typical Zigbee nodes having duty cycles of less than 5%. The result is significant energy savings and greater comfort for building occupants [13, 14]. Details of Zigbee's radio frequency characteristics, frequency bands, and modulation schemes are provided in Table 1.

3.2. Home Automation System. We developed a Zigbee-based home automation system [15] in order to demonstrate the utility of Zigbee-based home automation networks. Two-way communication was used to transmit readings from Zigbee end nodes to a data collection and control center (DCCC) and to pass control messages from the DCCC to the end nodes. Each end node is able to relay the collected data to the DCCC via distributed Zigbee routing nodes. The test bed architecture is shown in Figure 2. The Zigbee coordinator aggregates received data for display and processing and transmits control signals to the end nodes according to the selected power management strategy.

3.2.1. The Data Collection and Control Center (DCCC). The DCCC serves as the system controller, receiving input from the various sensors along with real-time power pricing. It also manages the loads for energy efficiency, demand response, and cost savings. A screenshot of the DCCC's user interface is shown in Figure 3. The DCCC is developed in MATLAB and utilizes a GUI front end to communicate directly with the Zigbee network coordinator and remote actuator modules. The DCCC provides the following functions:

(i) the display of received sensor data (temperature, light levels, room occupancy, etc.),

(ii) remote control of Zigbee modules,

(iii) user configuration of timing, pricing, and sensor data threshold values,

(iv) control of externally connected loads on the basis of user-determined price thresholds, time of day, and sensor readings,

(v) lighting control based on room occupancy and other variables.

3.2.2. Hardware System. Our hardware system consists of several meshbean Zigbee motes which we programmed to support the following functions:

(i) demand response,

(ii) lighting control,

(iii) ambient temperature sensing and control.

As shown in Figure 4, these modules combine an ATMEL 1281 V low-power microcontroller with 8 K of RAM and 128 kB of flash memory, an ATMEL RF230 Zigbee radio, onboard light and temperature sensors in a single battery-powered module with a USB interface. More details of our scheme can be found in [15].

4. Interoperability of Zigbee and Wi-Fi

Building and home area networks are only one of a variety of networks that make up the smart grid. Due to the multiplicity of networks and protocols within the smart grid, interoperability is a key issue. The availability of an interoperability framework is essential to end-to-end communication across and within smart grid domains, so a significant amount of work is being invested in interoperability frameworks for the smart grid.

The usage of IP within wireless sensor networks facilitates easy interconnectivity with existing networks, enables the re-use of existing TCP/IP protocols, tools, and programming paradigms, and permits the usage of IP friendly protocols such as BACnet and Modbus over WSN nodes. These goals sparked research into the use of IPv6 over WSNs, as the ability to connect even tiny wireless sensor nodes to the internet would facilitate ubiquitous computing in the home and throughout the smart grid.

Interconnection between WSNs and TCP/IP networks has primarily been by means of gateways [16], as it had been assumed that TCP/IP was too memory and bandwidth intensive for usage in resource constrained wireless sensor networks [17]. However, the development of uIP, the first lightweight IP stack for WSNs [18] demonstrated the viability of IP for wireless sensor networks and led to a flurry of work into on the use of IP for WSNs. The 6LoWPAN IETF standard defines a framework for deployment of IPv6 over IEEE 802.15.4 networks [19] by means of header compression and routing and forwarding at layers 3 and 2, respectively. This work is extended in [20] to address issues such as link duty cycling, network bootstrapping and node discovery to create a complete IPv6 architecture for WSNs.

The primary interconnection schemes proposed for connecting Zigbee WSNs to the Internet are proxy-based

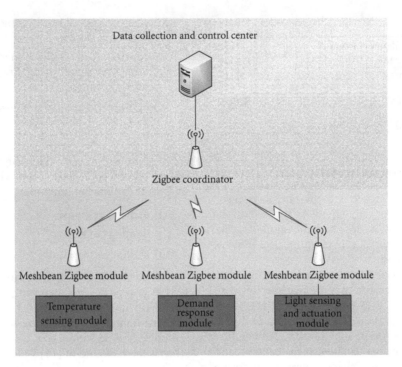

FIGURE 2: Zigbee HAN demonstration system architecture.

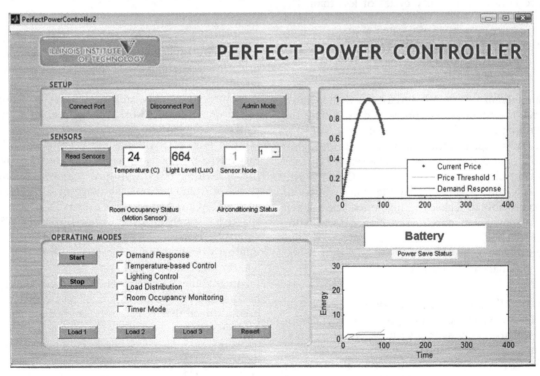

FIGURE 3: Perfect power controller GUI.

gateways [16, 21, 22] and sensor stack schemes [20, 23]. The issue of the inability of Zigbee to natively support IP is addressed by the compact architecture protocol (CAP) [24] in which the authors create a framework to enable the usage of Zigbee application layer protocols over any IP-capable network. We extend their work by creating a framework for interworking between Zigbee and Wi-Fi networks in HANs and BANs while providing QoS guarantees. The proposed interoperability network architecture is shown in Figure 5. Taking into consideration BASs application requirements, reliability and short delay are two most important factor related to the performance. In [25], the authors present

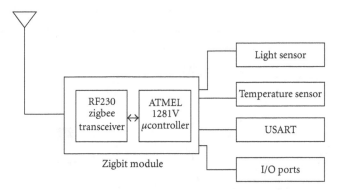

FIGURE 4: Meshnetics meshbean module block diagram.

an architecture for a medical information system which integrates WLAN and WSNs. In [26, 27], several QoS-enabling mechanisms present in the IEEE 802.11e provide us some ideas to design the frame work of the integration system. A two-tiered WSN and WLAN scheme with QoS guarantees is provided in [28], but the authors do not address IP-based interoperability.

4.1. Interworking. Interoperability is "The capability of two or more networks, systems, devices, applications, or components to exchange and readily use information—securely, effectively, and with little or no inconvenience to the user" [29]. The grid-wise architecture council (GWAC) [30] has defined an 8-layer interoperability framework encompassing all the facets of interoperability. Our primary focus is the 4 lowest layers of this framework (Figure 6), and we utilize it to develop an interoperability framework for HANs and BANs.

The internet engineering task force (IETF) 6LoWPAN working group defined the IPv6 over low-power wireless personal area networks (6LoWPAN) protocol to facilitate the use of IPv6 over low power and low data rate WSNs [31]. It was initially designed for usage over the 802.15.4 physical (PHY) and medium access layer (MAC) layers but can be extended for use over other PHY and MAC architectures (Figure 6).

In order to use IPv6 over 802.15.4 networks, an adaptation layer between the 802.15.4 data link and network layers [17] was developed to provide the following functions:

(i) stateless compression of IPv6 headers by means of HC1 compression [19] to reduce their size from 40 bytes to approximately 4 bytes, thereby reducing transmission overhead,

(ii) fragmentation and reassembly scheme to support the transmission of IPv6 packets over 802.15.4 frames. This is required as the minimum MTU of IPv6 packets is 1280 bytes, while the maximum size of a 802.15.4 frame is 127 bytes.

The benefits of 6LoWPAN over competing WSN implementations are its ease of connectivity with IP networks and its large addressing space (2^{128} compared with 2^{16} for Zigbee). In addition, the concept of device roles found in Zigbee is not applicable, with each device serving as a

router for its neighbor's traffic. Unlike Zigbee, 6LoWPAN permits duty cycling of routers, thereby extending device lifetime. The primary drawback of 6LoWPAN is its incompatibility with Zigbee, Zigbee's significant industry support, and very strong device interoperability guarantees across multiple vendors. A combination of the flexibility of IP networking and 6LoWPAN's power saving schemes with Zigbee's application profiles would marry the best features of both implementations to provide an industry standard, interoperable framework for HANs and BANs [32].

The compact application protocol (CAP) details a mapping of the Zigbee application layer to UDP/IP primitives [32, 33], permitting the usage of Zigbee application profiles over any IP capable network [24]. This removes the Zigbee application layer (ZAL) dependency on the Zigbee network layer and the 802.15.4 PHY and MAC layers. As shown in Figure 7, it preserves the excellent application layer interoperability features of public Zigbee application profiles while enabling end to end interoperability across the HAN/BAN using Wi-Fi, 802.15.4, and Ethernet. Rather than transmitting APS frames to the Zigbee network (NWK) layer for transmission to other nodes across the network using Zigbee addresses, the APS frames are now carried over UDP frames, necessitating modification to the addressing scheme to support communication with IP hosts using IP addresses and port numbers.

CAP is composed of four modules which correspond to the Zigbee application support sublayer (APS), Zigbee device objects (ZDO), Zigbee cluster library (ZCL), and APS security modules. The lowest layer of CAP is the Core module, which corresponds to the Zigbee APS layer. It frames data packets for transmission across the network, but now APS layer frames will be sent in UDP datagrams rather than in Zigbee NWK layer frames. In order to achieve this, Zigbee application profiles are rewritten to replace each Zigbee short (16-bit) and long (64-bit) address entry with a CAP address record. This consists of an IP address and UDP port pair, or a fully qualified domain name and UDP port number.

The data protocol is used to exchange data items and commands between communicating peer nodes. It encapsulates the ZCL and allows it to be used without modification, providing full ZCL support. The management protocol encapsulates Zigbee device profile (ZDP) command messages which are handled by the ZDO module, and provides service and device discovery and binding functionality. The final module is the security module which provides the same services as the APS security layer and is used to encrypt APS frames for secure transmission.

4.2. Gateway Router. Zigbee networks are primarily used for periodic data collection of low-bandwidth sensor and alarm data, while Wi-Fi networks support a variety of services with varying quality of service requirements. Based on this, a differential service medium access control scheme [25] is required to guarantee timely and reliable delivery of Zigbee traffic over building Wi-Fi networks. Thus, we design an enhanced distributed channel access-(EDCA-) based QoS model to achieve this.

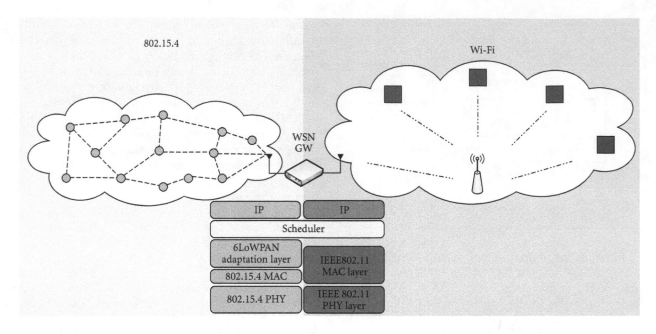

FIGURE 5: Interoperability network architecture.

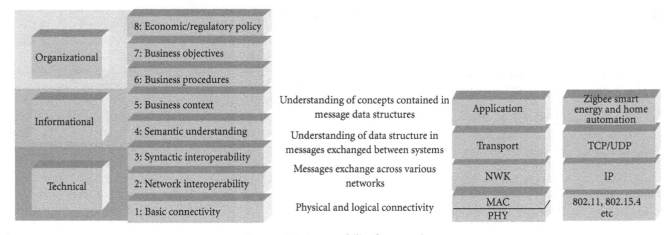

FIGURE 6: Interoperability framework.

Our framework facilitates the interconnection of the WSN to the BAN server via the in-building Wi-Fi system. This interconnection is achieved using a dual-stack gateway router (GR) node which performs QoS classification and packet aggregation on Zigbee application layer packets before tunneling them to the BAN server over Wi-Fi. As seen in Figure 6, we utilize the 802.11 and 802.15.4 MAC and physical layer protocols in conjunction with 6LoWPAN, the compact application protocol, and Zigbee application layer application profiles to provide end-to-end interoperability within HANs and BANs. Physical layer interoperability is provided by means of the GR's dual stack and 802.11 and 802.15.4 interfaces. Network layer interoperability is provided using IPv6 and the use of 6LoWPAN to enable the WSN to communicate using IP. Syntactic interoperability is achieved by the use of the CAP, which allows us to utilize publically defined Zigbee application profiles such as the smart energy or home automation profiles to provide application layer interoperability across multivendor devices. This frees us to use Zigbee application profiles across the HAN, on PCs, routers, and over any IP-capable device nodes all over the home or commercial building, rather than only over Zigbee 802.15.4 networks. In addition, the ability of our system to schedule 802.15.4 and 802.11 MAC frames enables us to provide quality of service prioritization to emergency Zigbee traffic.

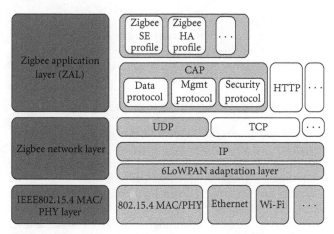

FIGURE 7: Zigbee, 6LoWPAN, and CAP stacks protocol stack [34, 35].

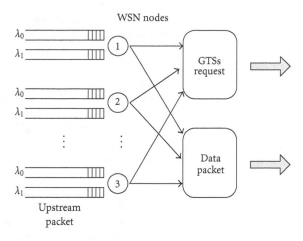

λ_0: Emergency packet
λ_1: Regular

FIGURE 8: Queuing model from WSN end nodes to WSN coordinator.

4.3. QoS of Service Framework.

The GR facilitates interconnection of the 802.15.4 and Wi-Fi networks to enable end-to-end communication. The GR contains an MAC scheduler in which can communicate with 802.15.4 MAC and 802.11 MAC layer. On the basis of these assumptions, we divide the queuing model into three parts. In the first part, traffic from WSN end nodes to the coordinator is considered; in the second part, packets from the Wi-Fi access point (AP) to the GR are discussed; finally, we will focus on the queuing model of packets sent from GR. In this scheduling scheme, the use of guaranteed time slots (GTSs) can combine the task of scheduling uplink and downlink flows of a naturally distributed carrier sense medium access with collision avoidance (CSMA/CA) environment into a central scheduler residing in the GR.

As shown in Figure 8, each WSN node has two traffic queues, one for emergency or alarm traffic and the second for normal traffic [25]. Class 0 (alarm packets) are higher priority emergency/control data, while Class 1 (normal packets) contains routine data. Nodes will typically transmit two message types. The first are GTSs requests to reserve slots in CFP, and the second types are data packets containing sensor data.

Data frames are assigned to their respective queue and contend for transmission over the channel. A node contends per information frame and can only send one packet each time. If the node has an emergency message in its queue, it will request a shorter back off exponent value to enable prompt transmission of emergency traffic. Nodes which do not have emergency traffic utilize the regular value of the back off exponent, resulting in longer wait times.

Traffic differentiation at the GR is performed on the basis of destination ports. As seen in Figure 9, we use different ports for normal and emergency traffic and map them to EDCA video (AC_VI) and voice (AC_VO) access categories, respectively, before transmitting over the Wi-Fi network. A dedicated BASs server is the final recipient of the entire off network WSN traffic, and this server filters traffic based on the ports the data is received on.

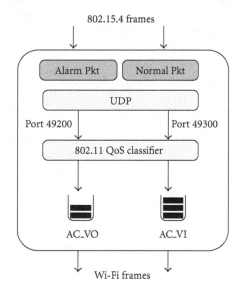

FIGURE 9: Queuing model from Gateway Router to Wi-Fi AP.

Due to the significant size difference between 802.15.4 and Wi-Fi frames, traffic aggregation is required for delay-tolerant traffic, while time sensitive WSN traffic is transmitted immediately. The encapsulation of individual 802.15.4 packets is very inefficient as the Wi-Fi header frame overhead is often larger than the useful information, necessitating packet aggregation to improve efficiency.

A hybrid scheduling model is used in the GR as shown in Figure 10. All packets received at the GR can be transmitted in either contention access period (CP) or contention-free period (CFP) modes. During the CP mode, nodes use a slotted CSMA/CA scheme to compete for the channel with other nodes. In CFP mode, up to seven GTS can be reserved and allocated by the coordinator. Devices which require the allocation of a new GTS transmit a GTS request command to the WSN coordinator and coordinator will assign GTS to each device. Our hybrid scheduling model adopts both EDCA in CP and point coordination function (PCF) controlled channel access (PCCA) in the CFP to achieve fairness and provide service guarantees. The GR assigns packets to different MAC schemes based on message type. Emergency/control messages which need to be sent out immediately will use EDCA contention access with smaller back off exponent. On the other hand, PCCA is used for routine messages, as these can wait for aggregation to be performed and are subsequently transmitted in reserved times slots.

Routine messages sent from the 802.15.4 PAN to the Wi-Fi access point are initially sent to the scheduler, where they are enqueued and time-stamped while a countdown timer initialized. The queue size is set to maximum size of a Wi-Fi payload, and if the queue is filled with routine messages before timer expiry, the scheduler reserves a GTS, aggregates all the enqueued traffic, and transmits them over the Wi-Fi radio. If the queue is not filled by timer expiry, then the GR reserves the number of GTSs required to transmit the queue and sends the accumulated data. The primary benefits of message aggregation with PCCA are collision and delay reduction for routine traffic.

5. Interference Avoidance Scheme

Zigbee networks operate in the license-free industrial, scientific and medical (ISM) frequency band, making them subject to interference from various devices that also share this license-free frequency band. These devices range from IEEE 802.11 wireless local area networks or Wi-Fi networks and Bluetooth devices to baby monitors and microwave ovens. Studies have shown that Wi-Fi is the most significant interference source for Zigbee within the 2.4 GHz ISM band [36, 37]. Zigbee and Wi-Fi networks are used extensively for BAN in smart grid applications, leading to coexistence problems as seen in Figure 11.

Therefore, we have performed a large amount of experiments to identify the "safe distance" and "safe offset frequency" to guide the Zigbee deployment [38]. The performance of Zigbee in the presence of IEEE 802.11 is defined and analyzed in terms of bit error rate (BER) and packet error rate (PER) by comprehensive approach including theoretical analysis, software simulation, and empirical measurement. Based on the concepts of "safe distance" and "safe offset frequency," we propose a frequency-agility-based interference mitigation algorithm [39]. PER, link quality Indication (LQI), and energy detection mechanisms are used to detect the presence of significant levels of interference within the current channel. Once interference is detected, the coordinator instructs all the routers to perform an energy detection scan on channels and then send a report to the coordinator. The coordinator selects the channel with the lowest noise levels and then requests all nodes in the PAN to migrate to this channel. In order to improve the detection time and power efficiency, all Zigbee channels are divided into three classes based on the offset frequency. The energy detection scan will be performed from high-priority class to low-priority class channels to quickly identify the channel with acceptable interference level. The testbed implementation shows that the proposed frequency-agility-based algorithm is simple but efficient, fast, and practical.

6. Opportunistic Load Scheduling

Demand response is the technology that manages customers' electricity usage to reduce electricity expenditure. Since customers are provided with the real-time power price by smart metering devices, load scheduling must incorporate real price in order to perform load control. The real-time price is an indicator of the system load. In general, the price is high when the load demand is high and vice versa. Some level of peak demand reduction may be automatically achieved by rational customers who aim to minimize the electricity cost. Naturally, the customers will choose to operate their flexible loads when the real-time price reaches the minimum. In this way, those flexible loads are shifted to the low demand time period, and consequently, the peak demand is reduced.

Nowadays, most existing load scheduling schemes are based on the assumption that future electricity prices are known or predictable. We propose to apply the optimal stopping rule [40] to perform distributed load scheduling. Our scheme to determines when to operate the flexible loads under the assumption that price signals are unknown and considered as random processes optimal stopping rule is proved to perform excellently in communication networks [41]. Thus, we extend the application of optimal stopping rule to power grids [42]. The time requirement of the load is taken into the consideration. If a user does not have time requirement, it will always choose to operate at the time when the electricity price is the lowest to minimize the electricity cost. However, many appliances, such as washing machine, are sensitive to the waiting time. Therefore, the spent time (which includes waiting time and service time) must be taken into consideration. The cost is modeled as the wait cost plus the electricity cost, and the objective is to minimize the total cost by choosing the best operating time. We show that the optimal scheduling scheme is a pure threshold policy; that is, each user needs to turn on the load when the electricity price is lower than a certain value; otherwise, the load remains idle. Simulation results show that the proposed low-complexity distributed scheduling scheme can dramatically reduce the cost. In other words, the loads are effectively shifted to low-demand time period. More details can be found in [6].

7. Open Issues and Future Work

7.1. Smart Grid Security. The smart grid requires detailed energy usage information in order to facilitate services such as real-time pricing and billing, customer energy management, and system load prediction. Unfortunately, as is the case with many other complex systems, the smart grid falls foul of the law of unintended consequences. The availability of such detailed usage data from every household every 5–15 minutes has created a massive security problem [43].

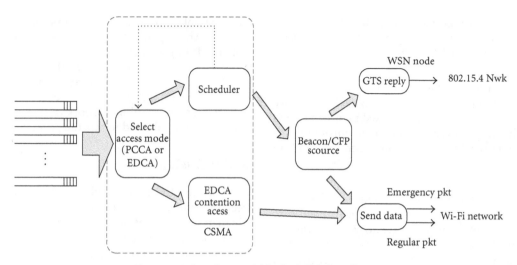

FIGURE 10: Queuing model in the WSN Coordinator.

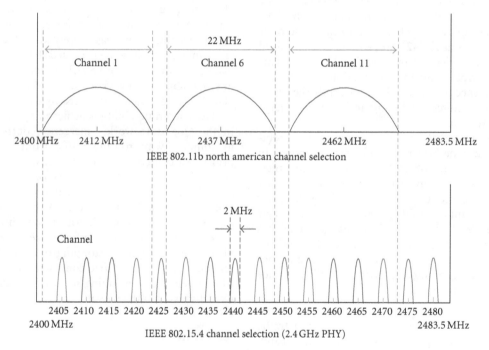

FIGURE 11: Zigbee and Wi-Fi channels in the 2.4 GHz band.

Smart meter data analysis provides the ability to determine which appliances are in use at any given time period. This has led to the fear that users can be spied upon by their meters, negatively impacting smart meter deployment [44]. The networking of smart meters with the electricity grid also raises the specter of smart meter fraud and increases the vulnerability of these devices to malicious attacks such as denial of service (DoS) attacks.

7.1.1. Privacy Issues. Research into nonintrusive appliance load monitoring technology (NALM) [45–47] has enabled the identification of appliances by means of their unique fingerprint or "appliance load profiles." By means of software analysis, it possible to determine which appliances are in

use and at what frequency. It provides access to information including the types of appliances a resident possesses, when he/she has their shower each day (by monitoring extended usage of the heater), how many hours they spend using their PC, or whether they cook often or eat microwave meals. This has led to the very valid fear that customers can be profiled and monitored by means of their smart meter. In addition, improper access to such data can lead to violations of privacy or even make one open to burglary.

7.1.2. Smart Meter Fraud. The desire for lower electricity bills provides a compelling incentive for smart meter fraud. The ability to report inaccurate data to the utility means that customers can reduce their bills by falsely claiming to supply power the grid or consume less power than their actually do. The possibility of commercially available smart meter hacking kits is also a reality [48].

7.1.3. Malicious Attacks. The internetworking of smart meters makes them especially vulnerable to denial of service attacks in which several meters are hijacked in order to flood the network with data in order to shut down portions of the power grid or report false information which can result in grid failures.

7.1.4. Smart Grid Security Solutions. Smart grid security issues can only be solved by a combination of regulatory and technological solutions. A regulatory framework is required to specify who has access to smart meter data and under which conditions as well as enforcement of penalties for data misuse [48]. Two technological solutions have been proffered. The first is to aggregate residential data at the neighborhood transformer and then anonymize it by stripping it off its source address before transmitting it to the utility [43]. Kalogridis et al. [42] propose the use of a third party escrow service which receives the detailed meter data, anonymizes it by stripping off any information that could be used to identify a specific household, then sends the utility the aggregate data required for billing and monthly energy usage for each customer.

We propose a digital rights management system-(DRMS-) based scheme which extends that proposed in [49]. Users license permission to the utility to access their data at varying levels of granularity. By default, the utility would have access to monthly usage and billing data, but customers have to grant the utility permission to access their data at higher levels of granularity in exchange for rebates or other incentives. Such a system eliminates the need for an intermediary between the utility and the consumer but requires a means of guaranteeing that the utility cannot access restricted customer data.

7.2. Data Compression. Mitigating data surges and traffic congestion due to catastrophic events is an open research area. When emergencies such as power blackouts occur, hundreds to thousands of smart meter flood the data collection center with traffic. Reliability is an important issue, since the data needs to be transmitted effectively and efficiently, and network coding is a promising approach to improving the reliability of the wireless networks under such conditions. By means of network coding, we could potentially introduce intraflow network coding into the data transmission in Zigbee networks; that is, routers mix packets heading to the same destination. As a result of this mixing, each received packet contains some information about all packets in the original file, and thus, no coded packet is special.

Conventionally, without coding, a transmitter needs to know which exact packets the destination misses so that it can retransmit them. When the network is unreliable, communicating this feedback reliably consumes significant bandwidth. In the presence of coding, no specific packet is indispensable, and as a result, a transmitter does not need to learn which particular packet the destination misses; it only needs to get feedback from the destination once it has received enough packets to decode the whole file. The reader may have noticed that the above applies to erasure-correcting coding applied at the source too. Indeed, source coding is just a special case of intraflow network coding, where the source is the only node allowed to mix the packets in the flow.

8. Conclusion

In order for the smart grid to achieve its potential, we need the resolve the problem of interoperability between the different communications technologies deployed in the grid. In this paper, we proposed an HAN architecture for energy management within smart grid environments. Zigbee-based building energy management was demonstrated to enhance building automation systems and permit granular control of electrical and HVAC systems in a smart grid context. An open architecture of an interoperability frame work for HANs and BANs was presented in the paper. Physical layer interoperability is provided by means of a router platform with 802.11 and 802.15.4 interfaces. Network layer interoperability is provided using IPv6 and the usage of 6LoWPAN to enable the WSN to communicate using IP. Syntactic interoperability is achieved by the use of the CAP. In the QoS framework, emergency/control message need to compete with routine traffic from other nodes. The prioritized contention algorithm ensured the high priority access the channel for these messages. Use of compression and scheduling increases the efficiency of the data transferred from Zigbee to Wi-Fi frames. A frequency-agility-based interference mitigation algorithm was introduced in the paper to guarantee the performance of Zigbee and Wi-Fi coexistence. Optimal stopping rule base load scheduling scheme as a distributed load control was present in the paper. More open issues including security and data compression were discussed in the paper.

References

[1] P. Yi, A. Iwayemi, and C. Zhou, "Developing ZigBee deployment guideline under WiFi interference for smart grid applications," *IEEE Transactions on Smart Grid*, vol. 2, no. 1, pp. 98–108, 2011.

[2] US Department of Energy, "Buildings Energy Data Book," March 2009, http://buildingsdatabook.eren.doe.gov/.

[3] T. J. Lui, W. Stirling, and H. O. Marcy, "Get smart," *IEEE Power and Energy Magazine*, vol. 8, no. 3, pp. 66–78, 2010.

[4] Office of the National Coordinator for Smart Grid Interoperability, NIST, "Framework and Roadmap for Smart Grid Interoperability Standards, Release 1.0," National Institute of Standards and Technology, 2010.

[5] "The Galvin Path to Perfect Power—A Technical Assessment: Report on the Galvin Electricity Initiative, Phase II, Tasks 1 & 2," Galvin Electricity Initiative, 2007.

[6] P. Yi, X. Dong, and C. Zhou, "Optimal energy management for smart grid systems—an optimal stopping rule approach," in *IFAC World Congress Invited Session on Smart Grids*, 2001, accepted.

[7] H. Farhangi, "The path of the smart grid," *IEEE Power and Energy Magazine*, vol. 8, no. 1, pp. 18–28, 2010.

[8] E. Santacana, G. Rackliffe, LE. Tang, and X. Feng, "Getting smart: with a clearer vision of the intelligent grid, control emerges from chaos," *IEEE Power and Energy Magazine*, vol. 8, no. 2, pp. 41–48, 2010.

[9] S. Amin, "For the good of the grid," *IEEE Power and Energy Magazine*, vol. 6, pp. 48–59, 2008.

[10] J. A. Gutiérrez, "On the use of IEEE Std. 802.15.4 to enable wireless sensor networks in building automation," *International Journal of Wireless Information Networks*, vol. 14, no. 4, pp. 295–301, 2007.

[11] A. C. W. Wong and A. T. P. So, "Building automation in the 21st century," in *Proceedings of the 4th International Conference on Advances in Power System Control, Operation and Management*, vol. 2, pp. 819–824, February 1998.

[12] D. Snoonian, "Smart buildings," *IEEE Spectrum*, vol. 40, no. 8, pp. 18–23, 2003.

[13] W. Kastner, G. Neugschwandtner, S. Soucek, and H. M. Newman, "Communication systems for building automation and control," *Proceedings of the IEEE*, vol. 93, no. 6, pp. 1178–1203, 2005.

[14] K. Gill, S. H. Yang, F. Yao, and X. Lu, "A ZigBee-based home automation system," *IEEE Transactions on Consumer Electronics*, vol. 55, no. 2, pp. 422–430, 2009.

[15] A. Iwayemi, P. Yi, P. Liu, and C. Zhou, "A perfect power demonstration system," in *Innovative Smart Grid Technologies Conference (ISGT '10)*, pp. 1–7, January 2010.

[16] J. J. P. C. Rodrigues and P. A. C. S. Neves, "A survey on IP-based wireless sensor network solutions," *International Journal of Communication Systems*, vol. 23, no. 8, pp. 963–981, 2010.

[17] J. W. Hui and D. E. Culler, "Extending IP to low-power, wireless personal area networks," *IEEE Internet Computing*, vol. 12, no. 4, pp. 37–45, 2008.

[18] A. Dunkels, "TCP/IP for 8-bit architectures," in *Proceedings of the 1st International Conference on Mobile Systems, Applications, and Services (MOBISYS '03)*, 2003.

[19] G. Mulligan, "The 6LoWPAN architecture," in *Proceedings of the 4th Workshop on Embedded Networked Sensors (EmNets '07)*, pp. 78–82, June 2007.

[20] J. W. Hui and D. E. Culler, "IP is dead, long live IP for wireless sensor networks," in *Proceedings of the 6th ACM conference on Embedded Network Sensor Systems*, pp. 15–28, 2008.

[21] M. Sveda and R. Trchalik, "ZigBee-to-internet interconnection architectures," in *Proceedings of the 2nd International Conference on Systems (ICONS '07)*, p. 30, April 2007.

[22] R. Wang, R. Chang, and H. Chao, "Internetworking between ZigBee/802.15.4 and IPv6/802.3 network," in *SIGCOMM Workshop "IPv6 and the Future of the Internet"*, Kyoto, Japan, August 2007.

[23] G. Mulligan et al., "Seamless sensor network IP connectivity," in *Proceedings of the 6th European Conference on Wireless Sensor Networks (EWSN '09)*, 2009.

[24] G. Tolle, "A UDP/IP adaptation of the ZigBee application protocol," http://tools.ietf.org/html/draft-tolle-cap-00.

[25] X. Yuan, S. Bagga, J. Shen, M. Balakrishnan, and D. Benhaddou, "DS-MAC: differential service medium access control design for wireless medical information systems," in *Proceedings of the 30th Annual International Conference of the IEEE Engineering in Medicine and Biology Society (EMBS '08)*, pp. 1801–1804, August 2008.

[26] A. Banchs, A. Azcorra, C. García, and R. Cuevas, "Applications and challenges of the 802.11e EDCA mechanism: an experimental study," *IEEE Network*, vol. 19, no. 4, pp. 52–58, 2005.

[27] Y. P. Fallah and H. Alnuweiri, "Hybrid polling and contention access scheduling in IEEE 802.11e WLANs," *Journal of Parallel and Distributed Computing*, vol. 67, no. 2, pp. 242–256, 2007.

[28] J. Leal, A. Cunha, M. Alves, and A. Koubâa, "On a IEEE 802.15.4/ZigBee to IEEE 802.11 gateway for the ART-WiSe architecture," in *Proceedings of the 12th IEEE International Conference on Emerging Technologies and Factory Automation (ETFA '07)*, pp. 1388–1391, September 2007.

[29] U. S. Department of Energy, Office of Electricity Delivery and Energy Reliability, "Recovery Act Financial Assistance, Funding Opportunity Announcement. Smart Grid Investment Grant Program Funding Opportunity Number: DE-FOA-0000058," June 2009.

[30] GridWise Architecture Council, "GridWise Interoperability Context-Setting Framework (v1.1)," 2008.

[31] IETF, "RFC 4944: Transmission of IPv6 Packets over IEEE 802.15.4 Networks," http://www.rfc-editor.org/rfc/rfc4944.txt.

[32] D. E. Culler and G. Tolle, "Compact Application Protocol (CAP): Uniting the Best of IP and ZigBee," http://www.rtcmagazine.com/articles/print_article/101065.

[33] Z. Shelby and C. Bormann, *6LoWPAN: The Wireless Embedded Internet*, Wiley, 2010.

[34] Parallax Inc., "Parallax PIR Sensor (#555-28027)," March 2010, http://www.parallax.com/dl/docs/prod/audiovis/pirsensor-v1.2.pdf.

[35] "Panasonic AQH Solid State Relay," http://pewa.panasonic.com/assets/pcsd/catalog/aq-h-catalog.pdf.

[36] Zensys, "White Paper: WLAN interference to IEEE 802.15.4," 2007.

[37] S. Y. Shin, H. S. Park, S. Choi, and W. H. Kwon, "Packet error rate analysis of ZigBee under WLAN and Bluetooth interferences," *IEEE Transactions on Wireless Communications*, vol. 6, no. 8, pp. 2825–2830, 2007.

[38] P. Yi, A. Iwayemi, and C. Zhou, "Frequency agility in a ZigBee network for smart grid application," in *Innovative Smart Grid Technologies Conference (ISGT '10)*, pp. 1–6, January 2010.

[39] G. Thonet and P. Allard-Jacquin, "ZigBee-WiFi Coexistence White Paper and Test Report," Schneider Electric White Paper, 2008.

[40] T. S. Ferguson, "Optimal Stopping and Applications," http://www.math.ucla.edu/~tom/Stopping/Contents.html.

[41] D. Zheng, W. Ge, and J. Zhang, "Distributed opportunistic scheduling for ad hoc networks with random access: an optimal stopping approach," *IEEE Transactions on Information Theory*, vol. 55, no. 1, pp. 205–222, 2009.

[42] G. Kalogridis, C. Efthymiou, S. Denic, T. Lewis, and R. Cepeda, "Privacy for smart meters: towards undetectable appliance load signatures," in *Proceedings of the 1st IEEE International Smart Grid Communications (SmartGridComm '10)*, pp. 232–237, 2010.

[43] E. L. Quinn, "Privacy and the New Energy Infrastructure," *SSRN eLibrary*, February 2009, http://papers.ssrn.com/sol3/papers.cfm?abstract_id=1370731.

[44] "IEEE Spectrum: Privacy on the Smart Grid," http://spectrum.ieee.org/energy/the-smarter-grid/privacy-on-the-smart-grid.

[45] G. W. Hart, "Nonintrusive appliance load monitoring," *Proceedings of the IEEE*, vol. 80, no. 12, pp. 1870–1891, 1992.

[46] J. G. Roos, I. E. Lane, E. C. Botha, and G. P. Hancke, "Using neural networks for non-intrusive monitoring of industrial electrical loads," in *Proceedings of the 10th IEEE Instrumentation and Measurement Technology Conference*, vol. 3, pp. 1115–1118, 1994.

[47] H.-H. Chang, C.-L. Lin, and J.-K. Lee, "Load identification in nonintrusive load monitoring using steady-state and turn-on transient energy algorithms," in *Proceedings of the 14th*

International Conference on Computer Supported Cooperative Work in Design (CSCWD '10), pp. 27–32, 2010.

[48] P. McDaniel and S. McLaughlin, "Security and privacy challenges in the smart grid," *IEEE Security and Privacy*, vol. 7, no. 3, pp. 75–77, 2009.

[49] Z. Fan, G. Kalogridis, C. Efthymiou, M. Sooriyabandara, M. Serizawa, and J. McGeehan, "The new frontier of communications research: smart grid and smart metering," in *Proceedings of the 1st International Conference on Energy-Efficient Computing and Networking (e-Energy '10)*, pp. 115–118, 2010.

18

Expected Transmission Energy Route Metric for Wireless Mesh Sensor Networks

YanLiang Jin,[1] HuiJun Miao,[1] Quan Ge,[1] and Chi Zhou[2]

[1] *Key Laboratory of Special Fiber Optics and Optical Access Networks of Ministry of Education, Shanghai University,*
  Shanghai 200072, China
[2] *Illinois Institute of Technology, Chicago, IL 60616-3793, USA*

Correspondence should be addressed to YanLiang Jin, jinyanliang@staff.shu.edu.cn

Academic Editor: Robert C. Qiu

Mesh is a network topology that achieves high throughput and stable intercommunication. With great potential, it is expected to be the key architecture of future networks. Wireless sensor networks are an active research area with numerous workshops and conferences arranged each year. The overall performance of a WSN highly depends on the energy consumption of the network. This paper designs a new routing metric for wireless mesh sensor networks. Results from simulation experiments reveal that the new metric algorithm improves the energy balance of the whole network and extends the lifetime of wireless mesh sensor networks (WMSNs).

1. Introduction

Wireless sensor networks are one of the most rapidly evolving research and development fields for microelectronics. A wireless sensor network potentially comprises hundreds to thousands of nodes. These nodes are generally stationary after deployment, with the exception of a very small number of mobile sensor nodes, as shown in Figure 1. Wireless sensor networks characterize themselves in their distributed, dynamic, and self-organizing structure. Each node in the network can adapt itself based on environmental changes and physical conditions. Sensor nodes are expected to have low power consumption and simple structure characteristics, while possessing the ability of sensing, communicating, and computing. For conventional wireless networks, high degree of emphasis on mobility management and failure recovery is located in order to achieve high system performance. However, as the power of sensor nodes is usually supplied by battery with no continual maintenance and battery replenishment, to design a good protocol for WSNs, the first attribute that has to be considered is low energy consumption that could promise a long network lifetime. The recent advances of WSNs have made it feasible to realize low-cost embedded electric utility monitoring and diagnostic systems [1, 2]. In these systems, wireless multifunctional sensor nodes are installed on the critical equipment of the smart grid to monitor the parameters critical to each equipment's condition. Such information enables the smart-grid system to respond to varying conditions in a more proactively and timely manner. In this regard, WSNs play a vital role in creating a highly reliable and self-healing smart electric power grid that rapidly responds to online events with appropriate actions. The existing and potential applications of WSNs on smart grid span a wide range, including wireless automatic meter reading (WAMR), remote system monitoring, and equipment fault diagnostics.

There are lots of topology for wireless networks, such as star topology, mesh topology, and line topology. Among these topologies, mesh has large throughput and excellent stability, which is upcoming to become the model of the future network. Mesh networks, inspired from wireless neighborhood networks [3, 4], are composed of static wireless nodes that own several features, such as ample energy supplying, a distributed infrastructure, self-organizing and self-configuring capability, and ease and rapidity of network deployment, as shown in Figure 2. Each of these wireless nodes can be equipped with multiple radios, called a multiradio/multichannel node, and each of the radios can be

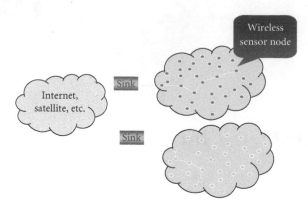

FIGURE 1: Wireless sensor network.

configured to a different channel to enhance network capacity. A wireless mesh network (WMN), possessing a more planned configuration, may be deployed to provide dynamic and cost-effective connectivity over a certain geographic area. Since its inception in the early years of this millennium, it has been in the limelight of all researchers.

The interest in wireless mesh networks has increased in recent years and several international standardization organizations are now developing specification for wireless mesh networking. IEEE 802.11 Task Group S (TGs), IEEE 802.16 Task Group, and IEEE 802.15.5th Task Group are standardizing wireless mesh networking. The Hybrid Wireless Mesh Protocol (HWMP) has been deemed as the mandatory routing protocol for WLAN mesh networks [5]. Although HWMP provides a mature routing scheme, merging the on-demand routing with the proactive routing, it does not present a method for WSNs, where limited energy is the crux and related works are barely done [6]. To achieve longevity in sensor networks, energy-aware architectures and protocols have been thoroughly investigated in the recent literature. The work in [7] introduced the NeLMUK algorithm to maximize the lifetime of 802.15.4-based wireless sensor networks. The work in [8] improved the ZigBee mesh routing protocol for energy-efficiency usage and proposed a routing algorithm combining AODV with the node residual energy. Mesh topology is not discussed. Sereiko firstly proposed the concept of wireless mesh sensor network (WMSN) by deploying wireless routers to connect sensor networks [9].

This paper studies the method of searching for the optimum routing paths of wireless mesh sensor networks by modifying the routing metric in HWMP. A new routing metric is proposed, considering the route effect on the energy distribution of the network, called expected transmission energy (ETE). We simulate the new metric algorithm compared with HWMP and min-hop in NS3 to evaluate the performance of the proposed routing method. Through experiments, we confirm that our proposed algorithm has better performance in prolonging the lifetime of WMSNs.

The rest of this paper is organized as follows. In Section 2, we describe on-demand routing, proactive routing, and HWMP, pointing out their advantages and disadvantages.

Section 3 introduces the ETX and ETT metrics and presents the proposed ETE metric. In Section 4, we introduce the ETE into HWMP airtime metric and analyze the simulation results. Finally, Section 5 concludes this paper.

2. Routing Protocols for Mesh Networks

Routing protocols can be divided into two categories: on-demand routing and proactive routing. Different routing protocols have different costs in terms of message overhead and management complexity.

2.1. On-Demand Routing. Originally proposed for ad hoc networks, on-demand or reactive routing protocols (e.g., DSR [10], AODV [11], MCR [12], LBAR [13], and DLAR [14]) only create a route between a pair of source and destination nodes when the source node actually needs to send packets to the destination. Network-wide flooding is usually used to discover routes when they are needed. For ad hoc networks, since there are frequent link breaks caused by the mobility of nodes, flooding-based route discovery provides high network connectivity and relatively low message overhead compared with proactive routing protocols. In wireless mesh sensor networks, however, links usually have a much longer expected lifetime due to the static nature of nodes. Since the frequency of link breaks is much lower than the frequency of flow arrivals in mesh networks, flooding-based route discovery is both redundant and very expensive in terms of control message overhead. Therefore, pure on-demand routing protocols are generally not scalable and inappropriate for mesh networks.

2.2. Proactive Routing. In proactive routing protocols, each node maintains one or more tables containing routing information to every other node in the network. All nodes update these tables to maintain a consistent and up-to-date view of the network. When the network topology changes, the nodes propagate update messages throughout the network to maintain routing information about the whole network. These routing protocols differ in the methods by which packets are forwarded along routes. Every node maintains a routing table that indicates the next hops for the routes to all other nodes in the network. For a packet to reach its destination, it only needs to carry the destination address. Intermediate nodes forward the packet along its path based only on the destination address. Due to its simple forwarding scheme and low message overhead, proactive routing is dominant in wired networks.

2.3. Hybrid Wireless Mesh Protocol (HWMP). IEEE 802.11s deems HWMP as the mandatory routing protocol for WLAN mesh networks and optionally allows other routing protocols such as the Radio Aware Optimized Link State Routing (RA-OLSR) protocol. HWMP supports the two routing modes of on-demand and tree-based proactive to be cooperated. HWMP uses a common set of protocol primitives, generation, and processing rules inspired by the Ad hoc On-demand Distance Vector (AODV) protocol [11].

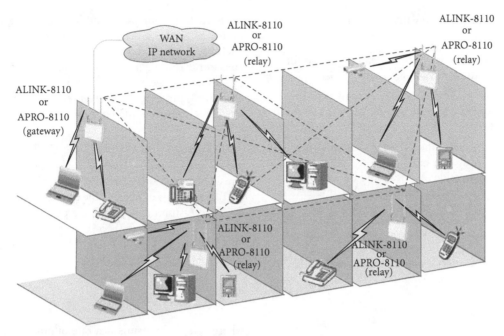

FIGURE 2: Wireless mesh network.

Four message frames are used in HWMP, namely, path request (PREQ), path reply (PREP), path error (PERR), and root announcement (RANN). Except for RANN that is only used in the proactive routing mode, these three message frames are mostly adopted from the AODV protocol.

HWMP, unlike traditional routing protocols on layer 3 with IP addresses, is operated on layer 2 using MAC addresses. When a routing protocol on layer 3 is used, data packets must be delivered to the IP layer to be routed. In the exchange between MAC addresses and IP addresses in the ARP table, overheads are also incurred. However, by adopting a layer 2 routing mechanism, HWMP can reduce overheads in forwarding data packets to destination nodes in WLAN mesh networks, based on multihop topologies. Consequently, high network throughputs can be achieved.

The operating method and the characteristics of the on-demand routing mode of HWMP are very similar to the existing AODV, except that HWMP uses layer 2 routing. In the on-demand routing mode, if a source node has no routing path to a destination node, it broadcasts a PREQ message inside the mesh network. The destination node that received the PREQ message sends a unicast PREP message back to the source node, and then a bidirectional routing path between the source and the destination nodes is established. During this procedure, the PREQ ID and the destination sequence number are used to prevent sending duplicated messages and to establish loop-free routing paths. The on-demand routing mode always provides the optimum routing paths by establishing its path when data transmission is required.

Figure 3 shows the instances of communication steps of mesh network. If mesh point4 wants to communicate with mesh point 9,

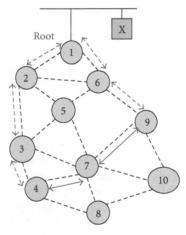

←-→ Proactive path
←—→ On-demand path

FIGURE 3: HWMP operation.

(1) MP 4 first checks its local forwarding table for an active forwarding entry to MP 9,

(2) if no active path exists, MP 4 may immediately forward the message on the proactive path toward the Root MP 1

(3) when MP 1 receives the message, it flags the message as "intra-mesh" and forwards on the proactive path to MP 9,

(4) when MP 9 receives the message, it may issue an on-demand RREQ to MP 4 to establish the best intramesh MP-to-MP path for future messages.

If MP 4 wants to communicate with X, who is outside of the current mesh cluster,

(1) MP 4 first checks its local forwarding table for an active forwarding entry to X,

(2) if no active path exists, MP 4 may immediately forward the message on the proactive path toward the Root MP 1,

(3) when MP 1 receives the message, if it does not have an active forwarding entry to X it may assume the destination is outside the mesh and forward on other LAN segments according to locally implemented interworking.

No broadcast discovery is required when destination is outside of the mesh. This efficient routing meets the severe energy constrains of wireless sensor networks and the flexible connectivity of mobile nodes.

3. Routing Metrics

Router metrics can contain any number of values that help the router determine the best route among multiple routes to a destination. A router metric is typically based on information like path length, bandwidth, load, hop count, path cost, delay, Maximum Transmission Unit (MTU), reliability, and communications cost. In this section, we discuss 3 traditional routing metrics that have been proposed and HWMP routing metric in 802.11s. After that, we propose a new metric which counterbalances energy consumption of the network basing on HWMP metric.

3.1. Traditional Routing Metric

3.1.1. Hop Count. Hop count is the most commonly used routing metric in existing routing protocols such as DSR [10], AODV [11], DSDV, and GSR. It reflects the effects of path lengths on the performance of flows. Efficient algorithms can find loop-free paths with minimum hop count, since hop count metrics are isotonic. However, hop count does not consider the differences of the transmission rates and packet loss ratios in different wireless links, or the interference in the network. Hence, using a hop count metric may not result in a good performance.

3.1.2. Expected Transmission Count (ETX). ETX, proposed by De Couto et al. [15], is defined as the expected number of MAC layer transmissions that is needed for successfully delivering a packet through a wireless link. The weight of a path is defined as the summation of the ETX of all links along the path

$$\text{ETX} = \sum_{k-1}^{\infty} k p^{k-1} (1-p) = \frac{1}{1-p}. \qquad (1)$$

Here, k means that the transmission times for node A send a packet to node B successfully. And p means error rate of the transmission.

Since both long paths and lossy paths have large weights under ETX, the ETX metric captures the effects of both packet loss ratios and path length. In addition, ETX is also an isotonic routing metric, which guarantees easy calculation of minimum weight paths and loop-free routing under all routing protocols. However, energy consumption of the devices is not taken into consideration in ETX.

3.1.3. Expected Transmission Time (ETT). The ETT routing metric, proposed by Draves et al. [16], improves ETX by considering the differences in link transmission rates. The ETT of a link l is defined as the expected MAC layer duration for a successful transmission of a packet at link.

The weight of a path p is simply the summation of the ETT's of the links on the path. The relationship between the ETT of a link l and ETX can be expressed as

$$\text{ETT}_l = \text{ETX}_l \frac{s}{b_l}, \qquad (2)$$

where b_l is the transmission rate of link l and s is the packet size. Essentially, by introducing b_l into the weight of a path, the ETT metric captures the impact of link capacity on the performance of the path. Similar to ETX, ETT is also isotonic. However, the remaining drawback of ETT is that it still does not fully capture energy consumption in the network. For example, ETT may choose a path in which energy of the devices is quite low. Though it may achieve high throughput, the lifetime of the WMSN may be awfully short as energy consumption focuses on some nodes.

3.2. HWMP Airtime Metric. In HWMP, the cost function for establishment of the radio-aware paths is based on airtime cost. Airtime cost reflects the amount of channel resources consumed by transmitting the frame over a particular link. This measure is approximate and designed for ease of implementation and interoperability.

The airtime cost for each link is calculated as

$$c_a = \left[O_{ca} + O_p + \frac{B_t}{r} \right] \frac{1}{1 - e_{pt}}, \qquad (3)$$

where O_{ca}, O_p, and B_t are constants listed in Table 1, and the input parameters r and e_{pt} are the bit rate in Mb/s and the frame error rate for the test frame size B_t, respectively. The rate r represents the rate at which the mesh point would transmit a frame of standard size (B_t) based on current conditions, and its estimation is dependent on local implementation of rate adaptation; the frame error rate e_{pt} is the probability that when a frame of standard size (B_t) is transmitted at the current transmission bit rate (r), the frame is corrupted due to transmission error, and its estimation is a local implementation choice. Frame drops due to exceeding TTL should not be included in this estimate as they are not correlated with link performance. This metric algorithm only takes the communication channel between nodes into account. However, it does not consider the condition of node's itself.

TABLE 1: Airtime cost constants.

Parameter	Value (802.11a)	Value (802.11b)	Description
O_{ca}	75 ms	335 ms	Channel access overhead
O_p	110 ms	364 ms	Protocol overhead
B_t	8224	8224	Number of bits in test frame
r			Current bit rate in use
e_{pt}			Packet error rate at the current bit rate

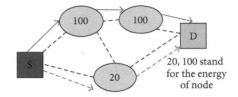

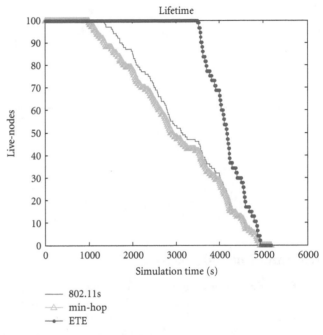

FIGURE 4: Route selection based on ETE metric.

3.3. Expected Transmission Energy (ETE).

All the algorithms mentioned above do not take the energy factor into account which is one of the most important problems of wireless sensor network. Our assumption is that all nodes are considered equally important in a WMSN. If a node died, we will lose control of a certain space in the sensing field. To prevent this situation, we would like to ensure that no node consumes energy at a rate significantly higher than other nodes, while simultaneously keeping the average power consumption rate low.

This conception can be formulated as two important parameters:

$$\sigma_E^2 = \frac{\sum_{i=1}^{n}\left(E_i - \overline{E}\right)}{n},$$

$$\overline{E}_c = \frac{\sum_{i=1}^{n_j} E_{ic}}{n_j}. \tag{4}$$

E_i is the remaining energy of node i after the transmission, E_{ic} is the energy consumption of the node i in the transmission which related to the distant, n is the number of nodes of the whole network, and n_j is the number of nodes along the selected route.

The route judgment can be concluded as the following four steps.

(1) $\overline{E}_c$ must be less than some maximum budget threshold $\overline{E}_t$.

(2) σ_E^2 should be minimized after the transmission.

(3) Once (1) and (2) are satisfied, the less $\sum_{i=1}^{n_j} E_{ic}$ it has, the better route it is.

(4) Once a node's energy is below a designated threshold, the node will not join the calculation of route metric which means it only sends his new packets and will not forward packets for others.

The routing metrics must ensure that optimum paths can be found by efficient algorithms with polynomial complexity. However, the expression of the σ_E^2 makes the algorithm too complex to realize. So the algorithm needs to be simplified. The minimization of σ_E^2 is equal to choosing route with the maximum $\overline{E}_c$. If the number is different, the situation could be simplified as Figure 4. The path with powerful nodes in

FIGURE 5: Lifetime of WMSN.

solid line will be chosen as the transmission path. While the dotted line path, though has less hop count, does not help to do energy balance of the network and will not be chosen.

Focusing the energy consumption on the route consisting of nodes with more power will help to the balance of the energy distribution of the whole network. But it will take a further path which contains more powerful nodes that help to increase the average energy $\overline{E}_c$. So, our simplified metric can be modified as $\sum_{i=1}^{n_j} 1/E_i$. To combine with the 802.11s airtime metric, it is normalized as $\sum_{i=1}^{n_j} 1/(100(E_i/E_{init}))$ and $\overline{E}_c$ is normalized as $\sum_{i=1}^{n_j} (E_{ic}/E_{init})/n_j$. And the full expression of our metric at last could be concluded as the following:

$$c_a' = \left[O_{ca} + O_p + \frac{B_t}{r} + \sum_{i=1}^{n_j}\frac{E_{init}}{100E_i}\right]\frac{1}{1-e_{pt}} + \frac{\sum_{i=1}^{n_j}(E_{ic}/E_{init})}{n_j}. \tag{5}$$

As $1/(1-e_{pt}) < 1$, $\sum_{i=1}^{n_j}(E_{ic}/E_{init})/n_j$ contributes less than $\sum_{i=1}^{n_j}(E_{init}/100E_i)$ to the result of c_a'.

In case there exist two routes with approximately equal energy. To prevent extra energy consumption in route establishment, the route metric will not be recalculated until the tenth transmission on the old route.

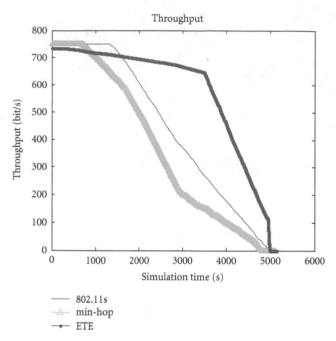

FIGURE 6: Throughput of WMSN.

4. Simulation and Analysis

All of our simulations are performed in the NS3 simulator. And the figures are printed by Matlab after the process of awk script. One hundred nodes are regularly placed over a 10×10 grid. The sources and destinations of the data flows are randomly located in the mesh network while the root of mesh network is designated. To simplify the simulation, we set the initial energy of a node 100. If a node sends a packet, it will cost 1, same as its receiving process. This means the node will lose 2 of energy when it forwards a packet. If a node's energy is less than 20% of E_{init}, this node will refuse to forward packets for other nodes. The remaining energy of it will only be used to send its own new data.

4.1. Lifetime. In Figure 5, the line with triangle, the leftmost one, represents the min-hop metric, and its lifetime is the shortest. This is because it just considers the minimization of hop count. However, even though some paths have less hop counts, the error rate is awful. Thus, forcing the nodes to retransmit their packets and causing a waste of energy. The line with asterisk in the rightmost represents the improved algorithm. Simulation result shows that the modified algorithm balances the energy consumption more effectively, that is, the lifetime of the WMSN is prolonged.

4.2. Throughput. As is shown in Figure 6, ETE achieves higher throughput. In the improved algorithm, the nodes with energy under the threshold will refuse to forward packets for others, helping extend the lifetime of low power nodes and balance the energy distribution of the network. Moreover, these nodes with low power will consume energy only when they have their own new data sent. Hence, we

have a higher throughput in the last part of the simulation, the rightmost one. Compared with ETE, low power nodes in 802.11s and min-hop routing die away more quickly and the total amount of data the nodes sensed become less which pull down the throughput.

5. Conclusion

In this paper, we study the traditional route metrics and point out their common deficiency-neglecting energy consumption. We proposed a new route metric called ETE and introduced it into 802.11s airtime metric. The simulation reveals that the new algorithm improves the energy balance of the whole network and extends the lifetime of wireless mesh sensor network. In the future, the proposed algorithm may be further considered for multichannel wireless mesh sensor networks. In addition, it will be used in the existing and potential applications of WMSNs on smart grid.

Acknowledgments

The authors would like to thank the reviewers for their detailed comments on earlier versions of this paper. This work was supported by Shanghai Leading Academic Discipline project (S30108, 08DZ2231100), Shanghai Education Committee (09YZ33), Shanghai Science Committee (08220510900, 10511501303) and Shanghai SMIT Fund.

References

[1] L. Lo Bello, O. Mirabella, and A. Raucea, "Design and implementation of an educational testbed for experiencing with industrial communication networks," *IEEE Transactions on Industrial Electronics*, vol. 54, no. 6, pp. 3122–3133, 2007.

[2] B. Lu and V. C. Gungor, "Online and remote motor energy monitoring and fault diagnostics using wireless sensor networks," *IEEE Transactions on Industrial Electronics*, vol. 56, no. 11, pp. 4651–4659, 2009.

[3] R. Karrer, A. Sabharwal, and E. Knightly, "Enabling large-scale wireless broadband: the case for TAPs," in *Proceedings of the Workshop on Hot Topics in Networks (HotNets '03)*, no. 1, pp. 27–32, Cambridge, Mass, USA, 2003.

[4] V. Gambiroza, B. Sadeghi, and E. W. Knightly, "End-to-end performance and fairness in multihop wireless backhaul networks," in *Proceedings of the 10th Annual International Conference on Mobile Computing and Networking (MobiCom '04)*, pp. 287–301, October 2004.

[5] IEEE Std 802.11TM–2007, "Wireless LAN Medium Access Control (MAC) and Physical Layer (PHY) Specifications," IEEE Computer Society, June 2007.

[6] J. D. Camp and E. W. Knightly, "The IEEE 802.11s extended service set mesh networking standard," *IEEE Communications Magazine*, vol. 46, no. 8, pp. 120–126, 2008.

[7] M. U. Ilyas and H. Radha, "Increasing network lifetime of an IEEE 802.15.4 wireless sensor network by energy efficient routing," in *Proceedings of the IEEE International Conference on Communications (ICC '06)*, pp. 3978–3983, July 2006.

[8] F. Zhang, H. Zhou, and X. Zhou, "A routing algorithm for zigbee network based on dynamic energy consumption decisive path," in *Proceedings of the International Conference*

on Computational Intelligence and Natural Computing (CINC '09), pp. 429–432, June 2009.

[9] P. Sereiko, "Wireless Mesh Sensor Networks Enable Building Owners, Managers, and Contractors to Easily Monitor HVAC Performance Issues," 2004, http://www.automatedbuildings. com/news/jun04/articles/sensicast/Sereiko.htm.

[10] D. B. Johnson and D. A. Maltz, "Dynamic source routing in AdHoc wireless networks," in *Mobile Computing*, vol. 353, Kluwer Academic, Boston, Mass, USA, 1996.

[11] C. Perkins, "Ad-Hoc on-demand distance vector routing," in *Proceedings of the IEEE Military Communications Conference on Ad Hoc Networks (Milcom '97)*, 1997.

[12] P. Kyasanur and N. Vaidya, "Multi-channel wireless networks: capacity and protocols," Tech. Rep., University of Illinois at Urbana-Champaign, Urbana, Ill, USA, 2005.

[13] H. Hassanein and A. Zhou, "Routing with load balancing in wireless ad hoc networks," in *Proceedings of the 4th ACM International Workshop on Modeling, Analysis and Simulation of Wireless and Mobile Systems (ACM MSWiM '01)*, pp. 89–96, July 2001.

[14] C. Perkins, E. Belding-Royer, and S. Das, "Ad Hoc On-Demand Distance Vector (AODV) Routing," IETF RFC 3561, July 2003.

[15] D. S. J. De Couto, D. Aguayo, J. Bicket, and R. Morris, "A High-Throughput Path Metric for Multi-Hop Wireless Routing," in *Proceedings of the Ninth Annual International Conference on Mobile Computing and Networking (MobiCom '03)*, pp. 134–146, September 2003.

[16] R. Draves, J. Padhye, and B. Zill, "Routing in multi-radio, multi-hop wireless mesh networks," in *Proceedings of the 10th Annual International Conference on Mobile Computing and Networking (MobiCom '04)*, pp. 114–128, October 2004.

Permissions

The contributors of this book come from diverse backgrounds, making this book a truly international effort. This book will bring forth new frontiers with its revolutionizing research information and detailed analysis of the nascent developments around the world.

We would like to thank all the contributing authors for lending their expertise to make the book truly unique. They have played a crucial role in the development of this book. Without their invaluable contributions this book wouldn't have been possible. They have made vital efforts to compile up to date information on the varied aspects of this subject to make this book a valuable addition to the collection of many professionals and students.

This book was conceptualized with the vision of imparting up-to-date information and advanced data in this field. To ensure the same, a matchless editorial board was set up. Every individual on the board went through rigorous rounds of assessment to prove their worth. After which they invested a large part of their time researching and compiling the most relevant data for our readers. Conferences and sessions were held from time to time between the editorial board and the contributing authors to present the data in the most comprehensible form. The editorial team has worked tirelessly to provide valuable and valid information to help people across the globe.

Every chapter published in this book has been scrutinized by our experts. Their significance has been extensively debated. The topics covered herein carry significant findings which will fuel the growth of the discipline. They may even be implemented as practical applications or may be referred to as a beginning point for another development. Chapters in this book were first published by Hindawi Publishing Corporation; hereby published with permission under the Creative Commons Attribution License or equivalent.

The editorial board has been involved in producing this book since its inception. They have spent rigorous hours researching and exploring the diverse topics which have resulted in the successful publishing of this book. They have passed on their knowledge of decades through this book. To expedite this challenging task, the publisher supported the team at every step. A small team of assistant editors was also appointed to further simplify the editing procedure and attain best results for the readers.

Our editorial team has been hand-picked from every corner of the world. Their multi-ethnicity adds dynamic inputs to the discussions which result in innovative outcomes. These outcomes are then further discussed with the researchers and contributors who give their valuable feedback and opinion regarding the same. The feedback is then collaborated with the researches and they are edited in a comprehensive manner to aid the understanding of the subject.

Apart from the editorial board, the designing team has also invested a significant amount of their time in understanding the subject and creating the most relevant covers. They scrutinized every image to scout for the most suitable representation of the subject and create an appropriate cover for the book.

The publishing team has been involved in this book since its early stages. They were actively engaged in every process, be it collecting the data, connecting with the contributors or procuring relevant information. The team has been an ardent support to the editorial, designing and production team. Their endless efforts to recruit the best for this project, has resulted in the accomplishment of this book. They are a veteran in the field of academics and their pool of knowledge is as vast as their experience in printing. Their expertise and guidance has proved useful at every step. Their uncompromising quality standards have made this book an exceptional effort. Their encouragement from time to time has been an inspiration for everyone.

The publisher and the editorial board hope that this book will prove to be a valuable piece of knowledge for researchers, students, practitioners and scholars across the globe.

List of Contributors

Omneya Issa
Communications Research Centre Canada (CRC), Ottawa, ON, Canada K2H 8S2

Prasad Calyam, Prashanth Chandrasekaran, Gregg Trueb, Nathan Howes and Rajiv Ramnath
Ohio Supercomputer Center/OARnet, The Ohio State University, Columbus, OH 43210, USA

Delei Yu, Ying Liu, Lixia Xiong and Daoyan Yang
Huawei Technologies, Shenzhen 518129, China

Xiaowei Li, Yi Cui and Yuan Xue
Department of Electrical Engineering and Computer Science, Vanderbilt University, Nashville, TN 37235, USA

Siamak Talebi
Electrical Engineering Department, Shahid Bahonar University of Kerman, Kerman 76169-133, Iran
International Center for Science, High Technology, and Environmental Sciences, Kerman, Iran
Advanced Communications Research Institute, Sharif University of Technology, Tehran 11365-11155, Iran

Hojjat Salehinejad
Electrical Engineering Department, Shahid Bahonar University of Kerman, Kerman 76169-133, Iran
International Center for Science, High Technology, and Environmental Sciences, Kerman, Iran

Jose Joskowicz
Universidad de la Rep´ublica, 11300 Montevideo, Uruguay

Rafael Sotelo
Universidad de Montevideo, 11600 Montevideo, Uruguay

Siok Kheng Tan,Mahesh Sooriyabandara and Zhong Fan
Telecommunications Research Laboratory, Toshiba Research Europe Ltd., 32 Queen Square, Bristol BS1 4ND, UK

Deze Zeng and Song Guo
School of Computer Science and Engineering, The University of Aizu, Fukushima-Ken 965-8580, Japan

Victor Leung
Electrical and Computer Engineering Department, The University of British Columbia, Vancouver, BC, Canada V6T 1Z4

JiankunHu
School of Engineering and Information Technology, The University of New South Wales at the Australia Defence Force Academy, Canberra, ACT 2600, Australia

Anh-Tai Ho and Jean-Francois Helard
IETR UMR 6164, INSA, Universit´e Europ´eenne de Bretagne, 35708 Rennes, France

Youssef Nasser
American University of Beirut, Bliss Street, Beirut 11-0236, Lebanon

Yves Louet
SCEE Team, Supelec, avenue de la Boulaie, 35576 Cesson-S´evign´e, France

Swapna Iyer
Department of Electrical and Computer Engineering, Illinois Institute of Technology, Chicago, IL 60616 3793, USA

Wei Ren and Jun Song
School of Computer Science, China University of Geosciences, Wuhan 430074, China

Min Lei
School of Software Engineering, Key Laboratory of Network and Information Attack and Defense Technology of MoE, Beijing 100876, China

Yi Ren
Department of Information and Communication Technology, University of Agder (UiA), Grimstad, Norway

Lei Guan and Anding Zhu
School of Electrical, Electronic & Communications Engineering, University College Dublin, Dublin 4, Ireland

Raghuram Ranganathan,Robert Qiu, Zhen Hu, ShujieHou, Marbin Pazos-Revilla, Gang Zheng, Zhe Chen and Nan Guo
Department of Electrical and Computer Engineering, Center for Manufacturing Research,
Tennessee Technological University, Cookeville, TN 38505, USA
Cognitive Radio Institute, Tennessee Technological University, Cookeville, TN 38505, USA

Frank X. Sun, Muhammad Ali Farmer and Abdul Waheed
British Institute of Technology & E-Commerce, 258-262 Romford Road, London E7 9HZ, UK

John Cosmas
Department of Electronic & Computer Engineering, School of Engineering and Design, Brunel University, Middlesex UB8 3PH, UK

Kaiqian Ou, Yinlong Xu, XiuminWang and Wang Liu
School of Computer Science and Technology, Key Laboratory on High Performance Computing, University of Science and Technology of China, Anhui Province 230026, China

RuiWang and Wanggen Wan
School of Communication and Information Engineering, Shanghai University, Shanghai 200072, China

Wenming Cao
School of Information Engineering, Shenzhen University, Shenzhen 518060, China

Michele Sanna and Ebroul Izquierdo
School of Electronic Engineering and Computer Science, Queen Mary, University of London, London E1 4NS, UK

Peizhong Yi, Abiodun Iwayemi and Chi Zhou
Electrical and Computer Engineering Department, Illinois Institute of Technology, Chicago, IL 60616-3793, USA

YanLiang Jin, HuiJun Miao and Quan Ge
Key Laboratory of Special Fiber Optics and Optical Access Networks of Ministry of Education, Shanghai University, Shanghai 200072, China

Chi Zhou
Illinois Institute of Technology, Chicago, IL 60616-3793, USA

Printed in the USA
CPSIA information can be obtained
at www.ICGtesting.com
JSHW051444221024
72173JS00006B/1580

9 781632 400482